Doing
RESEARCH

To Marjorie, Kathy, and Jamie

Doing
RESEARCH
Methods of Inquiry for Conflict Analysis

Daniel Druckman

SAGE Publications
Thousand Oaks ▪ London ▪ New Delhi

For information:

Sage Publications, Inc.
2455 Teller Road
Thousand Oaks, California 91320
E-mail: order@sagepub.com

Sage Publications Ltd.
1 Oliver's Yard
55 City Road
London EC1Y 1SP
United Kingdom

Sage Publications India Pvt. Ltd.
B-42, Panchsheel Enclave
Post Box 4109
New Delhi 110 017 India

Printed in the United States of America

Library of Congress Cataloging-in-Publication Data

Druckman, Daniel, 1939-
Doing research : methods of inquiry for conflict analysis / Daniel Druckman.
    p. cm.
Includes bibliographical references and index.
ISBN 0-7619-2778-6 (cloth) — ISBN 0-7619-2779-4 (pbk.)
    1. Conflict management—Resolution—Research—Methodology.
2. Social conflict—Research—Methodology. 3. Interpersonal
conflict—Research—Methodology. 4. International
conflict—Research—Methodology. I. Title.
HM1126.D78 2005
303.6'9'072—dc22

                              2004024120

This book is printed on acid-free paper.

05   06   07   08   10   9   8   7   6   5   4   3   2   1

Acquisitions Editor:	Lisa Cuevas Shaw
Editorial Assistant:	Margo Crouppen
Production Editor:	Denise Santoyo
Proofreader:	Gillian Dickens
Typesetter:	C&M Digitals (P) Ltd.
Indexer:	Kathy Paparchontis
Cover Designer:	Michelle Lee Kenny

Contents

Preface

There is no book on methods quite like this one. Having taught research methods in the Institute for Conflict Analysis and Resolution (ICAR) doctoral program for more than a decade, I recognize the need for a book that makes research interesting, worthwhile, and relevant while engaging the student in the debates concerning how to do it. Rather than discuss research methods in the abstract, as is done in most methods texts, this book presents methods in the context of actual research projects. More emphasis is placed on the way projects are done than on how to execute particular techniques. A central theme of the book is the value of multi-method approaches to research on conflict and related topics. Understood in the context of programs of research, this approach consists of moving vertically from small (single experiments or cases) to large studies (meta-analyses, comparative case analyses) and moving horizontally from simulations to case studies. Bridging a gap between theory and research, the approach provides the flexibility needed to bring scientific findings to bear on practitioner training and decision making. I include key insights derived from conflict research conducted with a multi-method approach.

Books on research methodology, like other kinds of books, reflect their authors' experiences and perspectives. This text is not an exception. My decisions about topic coverage and the way each of the topics is treated were influenced, to a large extent, by the teachers and texts that I have been exposed to and the experiences that I have had in a professional career that began on May 17, 1966, the day I was awarded a Ph.D. from Northwestern University. For this reason, it would seem useful to discuss briefly some of these influences.

My professors in the graduate department at Northwestern valued rigorous approaches to research, with a preference for quantitative over qualitative methods. Within this framework, however, there existed a tension between the experimentalists and the social psychologists. Tight laboratory controls, favored by Benton J. Underwood and his students, contrasted with the relaxation of controls reflected in the quasi-experimental designs proposed by Donald T. Campbell and his students. This tension between internal (represented by Underwood's approach) and external validity (emphasized by Campbell) strongly influenced the way I conduct research, develop theory, teach, and practice as a social scientist. The approach, which I elaborate on in Chapter 1, has emerged in recent years as part of a post-positivist culture of scholarship. It weaves through the treatment of topics in this book, not as a doctrine but as a flexible foundation for generating and accumulating knowledge.

I was exposed also at Northwestern to the use of simulation in international relations. Pioneered by Harold Guetzkow, simulation was construed both as an approach to modeling complex social processes and as a context for laboratory experiments. As a member of Guetzkow's team, I conducted research on the inter-nation simulation and constructed lifelike situations for exploring negotiation processes. This experience sensitized me to issues of generality of research, known also as external validity. A good deal of my research since graduate school has consisted of developing methodological approaches that would enhance the generality of findings from empirical studies. These concerns also weave through many of the discussions in this book.

I have benefited from exposure to other research traditions as well. A summer at the University of Michigan's survey research center introduced me to the intricacies of survey sampling and questionnaire design. As a research assistant on Donald Campbell and Robert LeVine's cooperative cross-cultural study of ethnocentrism (LeVine & Campbell, 1972), I was exposed to an ethnographic research tradition favored by many anthropologists. This experience taught me about the possibilities for comparative case or ethnographic studies as an approach for evaluating theory-based propositions. During this period, I learned about a wide variety of methodological issues and challenges, including the value of using unobtrusive measures in evaluation research designs. The captivating book on this topic by Webb, Campbell, Schwartz, and Sechrest (1966) was energized by Campbell working with several of his faculty colleagues during my time as a graduate student.

Courses on statistics stretched from undergraduate days through the doctoral programs at Duke in sociology and at Northwestern in social psychology. My first encounter with the analysis of variance occurred in a very difficult senior-level course in the statistics department at Michigan State. Concentrating primarily on the algebraic foundations for the technique, the professor used a text by Dixon and Massey (1957) to "introduce" the students to the topic. A more complete understanding of the technique was gained from the experimental perspective of Edwards's textbook *Experimental Design in Psychological Research* (1960), used in Albert Erlbacher's graduate course at Northwestern. The analysis of variance (ANOVA) was the primary technique used to analyze the data collected for both my master's thesis and doctoral dissertation and has been the primary statistical tool used in my research, especially in my earlier publications. Blalock's book *Social Statistics* (1960, 1979) was the foundation for my knowledge of correlation and regression, gained initially from a statistics course taught at Duke by a visiting professor from North Carolina State. I still use readings from this book in my research methods class at George Mason.

Although I have read and used a variety of other statistics texts, I have found several of the monographs in the Sage series on quantitative applications in the social sciences to be more helpful. In particular, Kruskal and Wish's (1990) monograph on multidimensional scaling, Klecka's (1980) book on discriminant analysis, and Wolf's (1986) treatment of meta-analysis have guided my analyses on several projects, which resulted in important publications. None of these books, however, has been more useful than Siegel and Castellan's (1988) excellent treatment of nonparametric statistics. Their wide-ranging survey of a variety of techniques and guidance in matching techniques to measurement assumptions is, I believe, unparalleled in this literature. Together, these texts have shaped my approach to teaching and, hence, the way I present statistical analysis in this volume.

Projects developed during my research consulting career have provided further opportunities for learning about methodologies. These "on-the-job" experiences sensitized me to applications of analytical tools. I learned about modeling during the conduct of projects on coalition formation in inter-religious councils and in Philippine group politics as well as in recent game-theory applications in the study of ancient diplomacy. The advantages of such complex statistical techniques as discriminant analysis and multidimensional scaling became evident in analyses of nonverbal behavior, political elite mobility, peacekeeping, and comparative case studies of international negotiation. The value of frameworks as conceptual tools and organizing devices was demonstrated in a variety of projects on negotiation, political stability, and human and organizational performance. Lessons learned from experience can also be a valuable source of insights as I discovered in analyses of practitioners' accounts of their diplomatic assignments. And my attempts to synthesize the research literature on bargaining have benefited from the advent of meta-analytical techniques. The techniques provided an answer to the question, "What does it all add up to?" These are some of the project experiences that have informed my yearlong graduate course on research. They are reflected in the treatment of many topics in this book.

All of these experiences make a book like this possible and, perhaps, useful. Thus, I am deeply grateful to all the teachers, mentors, colleagues, clients or sponsors, students, friends, and family members who inspired, challenged, and supported me as a teacher and social science researcher engaged in a lifelong quest for knowledge and understanding of conflict processes and conflict resolution approaches. I hope that they also take pride in the roles they played in its production.

The important contributions made by my colleagues Scott Keeter, Linda J. Seligmann, and Linda M. Johnston are gratefully acknowledged. Scott, a political scientist currently at the Pew Research Center for the People and the Press, prepared Chapter 5 on survey research. Linda Seligmann, an anthropologist in George Mason's Department of Sociology and Anthropology, wrote Chapter 8 on ethnographic methods. Linda Johnston, a conflict analysis and resolution scholar/practioner at George Mason's Institute for Conflict Analysis and Resolution, contributed Chapter 10 on narrative analysis. I thank each of them also for responding to my editing suggestions efficiently and with good cheer. I am sure that students will benefit from the many insights and guidelines provided in these chapters. I know that I have benefited, and am very pleased to include their work in the book. As well, special thanks go to the publisher's reviewers, whose excellent suggestions have further improved the book: Curt Signorino, University of Rochester; Brian Polkinghorn, Salisbury State University; William Donohue, Michigan State University; and Sean Byrne, University of Manitoba. I would be remiss if I do not also call attention to the contributions made by Lisa Cuevas-Shaw, Margo Crouppen, and Denise Santoyo at Sage, and Catherine Albano at ICC. Not only did they respond completely and quickly to all of my requests and questions, but they also made the whole experience of writing a textbook enjoyable. In my writing career, there has been no better publisher than Sage!

I would also like to recognize the contributions made by the recent cohort of doctoral students at the Institute for Conflict Analysis and Resolution. Thanks go to my "guinea pigs" in the 2002–2003 advanced research methods seminar. They were the first to be exposed to early drafts of the chapters and offered many suggestions that clarified arguments and added interesting examples to the text. Tatsushi Arai contributed a number of useful ideas based on his careful reading of some early draft chapters. Doga Eralp helped me to assemble the bibliography, often tracking down obscure references as well as making useful suggestions about organization. Landon Hancock helped with the SPSS boxes on calculation routines in Chapters 4 and 6. Special thanks go to Sascha Sheehan who helped me to make many of the chapters come alive with provocative graphics, easy-to-read charts, and other stylistic innovations as well as valuable information about library and web resources for students in this and allied fields of study. To each of these students, I have been privileged to know you and watch your professional development evolve from student to colleague.

It should, of course, be said that my wife Marjorie deserves a lion's share of the credit for encouraging a long career, starting with my thesis and dissertation work in the mid-1960s and winding its way to the book that I really wanted to write. She is also the co-producer of our children, Kathy and Jamie, both accomplished professional social scientists. The dedication is a small token of my appreciation for their lifelong support and love.

Prologue

In this prologue, I discuss what this book does and how it is organized.

The book is written primarily for students who plan to do research, first in the form of a master's thesis or doctoral dissertation and, later, as a significant activity in his or her professional career. This would cover practically all students enrolled in graduate social science programs. It is my hope that the topics treated will provide guidance for student research across the board. The methodologies discussed are broadly relevant to many types of projects. However, it is also targeted toward students in social science programs that emphasize the study of conflict as it occurs at all levels of analysis, from the interpersonal to the international. The examples used to illustrate applications are drawn primarily, although not exclusively, from research on conflict. For this reason, the book would be most appropriate as a text for courses in those programs, such as the program on conflict analysis and resolution at George Mason. The increased popularity of conflict analysis and peace studies in graduate schools around the world makes this a propitious time for a book of this sort.

The book represents, to a large extent, the kind of text that would have been helpful to me when I was preparing for a career in social science. I thought that I would like to have known more about several topics or issues. Before embarking on his or her own research projects, a student is likely to benefit from discussions about the value of research. These discussions would include both philosophical or epistemological issues and examples of important insights that have resulted from published studies in the field. They take the form of Chapter 1, which asks the motivational question, "Why do research?" However, although providing a needed foundation for doing research, the discussions do not convey the mechanics or skills involved in actually performing it. Thus, I launch into the practice of investigative inquiry, beginning with some guidelines on how to get started. Focusing attention on where ideas come from and how they might be investigated, Chapter 2 suggests options for the early decisions that shape an investigation or program of research. We are then ready to plunge into the technical issues concerning the design and implementation of investigations. Chapters 3, 4, 5, 6, and 7 cover many of these issues and are the heart of the text.

The social science landscape is covered by a wide variety of methodological approaches and analytical techniques. One approach, used by some writers of methods textbooks, has been to present a broad survey of this variety. One of the best surveys can be found in Robson's *Real World Research*, published by Blackwell in 1993 (first edition) and 2002 (second edition). I make no attempt to provide another survey of approaches. Rather, an attempt is made to present the methodologies shown to be most useful in analyses of conflict behavior and processes. These include experiments, case studies, and surveys. By dividing these broad categories further (e.g., simulations, quasi-experiments, qualitative and comparative case studies, probability and non-probability samples), we bring each approach to life with examples of published studies and dissertations that generated valuable insights about conflict and conflict resolution. The examples highlight design and analysis issues, and guide the student through the series of steps taken by the investigators of the studies that are reviewed. Readers are taken through similar journeys in Chapter 9 on content analysis and Chapter 11 on evaluation research.

The connection between research and practice is another issue that aroused my curiosity as a student and young professional but about which little guidance was provided. At that time (in the 1960s), psychology was sharply divided between basic and applied careers. Only limited attention was paid to bridging this divide. At the current time (shortly beyond the turn of the century), most social science fields recognize that research and practice are (and should be) connected in many ways. Some of the connections are discussed in Chapter 12. These include the use of evaluation methodologies to judge the impact of interventions in conflict, the increasing popularity of action research as an approach for strengthening the implementation of research products, training modules that utilize research findings, and the role played by research consultants in various policy contexts. The examples provided are drawn from both completed and ongoing projects conducted by professionals in the field, including recent doctoral graduates from George Mason's ICAR program.

The concluding part provides a summary of the various approaches discussed in the previous chapters, compares the methodologies, and highlights strengths and weaknesses of alternative sources of data. Emphasizing flexible approaches to doing research, I suggest that broad multi-method training would equip students to access methodologies that are suited to a variety of problems. The idea of a "tool kit" is compatible with spiral careers that exhibit thematic coherence in research with flexibility in the way that the themes are studied. This approach to scholarship, which moves away from older disciplinary paradigms, is open to the new ideas that can energize investigators and stimulate growth in theory, research, and practice. It is also useful for social scientists who prefer multidimensional careers, practiced in different settings within and outside the academy.

Many of the examples of studies described throughout the book come from research that I am familiar with, including my own published work and several of my students' dissertation projects. For those readers who may view these citations as self-serving, I want to assure them that my decision to include them was made following a consideration of available literature on the topic. Sometimes I concluded that my own studies, including collaborative and student projects, best illustrated the ideas being conveyed. At other times, studies done by others served to illustrate the techniques being discussed. Yet, despite this comparative evaluation, the decision may have been biased: It is certainly the case that I am more familiar with the way my own projects evolved than those done in other laboratories or field sites. It is also the case that my knowledge of the concepts and techniques discussed in many sections is derived from having conducted these sorts of studies. Thus, in my judgment, the reader will benefit from learning how my own understanding of methodologies developed from doing research that applies the relevant techniques. I do hope that you agree and regard the citations primarily as "hands-on" examples of the approach being discussed in a particular section.

A pedagogical device introduced by Robson for his 1993/2002 text *Real World Research* and used more recently by Schotz and Tietje in their 2002 text *Embedded Case Study Methods*, is to highlight key ideas in the condensed form of boxes. The boxed material appears at key junctures in several of the chapters, following a discussion of the topic. Like rests in music, the boxes give the reader a break before continuing on with the next section. In addition, the lessons to be learned from each topic are listed in the form of discussion questions at the conclusion of each chapter.

Part I

Doing Research on Conflict

The two chapters in this part of the book introduce the reader to the intellectual foundations for research and ways to prepare to do research projects. In the first chapter, I discuss some philosophical issues that influence the way we do research, motivations for doing research, the kinds of questions that can be answered by conducting research projects, and a sampling of findings from published studies on conflict analysis and resolution. An attempt is made to give the student a feel for the kinds of issues that are often debated intensely among social science researchers. The chapter also enlightens the student about certain features of the research enterprise, including ethics.

The second chapter is intended to get the student started to do research. Here, I come down from a philosophical perch to provide practical advice about how to review literature, use library resources, and choose a topic for investigation. Where and how to find information about a variety of topics in the field and how to organize the information in frameworks are discussed. Examples of recent dissertation studies are provided to give the reader a sense of the challenges facing these doctoral students in choosing a topic and implementing the research tasks. The chapter concludes with a discussion of how the framing of research questions goes hand-in-hand with the methodological approach taken, which could be conducting experiments, sample surveys, or comparative case studies.

The introduction to doing research provided by these chapters is a prelude to the more technical chapters about research design and analysis techniques to follow. You will notice that discussion questions are provided at the end of each chapter. These questions cover all parts of the chapter and provide an opportunity for review. This format reappears at the end of each chapter in the book.

1

1

Why Do Research?

Research Foundations: Debating Points

In trying to provide a foundation for doing research on conflict and conflict resolution (CR), I am struck by several tensions that take the form of controversies or debates in the literature and in academic conversations held in classes, colloquia, and informal hallway chatting. Some points of contention are discussed in the following sections.

ABSTRACT AND CONCRETE KNOWLEDGE

The distinction between abstract, or general, and concrete, or specific, knowledge is relevant to the study of conflict and CR. According to *Merriam-Webster's Collegiate Dictionary* (Mish et al., 2001), *abstract* as an adjective means "disassociated from any specific instance; difficult to understand; insufficiently factual; expressing a quality apart from an object; dealing with a subject in its abstract aspects; having only intrinsic form with little or no attempt at pictorial representation or narrative content." The antonym for abstract is *concrete*. As a noun, an abstraction is "the act or process of abstracting; the state of being abstracted; an abstract idea or term; absence of mind or preoccupation; abstract quality or character; an abstract composition or creation in art." As a transitive verb, to *abstract* is to "remove, separate; to consider apart from application to or association with a particular instance; to make an abstract of or summarize; to draw away the attention of; steal, purloin." Art and science are closely related by the activity of abstracting. Both include design, analysis (separating the elements), and synthesis (putting the elements together). Aspects of both art and science are present in social science and, particularly, in the field of conflict analysis and resolution (CA&R) where distinctions between basic and applied research and between scientific (or theory) and clinical (or practice) work are enthusiastically debated.

3

The field of CA&R consists of both scientific and clinical activities, and both are represented on faculties in academic departments that teach conflict analysis. When faculty members talk about applying research in practice or about the use of practice for research, they often confront the issue of moving from the general to the specific (or vice versa). The "general" refers usually to knowledge obtained from large-N or comparative analyses of data, as discussed in Chapter 7 on comparative case studies; the "specific" usually refers to knowledge obtained about a single case, which may be an individual, group, organization, or nation, and is the focus of Chapter 6 on enhanced case and time-series analyses as well as Chapter 8 on ethnographic methods. For example, when an investigator studies the relative effects of different techniques of mediation, he or she is doing general, or abstract, scientific research. When a person attempts to understand how a particular mediator handled a case, he or she is doing specific, or clinical, analysis. The former investigation seeks generality in order to contribute to theory; the latter seeks understanding in order to contribute to a satisfactory resolution or "cure." The tension between these approaches is due, in large part, to the difficulties in finding ways to connect them. One attempt is Kolb's (1984) idea of a learning cycle that connects concrete experience with abstract, analytic knowing. This conceptualization has influenced attempts to bridge the gap between researchers and practitioners in CA&R (see Cheldelin, Druckman, & Fast, 2003, chap. 2). I will return to this topic in Chapter 12.

This issue has been receiving a lot of attention in the educational research literature. It has pit a concerned group of cognitive scientists against a vocal group of educators who have been promoting an approach known as *situated learning*. The issue turns on different opinions concerning transfer of training. The cognitive scientists emphasize the transfer value of learning abstract concepts, such as mathematics or statistics (Anderson, Reder, & Simon, 1998). The situated learning group questions the transfer value of abstract concepts, claiming that effective learning takes place in work contexts and, thus, they herald the value of on-the-job or vocational training (Greeno, Smith, & Moore, 1993). The idea of understanding conflict behavior within its context is widely shared by conflict theorists. The most developed version of this assumption is the work on contingency models of conflict interventions (Fisher, 1997; Keashly & Fisher, 1996). However, an emphasis on the contextual or situational determinants of actions does not negate the importance of transferring learning from one situation to another. Contingency theorists share the view with cognitive scientists that similar processes are likely to take place in similar conflict situations. To claim that behavior is specific to situations, as I do (Druckman, 2003), is not the same as claiming that each situation is unique or even that the differences between situations are more important than their similarities. Thus, it is assumed in this book that abstract concepts are essential for understanding the way that conflicts unfold in particular settings.

Theoretical, or abstract, analyses of cases are discussed in detail in Chapters 6 and 7. Case examples are also used throughout the book as illustrations of the concepts.

Modes of reasoning may not, however, be universal. There has been a lively debate about the extent to which culture influences the way we reason, including preferences for abstractions. Nisbett, Peng, Choi, and Norenzayan (2001) found that East Asian and Western frameworks for reasoning differ substantially. In a variety of reasoning tasks, East Asians take a holistic approach. They make little use of categories and formal logic, focusing instead on relations among objects and the context in which they interact. The subjects from the United States, on the other hand, used an analytical perspective. They categorized objects by applying formal logic and rules, largely ignoring context. They looked for regular features of isolated entities. In another article, Peng and Nisbett (1999) found differences between Chinese and American students in their styles of reasoning about contradictions: The Chinese students tried to retain elements of opposing positions by seeking a middle way; the Americans tried to determine which position was correct and then rejected the other. Findings reported by Briley, Morris, and Simonson (2000) support these differences: The Hong Kong Chinese students in their study were more likely to prefer compromise solutions to problems than their American counterparts. This preference was stronger when the subjects were asked to provide reasons for their choices. These studies suggest that cultural experiences influence the way people reason. Yet despite the evident cultural differences, Atran et al. (1999) found that people can adapt to the preferred reasoning pattern of another culture, whether that pattern is holistic or analytic.

EPISTEMOLOGICAL FOUNDATIONS: POSITIVISTS AND CONSTRUCTIVISTS

Epistemology is the study of knowledge and how it is acquired. Alternative epistemological foundations for research can be found in the debates involving positivist and constructivist perspectives on knowledge. Perhaps the most relevant aspect of these approaches for doing research is their difference with regard to viewpoint. Positivists generally prefer analyst or outside observer interpretations of data. Constructivists prefer interpretations given by the subjects or respondents themselves. Based on the assumption that there is a world to be discovered, positivists prefer to use the tools and techniques of science to discover it. They seek a convergence, if not a consensus, among investigators on observations made and interpretations offered. Based on the assumption that the world is understood primarily through actors' perceptions, constructivists prefer to rely on reflections, perceptions, and stated beliefs of the actors themselves. They seek divergence of observations made and interpretations offered. By attempting to capture the relatively unique experiences of actors, constructivists attempt to illuminate the context of experience or the idea of multiple "realities." Both approaches are empirical. They differ on their adherence to the canons and use of tools for scientific investigation. Insights into conflict behavior have come from investigations conducted in both traditions.

The issues are drawn sharply in an earlier philosophy of science literature. The dramatic 10-minute argument between Wittgenstein and Popper, recounted by Edmonds and Eidinow (2001), captures the different viewpoints. Wittgenstein railed against causal and contextual reductionism; Popper embraced it. The key theme in Wittgenstein's philosophy was that language and thought cannot be separated from one another or from the context in which language is used to accomplish a goal. Meaning is not derived from the thought process concurrent with a speaker's words, but from the whole setting in which a speaker's words are embedded. Language makes sense only when subjects and observers share a common knowledge of the context in which they interact; this is referred to as *contextual inter-subjectivity*. If this is so, then language (or thoughts) is (are) not reducible, causal, or falsifiable. For Popper, however, the opposite is the case: Thoughts and language (or deeds) are assumed to be independent of one another. This, then, is the assumptive basis for causal analysis involving the falsification of hypotheses. By the time these two philosophers met in 1946, their views on these issues had solidified, resulting in a 10-minute conversational impasse. These views strongly influenced the continuing debate between the interpretive (or constructivist) and positivist traditions of scholarship.

In psychology, a similar debate occurred between the behaviorists and phenomenologists. An exchange between Skinner and MacLeod provides an illustration. Writing in 1964 about the difference between behaviorism (positivism) and phenomenology (constructivism), the psychologist Skinner argued that

> instead of concluding that man can know only his subjective experiences—that he is bound forever to his private world and that the external world is only a construct—a behavioral theory of knowledge suggests that it is the private world which, if not entirely unknowable, is at least not likely to be known well. The relations between organism and environment involved in knowing are of such a sort that the privacy of the world within the skin imposes more serious limitations on personal knowledge than on scientific accessibility. (p. 84)

He continues with a spirited defense of the importance of reinforcement contingencies for learning and suggests that "a person cannot describe or otherwise 'know' events occurring within his own skin as subtly and precisely as he knows events in the world at large" (p. 85).

Writing in the same collection of papers, MacLeod asserts that "the approach (of phenomenology) . . . always represents a fascination with the world of experience as it is there for us" (p. 67). He goes on to say that

> I do not care for the moment whether physiognomic meanings are learned or unlearned, whether or not a baby's smile in response to a friendly face is a product of some sort of conditioning. The fact is that there is essential components of communication which can be investigated. When we know a little more about them we may venture as psychologists into the even more entrancing fields of literature, poetry, and drama. But we had better hurry, because the electronic computer is gaining on us. (p. 71)

He adds, "what, in the old, pre-scientific days, we used to call 'consciousness' still can and should be studied" (p. 72). The difference of opinion between the behaviorist Skinner and the phenomenologist MacLeod turns on the issue of a proper functional unit of analysis, external or internal events. In this book, I will not take sides in this debate but, instead, argue that both units are relevant in the study of conflict. Indeed, these approaches have been unnecessarily estranged from one another as Jost and Kruglanski (2002) observe in their attempt to reconcile constructivism with experimental social psychology.

In an extreme form, referred to as *naive realism* (positivism) or *phenomenal absolutism* (constructivism), neither is tenable. When used together for informing empirical investigation, the approaches can provide a larger understanding. A number of studies in the field have benefited from a combination of behavioral and subjective data, suggesting the plausibility of a more integrated approach to doing research. For example, an investigator interested in the impact of alternative types of pre-negotiation experience on negotiating behavior can focus either on measured outcomes (type of agreement, impasse) or the bargainer's self reports about their strategies, perceptions, and feelings during negotiation. A focus on measured outcomes facilitates comparison and strengthens the argument for generalizable results. A focus on subjective events enhances our understanding the bases for decisions or choices made by individual bargainers. Together, the two types of data can be regarded as complementary, each contributing to a larger understanding of the negotiation process. Both types of data can be collected and analyzed systematically with procedures that can be used repeatedly. These kinds of studies would move the field in the direction of the kind of reconciliation of epistemologies envisioned by Jost and Kruglanski (2002).

QUANTITATIVE AND QUALITATIVE RESEARCH

The differences between quantitative and qualitative data or approaches are another source of contention in the field, and in social science more generally.

For many researchers, the distinction overlaps the difference between positivist and constructivist approaches to knowledge. Positivists generally prefer quantitative analysis, whereas constructivists mostly perform qualitative analyses. Although the difference is evident in work done within the frameworks of these traditions, there is nothing inherent in the epistemologies that would suggest a preference for either quantitative or qualitative analysis. Indeed, laboratory experiments have been conducted in the constructivist tradition (e.g., Gergen, 1982, 1984), and small-n focused comparisons have been conducted in the positivist tradition (e.g., Faure, 1994; Putnam, 1993). So, then, if epistemologies are not the central issue, what are some other reasons to prefer one or another type of data collection and analysis?

One argument made turns on the relative advantages of the approaches to provide a deeper understanding of a phenomenon. Qualitative researchers promote this advantage of their approach by arguing that nuance is missed or masked by quantification. Another argument made concerns the relative strength of the approaches for providing general (and generalizable) knowledge. Quantitative researchers lay claim to this advantage by arguing that quantification facilitates the comparison of a large number of cases sampled from a population. These arguments reflect different kinds of appreciation for the approaches, the one promoting understanding and the other, generalizability. But, for many scholars, both values are important, and the distinction between the approaches in terms of serving one or the other value is not so clear. Some in this "camp" prefer either quantitative or qualitative approaches based largely on training and skills development: Some people are more comfortable with numbers (or words) than others. I find value in both approaches and feel comfortable with both types of analyses. In fact, the distinction is not as sharp as many think. Quantitative studies have significant qualitative aspects, especially with regard to interpretation. As well, studies that are primarily qualitative often benefit from complementary analyses of quantitative data.

Several important qualitative decisions or activities inform most, if not all, quantitative projects. One is the use of previous research to frame the problem or hypotheses: Which studies are relevant? How are the previous results to be used to define a new, or the next, research question? Another concerns the decisions made with regard to the observational domain for the study, the unit of analysis, and the number of cases to use for data collection. Although previous studies often help an investigator with these decisions, other considerations are usually entertained when the new study is not a replication. A third set of qualitative decisions involves the categories to be used for coding behavior, events, discussions, or self-reports. Again, previous studies provide guidance but are usually not sufficient for all these decisions. Even for hypothesis-testing studies, implemented in a deductive tradition, decisions regarding acceptable criteria for rejecting the null hypothesis are not decided by formula. More generally, qualitative decision making plays a more substantial role in original, as contrasted to derived or replicated, research.

With regard to qualitative studies, quantitative methods can also play important roles as illustrated from some of my projects conducted with colleagues. One example is the use of formal analysis, such as game theory, to bolster interpretations based on thought experiments that ask "what if . . ." questions about verbal documents retrieved from archival sources about the distant past (see Druckman & Guner, 2000, for an example). Another example is to augment policy exercises, including simulations, with computer-based diagnoses of the situation (see Druckman, 1994a). A third is adding time-series analyses of data to the historical interpretations performed on single cases of conflict (see Mooradian & Druckman, 1999, for an example). And a fourth example consists of attempts to define more precisely elusive concepts used in complex analyses of conflict within or between societies (see Druckman & Green, 1995). The approach taken in this book advocates the combined use of quantitative and qualitative methods, and this is illustrated with many examples of studies in the chapters to follow.[1]

ETIC AND EMIC APPROACHES

A fourth issue concerns the debate about comparative research. For a number of researchers in the field, conflicts are unique events and must be understood within their own contexts. This opinion is similar to those anthropologists and linguists who hold to an emic approach to discovery. It also coincides with case-based or clinical research as discussed above, although it does not necessarily favor concrete over abstract analysis. A challenge to the emic approach is whether social phenomena can be understood without collecting data from participants. If not, then, secondhand accounts (including archival material), samples from populations, and artifacts from lost civilizations are irrelevant sources of data.

For other researchers, any particular case is seen as an instance of a larger class of conflict processes. It is the type of conflict—sources, dynamics, influences—that interests these researchers. This interest is similar to those comparative political scientists who favor an etic approach to discovery. It also favors statistical analyses of aggregate (large-N) data sets further removed from individual cases and, thus, more abstract. A challenge to the etic approach is whether large-scale social phenomena, including inter-group conflicts, can be understood without invoking intentionality. If intentions are important, then subjective probes of actors are needed. However, examples of unintended consequences of actions support the argument that intentions can be misleading. Examples include gun ownership for personal protection without any intention to increase the homicide rate, car ownership for convenience without an intention to worsen the greenhouse effect, and laying off workers without an intention to create an underclass (see Harris, 1990, for more examples). These sorts of unintended consequences are usually not considered by emic approaches to research. But, of course, it can also be argued that emic-inspired research is less concerned with broader societal consequences or with micro-macro linkages. It is concerned with the meaning assigned by individuals or other single units to their experiences. The key differences between these approaches are shown in the table below.

Etic	Emic
Language of science and linguistics	Language of culture and experience
Nomothetic, universal language	Ideographic, cultural language
Outsider vantage point	Insider vantage point
Observed behavior or events	Self-reported sense of meaning
Prediction (or post-diction) in a causal analysis framework	Prediction is irrelevant; avoids interpretations that suggest linear causation
Materialist and behavioral	Mentalistic, intentions, mental states or desires
Comparative analysis emphasized	Single case analysis preferred
Longitudinal analysis preferred with or without direct interviews	Short time periods with living participants and available information
Focus on social consequences of action	Focus on stated or inferred intentions

Although these issues will continue to stimulate debate, it would seem that a larger perspective on conflict would include aspects of both approaches. An example in the area of negotiation analysis is a two-stage study: In the first stage, analyses are performed across a large number of cases to establish a relationship between process and outcome; in the second stage, analyses are performed on a small number of cases to ascertain, through interviews, possible reasons for the relationships obtained in the first stage (see Irmer, 2003). Data collected in an emic tradition, often in the form of ethnographies, can also be used as cases for large-N statistical analyses in the etic tradition (e.g., Ember & Ember, 1992). This is discussed further in Chapter 7 in the section on aggregate case analyses (see Jones, 1979, for an early attempt to integrate these two approaches in the field of intercultural communication).

	Emic	Etic
Qualitative	Ethnography/ single case study	Focused comparisons (small-n)
		?
Quantitative	Case time series analyses	Experiments/surveys/ aggregate case comparisons (large-N)

Figure 1.1   Examples of Methodologies in Four Research Traditions

Research approaches have been closely aligned to these distinctions. For example, most ethnographies are qualitative studies done in the emic tradition (see Chapter 8). Laboratory experiments are usually quantitative studies done in an etic tradition (see Chapters 3 and 4). Many time-series analyses of single cases are quantitative analyses in an emic tradition, whereas small-n focused comparisons are qualitative analyses in an etic tradition (see Chapters 6 and 7). The methodologies are shown with these examples in the form of a 2 × 2 matrix in Figure 1.1. A challenge is to develop a methodology that combines the features of all these approaches as indicated by the question mark in the middle of the matrix.

BREAKING DOWN THE DUALITIES

Each of the issues discussed in the sections above illuminates a particular aspect of research. The abstract-concrete issue emphasizes the role of experience in knowledge acquisition. The epistemological issues call attention to the importance of vantage point, object or subject, in data collection. The quantitative-qualitative distinction highlights features of precision in measurement. And, the etic-emic distinction deals with matters related to comparison in research design. These aspects will be discussed in more detail in the chapters to follow. In particular, the abstract-concrete difference is discussed in the context of simulation modeling in Chapter 3. The quantitative-qualitative distinction is apparent in the discussion of case-study methods in Chapters 6 and 7. We return to the emic-etic issue in our discussion of ethnographic methods in Chapter 8.

A project on utilizing research findings in negotiation training programs illustrates the relevance of the etic-emic distinction in conflict analysis. Summaries of research findings from experiments conducted largely by

American investigators were organized by theme and presented in the form of narratives. The themes covered many of the aspects of negotiation found in most frameworks for research on the topic. They are then used by trainees in a series of real-world case analyses (see Druckman & Robinson, 1998, for details). This approach to the integration of research and practice has been used with participants from societies in most of the continents of the world. To the extent that it consists of viewing the negotiation process through the lenses of Western models and experiments, it is based on etic assumptions: The approach applies an "external yardstick" to a conflict resolution process that occurs in different places, even when translated into local languages.

A more recent application of the approach is being developed by colleagues in France. They decided that it would be more useful to adapt the general approach to their own research and training context. Thus, rather than translating the narratives and cases, they are constructing new narratives based on themes and research approaches used in the French literature. In contrast to the American literature on negotiation, French scholars have conducted research in historical, sociological, and industrial relations traditions. They often develop lessons from historical texts such as De Callieres (2000 [reprinted]) and view the negotiation process less in terms of its component parts and more in terms of complex systems of competing coalitions: For example, Petit (2003) views international trade negotiations as a process where governments respond to multiple, conflicting demands made by both domestic and external constituencies. As a result, they behave in ways that may appear to many as being irrational because it contradicts the apparent objective of the negotiation, such as increased trade liberalization. To the extent that these investigators develop an approach that reflects French research traditions, it is based on emic assumptions. The gain afforded by this approach in local relevance is offset by the loss in comparing training results from one country setting to another.

Yet despite assiduous attempts to avoid investigator biases in comparative research projects, it is virtually impossible to avoid "contamination." Research done in a positivist tradition on experimenter effects reveals that even the most disinterested and passive experimenters can influence the data at the stages of design, collection, and interpretation (Rosenthal, 1964). This research shows that the experimenter's assumptions and expectations play a role in subjects' behavior or decisions. Referred to in the experimental literature as demand characteristics (Orne, 1962), these expectations play a strong role when subjects are prone to speculate on the purpose of the experiment or when they seek guidance on how to act in the situation. Put in another way, investigators bring their own emics to the research situation. This can be especially problematic in research on conflict interventions where third parties take a more active role in the interactions. Clearly, there are opportunities here for influence; there are also challenges that can arise due to differences between researcher and researched on the emics that they bring to the situation. In this research, it may be difficult to identify the outsider role, thereby compromising an etic perspective.

Although the debates on each of these dualities are often spirited with little flexibility shown on either side, it can be argued that plausible points are made by proponents on both sides of the issues. It would seem that a larger perspective that incorporates elements of all the approaches would have advantages by covering many aspects of any research problem: abstract and concrete elements, outsider and insider data, scaled and categorical/narrative data, and in-depth or deep and comparative or wide probes. Such a perspective entails a multi-method, multi-paradigm approach to research in this field: Case studies, statistical methods, and formal models are complementary rather than competitive approaches to doing research. It is close to the sort of post-positivist paradigm of research advanced by Cook (1985). It is also similar to the idea of Boudreau's (2003) multiplex methodology, which is a "systematic inquiry into the multiple, simultaneous and often contradictory knowledge claims made by all significant parties to a violent human conflict" (p. 101). (Similar arguments emphasizing triangulation in social science research have been made by King, Keohane, & Verba, 1995; Stern & Druckman, 2000; and, most recently, by George & Bennett, 2004.) These are the perspectives that guide the discussion of research methods in this book.

An agnostic stance on preferred methods and paradigms would seem appropriate for a field such as CA&R. One reason is that the field is defined as much by its practical problems as by its theoretical issues. Confronted by a host of real-world problems, the conflict researcher benefits from a "tool kit" that can be used to perform analyses on a broad spectrum of problems. Another reason is that this is an interdisciplinary field. It seeks larger perspectives on conflicts, linking analyses at micro levels (individual, small groups) to macro levels (organizations, institutions, nations). Such a broad conceptual range requires comparable methodological breadth, where no particular methodology (experiments, surveys, or case studies) has a corner on this market. A third reason concerns the mission of many conflict scholars and practitioners to integrate theory, research, and practice (see Cheldelin et al., 2003). The scope of this challenge is apparent when we consider the variety of types of theories, methodologies, and practices that characterize the field. For this reason, frameworks for analysis must be elastic, by which I mean sufficiently general to integrate a number of configurations in the theory-research-practice tripod. Thus, an attempt is made in this book to help readers develop the skills needed to do research on a variety of problems that leads to robust findings and that contributes to an integration of theory and practice with research.

Research Motivations, Norms, and Assumptions

In this section, I discuss what research is, some motivations for doing research, features and norms of the enterprise, and faulty assumptions often made about research. According to *Merriam-Webster's Collegiate Dictionary* (Mish et al., 2001), *research* is defined as "studious inquiry or examination, especially investigation or experimentation aimed at the discovery and interpretation of facts, revision of accepted theories or laws in the light of new facts, or practical application of such new or revised theories or laws; the collecting of information about a particular subject." These definitions depict a goal-driven activity aimed at discovering new knowledge through a serious, organized strategic plan. The goal of discovery is to contribute to theory (understanding of a phenomenon) or practice (use of knowledge to improve conditions). The strategic plan is the method designed to produce the knowledge.

Although research has benefited from the discipline imposed by strategy and systematic processes, many researchers approach problems with a more playful attitude. Some argue that informality—as a kind of trial-and-error experimentation—encourages flexibility and creativity in scholarly work. There is a role for playfulness in doing research. That role is often thought about as the earlier, exploratory phases of research projects. Those phases are encouraged for developing ideas or formulating research hypotheses. However, there is also a role for playfulness in the later, more systematic, phases of research. This attitude can serve to stimulate questions that could be overlooked during the implementation of techniques, as well as suggest ideas for further investigations. In discussing research in the chapters to come, I show how both attitudes—playfulness and discipline—contribute to doing effective research.

MOTIVATIONS

Researchers are motivated by a variety of incentives and inspirations. My own reasons for becoming a social science researcher include making discoveries that would contribute to my understanding of behavior and group processes as well as a fascination with the drama of experimentation. In the first edition of his textbook on methods, Robson (1993) distinguishes between motivations that produce successful and unsuccessful research. Important contributions are more likely to result from a genuine curiosity, excitement about doing research, theoretical understanding, being part of a network of researchers with similar interests, seeing clearly the next steps in a progression of findings on a topic, and understanding the real-world value of research. Contributions are less likely to be made by researchers motivated by expedience, the promise of publication, using a particular method for its own sake, or a lack of concern for or understanding of theory. A key difference between these motivations is a long-term career commitment to doing research and a desire to attain short-term gains from assignments or contracts.

The distinction between basic and applied research is often raised by textbook authors as another source of motivation for social science research. At one time, it was fashionable to describe one's profession as either a basic or applied researcher. Social scientists did not "march to the same drummer." Some scholars wanted to understand the world. They were the basic researchers who measured their accomplishments in terms of contributions to the science or discipline. Other researchers wanted to solve practical problems. These applied researchers measured their accomplishments in terms of problems solved or practices improved. In the past, it was easy to distinguish between these researchers: Basic research was done mostly in universities; applied research in public or private "think tanks" or consulting firms. Today the distinction is blurred. Most researchers in social science—whether inside or outside the academy—construe their work in both basic and applied terms. A discernable trend toward a merging of theory, practice, and research is evident, particularly in the field of conflict resolution.

Yet, differences in emphasis exist among researchers. Those who are closer to the basic research "wing" prefer the slower pace of design, data collection, analysis, and peer review publication. For them, professional rewards are derived from publications in prestigious research journals. Those closer to the applied research "wing" engage in the faster-paced enterprise of solving problems for clients. They, too, derive rewards from publications but also strive to maintain relationships with clients and are more focused on the practical applications of their research. The standards of systematic inquiry, as defined by the philosophical traditions that inform their research, guide both of these types of researchers. They differ, however, with regard to the way their research is used: namely, to contribute primarily to theory or to practice.

FEATURES, NORMS, AND ASSUMPTIONS

In this book, research is construed as a public activity. Individual researchers are part of a community of social scientists. The community establishes norms, provides rewards for contributions, creates associations that hold scientific meetings, publishes professional journals, and provides opportunities for professional visibility and advancement. These features sustain an enterprise that contributes to the larger society, which includes people in a variety of professional and non-professional pursuits. Contributions from social science research have been made in teaching approaches, skills training, educational policy, welfare policy, politics (including public opinion polling), the workplace, organizational management, environmental policy, foreign policy, security studies, and conflict resolution. The research has also contributed to more general understanding of social processes as reflected in the development and refinement of theories of persons, groups, organizations, cultures, and nations.

As part of the larger social science community, CA&R professionals conduct their research and practice within the normative framework of these disciplines. This framework places a strong emphasis on the value of a peer-review process for judging the merit of contributions to the growth and development of the field. Original ideas are valued but so too are studies that take the next step in a cumulative process that builds on existing knowledge. However, the norms provide only general guidelines for judging merit or contribution; they do not offer precise criteria. Thus, it is not surprising that members of peer-review panels disagree about the value of the same piece of work. Their disagreement is often along the lines of preferences for different paradigms or methodologies. Nonetheless, the debates are open, and the "debaters" (peer reviewers) typically accept their responsibility to render a fair judgment about the value of the research being evaluated. After all, peer reviewers are also researchers eager to make their own published contributions.

The framework also places value on ethical considerations in the conduct of research. Ethics refers to the treatment of all those involved in a particular research enterprise. Issues with regard to research subjects include disclosing information about the purpose of the research and any possible short- or long-term consequences that may arise from participation. There are strong norms against deception in the conduct of scientific research. These norms are implemented by human subject review boards at academic and research organizations (see Kelman, 1967, for an early statement about deception in research). Issues that arise with regard to collaborators include proper credit for contributions, including authorship on publications and openness among all members of the research team in discussing design, data collection, and analysis issues. Unlike treatment of research subjects, collegial relations are self-monitored, with avenues of complaint available in most departments.

Another area in which ethics are important concerns matters of trust in reporting findings. These include the very serious charges of plagiarism and manipulating or creating false data. When these matters arise, they are usually prosecuted through legal channels and can result in exclusion from the community or a loss of professional recognition. More difficult to detect are the subtle attempts to manipulate procedures or analyses that change non-significant results into significant findings. Pressures for promotion and recognition may encourage these forms of deception. The frequency of this behavior is difficult to calculate. A low frequency, if it were discovered, would indicate that most investigators subscribe to the community's ethical norms.

Research is a difficult profession. The knowledge accumulation process is slow and labor intensive. Resources are rarely sufficient to carry out many investigations or to build a program of research. The peer-review process is neither perfect nor efficient, and often leads to disappointment. Progress is usually apparent only after many years of painstaking investigation. Yet, despite these frustrations, the larger body of social science research is quite impressive—with regard to the scope of issues studied, the depth of analyses, and the practical implications of findings. Seasoned investigators can take pride in their contributions to this enterprise. New researchers can look forward to rewarding careers if they recognize that they are part of a much larger endeavor and appreciate the long-term value of doing research.

New researchers can also benefit from knowing about some faulty assumptions made about research. These include the following:

1. A critical experiment can be designed and conducted in order to confirm or disconfirm a theory.

2. Results of experiments can identify the single factor that explains social behavior.

3. Any concept can be defined in terms of a single measurement or by its operational definition.

4. At some level of abstraction, we can discover universal laws that apply across time and space.

5. A deeper understanding of a social process can be gained only through the use of ethnographic methods and participant observation.

6. Applications flow directly from the results of scientific research.

In fact, the research process is more complex than these statements suggest. Statistical findings reveal many interaction effects that indicate contingent (it all depends on the situation and time frame) relationships among variables. Surveys show many differences among sub-groups within any population with regard to values, preferences, and activities. Ethnographic studies reveal that behavior patterns are anchored in specific cultural contexts that can change. These and other findings move us away from the chimera of grand, all-encompassing theories and toward an appreciation for variety in expression for different groups and for the same group in different periods of time.

Some Contributions From Research on Conflict

A motivation for writing this textbook is the hope that it will help students conduct high-quality research on topics of CA&R. This hope is based on the opinion that it is worth investing the time and effort to do research on these topics. Because I have pursued a career along these lines, it would be dissonant for me to reject that opinion. I continue to be sufficiently stimulated by my own and others' research to enthusiastically endorse the value of the CA&R research enterprise. This enthusiasm springs from the insights generated by many of the projects completed to date. It may be infectious, not because you interact with me in the classroom, but because you appreciate the products. In this final section of the chapter, a sampling of some of these products, obtained from studies using various methodologies, is presented. Before the findings are presented, however, a brief overview of the range of conflict situations represented by them is provided.

The sampled studies cover a variety of situations and contexts in which conflict occurs. These include divorce mediation and custody disputes, mediation in community dispute resolution clinics, conflicts in schools, interactions between feuding departments in organizations and between nations, inter- and intranational war zones, formal negotiations that occur in laboratory and field settings, and disputes among political interest groups and ideological constituencies.

Issues include economic competition, power or status rivalries, national or cultural autonomy, environmental regulation, health policy, and nuclear arms control. Some matters are more tangible than others, such as the difference between disputes over money or land and those concerning recognition or identity. Variety exists also in levels of analysis: Divorce mediation is an interpersonal conflict, feuding gangs in schools are inter-group conflicts, department competition for resources is an intra- organizational conflict just as ethnic conflicts occur usually within national boundaries, and inter-organizational or inter-governmental conflicts occur when different firms consider mergers or nations attempt to negotiate membership in a regional alliance.

This complexity is captured by Sandole's (2003) three-pillar framework (elements of conflict, causes and conditions, design of interventions). It is also reflected in the framework devised to organize the chapters in Cheldelin et al. (2003). At the core of this framework are types, sources, and dynamics of conflict: What is the conflict about? Where does it come from? How does it unfold through time? The framework expands to consider the various influences on this core—situations, identities, cultures, structures, and institutions. All of these factors inform the choice among various formal and informal interventions to resolve conflict. CA&R research scholars navigate in this complex conceptual world. The analysis ("A") challenge is to gain an understanding of it. The resolution ("R") challenge is to improve upon (and evaluate) tried ways of dealing with it. The route to A&R advanced in this book is twofold: develop complex theoretical frameworks and subject them to evaluation by multiple (and often complementary) methods. This may indeed require more thought in preparation and execution of studies than is given to research in many other fields of social science. Let us turn now to examples of the progress made to date.

- From experiments on mediation in field settings, we know about some consequences of taking a problem-solving approach (with information search intended to explore mutual interests and goals) compared with a settlement orientation (emphasizing moving toward compromises) to disputes. The former usually produces better outcomes (Kressel, Frontera, Forlenza, Butler, & Fish, 1994).

- From a series of studies on peer mediation, we learned that students trained in the procedures chose an integrative rather than distributive approach to negotiation and developed more positive attitudes toward conflict. Further, the investigators found that integrating conflict resolution and peer mediation training into an academic course produced higher achievement, greater long-term retention of the academic material, and greater transfer of academic training in the social sciences and language arts (Stevahn, Johnson, Johnson, & Schultz, 2002).

- From a meta-analysis of 25 years of experimental research on bargaining processes, we know that such variables as negotiator orientation, pre-negotiation experience, and time pressure have considerably stronger effects on outcomes than representation, accountability, and visibility of the bargaining process (Druckman, 1994a).

• From content analyses of negotiation transcripts, we know that when delegates engage in sustained problem-solving behavior through the middle phases of the talks, the outcomes are more likely to be integrative (all benefit) than compromise (all sustain some losses) or impasse (Wagner, 1998).

• From complex simulations, we know that when representatives choose between courses of action that favor their interests or their ideologies, their interests usually prevail (Druckman, Rozelle, & Zechmeister, 1977).

• From events analyses of interactions (including negotiations) between nations, we know that actors adjust their moves toward each other's previous move (or concession) in order to achieve synchrony and reduce any perceived unfair advantage. This behavior can produce impasses (Patchen & Bogumil, 1995).

• From both comparative case studies and simulations, we know that bilateral negotiating structures lead to better outcomes than multilateral structures, especially when the bilateral interactions occur between relatively weak parties whose power is roughly equal (Beriker & Druckman, 1996; Druckman, 1997a).

• From a simulation of the dispute in Cyprus, we know that cooperative negotiation processes result from confronting and discussing differences in values prior to negotiation (referred to as *facilitation*) as compared with de-emphasizing those differences both before and during the negotiations (referred to as *fractionating the issues*) (Druckman, Broome, & Korper, 1988). This has been found to be due to both increased liking of and enhanced familiarity with the opposing negotiator (Druckman & Broome, 1991).

• From a score of laboratory experiments, we see the ease with which subjects develop ingroup-outgroup perceptions and biases (even in temporary groups formed on the basis of trivial issues). We also know about the difficulty of changing these perceptions and biases (Brewer & Kramer, 1985).

• From time-series analyses of violent conflicts between former republics of the Soviet Union, we know that timing of mediation efforts is critical. They are more likely to work following a series of military campaigns that produce a hurting stalemate (Mooradian & Druckman, 1999).

• From field experiments of community conflict resolution centers, we know that the anticipation of arbitration can either chill or hasten movement toward reaching agreements. Chilling effects occur when bargainers fear looking weak by making concessions, when they expect a split-the-difference solution, and when they have had favorable experiences with (or actually choose) the arbitrator (McGillicuddy, Welton, & Pruitt, 1987; Pruitt, 1981).

- Studies within organizations show that team-building exercises reduce conflict within units but can increase inter-unit conflict throughout the organization (Buller & Bell, 1986; Insko et al., 1988).

- Based on results from simulated environmental conflicts, we know some conditions that lead parties down a path toward agreement and other conditions that traject them toward impasses (Druckman, 1993, 1995).

- Social-psychological research identifies the conditions under which contact between adversaries should take place if changed attitudes are to occur—for example, equal status of participants, institutional support for such contacts, common goals, and inter-dependence between the parties (see Rouhana, 2000, for a review of the evidence).

- From ethnographic descriptions, we have a richer but context-specific understanding of people's coping mechanisms in times of war. One researcher observed the ways in which people living in the midst of brutal conflict creatively resist violence through their personal stories, songs, poetry, and dance. These acts, she argues, when taken together, constitute "politics in the making" that counter violence and build the foundation for the restoration of peace (Nordstrom, 1997).

- By using narrative and discourse theory, one researcher analyzed the stories of individuals involved in the tobacco conflict, paying particular attention to power. She examined and conceptualized types of discourse in conflict (generalized, specialized, dominant, and demotic) in order to understand the stories of those in the conflict. She found, however, that these categories were not static, and individuals could choose to move among the categories, exercising influence over the course and dynamics of the conflict in the form of power or knowledge (Johnston, 2000).

From findings such as these, by using a wide range of methodological approaches, we can draw implications for both theory and practice. Some contributions to theory include the prevalence of equilibrium-seeking behavior, trajectories toward escalatory or de-escalatory paths, and structure (macro-level)–behavior (micro-level) linkages. With regard to practice, the findings suggest ways for third parties and negotiators to arrange situations, construe issues, and encourage certain behaviors that are more likely to produce beneficial agreements or improved relationships.

Discussion Questions

Several discussion questions are suggested by the topics treated in this chapter. Use these questions to provoke class discussion or student review of the key ideas in the chapter. This review format will be used at the conclusion of each of the chapters to follow.

1. Discuss the relationship between the contrasting epistemologies and choice of research methodologies in conflict analysis. How might the different epistemological approaches be combined in doing research?

2. How might the gap be bridged between abstract and experiential approaches to learning concepts in conflict resolution? What are some ways in which abstract concepts or findings can be used in the practice of conflict resolution?

3. What are some differences between etic and emic approaches to research? How might these approaches be combined in a project?

4. What are some examples of qualitative contributions to quantitative research? How can quantitative analysis contribute to qualitative research topics?

5. List various reasons for doing social science research. Distinguish among the reasons in terms of those likely to lead to more and those that may lead to less important contributions to the field.

6. Describe some key features of the research enterprise. What can consumers of research products expect to learn? What are they unlikely to learn from results of projects?

7. Describe two conflict settings, an interpersonal conflict of interest and an inter-organizational conflict of values or worldviews. Which is likely to be more difficult to resolve and why might this be the case?

8. Discuss some new insights generated by the sample of research findings listed in this chapter. Which findings contribute primarily to understanding or theory? Which findings have more practical relevance?

Note

1. Many students and professional researchers have the impression that quantitative research is systematic and qualitative research is not. The approach to research taken in this book emphasizes the systematic features of both kinds of studies: Both are guided by widely accepted paradigms, are goal-driven activities, and are conducted within the context of research designs or rule structures. Responses by interviewees or respondents to open-ended questions, frequently used in qualitative research, acquire meaning in relation to planned designs or probing procedures. (For example, see the discussion of focused case comparisons in Chapter 7.)

2

Getting Started to Do Research

Where Ideas Come From

Ideas for research can come from a number of sources. Perhaps the most popular source is from a review of literature on a particular topic of interest. Becoming familiar with a body of published work is an essential task for the researcher. It provides a basis for discerning gaps in knowledge, learning about methodological strategies used by other investigators, and developing frameworks that can organize the new research. Research methods textbooks devote very little, if any, space to discussing the uses of literature reviews. Attempts are rarely made to connect reviews of literature to the process of doing research. Nor do teachers of methods courses develop students' skills in the mechanics of doing reviews of literature. In this section, I discuss how literature reviews are used and performed, the library resources that are available to facilitate searches, how frameworks are developed, and the role of theory in doing research.

THE LITERATURE REVIEW

Reviews of research can be discussed from the standpoint of the user as well as the reviewer. Published reviews are a valuable source of ideas for both teaching and research. However, reviews can be done only on topics that have benefited from completed research. In CA&R, reviews can be found on domestic and international negotiation, third-party influencing—including mediation, adjudication, and social-psychological approaches to conflict resolution—and social identity (see, for example, Zartman & Rasmussen, 1997). These topics have benefited from both experimental and case study research accumulated over several decades. Other, newer topics that have received attention by researchers since the end of the cold war include investigations of ripeness, interactive conflict resolution, peacekeeping, and electoral systems (reviews of some of these topics can be found in Stern & Druckman, 2000). For many other topics of interest to CA&R researchers, however, the research base is limited. Examples are peace-building processes, nongovernmental organizations' roles in conflict resolution, religion and conflict, roles played by regional organizations, and environmental conflict resolution. To the extent that researchers are drawn to the more developed topics, the field's coverage is likely to remain uneven for some time to come.

Two features of literature reviews make them useful for generating research ideas. One is the information provided about the particular studies that are summarized. Another is the organization of the review itself. These features can be illustrated with the help of a literature review done by me on international negotiation (Druckman, 1997b). With regard to specific studies, the review presented findings on the details of negotiation processes and influences. Many experiments provided a window into concession-making dynamics, tactics, and stages. They also illuminated the effects of task framing, pre-negotiation activities, time pressure, culture, and issue type, size, and complexity. Comparative case studies showed how turning points may occur, the impact of number of parties or conference size, forms of reciprocation, and negotiating objectives. Of equal importance in the review was the way these studies were organized—that organization provided a larger perspective on negotiation: what it is, how it occurs, and the ways in which it is influenced. The studies are woven into the fabric of a framework that defines the domain in terms of alternative perspectives, depicts processes as rhythms and patterns, and expands the domain to a consideration of new (and more complex) forms. The reader or researcher benefits from both features of the review. The studies provide the research specialist with knowledge accumulated to date as well as access to the technical information needed to design new studies. The organization of the review provides the reader with a larger perspective on the topic that, in this example, is negotiation processes and influences.

The two features of reviews are also relevant for the reviewer. The crafting of a review article includes both coverage of relevant studies and organization. From the standpoint of mechanics, coverage is accomplished in the following way: (a) doing keyword searches; (b) developing a bibliography of articles in each of the keyword categories; (c) summarizing the methods, findings, and implications of each article; and (d) reviewing the match between articles and keyword categories. These tasks are aided considerably by citation patterns. Citations provide a window into the research that has been done on the topic. Articles that appear in refereed journals usually build on previous research in a cumulative manner. For many topics, such as, for example, reciprocity in bargaining or mediation approaches, the reviewer gets a snapshot of the body of research by just reading a few papers. For other (usually newer) topics, such as, for example, peace-building or conflict transformation, the reviewer has a larger challenge of searching for relevant studies. The process of searching and summarizing often suggests new ways of thinking about a field. The tasks involved in covering a field of research are related to those that serve to organize the review.

The organization of a literature review is a perspective on the topic. The reviewer often attempts to achieve thematic coherence in the form of a framework. Section headings may resemble the keyword search categories or they may be the central variables explored in the studies. But as a field develops, other categories and forms of organization may emerge as illustrated by a set of reviews that I have done on negotiation. In my first published review (Druckman, 1971), I summarized the findings of the key studies in tabular form at the beginning of the article. The article then discussed the studies in each of 10 variable categories. My second published review (Druckman, 1973) organized the literature according to a version of a well-known framework developed several years earlier (Sawyer & Guetzkow, 1965). This framework was used also to organize the chapters of a book on the subject that appeared a few years later (Druckman, 1977b). Another review organized a similar literature according to the distinction between person, role, and situation influences on negotiating behavior (Druckman, 1977a). And, a more recent review (Druckman, 1997b) provided a threefold distinction between defining the domain, capturing rhythms and patterns, and expanding the domain. The reader of this set of reviews can discern the way this field has developed from early experimental research (in the 1960s and 1970s) to later comparative case research (in the 1980s and 1990s). The growth of the field is reflected also in the way conceptualizations of the phenomenon have changed.

For more detailed treatments of ways to perform literature reviews in the social sciences, see the various recent Sage books, including Fink (2004); Locke, Silverman, and Spirduso (2004); Hart (2001); and Cooper (1998). For guidelines on the process of evaluating research articles, Girden's (2001) book provides valuable suggestions. A particularly useful Web tutorial developed by the George Washington University's Graduate School of Education and Human Development can be found at http://www.gwu.edu/~litrev/. This site provides a series of lessons on critical aspects of searching for research literature, assessing the quality of reports, and integrating across several reports or articles on a topic. The searching task is discussed next in the context of CA&R.

USING LIBRARY AND WEB RESOURCES

Library resources can facilitate the process of doing literature reviews. Over the past 10 years, information and computer technology have revolutionized the way people gain access to and collect information. A growing number of online databases and indexes allow easy navigation and the rapid retrieval of a wealth of information across multiple disciplines. If used correctly, these online resources can be useful tools for performing keyword searches and literature reviews. However, despite the increasing accessibility of online information,

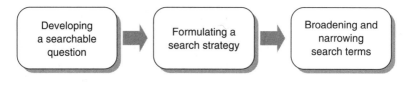

Figure 2.1   Search Strategy Process

many remain hesitant about utilizing these resources in their research for fear that they will become lost forever in the vast world of cyberspace. This section provides insight into the tools and procedures needed to provide access to the global world of online research. It is not meant to be a comprehensive guide to performing searches but rather a brief overview for those who wish to use online resources to improve their reviews.

Whether conducted in the library or on the World Wide Web, a search contributes to research planning. The contribution depends, however, on how well a research question is formulated and the search strategy used, including the broadening and narrowing of search terms. This process can be depicted as shown in Figure 2.1.

Searches are more useful for topics that have received attention in the research literature. The more obscure the topic, the less fruitful the online search is likely to be. For example, topics such as conflict resolution skills, stereotypes and the media, and human rights are likely to yield many citations, referred to also as *hits*. Considerably fewer hits are likely to be found when these topics are narrowed, as with sustainable conflict resolution skills, stereotypes and terrorists, or religion and human rights.

An example of a more specific search is the problem of post-conflict Afghanistan. This search addresses the question, What are the conditions for enhancing peace and stability in the aftermath of violent conflict? An initial choice of keywords includes the following broad categories: post conflict, war termination, peace, security, stability, and challenges or obstacles. Searches were conducted in two online databases, Columbia University's International Affairs database (CIAO) and the Social Science Citation Index (SSCI). The former, CIAO, includes a large variety of types of sources; the latter, SSCI, is limited to journals in the social and behavioral sciences. Both can be accessed through most university library home pages by clicking on the "Database" heading and, then, clicking on the particular database of interest, "CIAO" or "SSCI." Often the databases are sorted alphabetically, and some university Web sites will require you to first select "S" for the Social Science Citation Index or "C" for the Columbia International Affairs Online database. By further choosing to perform an "Advanced Search," the user can reach a wider sampling on the topics of interest. This search produced over 11,000 hits on the keywords.

A more useful result was obtained by narrowing the search terms by adding "Afghanistan" (31 hits from CIAO) or stipulating an interest in articles that focused on the creation and maintenance of "economic infrastructure" (a couple hundred from SSCI). Other terms that would limit the hits are democracy, legal reforms, market reforms, public health, and refugees. Further narrowing would occur if specific authors or institutions were included or if particularly broad terms, such as *peace-building* or *relief,* were excluded.

Useful searches occur when keywords are closely related to the research question and when those words open a window on relevant research literature found in the chosen databases. The "right" keywords searched in the "wrong" database may be misleading; similarly, the "wrong" keywords searched in the "right" databases can be misleading. The keyword *conflict* is too broad; the phrase *trauma healing in post-conflict societies* is likely to be too narrow. The phrase *interpersonal conflict* narrows the search to some degree; *interpersonal conflict in divorce mediation* will produce a more limited, and perhaps relevant, set of articles. *Trauma healing* will produce a larger number of hits in databases that cover psychology, but not those that focus on international affairs. The opposite would be likely for *post-conflict societies.* Descriptions of 12 databases that may be useful for searches on CA&R topics are shown in Table 2.1.

Table 2.1   Databases for CA&R Searches

Online Database/Index	What It Searches	Notes
Social Science Citation Index	Online index of journals in the social and behavioral sciences.	Covers the journal literature of the social sciences from 1980–present. Over 2.8 million articles, with 2,800 added each week.
Columbia International Affairs Online (CIAO)	Full text of more than 400 working papers, 40 conference proceedings, and 10 books annually, as well as abstracts from leading international relations research journals, brief reports, monthly statistics, and maps.	The CIAO database covers 1991–present and collects papers from a spectrum of different sources, including universities, research institutes/foundations, NGOs, academic journals, and books on international affairs.
Database Abstracts	Complete range of academic subjects appearing in dissertations accepted at accredited institutions.	Abstracts on all dissertations from 1861–present.

(Continued)

Table 2.1 (Continued)

JSTOR: The Scholarly Journal Archive	The complete text of core scholarly journals in the fields of anthropology, Asian studies, ecology, economics, education, history, philosophy, political science, population studies, sociology, and more.	Coverage varies.
Social Research Methodology (SRM)	A bibliographic database of references on social research methodology, statistical analysis, and computer programs used in the social and behavioral sciences.	Database chronicles articles from 1997–2000.
Stockholm International Peace Research Institute (SIPRI) Article Databases	Indexes multiple databases. Contains full-text search in NATO Review articles and wide range of articles related to international peace and conflict.	Database chronicles articles from 1991–1997.
Lexis Nexis Academic	Provides access to a wide range of news (including *New York Times, Washington Post, L.A. Times*), business (company news, industry forecasts), government (legislative news, tax information), legal (news, case law), and reference information.	Coverage varies. However, it is quite extensive and updated daily.
Global NewsBank	An index of several hundred international newspapers, news services, and broadcast media.	Database chronicles articles from 1996–present.
Statistical Lexis Nexis	Chronicles all statistics issued by the U.S. government since 1973. 1,000 of the best statistical publications of private and state government sources and approximately 2,000 titles from international agencies.	Full text documents, 1973–present.
Sociological Abstracts	The premier online resource for researchers, professionals, and students in sociology and related disciplines. Contains citations and abstracts from over 2,000 journals.	Abstracts only. 1963–present. 514,000+ records.
Worldwide Political Science Abstracts	Provides citations, abstracts, and indexing of the international serials literature in political science and its complementary fields, including international relations, law, and public administration.	Abstracts from 1975–present.
Peace Research Abstracts	Abstracts of literature concerning peace studies, conflict studies, and international relations.	Abstracts on CD-ROM only. 1964–present.

A particularly useful reference guide for performing keyword searches has been assembled by the Duke University library and can be accessed on the World Wide Web at http://www.lib.duke.edu/libguide/adv_searching.htm. Table 2.2, adapted from a table in the reference guide, helps with the process of combining search terms and broadening or narrowing a search.

A number of other tips may aid the search process, including the following:

1. Always begin an online search by selecting broad parameters, then narrowing subsequent searches. Be cautious when choosing the narrowing terms, as they may eliminate important articles that may be relevant.

2. Truncation is another little known trick that is useful in performing online searches. Typing econom* in the search box will look for any keywords containing the root word selected, such as "economist," "economy," or "economical."

3. Proximity operators are useful in searches for specific words that appear within two words of one of your search terms. For example, an interest in the word "development" within two words of your search term "sustainable" would appear in your search as sustainable w/2 development.

4. Use Boolean operators (and, or, not) to combine terms in broad searches. For example, the search "conflict resolution skills" searches for records containing "conflict" and "resolution" and skills" (i.e., all terms must be present in the record). The search "conflict or war" searches for records containing either "conflict" or "war." The search "conflict not war" searches for records that contain the term "conflict" but do not contain the term "war" (see Table 2.2).

5. When searching for an exact phrase to appear in a document, title, or abstract, use quotation marks around the phrase. For instance, information on "sustainable international development" requires quotation marks around the text in order to generate hits that use that exact phrase.

6. Generally, online searches are case insensitive. Using either upper- or lower-case letters will yield the same result set. However, it should be noted that this is not always the case.

7. Some search engines also offer "subject trees" or "directories." These are categories of information that can be used to narrow the scope of your search. These resources are often useful guides to the contents of particular databases.

8. If few hits are generated during a first search, consider searching for different keywords in the same database or perhaps the same words in a different database.

9. In developing keywords, remember to use lateral thinking. If the word "development" yields little, try "underdevelopment" or "developing

Table 2.2   Alternative Search Operators

Boolean Operators	Example Search	The Search Will Find . . .	Venn Diagram
AND	conflict resolution AND culture	Items containing "conflict resolution" and "culture." Note that AND narrows a search, resulting in fewer hits.	
OR	war OR peace	Items containing either "war" or "peace" or both. Note that OR broadens a search, resulting in more hits.	
NOT	conflict NOT warfare	Items containing "conflict" but not "warfare." Be careful. It is easy to end up excluding relevant keywords that may generate important hits.	

countries." It is also possible that an antonym ("peace" instead of "war") will yield the desired sources.

10. If only one source is a good match, read that source carefully. Pay attention to the list of references, as it may lead you to other articles as well as the names of experts in the field.

11. Citations found from a keyword search can be retrieved for later use by importing them into a program such as Endnotes.

It is important to remember that a search is not a substitute for the research. An investigator should not aspire to knowing all that has been done on a topic before conducting his or her own project. Of equal importance is the development of a framework to organize the project, which is the topic of the next section.

CONSTRUCTING FRAMEWORKS

Frameworks are organizing devices. They may be used to organize literature reviews, as discussed above. But they also serve to organize other aspects of the research process by providing categories for data collections and analyses. For CA&R researchers, frameworks identify and relate elements of structure or contexts, interactive processes, and dynamics. By aiding the tasks of conceptualizing, analyzing, and interpreting, frameworks enable an investigator to get his or her "mind around a topic." Each of these functions of frameworks is discussed in this section followed by an example of how a framework may be constructed.

Before engaging in the technical aspects of a research project, an investigator must develop a conceptual understanding of the phenomenon to be explored. Literature reviewing is a necessary part of this process. It is not, however, sufficient. Also needed is a way of organizing the knowledge accumulated to date and providing an abstract representation of that knowledge. This process can be illustrated. In 1965, Sawyer and Guetzkow presented a framework for research on international negotiation. These theorists first identified the key negotiation processes and outcomes and the many factors shown by the early research (prior to 1965) to influence them. This panoply of factors was organized by a structure that captured the various parts of the phenomenon, relations among the parts, and dynamics as the flow from antecedent to concomitant to consequent factors. The relational and dynamic features of this framework, shown in Figure 2.2, render it an abstract representation of

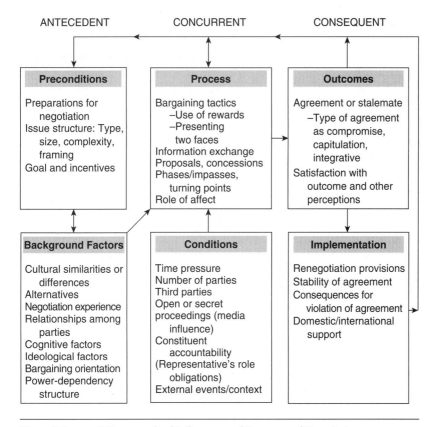

Figure 2.2   A Framework of Influences and Processes of Negotiation

negotiation. As such, it can be applied to a wide variety of types and cases. Indeed, versions of this framework have been very useful for organizing literature, guiding analyses of cases, and for comparative research.

Another function served by frameworks is to guide the collection and analysis of data. This function is illustrated by Bonham's (1971) simulation of an arms control negotiation. His interest in reproducing an actual case in the laboratory was intended to capture the advantages of experimental controls and real-world relevance. He used the categories of the Sawyer-Guetzkow (1965) framework to ensure that the simulation was a reasonably good replica of the case. The categories were used to compare the framework with the case: Examples of categories were goals, issues, background of negotiators, media coverage, and time pressure. Direct comparisons were afforded by using the same categories to analyze the content of the discussions in the simulation and in the actual case. Other examples of framework-driven analyses are Graham, Mintu, and Rodgers's (1994) 10-culture comparison of process-outcome relationships, Chasek's (1997) 11-case comparison of processes used in environmental negotiations, and the evaluation of Iklé's (1964) framework of negotiating objectives with 34 cases drawn from the Pew case studies series (Druckman, Martin, Allen Nan, & Yagcioglu, 1999). In the former two studies, a framework guided the operational definitions of the variables used in the comparisons. In the latter study, 16 coded aspects of the cases were analyzed to detect whether or not the framework was effective in distinguishing among them. The statistical analyses indicated that the five negotiating objectives separated the cases. Sometimes, an initial framework based on past research is modified by the results of new data collections, as shown by Allen Nan's (1999) comparison of 3 cases involving third-party coordination.

A third function of frameworks is interpretation. Two studies illustrate this function. Ramberg's (1978) analysis of tactics used in the Seabeds Arms Control talks (1967–1970) was informed by the Sawyer-Guetzkow (1965) framework. Rather than using the categories to guide the analysis or coding of process, he placed the tactics in the larger context of processes and influences highlighted by the framework. As a result, he provided a more comprehensive interpretation of the case. A simulation experiment reported by Druckman et al. (1988) shows how a framework can be induced from findings. They compared alternative approaches to resolving value conflicts referred to as *facilitation* and *de-linking*. Although the approaches did not differ in their influence on the outcomes, they did produce different kinds of processes. These differences suggested alternative routes to agreements that were interpreted in the form of "models." In turn, the models can be used as frameworks to guide further research. This connection between the interpretive and generative functions of frameworks suggests a cyclical pattern among the three functions of frameworks—conceptualizing, analyzing, and interpreting.

Framework construction can best be understood perhaps in terms of an example. Suppose that you were preparing to do research on integrative bargaining, which refers to a problem-solving process leading to favorable joint outcomes. Your research questions presume a familiarity with what is and what is not known about this process. Familiarity is gained by a literature review on the subject. Understanding is further developed by embedding the knowledge gained from studies in a conceptual framework that also specifies relationships among the variables uncovered in the review. The framework can be constructed in the following way.

1. In reviewing existing frameworks, you have discovered that negotiation is usually conceived as a dynamic process that moves from antecedent to concomitant to consequent factors. The factors are defined more specifically as pre-conditions, background factors, processes, conditions, outcomes, and implementation.

2. Since those frameworks were developed, you have become aware that the research has moved away from bargaining and toward problem solving as the key process in negotiation. Problem solving processes have been shown to lead to integrative or optimal rather than compromise outcomes.

3. In reviewing the published literature, you have found many experiments designed to identify the factors that lead toward or away from integrative outcomes. These factors are delineated more specifically in your summaries of the experimental findings.

4. Returning to the general framework, you can organize the factors into their categories, placing them appropriately in the boxes under antecedent, concomitant, or consequent factors.

5. Drawing on the literature review, you can judge the way these factors relate to one another in a causal direction. Causality, indicated by arrows between the boxes, may be complex with recursive or circular relations indicated.

6. The framework that emerges from these steps may take the form of the diagram referred to as "the anatomy of integrative bargaining" in Figure 2.3. This sort of framework identifies the factors that influence integrative bargaining, shows how they relate to each other, and suggests a practical strategy for encouraging such processes and outcomes. It services research by calling attention to what is and is not known. It also services training by providing a path to explore in exercises intended to give trainees experience in negotiating.

7. An alternative way of thinking about integrative bargaining was proposed by Walton and McKersie (1965). This process, shown in

Figure 2.4, proceeds through stages of problem recognition, searching for alternatives, evaluating alternatives, and agreeing on a solution to the problem. This framework focuses entirely on the process box in Figure 2.3. The stages and feedback loops depicted in this framework elucidate the information search process that is at the heart of integrative bargaining.

Taken together, the three frameworks proceed from the general to the specific. Each figure opens a box from the previous framework for more detailed examination. Integrative bargaining is one of several processes indicated in Figure 2.2. It is isolated for study in Figure 2.3, where an information search is recognized as the key process. That process, then, is further decomposed into its parts in Figure 2.4. This figure can also be used to guide negotiators through the steps. Each is an example of a framework that has been used to guide empirical research in experimental and case study traditions on negotiation and problem-solving processes.

THE ROLE OF THEORY

The discussion in the previous section trumpeted the value of frameworks for organizing thinking about a topic. Useful frameworks are usually those that include a large number of factors or processes. They are expansive depictions of a topic, approach, or concept, and they can be used to guide the generation of observable data. But they are not theories. Differences are the degree of

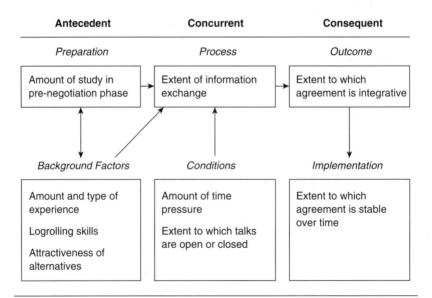

Figure 2.3   Anatomy of Integrative Bargaining

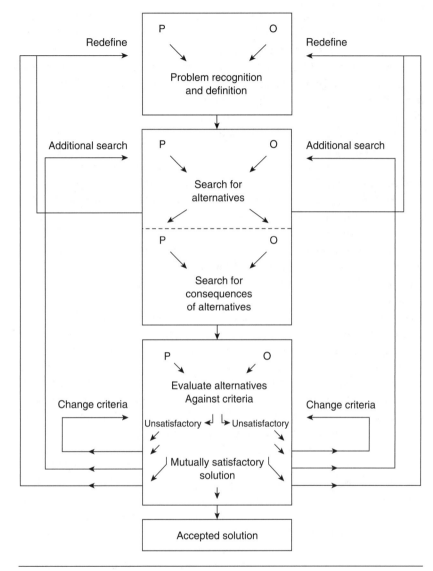

Figure 2.4   Joint Problem-Solving Process

Note: P = party; O = other

Source: Walton, R. E., & McKersie, R. B. (1965, p. 138). *A behavioral theory of labor negotiations: An analysis of a social interaction system.* New York: McGraw-Hill.

precision in specifying relationships among factors as well as providing explanations (or understandings) for those relationships: A theory is both more precise and more explanatory than a framework. These differences can be illustrated.

The relationships depicted in Figure 2.3 indicate that certain kinds of preparation, background factors, or conditions influence the process of negotiating which, in turn, lead to particular outcomes. For example, studying the issues prior to negotiation increases the chances of engaging in an information-exchange process, leading to an integrative outcome. This hypothesis has been evaluated and confirmed in several experimental studies reviewed in my meta-analysis article (Druckman, 1994a). Thus, hypotheses about relationships between independent (preparation) and dependent (process, outcome) variables can be derived from frameworks. The hypotheses can also be evaluated with the research methodologies discussed in this book.

But why is this not the same as evaluating a theory? First, the variables are insufficiently specified by the framework: How much studying (vs. strategizing)? How much and what kinds of information should be exchanged? To what extent must joint benefits be realized to qualify as an integrative agreement? Second, the reason for hypothesizing this relationship is not articulated. Alternative explanations highlight cognitive or motivational factors. A cognitive theory would emphasize the rigidity (flexibility) induced by strategizing (studying). A motivational theory would emphasize the competitiveness (cooperativeness) sparked by strategizing (studying). A more complex contingency theory may specify the conditions under which either cognitive or motivational factors are more or less important. Research designed to evaluate these theories would go beyond demonstrating the relationship posited by the framework.

Another example of the distinction between a framework and a theory is drawn from research on the sociology of conflict. This research has addressed propositions about the interplay between conflicting interests and values suggested by Coser (1956) and Aubert (1963), among others. Interests are represented in the framework shown in Figure 2.2 in the box on pre-conditions as issue structure (type of issue) and goals (to satisfy interests). Values are represented in the box on pre-conditions as issue structure (type of issue) and in the box on background factors as cultural similarities and differences as well as ideological factors. Both are hypothesized to influence the negotiation process leading to particular outcomes. These relationships are not specified precisely. Nor are they explained in the framework.

A theory about the interplay between interests and values would cover the types, sources, and dynamics of conflict as these terms are discussed in Chapter 1: What is the conflict about? Where does it come from? How does it unfold through time? This particular theory has other important features as well:

1. The two sources of conflict (independent variables) are interdependent through time.

2. It focuses attention on the intensity of the conflict (dependent variable).

3. Conditions (contingencies) are defined in terms of moderating and enhancing influences on conflict intensity.

4. A mechanism is defined in terms of a dynamic equilibrium (counter-vailing effects of the moderating and enhancing conditions).

5. The propositions derived from the theory have been evaluated empir-ically in both experiments and case studies.

6. The theory is distinguished from other theories of conflict by its attempt to connect micro-level processes (negotiation) to macro-level structures (organizational dynamics).

These features are evident in the description of the theory (see Druckman & Zechmeister, 1973). Of particular interest, however, is the way that research methodologies have been used to address the theory's propositions.

Two approaches have been used to evaluate this theory—experimental sim-ulation and a case study. The experimental work was intended primarily to assess the impacts of the link between values and interests on attempts to reach agree-ments in simulated talks. A series of experiments (simulations of political decision making) showed that when value differences are linked explicitly to conflicting interests, the conflict is more difficult to resolve than when values are not invoked (e.g., Druckman et al., 1977). This replicated finding supports the first proposi-tion drawn from Coser (1956) and stated in Druckman and Zechmeister (1973). Further, competing hypotheses about interventions were evaluated within the context of this theory: Facilitation, in the form of confronting value differences during pre-negotiation, works better than fractionation, in which parties focus only on their interests, not their values (Druckman et al., 1988).

Laboratory experimentation is limited, however, to relatively short-term interactions among conflicting parties. The theory's other propositions describe unfolding processes through longer periods of time, for example, waves of increases and decreases in the intensity of conflicts as the parties con-tinue to interact. A window on these processes is provided through the course of an extended case. Indeed, a case of negotiation between the new Aquino administration and the National Democratic Front in the Philippines provided this opportunity (see Druckman & Green, 1995). This enhanced case study is described in Chapter 6. For purposes of this discussion, the example illustrates theory-driven research with complementary methodological approaches. It also underscores the value of multi-method research on conflict processes.

Of course there are other theoretical perspectives that can inform research in CA&R. A recent count, made in conjunction with a course that I teach on integrating theories, research, and practice, lists 20 theories. Although they dif-fer on the theory criteria stated above—in other words, some are better theories than others—all contribute ideas to our understanding of conflict. They can be grouped into five categories according to their key concepts. Equilibrium theories of conflict posit cyclical processes that bounce back toward a stasis or ideal state: Game theory, exchange theory, the dual concern model, and (at a macro level) structural-functional theories are examples. Utility theories of conflict posit rational, calculating actors who are moved to action by incentives: examples include social learning or reinforcement theories, decision and game theory, and various forms of contingency theories. Consistency theories emphasize tensions between competing cognitions and the accompanying motivation to reduce these tensions: These theories are pitched at both a micro (cognitive dissonance) and macro level (rank disequilibrium, structural violence) as well as bridging the levels (relative deprivation). Cultural theories stress identities, ideologies, and worldviews and include the various perspectives on social identity as well as discourse analysis. Psychosocial theories focus primarily on the individual and tend toward being reductionist: Examples are human needs, psychoanalysis, and frustration-aggression.

With all of these theories, there would seem to be no limit on sources for research ideas. However, only a few have received much empirical attention, and these are mostly at the micro level of analysis: They include game theory, exchange theory, cognitive dissonance and related entrapment processes, social identity, and the dual concern model. Each of these theories has yielded hypotheses similar to those developed from the literature on the sociology of conflict. These hypotheses have been addressed in the laboratory and in the field, with experiments, surveys, and case studies. Indeed, a large body of research has accumulated on these topics, and the studies have been synthesized with meta-analytic procedures. (For example, De Dreu, Weingart, & Kwon, 2000, on the dual concern model; Druckman, 1994a, on group identification; meta-analytical procedures are discussed in Chapter 3.) Unlike the many other theories largely immune to empirical testing, these theories are characterized by clearly defined variables, explanatory concepts, and accessible venues (or levels of analysis) for exploration. Clearly, theories are an importance source of ideas for research. Many would argue that sound research depends on connections to a theoretical context, performed either as "tests" of propositions and assumptions or to generate new theories.

A number of the studies used in later chapters to illustrate methodologies are examples of theory-inspired research. However, this book is about doing empirical research for making inferences that may have relevance for various theories of conflict. It is not intended to generate the theories to be evaluated. The research approaches to be discussed should apply to any theory of conflict constructed to produce observable implications. The results obtained from well-designed and implemented studies intended to evaluate a theory (or decide between competing theories) should contribute to a "verdict" about the quality of that theory (or theories). (See also King, Keohane, & Verba, 1994, for a similar distinction between theory generation and theory evaluation. Their book on qualitative research is intended primarily to develop the logic of inference rather than to propose new theories for political science.)

Choosing a Research Topic

Doctoral students are often in a quandary about how to go about selecting a research topic for their dissertation. I have observed many students dealing with the tension of trying to satisfy the criteria of (a) doing what they find to be interesting, (b) doing what needs to be done in order to make a contribution to the field, and (c) doing a project that can be completed in a reasonable period of time given available resources. When three of these criteria are satisfied, the ideal project has been found. When all of them cannot be satisfied, trade-offs must be entertained. This decision-making process is, however, rarely a choice among the criteria. Rather, it consists of making adjustments that attempt to satisfy all of them in varying degrees. This process can be illustrated with a few dissertation projects.

During the course of his project, Weiss (2002) confronted these three criteria. Initially, he was interested in the problem of the way various mediation strategies are implemented and the impacts of those strategies on international peace processes. This is, of course, not an entirely new problem for researchers in CA&R. But, by identifying the problem even in very broad terms, he has satisfied the criterion of interest. The next questions asked were, What do we know about various strategies? What remains to be known about them? These questions led to the task of reviewing a very large body of research on mediation. The review made evident the strategies that have received attention in earlier research. It did not point to strategies used in actual cases of international peace agreements. For this information, Weiss conducted interviews with international mediators. The strategies they discussed received scant attention in the research literature. Investigating them systematically would satisfy the second criterion of making a contribution to the field.

The next challenge for Weiss was to refine his questions in a way conducive to carrying out and completing the research in a reasonable period of time. He did this by (a) limiting the investigation to the three strategies most commonly used, (b) developing indicators that would distinguish the strategies, (c) choosing cases that would serve as exemplars of each of the strategies, (d) searching for detailed published reports of the negotiation process in each case, (e) developing a system of categories to content analyze the process, and (f) performing statistical analyses of relations among variables that distinguished the cases. By limiting the strategies chosen for investigation (based on frequency of use) and limiting the number of cases to investigate (based on relevance and available information), he satisfied the third criterion of completing the project in a reasonable period of time. Further, by limiting his goal to the development of a taxonomy of alternative mediation strategies, he justified the use of a small number of different cases. In a later chapter, we will discuss this research approach; it is referred to as the "most different systems design" (Faure, 1994).

Another example of narrowing the focus of a project in order to complete it in a reasonable period with limited resources is the dissertation study by Jackson (2001). Her interest in studying the development of identity and the self concept led to an extensive literature review of the subject. The review helped to refine her understanding and discover gaps in knowledge. However, she was challenged by having to decide which of the many avenues for research to pursue. Working with members of her committee, she decided to investigate the relationship between perceived control beliefs and conflict management preferences; she would leave other interesting problems for further research. This decision was a turning point in the project: She formulated hypotheses, identified the key variables, and began to develop indicators for assessing the variables.

It then became evident that the problem could best be investigated by conducting an experiment with children. Taking into account opportunities and resources, she prepared a strategy for data collection and analysis. She sought and obtained the cooperation of a school's administrators and classroom teachers as well the necessary permissions for participation from the children's parents. Timelines for data collection and analysis were developed, procedures were piloted, and the experiment was carried out. The study satisfied the three criteria—interest, contribution, and implementation—while also providing a road map for a research program that addresses issues of context, self concept, and conflict behavior.

A lesson learned from these projects is that doing research depends as much on implementation as it does on conceptualization. Knowing the setting within which the research will be conducted is important. This includes surveying the opportunities available for data collection and analysis—for example, subject pools for experiments, administrative support for surveys, and establishing trust from group members for participant observation. It also includes the constraints that exist in the organization or culture such as the availability of financial support for a project and faculty members who are both knowledgeable about and interested in the project. Opportunities and constraints may be regarded as the pre-conditions for implementing projects. They define the context for research as illustrated by other dissertation projects.

Larson (2003) developed a framework for analysis of multilateral environmental negotiations. The successful implementation of the project depended on seizing opportunities that were available. It also depended on dealing with some constraints that would limit the scope of the study. The opportunities included recruiting interested committee members who were also knowledgeable about the topic, securing records of the proceedings of the cases chosen for analysis, and using her network of contacts in the environmental diplomacy community to arrange interviews. These opportunities enabled her to assemble a data set and perform content analyses of the discussions in two cases. The discussions with committee members and informants also contributed to the further development and refining of her framework. The constraints included a small number of cases available for analysis and limited coverage of the discussions in each case. Although these limitations created problems for generalizing the results, Larson presented plausible claims that favored the selection of these cases and material. The cases were considered exemplars of types of negotiation; the information was sampled for parties and time periods. The study also succeeded in demonstrating the usefulness of her more general framework of multilateral negotiations.

Hancock's (2003) study of identity change in the Northern Ireland peace process illuminates trade-offs between opportunities and constraints. An earlier comparative analysis done by the author in other country contexts set the stage for the study design. Faculty interest in the topic, coupled with peer-group support, provided the needed encouragement to go forward. A key opportunity was the network connections between faculty members and similar organizations in Northern Ireland. These connections opened the door to interviews conducted in the field. A dissertation grant enabled him to direct his energies to the dissertation project rather than on other tasks in a workplace environment unrelated to the topic. The research was, however, constrained by limited funds. It was difficult to spend enough time at the research site to obtain a large amount of primary data from interviews with participants. This limitation was offset, to some extent, by a rich volume of secondary sources on this conflict available for analysis.

Research on new topics or areas that have received little attention in the literature may be more preliminary. An example of such a topic is peace building. The developing literature to date is quite scattered, both in terms of where articles on the topic appear and in terms of conceptual clarification. It is difficult to know what accounts for the success or failure of post-conflict peace-building activities taking place in many parts of the world. An ongoing dissertation project at George Mason by Monica Jacobsen takes an important first step by organizing the various processes that spin into motion following a peace agreement. These processes include (but are not limited to) building democratic institutions, reforming the military, sustaining the peace, growing the economy, ensuring health care and educational opportunities, and building the infrastructure of a civil society. To better understand this complex web of activities, a project would consist mostly of constructing a framework that draws connections among the various parts of peace building and developing indicators for these parts (for example, election monitoring, trade flows, progress in transforming militant groups into political organizations). A next phase of the project could use these indicators to evaluate progress followed by confirmatory research into the reasons why particular programs succeed and others fail.

DEVELOPING RESEARCH QUESTIONS

There are many sources for research ideas. Many of my own projects have been developed from immersions in particular research literatures. Previous studies or theoretical debates about sources of conflict and interventions have often stimulated new ideas that lead to important studies. One example is the debate between Roger Fisher and John Burton over the best strategy for reconciling value conflicts. Fisher's (1964) well-known fractionation approach contrasts with Burton's (1986) facilitation approach: The former emphasizes separating the negotiable interests from the non-negotiable values; the latter promotes confronting the larger values and discussing them outside of formal negotiations. These approaches can be presented as competing hypotheses subject to empirical investigation. A simulation experiment was designed as a contest between the competing hypotheses. The results showed that although the approaches produced about the same number of agreements, Burton's strategy was more effective in inducing a cooperative process with implications for beneficial long-term relations between the parties (see Druckman et al., 1988). This research also stimulated further questions about the reasons for the positive effects of the facilitation condition. This condition served to increase both liking and familiarity between the conflicting parties. In another simulation experiment, we separated these factors and explored their relative and combined effects on the resolutions that were achieved (see Druckman & Broome, 1991).

These experiments provided vehicles for confronting alternative approaches or competing hypotheses. Through the years, I have gained an appreciation for this contribution made by experiments. Starting with a master's thesis on ethnocentric bias in groups, I have conducted a string of experiments designed to shed light on alternative explanations. My dissertation study examined the relative effects of the person, role, and situation in simulated collective bargaining. Other studies included the relative plausibility of alternative models of responsiveness in negotiation, effects of different configurations of power among negotiating parties, and the relative strength of competing explanations for stopping wars—mediation or hurting stalemates. This function of experimental work is amplified by the results of a meta-analysis that compared the impact of 10 variables on subjects' bargaining behavior (Druckman, 1994a).

There are other sources for research ideas. A number of examples illustrate the value of preliminary investigations in an inductive tradition. Interviews with international mediators suggested that they used a number of strategies for sequencing issues in negotiation. Three of the most frequently used strategies—referred to as gradualism, "boulder in the road," and committee— were investigated further with a more systematic content analysis of case material (Weiss, 2002). Newspaper reporting of day-by-day developments in an internal negotiation during the 1980s in the Philippines provided useful accounts of the process. This information was used to develop a chronology of events that was used as "data" for more systematic analysis. The analysis consisted of an evaluation of a theory about the interplay of values and interests in conflict (Druckman & Green, 1995). Panel interviews with delegates to several international negotiations provided useful information for developing lessons learned from practice. The panel inferred lessons from the discussions and presented them in proposition form for evaluation in a more deductive research tradition (Bendahmane & McDonald, 1986; McDonald & Bendahmane, 1990).

Informal participant observation of processes provide another source for research questions. One example is an insight that occurred in the context of conflict resolution training sessions. Participants in simulated multilateral negotiations appeared more willing to engage in joint problem solving when representatives from the different teams discussed the issues away from the negotiating table. This observation led to an hypothesis: Fewer (more) agreements would be reached when representatives negotiate around tables (chairs). A systematic test of this hypothesis was then arranged with replicated negotiation sessions and random assignment to conditions in a simulation and in a field setting. The hypothesis was strongly confirmed in the simulation but not in the field setting. Another example comes from professional social science annual conventions. Informal observations made at the 2000 meetings of the American Psychological Association, the American Sociological Association, and the American Political Science Association, all held in Washington, D.C., suggested research questions about similarities and differences among these fields. The questions pertained to types of themes emphasized, demographic representation, preferred dress, formality of sessions, professional compared to academic panels, ease of circulating among sessions and events, and opportunities for networking. The observations were collected and organized in a format that would facilitate more systematic evaluation at future conventions.

The research questions that developed from these sources of information had several features in common. One is clarity in the definition of terms. For example, *fractionation* refers to the perceived size of issues; *facilitation* refers to particular procedures administered in non-negotiation settings. Another is that relationships between variables are specified. For example, strategizing prior to negotiation leads to impasses, whereas while studying the issues produces agreements. Third, the conditions for comparison are evident. For example, in the experiment comparing furniture configurations in the negotiating room, a condition in which the parties sit around a table is compared to a condition in which the parties sit in chairs arranged in a circle. And fourth, data collection and analysis procedures follow from the question. An example is the choice of appropriate cases for comparing the impact of each of three mediator sequencing strategies. Each case was an exemplar of one of the strategies. Published descriptions of the round-by-round discussions were sampled for coding according to appropriate content analysis categories, and the results were shown to have implications for the investigator's research questions or hypotheses. In guiding the development of research questions, these four features facilitate the conduct of research projects. They provide criteria for distinguishing between good (or useful) and bad (or misleading) research questions.

Alternative Methodological Approaches

There is a considerable amount of variety in the way social science research is conducted. Variety is characteristic as well in the CA&R literature. Most of the studies can, however, be regarded as variants on three general approaches to doing research: experimentation, survey research, or case studies. Although there are generally accepted standards for doing research in any of these traditions, there are also important differences with regard to how the research is conducted and used. Generally accepted standards, discussed earlier in Chapter 1, include public reporting of the research, a peer-review process, adherence to ethical norms, and sensitivity to issues of validity in making inferences from the research findings. The differences fall along a number of dimensions, several of which are discussed in the paragraphs to follow and elaborated further in the concluding chapter.

One dimension of difference concerns form. Experiments and surveys are more structured than most case studies. The quality of an experiment or survey depends on maintaining the stability of a research design throughout the data collection and analysis process. For experiments, stability consists largely of control over independent variables in order to evaluate causal hypotheses. For surveys, stability refers to maintaining the sampling design and uniformity of question wording and administration for purposes of inference and comparison. Inference emphasizes internal validity; comparison deals mostly with external validity. Case studies are typically less structured projects. They are usually conducted in an inductive tradition that seeks insights rather than tests hypotheses.

Another difference concerns the role of the researcher and related logistics. The role of experimentalist is generally passive during the research process. He or she adopts the role of outsider in order to avoid influencing subjects during their participation in the experiment. Ideally, the person who collects data should be blind with regard to research design and hypotheses. The ideal experiment separates the activities of design, data collection, and analysis by having different members of the research team participate in each of the phases. The role of the survey researcher is also relatively passive if he or she does not conduct interviews. Mail surveys are the least intrusive; face-to-face open-ended interviews are the most intrusive. But the best surveys, often conducted by organizations, are those that employ interviewers unaware of the research design or purpose of the questions being asked. Similar to experiments, carefully implemented surveys attempt to separate design, collection, and analysis activities. These considerations are consistent with the assumptions of the etic approach to research discussed in the first chapter.

In contrast to experiments and surveys, the role of the case study researcher is generally active. Because the insights achieved from case studies come from the researcher's experience, he or she must be involved in the groups being studied. Of course, involvement may vary from being relatively intrusive to being unobtrusive. For many research questions, participant observation in an emic tradition is needed. These questions deal with such aspects of culture as norms, traditions, and functions of activities. Other kinds of questions depend less on direct involvement. These questions deal with documented events or activities described in archival sources. For both types of involvement with the subjects of research, case study researchers seek connections between design, collection, and analysis activities. They prefer a flexible design that provides opportunities for feedback from observations (analysis) to collection. A discovery made during the course of participation in a group may suggest new questions, observation sites, or informants. In the tradition of theory building, rather than theory testing, case studies allow for ideas to emerge during the research process.

Differences exist also with regard to issues of validity, sampling, and analysis. These issues are discussed in some detail in the chapters to follow. Generally, the debates concern matters of emphasis. Experimentalists emphasize the importance of precise comparisons of conditions, random assignment to conditions, and the use of inferential statistics. Survey researchers emphasize the importance of representative sampling from defined populations to compare pre-defined groups on preferences, attitudes, perceptions, or reported behavior. Case study researchers usually trade the generality that comes from population sampling or the precision that results from random assignment for depth of understanding. Although surveys and experiments can be conducted in case contexts, the primary strength of the case study is description. For CA&R, many important insights have been generated from observations made over time in particular cultures. These insights can be regarded as hypotheses to be evaluated with other approaches.

Other differences are less in the vein of defining features of the approaches but more matters of preference by researchers who use them. One type of difference concerns techniques for data collection and analysis. Experimentalists and survey researchers prefer to collect data that can be scaled for quantitative analysis. Both approaches rely primarily on statistical analysis for making inferences about relationships between variables. Experimentalists have pioneered the development of multivariate designs that allow for the evaluation of complex interactions among variables as well as evaluation research designs. Survey researchers have developed panel techniques for analysis of change in attitudes or events over time. Case study researchers, on the other hand, prefer to collect qualitative information. They have invented a variety of systematic techniques for design—such as focused case comparisons—and analysis—such as textual and narrative analysis.

Researchers also differ with regard to their preferences for matters of philosophy and application. The empirical work done by experimentalists and survey researchers are largely, although not entirely, in a positivist tradition. Case study researchers show more variation in the philosophical assumptions guiding their work: Comparative case-based research develops from positivist, etic assumptions; text analysis and ethnographic research is closer to a constructivist, emic tradition. With regard to applications, experimentalists have contributed models for evaluating interventions; survey researchers have refined techniques that monitor societal change in sectoral preferences regarding political and economic issues, and, through the use of action research models, case study researchers have contributed to planned change in the communities within which they work.

The approaches have evolved in different social science disciplinary contexts: experimentation in psychology and economics, survey research in sociology and political science, and case studies in political science and anthropology. Although CA&R researchers cannot claim to have pioneered any of these approaches, they are in the forefront of a growing movement toward combining them in addressing a host of real-world problems. The field's multidisciplinary roots are reflected in its preference for an amalgam of methods, preferring to combine the different strengths of multiple approaches in doing research. This research strategy is also evident in the way that the approaches are presented in the chapters to come.

Choosing an Approach

The overview provided in the previous section calls attention to some of the considerations that a researcher may entertain when deciding on an approach to a research question. This decision is based on the kind of question being asked. It is also based on experience or familiarity with the different approaches, opportunities in the setting for implementing the approaches, and the larger, more programmatic, goals of the project. Each of these considerations is discussed in this section.

Experimental methodologies are usually used at a relatively advanced stage of conceptualizing about a topic. Referred to as fixed designs or theory-driven designs, experiments "specify in advance the variables to be included in our study, and the exact procedures to be followed, (made possible) by having a reasonably well-articulated theory of the variables we are investigating" (Robson, 2002, p. 96). Some topics in CA&R are at this stage of conceptualizing. Experiments have been particularly useful in obtaining knowledge about conflict-resolving activities that occur in small groups. Sophisticated frameworks and models of negotiation and mediation have been developed in concert with experimentation. The models identify critical variables and, more important, specify dynamic relationships among these variables, as will be discussed in the next chapter.

Research questions suited for experiments specify independent (conditions, mediator approaches) and dependent (agreements, improved relationships) variables as well as the expected relationship between them. The distinction between independent and dependent variables is an attempt to isolate causes (independent) from consequences (dependent). For example, an experiment can be designed to investigate the influence of alternative organizational designs—hierarchical, horizontal, mixed—(independent variable) on the incidence of conflict within an organization (dependent variable). An hypothesis might be that a higher incidence of interpersonal (or intergroup) conflict occurs in hierarchical organizations than in either horizontal or mixed organizations. Following are examples of other questions, stated in the form of relationships between independent and dependent variables, that have been evaluated with experiments.

1. Do more satisfactory agreements (dependent variables) result from the following combination of conditions (independent variables): when negotiating teams study the issues (rather than strategize) prior to negotiation, when they explore their different values in pre-negotiation discussions (rather than ignore these differences), and when they are equal (but relatively weak) in power?

2. Are mediators more effective in improving the relationship between disputants (dependent variable) when they use a problem-solving, rather than a settlement-oriented, approach (independent variable) to the dispute? (A problem-solving approach encourages a vigorous search for information that can lead to mutually satisfactory outcomes. A settlement-oriented approach encourages efficient bargaining leading to compromise solutions.)

3. Will more agreements, and fewer impasses, occur in multilateral conferences (dependent variable) when delegation representatives discuss the issues in a circular chair configuration than when they negotiate behind tables (independent variable)?

Survey designs are also relatively fixed in terms of a chosen sample of respondents, data collection instruments, and analysis procedures. Their main advantage is coverage of a cross section of a defined population. This approach can be used at either an early exploratory, theory-developing stage or at a later, more advanced, theory-testing phase of research. Complex models often result from analyses of survey data or can provide a structure for data collection. These issues are discussed in Chapter 5.

Research questions suited for surveys specify relationships between variables to be investigated across a broad sampling of a population (American citizens, family mediators, nongovernmental organizations [NGOs] in the questions asked below). The relationships are stated in correlational, rather than causal, terms. Thus, the independent-dependent terminology is inappropriate for describing hypothesized relationships in most surveys. However, if the assessments are made at several time periods (as in panel surveys), it would be possible to infer direction or causality. For example, a survey can be used to explore relationships among alternative organizational designs (hierarchical, horizontal, mixed), size (small, medium, large), sector (industrial, service, governmental), and the incidence of conflict within a stratified sampling of organizations in the United States. Examples of other survey questions in CA&R are the following:

1. What are the relationships among values about the environment, occupation, and political preferences of American citizens?

2. What is the relationship between the preferred theoretical approaches of family mediators and their effectiveness in helping families settle their disputes?

3. What are the relationships among organizational characteristics, mandates, and activities of NGOs and the likelihood that they will be targets of violent attacks?

Case study designs are flexible in the sense that they can be refined or revised during phases of data collection. Flexibility allows for new insights to emerge during the research process. Although there is considerable variation in the extent to which case studies are open-ended, most are intended to provide opportunities for close observations of social behavior over relatively long periods of time. The singular focus of these studies may provide a deeper appreciation for the way a conflict process unfolds. These issues are discussed further in Chapters 6 and 8.

Research questions suited for case studies focus attention on processes that occur in a particular setting. The question being asked is more descriptive (What happened? How did it happen?) than explanatory (Why did it happen?). Many researchers consider the case as a whole rather than as part of a larger comparative research design. This focus entails following the development of events through the course of an entire negotiation or successive attempts at mediation. But this does not preclude comparisons between time periods, mediators, or parties. For example, the organizational-impact questions stated above for experiments and surveys would take a different form for investigation with case studies: How often does conflict occur at different times or in conjunction with specific events that occur in an organization? Other case study questions include the following:

1. What conditions accompanied turning points that moved a negotiation over base rights to an agreement?
2. What did successive mediations do to attempt to resolve the conflict between Azerbaijan and Armenia over Nagorno Karabakh?
3. What did the small island states do to achieve favorable concessions from the developed countries in the multilateral global environmental conference at Kyoto, Japan?

Another reason for preferring one research approach over another is familiarity. Training in research methods varies from one social science discipline to another. For example, students trained in psychology (sociology) will probably have more experience with experimental (survey) designs than survey (experimental) designs. Case study methods are becoming more popular in sociology, political science, and international relations; they have been the method of choice in anthropology for a much longer time. A trend in most of these disciplines toward the use of multiple methods is reflected in recent textbooks. It is emphasized in this book, not only because it reflects a trend, but because it advocates flexibility for the field of CA&R. Therefore, students who read this book will become familiar with each of the major approaches. Familiarity and confidence should encourage researchers to choose the approach best suited to answer the questions that interest them.

Opportunities for doing research were discussed in the "Choosing a Research Topic" section. In that section, I discussed the setting in which the research is to be conducted, including availability of subjects or respondents and materials. These sorts of opportunities also have implications for the research approach chosen. For example, captive populations are needed for both experiments, in the form of subject pools, and surveys, in the form of cooperative respondents chosen to be in the sample. Other opportunities include appropriate archival documentation for secondary data analysis, access to relevant groups for interviews or participant observation, and knowledgeable mentors or colleagues to advise and critique the research design and analysis. But, in addition to familiarity with an approach and opportunities for implementing it, choices depend on the programmatic goals for the research. These goals are influenced by the preferences of sponsors. They are also influenced by the way a student envisions his or her career path.

Sponsors make it possible to conduct programmatic research through multiple-year grants. Career goals can be defined by a framework that organizes various parts of an extended program. The earlier discussions on literature reviews and frameworks are relevant. A framework can organize a review of literature by connecting aspects of a topic, such as negotiation or third-party intervention, with the research approach and data sources used in the earlier studies. This exercise provides a foundation for a new research program by revealing the variety of approaches used to investigate the topic. The next step is to develop a coherent multiple-method approach for generating the needed knowledge. This task can be helped by imagining that you have been given a lifetime achievement award for your work in CA&R. How would you describe the research program that led to such a recognition? You never know: The careful planning and dedication to the implementation of the research may in fact eventuate in an award! It is hoped that this book makes a contribution toward putting you on this path (note Druckman, 2003).

Discussion Questions

Several discussion questions are suggested by the ideas presented in this chapter about getting started in doing research. This chapter has covered literature reviews, conceptual frameworks and theories, opportunities and constraints for conducting projects, and research questions suited to each of the major methodologies to be discussed in this book. You should review the questions and discuss them in class before moving to the next part on performing experiments.

1. Discuss some functions served by a review of literature on a topic. How would you plan to conduct a review on a CA&R topic in terms of the mechanics of literature coverage and organization?

2. Develop a strategy for retrieving information about a research topic of your choosing. Include a plan for progressing from broad to narrowly defined questions.

3. Describe some functions served by conceptual frameworks. How would you construct a framework on a CA&R topic of your choice? Outline the steps needed to build the framework.

4. How might you develop a research project that can be implemented in a reasonable period of time with available resources? Describe the various decisions that must be made to achieve this goal.

5. What kinds of projects are more or less likely to be successfully implemented in your setting or institution? What opportunities are

available to encourage certain kinds of projects? What are some constraints that may discourage other kinds of projects?

6. Which CA&R theories have generated a body of empirical research? Which theories have not benefited from research?

7. What considerations would you entertain in the design of a research project that is intended to evaluate a theory or theories?

8. What sorts of factors should be considered in developing questions for research? Give examples of questions on several CA&R topics.

9. What are some reasons why you would choose to conduct an experiment rather than a survey or case study? Similarly, why might you decide to conduct a survey or case study rather than one of the other approaches to doing research?

10. Give examples of other research questions (in addition to those listed in this chapter) that are best suited to be investigated by conducting experiments, surveys, or case studies. What are some other considerations that should be entertained in deciding on a particular approach to doing research?

11. What are some differences between designing a single, one-shot study, using any of the approaches discussed in this chapter, and developing a long-term program of research? How might the approaches be used together in a research program?

Part II

Performing Experiments

The two chapters in this part are about the design and analysis of laboratory and field experiments. Chapter 3 covers a number of topics on design. Starting with an overview of the experimental method, the chapter proceeds with a discussion of internal and external validity issues that bear on the value of an experiment: Do the results follow from the procedures? Do the findings have relevance for other situations? At the heart of the chapter is a discussion of the various experimental designs used in CA&R and related research areas. Examples of classical and quasi-designs are used to illustrate ways to control for possible threats to validity: These include randomized pre-test–post-test designs, repeated measures, and simulation designs. The chapter then moves to a discussion of modeling. It covers both relatively simple and complex models with examples from game theory, bargaining, stochastic processes, and system dynamics. The reader should come away from this chapter with an appreciation for the many ways that experimental and modeling techniques can be used to address problems of conflict and approaches to resolution.

Chapter 4 concentrates on the analysis of experimental data. It begins with what I consider to be the essential ideas of statistical analysis, bringing them to life in the following sections with applications. The sequence of the discussion may be regarded as a progression in design and analysis complexity. From relatively simple two-group designs, I move to three-group and factorial analyses of variance (ANOVA). The connections between these techniques are made by using the same CA&R example—a mediation experiment—for each application. These analyses do not, however, cover all the problems faced by the CA&R experimentalist. The next section discusses how repeated measurements on the same unit (person or group) can be analyzed with ANOVA, and the following sections deal with statistical control issues in the form of randomized blocks of subjects and co-variates. Elegant designs such as Latin square are also illustrated. I wind up the chapter with a treatment of how a researcher can estimate the size of effects across experiments. Strengths and limitations of meta-analysis are highlighted. This chapter should not be read as another exposition of tried-and-true techniques. Many statistics books do that job well. Rather, it should be appreciated for the way these techniques are applied to problems in our field. Similarly, the reader will have an opportunity to learn about applications of other statistical techniques in Chapters 6 and 7 on case study analyses.

3

Designing Experiments and Conducting Simulations

The Experimental Method: An Overview

Although experimental methodologies have become very sophisticated during the latter part of the 20th century, only a few essential ideas characterize the approach. It has been regarded historically as being synonymous with the scientific method. Experimentation is a technology for assessing causality; it is supported by philosophical approaches that emphasize explanation. The *essentials* have not changed much since John Stuart Mill wrote about reconciling syllogistic logic with the methods of inductive science in his 1843 book titled A *System of Logic*. Favoring deduction over induction, experimentation has the following key features:

1. Experimental treatments can be applied independent of the prior states of the persons or groups being studied. This is accomplished through random assignment to the treatments being compared.

2. Experimental subjects are unaware of the purpose of the experiment or that other units are getting different treatments.

3. The experimental investigator has control over the administration of the treatments, referred to also as the *independent variables*. This administration occurs before measurements are made.

4. The same aspects of subjects' behavior, decisions, or perceptions are measured in each condition. These aspects, referred to as dependent variables, are free to vary.

5. Each condition of the experiment is repeated or replicated many times— usually at least 10 times—in order to assess variation in the dependent variables within and between the conditions.

These features facilitate the comparisons that are needed to infer causal relations between the treatments (independent variables) and the measurements (dependent variables). The key advantage of controlled comparisons is reduced ambiguity or increased confidence in specifying the direction of a relationship between variables. Confidence in making these inferences is increased to the extent that threats to internal validity are reduced (Campbell & Stanley, 1963). This subject is discussed widely in contemporaneous methods textbooks. I will have more to say about it shortly. But another advantage of experiments, discussed less frequently in texts, is the opportunity to make careful observations of the details of a process (such as negotiation) largely inaccessible in field settings. The human-subjects laboratory experiment provides a window into unfolding processes similar to the natural scientist's microscope. This advantage is discussed further in Chapter 9 on content analysis. The laboratory experiment is also a vehicle for exploring novel conditions and strategies in a relatively safe environment (Mahoney & Druckman, 1975, refer to this as a "test drive before you buy"). Many forms of third-party intervention in conflicts would benefit from a trial run in the laboratory before implementation in the field.

There is, however, another side to the well-known experimental coin, which is often used to assign subjects to conditions on a random basis. The setting is contrived: Experimental subjects are usually college student role players, time is often greatly compressed, past and future relationships are typically non-existent, issues and options in a conflict are usually assigned to subjects who play roles, and conflicts take the form of games or scenarios devised by the research team. These features pose a problem for generalizing results to real-world situations. Confidence in making the case for relevance turns on reducing threats to external validity (Campbell & Stanley, 1963). The issue is less about the obvious differences between the settings in scale and scope but whether these differences are critical variables in terms of influencing the experimental findings. A related issue is whether the experimental results suggest mechanisms that operate also in similar field settings. These issues can be understood in terms of trade-offs between internal and external validity.

Internal and external validity are important considerations in experimental design and analysis. They are discussed in the next section. The other major section of this chapter deals with the variety of designs and models that are relevant for addressing issues in CA&R. The discussion in these sections is intended to address questions often asked by new researchers in CA&R: Can experiments provide useful information about conflict and conflict resolution processes? Which designs are most appropriate for addressing particular issues in the field? What is involved in designing and implementing experiments? Understanding the strengths and limitations of experiments helps a researcher decide whether to use this approach to doing research. Knowing how to perform an experiment increases a researcher's confidence in using the approach. This chapter contributes to both these skills.

Internal and External Validity

The randomized control design gives an experimenter confidence in inferring causation from results of analyses, namely, that the manipulated treatment (problem-solving procedures) causes the measured outcomes (change in attitudes toward another group). This design has been regarded as a kind of panacea for the plausibility of alternative explanations for findings, namely, that another, extraneous factor that may be correlated with the treatment (contact with another group's members) caused the measured outcomes (changes in attitudes). But there is a limit to the number of controls that can be instituted in any experiment and, because of this, arguments that favor the hypothesized causal relationship between the treatment (problem-solving procedures) and outcomes (attitudes) can almost always be challenged. An experimenter's confidence in findings that support an hypothesized relationship between alternative treatments and outcomes increases to the extent that threats to internal validity are reduced.

The most well-known list of factors that may pose threats to internal validity was suggested by Cook and Campbell (1979). Among the 12 factors in their list are external events, referred to as *history;* aspects of measurement, referred to as *testing, instrumentation, and regression;* changes in the study's participants, referred to as *mortality or dropouts,* and *maturation;* and suspicions aroused by conversations among participants about the experiment, referred to as *diffusion of treatments, compensatory equalization of treatments,* and *compensatory rivalry* (see also Robson, 2002, for further discussion of these threats). I have added several other threats to the Cook and Campbell list. One of these is a participant's self-consciousness about being in an experiment, known as a *Hawthorne* or *placebo* effect. Another is suspicions about the experimental hypothesis aroused by subtle communications during the experiment, referred to as *demand characteristics.* A large research literature on the influence of expectations shows that experimenters often send signals, verbally and non-verbally, that influence subjects' behavior (see Harris & Rosenthal, 1985). Two other threats deal with measurement issues. One is the preference to choose socially desirable responses to questions about attitudes. Another is a preference for responding to items in a positive or affirmative direction. (For a discussion of these response biases, see Rokeach, 1963, and Druckman, 1970.)

Experimentalists have been inventive in developing controls for many of these threats, particularly those concerning dropouts, measurement issues, and response biases. Others have been more difficult to control, particularly those involving external events, maturation (in longitudinal experiments), and diffusion of treatments. In any event, it is not possible to perform an experiment in a vacuum; controls are a matter of degree. It is possible, however, to compare results obtained from experiments that control for different kinds of threats to validity. It is also possible to replicate experiments. Replicated findings—the same results obtained in repeated experiments—increase an investigator's confidence in them. Knowledge develops from programs of research, not from a few non-replicated experiments.

Confidence in experimental research findings is one part of the validity issue. The other part refers to relevance of the findings for other settings. Referred to as external validity, relevance may be limited by several features of an experimental design. LeCompte and Goetz (1982) suggest four threats to external validity. Findings may be limited to the particular groups studied (*selection*), the particular *setting* in which the study took place, or the specific *historical circumstances* that existed at the time of the study. These threats are magnified when college students play assigned roles in simulated conflicts. They are addressed, but not resolved, by assessments of similarity between the experimental setting and a comparable real-world situation. (A compelling case for external validity of an arms-control simulation was made by Bonham, 1971.) A fourth threat is that the particular *constructs* studied may be specific to the groups in the investigation. For example, problem-solving procedures may be understood differently by students in a role play and by policymakers wrestling with similar issues in actual conflicts. Two other threats to external validity are *investigator perspectives* and *non-representative sampling*. The former refers to the particular interpretive preferences held by the study's investigative team. This threat can be addressed by including different perspectives on the research team or by soliciting comments from colleagues on early drafts of articles. The latter refers to missing aspects of the population from which the experimental sample is drawn or is presumed to represent. This threat is reduced by choosing participants according to a sample design. This is accomplished to a degree when experiments are embedded in random-sample surveys (see Chapter 5 on survey research).

The two validities can be considered as being complementary. The more controls instituted in an experimental design to reduce threats to internal validity, the less the experimental setting is likely to resemble other (non-experimental) situations. Internal validity is often gained at the expense of external validity. In their attempt to reduce the plausibility of alternative explanations for findings, or to reduce threats to internal validity, experimentalists often simplify the tasks and settings of their experiments. A CA&R example is a simulation of the conflict between the Greek and Turkish communities in Cyprus (Druckman et al., 1988; Druckman & Broome, 1991).

In order to implement the Cyprus simulation in a reasonable amount of time (2 hours), a limited amount of background information about the conflict was presented, preparation time for the negotiations was limited, the role-playing students negotiated only three issues presented in the form of scaled options, and a time limit of 35 minutes was imposed on the negotiations. In order to control for the effects of testing, no attitude pre-test was administered; this was a randomized post-test design. Further, in order to separate understanding differences between the parties in values (the research question of interest) from familiarity or contact with the opponent, a simulated pre-negotiation workshop was described for one of the experimental conditions. An actual workshop would have required interaction before the negotiation.

These design features lend confidence in the findings at the expense of generality. The situation being simulated consisted of knowledgeable representatives of the parties, extended negotiations over many interrelated issues, changing attitudes over time, and participation in actual workshops in which both familiarity and liking are influenced. The controls instituted to reduce threats to internal validity (e.g., external events, testing, maturation, diffusion of treatments, and compensatory equalization of treatments) increased the threats to external validity (selection, setting, and history or a specific period of time). A more realistic simulation, on the other hand, would have raised questions of extraneous variables and comparability among the conditions. In this example, increases in one type of validity lead to decreases in another. This idea suggests that designers aspire to a balance between the validities. Rather than attempt to optimize either validity, an experimentalist can tweak both in order to achieve reasonable verisimilitude or generalizability without forfeiting interpretability of the findings. Some examples of designs that address issues of balancing are discussed next.

Experimental Designs: Examples From CA&R

Many CA&R researchers prefer the case study method. A question of interest is, why not perform experiments that address issues about conflict and conflict resolution? There are plenty of hypotheses to evaluate, and the method is relatively inexpensive and easy to implement. The methodology has the advantage of encouraging careful, precise thinking, usually in a deductive form. Randomized control group designs address issues of internal validity. Although threats to external validity are difficult to reduce, the issues are addressed with experiments that take the form of simulations: Experimental simulations are attempts to reproduce complex real-world situations and allow for a comparison with findings obtained in those settings. In this section, I introduce the CA&R researcher to alternative experimental designs and then discuss some simulations that have been used to evaluate hypotheses about conflict behavior.

A clear exposition of alternative designs can be found in Creswell (1994). His distinction between pre-experimental, quasi-, and classical experimental designs can be regarded as a progression from weak to strong attempts to reduce threats to internal validity. The pre-experimental design is particularly weak on comparisons or controls. It may take the form of a one-shot case study in which one treatment (designated as X) is evaluated (designated as O) with (O1 ——— X ——— O2) or without a pre-test (X ——— O). Or, it may compare non-equivalent groups where participants are not assigned randomly to a treatment or no-treatment group (Group A: X ——— O; Group B: ——— O), or two treatments are compared without random assignment (Group A: X1 ——— O; Group B: X2 ——— O).

Quasi-experimental designs add the feature of control groups. They may take the form of a pre-test, post-test comparison of two groups, one receiving a treatment, the other not receiving the treatment as follows:

Group A: O ——— X ——— O

Group B: O ——————— O

Because participants are not assigned randomly to these groups, the comparison is between non-equivalent groups. This feature enhances the plausibility of alternative interpretations for any differences found between the groups. Each alternative interpretation is a threat to the internal validity of the experiment. This sort of design is frequently used in field experiments where opportunities for random experiment are limited. For example, questionnaires that ask about attitudes toward the other group can be administered prior to (pre-test) and after (post-test) a problem-solving workshop (Group A). The same questionnaire can be administered, with the same time interval between administrations, to another group (B) not exposed to the workshop. It would be unlikely that participants are randomly assigned to these groups: Most workshops are intended to address relational issues between members of actual groups in conflict; random assignment to treatment and control groups would raise ethical issues in this context. It is also unlikely that Group B's activities between the pre- and post-test are similar to Group A's activities in all ways save for the problem-solving procedures. Thus, differences found in the change scores (pre- to post-test) can also be attributed to factors other than the workshop procedures.

A somewhat stronger quasi-experiment is the time-series design. Its strength derives from the feature of multiple measures before and after an intervention. Although randomization is missing, the time-series design enables a researcher to evaluate change in the context of a longer history of events or relations between groups. It also allows for an evaluation of the extent to which the change is sustained through time as well as compared to other groups repeatedly assessed without the intervention. Examples of time-series designs are discussed later in this chapter. (For more on a variety of quasi-experimental designs used in other areas of social science, see Cook & Campbell, 1979.)

The strongest design is the classical experiment. Random assignment (R) is intended to ensure that the comparison groups are equivalent. A popular form of the randomized control group experiment is called the Solomon four-group design. Participants are assigned randomly to one of four groups as follows:

Group A: R ———— O ———— X ———— O

Group B: R ———— O ———————— O

Group C: R ———————— X ———— O

Group D: R ———————————— O

In this design, randomization ensures equivalent groups, and the groups without pre-tests (C and D) provide controls for the effects of testing. Supporting evidence for the hypothesis that the treatment (X) makes a difference would consist of the following results of group comparisons: Group A change scores (pre-test to post-test) are greater than (>) Group B change scores, Group C post-test scores are greater than (>) Group D post-test scores, and Group A post-test scores equal Group C post-test scores. These results would provide compelling evidence for the hypothesis, particularly because they eliminate an interpretation based on experience with a pre-test.

An application of this design would be an evaluation of the effects of mediation skills training on the acquisition of the desired skills. A pool of 48 trainees is assigned randomly to the four groups, 12 per group. Trainees in Groups A and C receive the training procedures; those in Groups B and D do not. A day before the training, Groups A and B are administered a pre-test that covers the kinds of mediation skills in the training package; Groups C and D do not get a pre-test. A day following the training, Groups A and C are given a post-test. Testing occurs at the same time, and with the same interval, for Groups B and D. Evidence for effective training would take the following form: Group A > (larger change in the direction of improved skills) Group B, Group C > Group D, and Group A (post-test) = Group C (post-test). However, these results do not provide evidence for the long-term effects of training. Such an evaluation would entail repeated post-tests given to each group through the course of several weeks or months. This design combines the features of the Solomon four-group design with before and after repeated measures. The form taken by this design is as follows.

Group A: R — O — O — O — X — O — O — O

Group B: R — O — O — O ———— O — O — O

Group C: R   X — O — O — O

Group D: R   O — O — O

The Solomon four-group design does not include a comparison of alternative training packages or other interventions. In order for such comparisons to be made, the design would have to be repeated for each of the several alternative procedures. Suppose that the training procedures (X1) used in the first design emphasized a settlement-oriented style (SOS) to mediation: According to Kressel and his colleagues (1994), this approach emphasizes the value of efficient, compromise solutions to conflicts. An alternative set of procedures, referred to as a problem-solving style (PSS), emphasizes the value of searching for information that can be used to reach an integrative (increased joint benefits) outcome. A question of interest is whether SOS (X1) is easier to learn than PSS (X2). The comparison would entail two Solomon four-group designs, one with SOS (X1) and the other with PSS (X2). An advantage of this comparison is that it controls for the threat to validity posed by testing effects. The key comparison would be the relative size of the differences between Groups A and B change scores (for X1 and X2) and between Groups C and D post-test scores. Larger differences for X1 than X2 would support the hypothesis that SOS skills are learned better than PSS skills. It would not indicate that SOS is a more effective approach to mediating disputes.

A disadvantage of comparing two or more Solomon four-group designs is the number of participants (or trainees) needed to fulfill the design's analytical requirements. The PSS (X2) design requires another 48 participants, bringing the total number of subjects for the experiment to 96. There is an alternative way of comparing the effects of different treatments. It is a short-cut with the attendant shortcomings. It consists of three groups, instead of the eight called for by the Solomon four-group design. A third group is a no-treatment (neither SOS nor PSS) control. Participating trainees are assigned randomly (R) to one of the following groups:

Group A: R   X1 (SOS) ——————————— O

Group B: R   X2 (PSS) ——————————— O

Group C: R   X3 (control) ——————————— O

If 12 trainees are assigned to each group (as in the designs above), only 36 participants are needed to implement the experiment. Support for the hypothesis that SOS is easier to learn than PSS would be indicated by higher post-test scores for SOS than for PSS and the control group (SOS > PSS = control); somewhat weaker support would also be obtained by the finding that SOS > PSS > control.

Although this design is easier to implement, it is a weaker evaluation of the hypothesis. When the pre-test is eliminated, no evaluation of changes resulting from the treatments exists. When a pre-test for each condition is installed, control for its effects independent of the treatments becomes necessary; hence, the preference for the Solomon four-group design. If, on the other hand, it is assumed that random assignment eliminates all pre-test differences (referred to also in the training literature as "baseline data"), then it follows that all post-test scores are deviations from the same pre-test result or baseline.

These are some of the considerations entertained by researchers torn between arguments that emphasize the value of reducing threats to internal validity at the cost of design efficiency (the Solomon four-group design) and those that promote design efficiency at the cost of dealing with alternative explanations for findings (the three-group comparison). It also gives the new researcher a glimpse into the way that decisions about research designs are made.

The mediation training example is an evaluation experiment that is concerned with impacts of mediation procedures on the development of skills. It focuses on outcomes rather than on the processes of skill acquisition. By paying attention to process, the researcher may gain insights into the way that the mediation procedures work. This sort of design would take the following form.

Group A: R X1 (SOS) ——— O1 (process coding) ——— O2 (outcomes)

Group B: R X2 (PSS) ——— O1 (process coding) ——— O2 (outcomes)

Group C: R X3 (control) ——— O1 (process coding) ——— O2 (outcomes)

Two types of assessments are made in this design, a coding of the process (O1) and outcomes (O2). The process may be captured by, first, observing the way trainees perform in role-play exercises during training and, second, developing codes that capture their progress. The outcomes are summary indicators of the mediation skills acquired. The analyses may include correlations between the process and outcome indicators, perhaps showing different paths (process) to acquisition (outcomes) for the different treatments. Some paths may hinder skill acquisition, whereas others may facilitate it.

The same type of experimental design was used in the simulation experiment by Druckman et al. (1988) discussed earlier. Recall that this experiment was a comparison of three conditions hypothesized to influence negotiation: interests derived directly from values (referred to as an "embedded" condition), values separated from interests (referred to as a "de-linked" condition), and a pre-negotiation workshop intended to understand the contrasting values from which interests were derived (referred to as a "facilitation" condition). The post-test-only random-assignment design took the following form.

Group A: R X1 (embedded) ——— O1 (process) ——— O2 (outcomes)

Group B: R X2 (de-linked) ——— O1 (process) ——— O2 (outcomes)

Group C: R X3 (facilitation) ———O1 (process) ——— O2 (outcomes)

Equivalence—meaning that the average pre-test scores would be the same—among the conditions was assumed through random assignment. The embedded condition was hypothesized to generate the most competitive negotiations and, thus, regarded as the standard against which the other conditions were compared; the de-linked and facilitation conditions were hypothesized as variations in the direction of less competition. For these reasons, a pre-test was not necessary and would, in any event, be difficult to administer because the negotiation had not begun. No-treatment controls were also difficult to design because Groups B and C were variants on a theme much like a control condition would be. Process variables included codes for the types of statements made during the negotiation and self-reported perceptions. These variables intervened between the conditions and the outcomes (agreements reached, types of agreements, time to settlement).

The results showed that more agreements were reached in both Groups B and C than in Group A. However, these conditions (Groups B and C) differed in terms of process: more statements indicating agreement, more appeals to joint interests, and fewer statements indicating dominance by one negotiator over the other in the facilitation condition. These findings were interpreted as showing different paths to the same outcome, suggesting two models of negotiation, expedient bargaining for short-term agreements (in the de-linked condition) and cooperative bargaining for long-term relations (in the facilitation condition). The process paths are the "mechanisms" that connect the negotiating situation with outcomes. These results were generated from both the arrangement of the groups and the multiple assessments—processes, perceptions, outcomes—made possible by the experimental design. They contribute to the evaluation of interventions (see Chapter 11) and to theories of negotiation.

A way of bridging the two validities is by conducting field experiments. Two well-known examples from CA&R are the studies by McGillicuddy, Welton, and Pruitt (1987) and Mooradian and Druckman (1999). The former study was conducted in a New York state community dispute resolution clinic. This is a rare example of a field study that implemented a classical design by permitting random assignment of 36 disputant pairs and mediators to one of three experimental conditions: mediation without arbitration (med), mediators become arbitrators if the dispute is not settled (med/arb same), and a new party is appointed to be an arbitrator if the dispute is not settled (med/arb diff). A problem, however, was subject mortality: 68% of the participants dropped out of the study before it was concluded. Although this is a serious threat to the internal validity of the experiment, the investigators showed that the dropouts were not related systematically to the experimental conditions; the conditions did not differ in number of dropouts. Strong results were obtained on process but not outcomes: Med/arb (same) condition disputants were less hostile, made more new proposals and more concessions, agreed more often with the other disputant, and were more satisfied with the outcome than disputants in the other two third-party configurations. This condition induced more cooperative motivation than the other conditions (see also Pruitt, McGillicuddy, Welton, & Fry, 1989).

The Mooradian and Druckman (1999) quasi-experimental study was an attempt to compare the effectiveness of mediation (de-escalation hypothesis) versus a hurting stalemate (escalation hypothesis) in reducing violence between nations engaged in combat over Nagorno Karabakh. A large events data set was assembled (3,856 events during the period 1990–1995) and coded on a six-step scale ranging from most peaceful to most violent. These data were analyzed as a time series (dependent variables) influenced by the interventions—mediation or hurting stalemate (independent variables). The interventions were construed as experimental treatments in a sequence of before-and-after quasi-experimental designs without control groups. Significance tests (see Chapter 4) were used to assess the changes from before to after an intervention (mediation, hurting stalemate) in a manner similar to the way data would be analyzed from a laboratory experiment where control groups could also be included in the design. Results showed that the casualties suffered from the hurting stalemate reduced violence more than the attempts at mediation, leading to a cease-fire negotiation. The quasi-experimental design was useful for organizing comparisons in time (before and after interventions) and space (mediation vs. hurting stalemate).

For both studies, experimental designs contributed to knowledge about mediation. The internal validity threat incurred by dropouts in the study by McGillicuddy and associates (1987) was reduced by showing that the distribution was random across the conditions. The lack of random assignment and control groups in the Mooradian and Druckman (1999) study was offset to an extent by the number of opportunities to disconfirm the hurting stalemate hypothesis (six mediation efforts) and by the clarity of the definition of the stalemate (as offensives resulting in significant casualties; neither the casualties nor the mediators' behavior during the offensives were included in the events data set). Both studies are examples of opportunities to conduct well-designed experiments in the field. They are discussed further in Chapter 9.

Another approach to field experimentation is randomized field trials (RFTs). This approach avoids selection biases that occur in observational studies, including ethnographic research (see Chapter 8). However, RFTs have rarely been used in CA&R research to date. Researchers can benefit from the experience gained from RFT applications in other areas of social science. Several of these applications are discussed in the collection of articles edited by Green and Gerber (2004) for a special issue of the *American Behavioral Scientist*. That collection includes examples of field experiments on health behaviors, social welfare programs, criminology, and school vouchers. A particularly interesting methodological innovation discussed by Baruch et al. (2004) is random allocation of such macro-level units as villages and communities, housing developments, hospital units, schools, and other large administrative units. A good deal of conflict research is done at a macro level of analysis, with entities or places rather than individuals or small groups; very little of the research employs RFT (or place-randomized trials) procedures. The progress made to date in other areas bodes well for research that addresses conflicts between communities, organizations, or nations. These methods would also refine data collection strategies geared toward exploring connections between micro and macro levels of analysis. But a more popular approach to bridging the validities in CA&R research is simulation. We turn now to a discussion of simulation research and design with examples drawn from CA&R.

BRIDGING INTERNAL AND EXTERNAL VALIDITY: SOME SIMULATION DESIGNS

Simulation is another approach to experimentation intended to address threats to both internal and external validity. It is an attempt to represent a real-world context in the laboratory. The laboratory aspects of simulation consist of the experimental design. The contextual aspects of simulation consist of the scenario within which the experiment is embedded. A variety of randomized control group designs can be embedded in simulations. By employing these designs, a researcher reduces threats to internal validity.

Simulation experiments are also useful vehicles for exploring new conditions not present in a particular real-world setting. This feature is illustrated by the experiments discussed just below.

A variety of contexts have been simulated, although many simulations are over-simplified versions of those contexts. Examples are collective bargaining interactions, decision making in city councils, space missions, organizational departments, and diplomatic relations among national representatives in an international system. (Many other examples can be found in Crookall and Arai [1995], and Druckman [1994b] as well as in the journal *Simulation & Gaming*.) To the extent that these simulated settings resemble the setting being simulated, the researcher reduces threats to external validity. A simulation is realistic to the extent that fundamental properties of the system (or context) being simulated are incorporated in the laboratory scenario. But this is also an empirical issue that can be evaluated by comparing findings obtained in the different settings. In making these comparisons, it is particularly important to specify clearly what is being compared (see Drabek & Haas, 1967). Several projects illustrate how this is done.

The most ambitious program designed to address issues of external validity is the research on simulated international processes conducted by Guetzkow and his colleagues. These researchers were able to collect comparable data from simulated and field settings. Their comparisons, made across more than 20 studies, showed considerable correspondence: 16 of 20 comparisons yielded judgments of much or some correspondence of findings between the settings (see Guetzkow & Valadez, 1981). Another interesting comparison of simulation and laboratory findings was made by Hopmann and Walcott (1977). They explored the relationship between external stress and negotiating behavior in a simulation of the Partial Nuclear Test Ban Treaty of 1963 and in the actual negotiations. In this study, the effects of three experimental conditions—benign, neutral, and malign systemic tension levels—were compared on a number of intervening process variables and dependent outcome variables. They also coded the negotiation transcripts on similar process and outcome variables. Variations in external stress as events unfolded during the course of the talks were tracked; this is different from creating experimental variations of stress. Convergences were found between the experimental and field results, indicating that stresses were dysfunctional for negotiations: High stress produced greater hostility, harder bargaining strategies, and fewer agreements than low stress. The experimental findings showed that the malign condition (high stress) produced significantly fewer solutions than both the benign (low stress) and neutral conditions. This kind of controlled comparison is a strength of experiments. It indicates that low stress does not improve the outcomes, but high stress hinders attempts to reach agreements.

A third study by Beriker and Druckman (1996) provides another example of the value of laboratory-field comparisons. These researchers compared findings obtained from a simulation of a post–World War I peace conference with the actual conference held at Lausanne, Switzerland in 1922–1923. A key feature of this conference was the power asymmetry among the parties. Symmetric (equal power) and asymmetric (unequal power) structures existed on two important issues in the talks, passage to the Black Sea through the straits and the question of civil rights for minorities. A content analysis of the transcripts showed some differences in bargaining behavior between the two power structures.

These structures were then simulated and compared to a third condition, bilateral negotiation between relatively weak parties of equal power. The additional condition created for the simulation provided insights not likely to be obtained from an analysis of the actual talks. Negotiators in the bilateral condition were more satisfied with the outcome, achieved faster resolutions, disagreed less, and made fewer competitive statements during the discussions than those in the multilateral (coalition) conditions. Similar to the Hopmann and Walcott (1977) simulation, this study illuminates an advantage of experiments: They allow for exploration of new conditions not present in the setting being simulated; these explorations often produce interesting findings with practical implications. The comparison between the two power-configuration conditions that existed in both simulation and field showed some similarities and some differences in the findings. The similarities bolster support for the relevance (or external validity) of the simulation to the case being simulated.

External validity can also be understood in terms of how much complexity is captured in the simulated experimental environment. Most field settings are more complex than experimental settings, and many conceptualizations of conflict resolution processes include more factors or variables than can usually be investigated in an experiment. Thus, experiments are usually only limited evaluations of these frameworks.

An example is a study that attempted to evaluate the framework constructed by Sawyer and Guetzkow (1965) to encompass a variety of processes and influences of negotiation. This framework depicts pre-conditions, background factors, conditions, processes, and outcomes of negotiation (see Chapter 2). The challenge is to evaluate the impacts of these multiple interacting influences on negotiating behavior. This was done by constructing "packages" of variables in a simulation scenario of a multilateral environmental conference (Druckman, 1993).

Three packages were developed for each of four stages of the conference: *pre-negotiation planning, setting the stage, the give-and-take,* and *the endgame.* Each of the packages contained five or six variables hypothesized to influence the flexibility of the negotiators. The design enabled me to compare the effects of three different types of packages at each of the stages: one in which the variables in all the stages were arranged to encourage flexibility, another where they were arranged to encourage inflexibility, and a third where the variables in the earlier stages were arranged for flexibility and those in later stages toward inflexibility. The three packages were regarded as experimental conditions. This was a 3 × 4 design in which the three conditions were combined with the four stages (a repeated measure).

Effects of these conditions were evaluated for their impacts on the flexibility of the negotiators in the simulation. However, this evaluation did not reveal the relative importance of the variables contained within the packages. For this evaluation, a procedure known as a "halo error" technique (Guilford, 1954), was used to unpack the variables, providing weights that indicated the relative impact of the variables on flexibility within the stages. This experiment is a good example of how simulation can be used as a device to evaluate the sorts of combinations of variables depicted by frameworks. It shows how complexity can be incorporated in experiments. To the extent that this goal is achieved, external validity is enhanced.

Simulations are a way of addressing issues of external validity raised by laboratory experiments. In this section, I have shown how some researchers evaluate the correspondences between findings obtained in simulation experiments and in the settings being simulated. To the extent that correspondences are found, a case can be made that the simulation is an accurate model of the real-world setting. The strong correspondences found for both international decision making and negotiation processes bolster confidence in the external validity of the simulations. This does not mean that other simulations are also good replicas of the settings being simulated; the evaluations must be done separately for each simulation. However, some design guidelines intended to enhance external validity can be suggested.

One guideline is to incorporate complexity in the simulation, as illustrated by the environmental conference discussed above. Another is to recruit participants for the simulation from the real-world setting, for example, diplomats for a study of international negotiation or scientists for a study of environmental policymaking. A third is to perform multi-method research by analyzing data collected from both the simulation and field settings. The field experiences are likely to suggest structures and variables that would improve the validity of the simulation; the simulation may contribute methods of analysis useful for the field study as well as evaluate the impacts of new situations not readily available for analysis in the real world. For more reading on the issues and challenges of evaluating a large variety of types of simulation validities, see Feinstein and Cannon (2002). One interesting distinction made by these authors is between the structure of the game and the effects it has on those who play it. The former is referred to as representational validity, the latter as educational validity. The questions asked are as follows: How similar are the simulated and referent (real-world) environments? Do participants in both environments behave in similar ways? Both are important questions.

Simulations as Models

The scenarios discussed above are attempts to represent complex activities or social systems. To the extent that they succeed in doing this, the simulation is regarded as being externally valid. The research reviewed in the previous section shows that one way to evaluate success is to compare results obtained in simulated and real-world environments. Judgments of external validity turn on the similarity of results.

Another way of thinking about this issue is in terms of simulation design. With Robert Mahoney, I proposed a taxonomy for distinguishing among types of simulation designs (Mahoney & Druckman, 1975). It consists of two dimensions referred to as range and extension. *Range* refers to the number or variety of situations that are modeled. Simulations that are applicable only to a few well-defined situations are said to cover a narrow range. Those that represent many types of situations cover a wide range. *Extension* refers to the amount of detail incorporated in the simulated environment. When many details are written into the scenarios, the simulation is said to have deep extension; when few details are included, the simulation has thin extension. The simulations of international processes, discussed above, cover a narrow range and have deep extension. The popular prisoner's dilemma game (PDG), on the other hand, is a wide-range, thin-extension simulation. Both of these types of simulations can be thought about as models. Examples of these models are presented in this section, focusing first on game-theoretic models, second on computer simulation models, and third on more complex computer and human simulations on problems of conflict.

GAME-THEORETIC MODELS

Game-theoretic models are parsimonious in the sense that they derive their power from simplicity. Osborne (2004) notes that "the assumptions upon which (game-theory models) rest should capture the essence of the situation, not irrelevant details" (p. 1). The key assumption is based on the theory of rational choice: It posits that a decision maker chooses the best action according to his or her preferences among all the available actions. Preferences are often represented by payoff functions, as shown in the examples below. But there is another important assumption based on the idea of interdependent decision making: It posits that the best action for any given player depends on the other players' actions. This means that a player must have in mind (or form a belief of) the actions that the other players will take. These assumptions are the underlying bases for the most popular solution concept, which is referred to as a *Nash equilibrium.*

Nash (1950) showed that a unique solution to the bargaining problem can be identified for all two-person games. The characteristics of this solution can be summarized simply as the outcome that maximizes the product of the preferences (utilities) of the two parties. Expressed differently, this solution minimizes the losses incurred by players who choose other outcomes in a game. As such, it may be regarded as a steady state or a social norm in the sense that if everyone else accepts it, no person prefers to deviate from it. Although other solution concepts have been proposed, the simplicity and elegance of the Nash concept has given it the longest "shelf life." (For a review of various solution concepts and the studies designed to evaluate them, see Schellenberg & Druckman, 1986.)

An advantage of game-theoretic analysis is that conclusions or solution concepts are derived from general models that cover a wide range of choice dilemma situations, in which a person must decide between making an offer or remaining silent, voting for one candidate or another, or intervening versus standing aside. It does not depend on knowledge of particular features of the specific environment in which actions are taken. (Recall the distinction made between etic and emic approaches to research in Chapter 1.) For example, social-psychological analyses of bystander apathy attempted to understand the circumstances in which a bystander would help a person in trouble. The analyses revealed that group size mattered, and the investigators posited alternative hypotheses to explain why there is a decline in offering assistance as the number of witnesses increase: Alternative explanations include diffusion of responsibility, audience inhibition, and social influence. A more parsimonious explanation is based on the idea of an equilibrium. Following Osborne (2004),

> Whether any person intervenes depends on the probability she assigns to some other person's intervening. In an equilibrium each person may be indifferent between intervening and not intervening, and . . . this condition leads inexorably to the conclusion that an increase in group size reduces the probability that at least one person intervenes. (pp. 133–134)

This conclusion is based on fewer assumptions and follows logically from them. These abstract concepts may come to life in the illustrations of various types of games to follow.

The prisoner's dilemma is a two-person (or player) game that models the tension that often exists between trust and risk. In order to achieve the best outcome or highest payoff, players must trust each other to cooperate rather than to compete in an exploitative fashion. The best individual outcomes result from playing the game competitively; the best joint outcomes occur when the players choose cooperatively. This dilemma is reflected in the game matrix presented to the players. It takes the form illustrated in Figure 3.1.

The numbers represent payoffs to each player, Suspect 1 and Suspect 2. The highest payoff is 4; the lowest is 1. In terms of the game story, an outcome of 4 means no time spent in prison; an outcome of 1 means a stiff sentence with lighter sentences imposed for the intermediate outcomes of 2 and 3. It can be seen that each player (suspect) receives the highest payoff (4) when he or she confesses and the other remains silent. The highest joint payoff (known as the optimal outcome) occurs when both remain silent (total of 6), the lowest when both confess (total of 4). The idea of trust is represented in the game by a prediction that the other will remain silent. The idea of risk is reflected in acting on this prediction by remaining silent. If the other thwarts my prediction by confessing, I receive the lowest payoff of 1 (maximum prison sentence) while he or she gets the highest payoff of 4 (or freedom). This is the dilemma confronting

	Suspect 2	
	Remain silent	Confess
Remain silent	3, 3	1, 4
Suspect 1		
Confess	4, 1	2, 2

Figure 3.1   The Prisoner's Dilemma Game

both players. Most outcomes of PDG experiments are confess-confess (a total payoff of 4). Players tend to be risk averse or competitive rather than trusting. This is also known as the equilibrium outcome, defined as the outcome that minimizes the players' losses rather than maximizes their gains.

The reason why this is regarded as a wide-range, thin-extension model is that it captures a dilemma present in a variety of conflict situations. It highlights the mixed motives of cooperating and competing found in many negotiating situations. This dilemma is reflected in a simple matrix form, without the need for elaborate substantive information about issues, history, and situations. For this reason, however, the PDG does not capture the complexity of detail found in any particular conflict situation. Thus, it differs from the examples of role-play simulations, such as collective bargaining, discussed in the section above. It is one of a family of matrix games, each of which illuminates a particular dilemma faced by parties in conflict. These games include chicken, deadlock, bully, maximizing differences, coordination, and battle of the sexes (for a lucid presentation of these games and their applications to actual international conflicts, see Snyder & Diesing, 1977).

The game of chicken takes the form illustrated in Figure 3.2. In this game, the best outcome for each of the players is obtained when he or she does not swerve and the other swerves (4). The best joint outcome occurs (each gets 3) when both swerve, and the worst outcome occurs, of course, when neither swerves. Similar to the PDG, the dilemma is between trust (predicting that the other will swerve) and risk (acting on the prediction by not swerving). A difference between the games, however, is that the consequences are more severe for making the wrong prediction in chicken: Collision occurs. Another difference is that the equilibrium solution is the swerve-swerve outcome in the upper left box rather than the confess-confess outcome in PDG's lower right box. This format has been used to capture the interactions between President Kennedy and Premier Khruschev in the famous historical situation of the Cuban Missile Crisis. A question raised by historians is whether the outcome

		Player 2	
		Swerve	Do Not Swerve
	Swerve	3, 3	2, 4
Player 1			
	Do Not Swerve	4, 2	1, 1

Figure 3.2   The Chicken Game

of that crisis was the equilibrium solution, swerve-swerve (both removed missiles; the United States from Turkey, the Soviet Union from Cuba), or the solution favoring the United States, swerve-do not swerve (Soviets remove missiles as United States stands firm). Another historical situation that has been modeled as a game of chicken is the Berlin Blockade of 1948–1949. The outcome of this crisis was swerve (the Soviet Union conceded)—do not swerve (the United States held firm) (see Snyder & Diesing, 1977, p. 114).

The maximizing-differences game takes the form shown in Figure 3.3. This is an interesting game from the standpoint of revealing the social motivation of players. The "rational" choice for both players is A: Both maximize their payoffs with this choice. Yet, despite the obvious, many players choose B, not because they do not understand how payoffs result from choices, but because they prefer a solution that maximizes the difference between them for relative gain rather than obtain the highest individual and joint payoff for absolute gain. McClintock and Nuttin (1969) showed that the frequency of relative gains choices differs for Dutch and American children. Hopmann (1995) discusses the prevalence of a relative-gains approach taken by nations in foreign policy decision making and negotiations, particularly during the cold war.

		Player 2	
		Choice A	Choice B
	Choice A	6, 6	0, 5
Player 1			
	Choice B	5, 0	0, 0

Figure 3.3   The Maximizing-Differences Game

		Player 2	
		Choice A	Choice B
Player 1	Choice A	2, 3	1, 4
	Choice B	4, 2	3, 1

Figure 3.4   The Bully Game

The payoff configuration for the bully game is as shown in Figure 3.4. This game illuminates a dominant choice for Player 1. This player can never lose if he or she chooses B: The difference in payoffs is between 4 and 3, depending on whether Player 2 chooses A (1 gets 4 units) or B (1 gets 3 units). This game depicts interactions between parties with different amounts of power. It is particularly relevant to negotiations between hegemonic powers and lesser powers who depend on them. An example from ancient diplomacy involved negotiations between the pharaohs of Egypt and emissaries from lesser kingdoms, as illustrated by Druckman and Guner (2000). (See also Guner & Druckman, 2000, for further elaboration of the model.) It is also illustrated by Leng (1998) in terms of influence strategies used by 20th-century powers in recurring crises between pairs of nations.

This family of games models relatively simple conflicts. They can be compared to one another in terms of the symbolic notation given in Figure 3.5. In this notation, R is reward, T is temptation, S is a sucker's choice, and P is punishment. The sequence of outcomes for the PDG, ranging from best to worst for each player, is $T > R > P > S$. This means that the highest payoffs go to Player 2 in the upper right-hand box; the highest payoffs go to Player 1 in the lower left-hand box. These payoffs result from the combined choices of both players. The sequence of outcomes for chicken is $T > R > S > P$. In this game, the punishment is quite severe and worse than making the sucker's choice to swerve when the other does not. Notice the difference between these games: S and P are reversed, with S being better (worse) than P in chicken (PDG). Each of the other games is defined by a sequence of these outcomes. For example, the sequence for the game of deadlock is $T > P > R > S$: PP (in the lower, right-hand box) is the equilibrium outcome.

The configuration of outcomes in matrix games has a strong influence on the way that the games are played. In most games, however, the best joint outcome (which is often the R, R choice combination) is not the same as the

	Player 2	
	R, R	S, T
Player 1		
	T, S	P, P

Figure 3.5   Symbolic Representation of Game Payoffs

best individual outcome (which is often the S, T or T, S choice combination). Thus, advice would be tailored to game-playing goals that can be competitive/ individualistic or cooperative/collective. These goals are easily manipulated through instructions about how the game is to be played. But there are a number of other variables shown in experiments to influence outcomes. The long list includes the size of payoffs, whether choices are made sequentially or simultaneously, whether feedback is provided, the number of games, the relationships between players, framing of the payoffs as gains or losses, whether the player roles are representative of others, and so on. This has been a popular line of research due, at least in part, to the ease with which experiments are conducted and embedded in very simple scenarios. It is also a flexible form of modeling that reduces a large variety of real-world conflicts to their essentials. (In addition to the 20th-century applications given in Snyder & Diesing, 1977, see Guner & Druckman, 2000, for analyses of four games representing different assumptions about information exchanged in diplomatic correspondences between representatives of the kingdoms living during the Bronze Age [circa 1400 BCE].)

Game-theoretic analyses have also been used to demonstrate some counterintuitive aspects of the mediator role. In his analysis of mediator bias, Kydd (2003) showed that communications may be more credible when the mediator is biased toward one or another disputing party. In bargaining situations, where the interests of the parties are at least partially opposed, there is an incentive to bluff: A party is encouraged to tell the mediator that it has high resolve and will fight unless it receives a concession, regardless of whether or not this is the case. The question then is under what conditions can a mediator credibly communicate information to the negotiators about the other party's resolve? Much of the literature on mediation promotes the idea that an impartial mediator can be trusted by all parties because he or she neither favors nor disfavors any party.

Kydd's (2003) game-theoretic model demonstrates the opposite of this conventional wisdom—that a partial mediator is likely to be a more effective communicator. The model implies that a mediator who favors the side he or she is communicating with is more credible, and thus persuasive, about the other side's resolve. This then encourages the favored party to make a concession. The model also shows that a certain degree of bias is not only acceptable but actually necessary in some roles the mediators play and that the function of providing information can be implemented better, in some circumstances, by powerful, biased mediators. (For a readable introduction to the many facets of game theory, including games with perfect and imperfect information as well as variants and extensions, see Osborne, 2004.)

COMPUTER SIMULATION

Another form of modeling is computer simulation. Instead of having people play games in assigned roles, the computer performs computations based on assumptions specified in a model. The assumptions may, for example, consist of preferences for alternative possible agreements that would settle conflicting claims between two or more parties. The preferences are often expressed as probabilities assigned to each proposal or as a probability distribution across the complete set of possible proposals. In an interactive context, the probabilities or preferences determine the proposals (referred to also as demands) made by each of the disputing parties. Agreements or impasses emerge from sequences of proposals and counterproposals. The key to agreement is the extent to which the parties change their proposals or make concessions. According to one model, concessions are a function of three parameters: desire to reciprocate, desire to initiate reciprocation, and friendly feelings toward the opponent.

Bartos (1995) expresses these parameters in the form of an equation:

$$dD = -k * dO - a * D + g \quad 0 < k, a < 1 \tag{1}$$

where D is the current demand, dD is the current change in demand, and dO is the current change in the opponent's offers. Parameter k controls the tendency to reciprocate; a, the tendency to make unilateral concessions; and g, the level of feelings. This model specifies the conditions under which concessions will be made: The larger the reciprocation parameter (k), the larger a party's concession will be in response to an opponent's concession; unilateral concession making (a) is most pronounced during the early stages of negotiation when demands are high, and the larger the friendliness or feelings parameter (g), the larger the concession. The model is evaluated by varying the values of these parameters and observing when an (and what) agreement is reached. Bartos (1995) used this equation to determine paths of demands: The computer generated a series of demands that, according to the probabilities specified by the program, each negotiating party would make. He then evaluated the relative merits of two approaches to negotiation, a *distributive* (concession exchange) and *integrative* (information search) approach. He concluded that the distributive process is faster, but the integrative process may be more productive because it can increase the chances of an agreement.

A second example of computer modeling involves stochastic processes. These processes assume sequential dependence of events. A number of social conflict processes have been modeled as a continuous-time Markov chain. This model assumes that the outcome of one event places an individual in a particular state, and the probabilities of new events depend on that state. It construes conflict as a dynamic process in which parties transition between states of antagonism and cooperation. A key analytical question is, What influences the rates of transition from one state to another? Earlier work by Coleman (1973) on causal modeling made progress on this issue. He showed that transition rates are a function of two parameters expressed by the following equation:

$$q(t) = q_0 e^{-at} \tag{2}$$

where q_0 is the transition rate at the time of the initiating event, a is the rate of decline, and $q(t)$ is the transition rate at time t after the initiating event. This equation captures exponential decay in rates of change from one state to another. Decline in rates is a function of time since the last move: The longer a process remains in a state of cooperation between parties, the lower the probability that it will move to a state of antagonism between them. Empirical examples given by Coleman (1973) illustrate that the longer parties remain in a state, the less they attend to cues that may signal a change in process or relationship. However, this process is reversed when there is a terminating event such as an election or a negotiating deadline. In this case, transition rates increase over time in a systematic fashion. The exponential growth function that captures this process takes the following form:

$$q(t) = q(0) e^{at} \tag{3}$$

where $q(0)$ is the value of q when $t = 0$, and the other terms are same as that in Equation 2.

These two situations of initiation and termination can be studied with computer simulation or experimental methods. One example would be to manipulate the time spent in each of several stages of a conflict process, with and without an imposed deadline. Calculations of rates of change (q_0 and $q(t)$) would be made for the same time period when a deadline has been imposed and when it has not. Simulation data showing that rates slow down with time from initiating events and speed up with time to a terminating event would have implications for third-party interventions intended to move disputing parties out of antagonistic states. Creating a terminating event can move the parties quickly out of a state toward agreements. When terminating events are not available or cannot be manufactured, early interventions that are less direct or more facilitative may work. Later interventions may work better if they are more direct, including the use of combinations of mediation and arbitration (see McGillicuddy et al., 1987).

An application of stochastic modeling to international interactions was developed by Duncan and Job (1980). By using coded data on tensions, they calculated transition probabilities—modeled as a continuous-time Markov process—for estimating shifts from one state (minor tension) to another state (major tension) of the interaction system. The probabilities provided additional information about trends in the interactions between Israel and Syria and between Rhodesia and Zimbabwe. The information is useful for forecasting when changes are likely to occur, contributing to the technology of early warning of escalations or de-escalations in the ongoing relationships.

The models discussed to this point in the section are relatively simple. They deal with only a few variables or parameters: Demands, offers, reciprocation, and feelings in Bartos's bargaining model (1995); time from initiating events and to terminating events in Coleman's and (1973) model of transition rates. The game-theory models focus on two choices made by each of two players confronted with a dilemma of balancing trust against risk. The relationships specified by these models can be evaluated with two-person game experiments conducted over a brief period of time. They can also be evaluated in terms of assumptions about expected payoffs to the players. An example of this kind of strategic analysis is Sandler and Arce M.'s (2003) game-theoretic treatment of terrorism. They developed alternative scenarios, based on different types of games (e.g., PDG, coordination), for assessing the benefits of proactive or reactive government policies. They also explored some implications of granting concessions to terrorist organizations with differing proportions (p and $1 - p$) of moderate and hard-line members. These implications include answers to the following question: What kind of offer should a government make to a terrorist organization? By addressing these issues, the models provide a means for evaluating the effectiveness of antiterrorist policies.

COMPLEX MODELS

More complex models are needed when the number of conflicting parties in a system increases (e.g., Mosher, 2003) or when general variables (such as terrorist incidents) are decomposed into their various components (such as intensity and location of incidents, type as own or foreign terrorism, effects on market share and spillover; e.g., Drakos & Kutan, 2003). These kinds of models are often tested with archival data over time. They can also be evaluated with simulated data, as illustrated by Clarke's (2003) attempt to discriminate among different models of international relations. (He performed Monte Carlo experiments with randomly generated simulation data.) Further opportunities for simulation modeling are provided by Internet technologies. Dasgupta (2003) provides an example of the use of Internet-mediated simulations for providing uncontrolled environments for the study of group decision-making processes. For a survey of various applications of Internet technologies, see the other articles in the special issue of *Simulation & Gaming* edited by Dasgupta (2003b).

As well, data collected from human role-playing simulations can be used to evaluate complex models. Typically, however, the models evaluated by role-play simulations take the form of schematic diagrams or flowcharts rather than sets of equations. Examples include Wolfe's (1995) evaluation of the management development process; the Klabbers, Swart, Van Ulden, and Vellinga (1995) use of gaming to evaluate problem-solving models for addressing climate change and policy; and the Garris, Ahlers, and Driskell (2002) use of instructional games to demonstrate the value of an input-process-outcome model of learning. In addition to model precision and calibration or measurability, the computer and human forms of simulation differ in terms of the number of variables in the model and the consistency of the behavior observed. Computer simulations—especially those based on mathematical models—deal with fewer variables and focus attention primarily on the rational or ordered aspects of decisions or behavior (see Armstrong, 1995, for a taxonomy of simulation approaches).

Of particular interest in this discussion of simulation approaches to modeling is the trade-off between broad and narrow applicability of computer or role-play results. The broad applicability of game models is gained at a price of relevance to particular conflict situations. Relevance is less at issue when simulations are used primarily as vehicles for theory development, as in the examples of the Bartos (1995) and Coleman (1973) models. It is more important when simulations are used to accomplish training or policy goals, as in the example of climate-change policy or instructional simulations. In Chapter 1, I discussed the difference between abstract or general and concrete or specific concepts. The game models—and other wide-range thin-extension approaches—are closer to the abstract end of this continuum. Many policymaking simulations, as examples of narrow-range, deep-extension models, are closer to the more concrete end. Abstractions are useful for theory construction. They are less useful for giving advice about particular issues or situations. They may also be less useful for participant learning about how to perform well-defined tasks in other settings. (For more on issues of transfer of learning, see Reder & Klatsky, 1994; on types of learning, see Kolb, 1984.)

Summary

The discussion in this chapter reviews the variety of designs that have been used in experiments. Examples of experiments that address CA&R issues are used to illustrate the designs, which vary in complexity from simple pre-post test comparisons to elaborate controls with repeated before-and-after treatment assessments. The key idea for experiments is random assignment of participants to conditions. This idea is the primary distinction between quasi and classical experiments. It bolsters confidence in the internal validity of an experiment, especially when efforts are made to control for various possible threats to validity. It does not ensure external validity, however. Two ways of bridging internal with external validity is through field experimentation and simulation design. The advantages of randomized field trials have not been exploited by CA&R researchers to date. Simulation, on the other hand, has been a popular approach to doing research and modeling.

Simulation designs are attempts to reproduce real-world environments, including historical negotiations, political decision making, and organizational processes. To the extent that they are effective in doing this, external validity is improved. The examples given show how experiments can be embedded in simulations of conflict. Simulations are also models of social processes. The models discussed include both relatively simple games such as the popular prisoner's dilemma and the more complex designs that capture many details of the settings being simulated. The former are thought to apply to a wide range of situations and, thus, may be useful devices for theory testing and development. The latter models, which include both computer and human simulations, focus on particular situations and may thus be useful for practice and training.

In this discussion of experimental designs, methods of analysis have been mentioned but not developed. Let us turn to the next chapter to consider how data collected from experiments and simulations can be analyzed.

Discussion Questions

It is hoped that you now have an appreciation for both the strengths and limitations of experimentation. The strengths may lead you to consider performing experiments on CA&R topics. The limitations should lead to a consideration of using a multi-method research strategy that includes doing experiments. Several discussion questions are suggested by this presentation of the experimental and modeling approaches to research. You may want to use them as a basis for class discussion and review before moving on to the next chapter on methods of analysis.

1. What is the primary goal of experiments? What are the key features of this approach to doing research?

2. Internal and external validity are often regarded as being complementary considerations in experimental design: Give examples of how you might attempt to reduce some threats to both types of validity. What are some trade-offs between the two types of validity?

3. What are the key distinguishing features of pre-experimental, quasi-experimental, and classical experimental designs? Under what conditions would one or the other of these types of designs be used?

4. Design a CA&R experiment that combines the Solomon four-group design with time-series data. What are some advantages of using this type of design compared, for example, to a one-shot, pre-test–post-test design?

5. Many experiments are designed to explore the connection between the experimental variable or treatment and outcomes. What other kinds of data might be useful for explaining this connection? Give examples from studies of conflict resolution.

6. How can experimental simulations be used to bridge the gap between internal and external validity? What are some strengths and limitations of simulation techniques?

7. What is the relevance of the distinction between models that have wide range and thin extension and those that have narrow range and deep extension? Give examples of models in each of these categories.

8. Describe some contributions made by game-theoretic analyses to the field of CA&R. Illustrate these contributions with games such as prisoner's dilemma, chicken, or bully.

9. What is the value of computer simulation approaches to understanding (theory) and resolving (practice) conflicts? What are some gains (and some losses) from using computer platforms rather than human role players in modeling?

10. Compare relatively simple (a few parameters) with complex (many parameters) simulation models. What are the relative advantages and disadvantages?

4

Evaluating Data From Experiments

Methods of Analysis

The discussion in the previous chapter has been about issues of designing experiments, with special attention paid to matters of internal and external validity. Of equal importance in conducting experiments is the way that data are collected and analyzed. More than any of the other methodologies used in social science, experiments are intended to forge a tight connection between design, data collection, and analysis. The connection is important if threats to internal validity are to be reduced. This means that the planned comparisons between conditions (referred to as independent variables) can be evaluated with quantitative data generated in keeping with the plan (referred to as dependent variables). Experiments work best when they serve as vehicles for evaluating hypotheses; they provide a technology for judging the validity of deductions from theories. I am particularly impressed with the power of experiments for deciding between plausible rival hypotheses drawn from different theoretical perspectives. For example, an experiment was helpful in deciding whether Piaget's hypothesis about the development of fairness norms was more plausible than competing hypotheses from equity theory (Solomon & Druckman, 1972; for other competing hypotheses arbitrated with experimental techniques, see Druckman, 2003). The answers are provided within the framework of inferential statistical analysis discussed in this chapter.

Various tools for evaluating experimental data are presented in this chapter. The discussion begins with the essential ideas of statistical analysis. It then proceeds to illustrate a trade-off between precision in measurement and power of a statistical test. The remaining sections discuss the popular family of analysis of variance (ANOVA) techniques.

Essential Ideas of Statistical Analysis

There are many good books on statistical analysis. Some of my own favorites are mentioned in the Preface: I particularly like Siegel and Castellan's (1988) treatment of nonparametric statistics, Edwards's (1960) presentation of the analysis of variance, and Blalock's (1979) discussion of correlation and regression; I have also benefited from many of the Sage papers on quantitative analysis. Valuable features of these books are their clear exposition of underlying theory, assumptions to satisfy for use of each of the techniques, and application examples. No attempt is made here to repeat those expositions. Rather, an attempt is made to cull from these and other treatments the essential ideas of probability theory. I suggest that an understanding of four ideas is sufficient to appreciate the purpose and value of statistical analysis.

Inferential statistics. Statistics is a branch of applied mathematics based on probability theory. This is a theory of chance expressed in the form of a distribution of all possible occurrences of events over the long run. The idea of a distribution, referred to as a *probability distribution,* is central to inferential statistics as distinguished from descriptive statistics. The goal of inferential statistics is to infer properties of populations (of people, cases, situations, or events) from samples taken from these populations. Descriptive statistics consists of numerical descriptions of samples with no intention to generalize to larger populations. Inferential statistics is used to evaluate experimental hypotheses and are, thus, the focus of this discussion.

A popular example of a distribution is the occurrence of heads or tails that results from the flipping of an unbiased coin—heads or tails are equally likely to occur on any flip. The question of interest is how often heads (or tails) are likely to occur in N flips. Suppose that N is 12. The most frequently expected outcome would then be 6 heads and 6 tails. However, it is unlikely that this outcome would occur each time we flipped the coin: 7 heads, 5 tails; 8 heads, 4 tails; 9 heads, 3 tails, 10 heads, 2 tails; 11 heads, 1 tail; and 12 heads, no tails will occur in some samples of 12 flips. The deviation from an equal split outcome can be calculated from many samples. In fact, across many samples or over the long run, the alternative outcomes will occur with certain probabilities (p), defined as the number of times heads (or tails) occurs in N samples of 12 flips. Siegel and Castellan (1988, pp. 16–17) calculated the probabilities by using the formula for the binomial (normal) distribution. The probability distribution that they obtained for 4,096 (2^{12}) samples of size 12 is shown in Figure 4.1.

The figure shows that the set of frequencies and probabilities takes the form of a normal distribution characterized by symmetry. A normal curve is superimposed on each of the columns. The same set of probabilities occurs on both sides of the most frequently occurring event, 6 heads. Each probability is

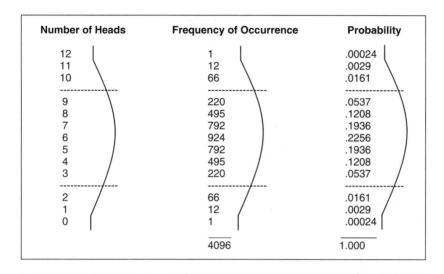

Number of Heads	Frequency of Occurrence	Probability
12	1	.00024
11	12	.0029
10	66	.0161
9	220	.0537
8	495	.1208
7	792	.1936
6	924	.2256
5	792	.1936
4	495	.1208
3	220	.0537
2	66	.0161
1	12	.0029
0	1	.00024
	4096	1.000

Figure 4.1   Frequencies and Probabilities for Samples of Coin Flips

Source: Adapted from Siegel and Castellan (1988, Table 2.2).

arrived at by dividing the frequency by the total number of samples (1/4,096 = .00024). The probability of obtaining 10 heads or more is 1/4,096 + 12/4,096 + 66/4,096 = .019. This calculation shows that in any set of 12 flips of a coin, the chance of obtaining 10 or more heads (or tails) is very low. If this outcome were to occur frequently, across many samples, it would raise questions about whether the coin is unbiased. This procedure is the basis for statistical hypothesis testing. It is referred to as a *sampling distribution*.

Sampling distribution. The sampling distribution is the most important concept in inferential statistics. In theory, it is the distribution of probabilities calculated from all possible samples of a given size drawn randomly from a population of events or other variables. In the coin-flipping example, this would be the number of heads obtained from an infinite number of samples of size 12. Of course, it is impossible to compute values from an infinite number of samples. And, in any event, this is unnecessary for many characteristics of samples because the sampling distribution is very close to the expected population distribution when many samples are drawn. For most events, including statistical tests, the sampling distribution approximates a normal distribution, as in the coin-flipping example above. Proof that this is the case is provided by a mathematical theorem known as the *central limit theorem;* it has also been referred to as the *law of large numbers.* This theorem states that when the number of samples approaches infinity, the distribution becomes normal. However, because samples are finite, the term *approximately* is appropriate (see also Chapter 5 for a discussion of the sampling distribution in the context of survey research).

Rejection region. The tables found in appendices of statistics textbooks contain the values of the statistic (or statistical ratio) located in the tails of the sampling distribution for each of a number of commonly used statistical tests. The tails are the parts of the distribution that consist of the smallest probabilities, where the distribution *tails off*. These are the values that have the smallest probabilities of occurring by chance, for example, the probabilities of getting either 0, 1, 2 or 10, 11, 12 heads in the coin-flipping exercise (see Figure 4.1). Because these values occur so infrequently, or in so few samples, a question arises about whether they are indeed chance occurrences. This part of the sampling distribution—or area of the curve—is known as the *rejection region,* indicated by the lines drawn on the normal distributions in Figure 4.1.

It has become a custom in social science to regard values that occur in less than 5 out of 100 samples, such as 10 heads, as being in the rejection region of the sampling distribution. This means that these values are unlikely to occur by chance alone. This is the significance threshold indicated by the symbol $p < .05$. (The probability of occurrence by chance is less than 5 in 100.) A statistically significant finding obtained from an experiment leads the investigator to reject the null hypothesis of no differences between conditions in favor of the alternative hypothesis of differences between the conditions. The differences between experimental and control conditions are not regarded as mere chance variations. For example, mediation training (an experimental condition) resulted in significantly more dispute settlements than no training (a control condition). In statistical terms, this finding indicates that the two samples, people with or without mediation training, come from different populations. Alternative hypotheses can be stated in directional terms, such as mediation training results in more agreements than no training: When stated in one direction, the problem is a one-tail test of the hypothesis. The alternative hypothesis can also be stated in non-directional terms, which is referred to as a *two-tailed test:* For example, a particular type of mediation training will produce either more or less agreements than another type of training. Two-tailed tests are more stringent in the sense that a larger statistical ratio is needed for significance: For example, a *t* ratio of 1.94 is significant at the .05 level for a one-tailed directional test but only at the .10 level for a two-tailed non-directional test of an hypothesis. These ideas are discussed further in the next section on statistical ratios.

Statistical ratios. Statistical inference depends on an understanding of the meaning of a statistical test. Most tests are ratios of values that summarize differences between conditions to values that reflect variation within conditions of an experiment. This comparison may be between two conditions, such as an experimental and control group (with and without training) or among three or more groups, as when several different interventions are compared for effectiveness (see the examples of alternative research designs in the previous chapter).

Some statistical tests are designed for making two-condition comparisons. The most popular parametric test is probably the *Student's t-test*. This test was invented by the English statistician W. S. Gosset (1876–1936). He worked in the experimental unit at the Guinness Breweries in Dublin, Ireland after taking a degree at Oxford. His task was to ascertain the best varieties of barley and hops for the brewing process from small samples. He published his work under the name Student. According to Agresti and Findlay, this name was used because of "company policy forbidding the publishing of trade secrets" (1997, p. 181). Apparently, his employers did not want the competition to realize how useful the results might be.

The *t*-test is a ratio of the difference between the means (averages) of the two conditions to a measure of variation within each of the conditions, referred to as the standard error of the difference. The former (difference between the means) appears in the numerator; the latter (standard error) appears in the denominator. The larger the numerator relative to the denominator, the larger the value of the *t* ratio. The key idea is that when the difference between the condition means is larger than the variation of scores within those conditions, the value of the *t* ratio is more likely to be found in the rejection region of the sampling distribution—and, thus, be significant. An example may help in understanding this idea.

Suppose that we are interested in evaluating the effects of mediation on a dispute settlement. Only eight trainees are available for the experiment. They are assigned randomly to one of two conditions, a simulated dispute with mediation and the same dispute without mediation. The dependent variable consists of ratings of the process on a scale ranging from 0 (poorest quality) to 12 (excellent quality). The resulting ratings for the two groups are as follows:

Group A (With Mediation)	Group B (Without Mediation)
12	8
10	6
8	2
4	0
Mean (sum of scores divided by 4) = 8	Mean = 4

The difference between the means is 4. The task is to evaluate the hypothesis that mediation makes a difference: The one-tailed hypothesis is that mediation procedures produce a better quality process than no mediation. What do you think? An average difference of 4 units on the scale in the hypothesized direction would seem to lend support to the hypothesis. However, this observation does not take into account the variation that exists within each of the groups. Although the rating scores are different, the groups have the same variation. (The standard deviation is 3.65 for both groups.) Recall that a measure of variation appears in the denominator of the t ratio; the difference between the means appears in the numerator. For this example, the ratio consists of 4 (difference between the means)/9.46 (standard error of the difference). This results in a t ratio of .42. Consulting the table of critical values for t (the tails of the sampling distribution) reveals that a value of 1.943 is needed for significance for an n of 8. (This is equivalent to 6 degrees of freedom in the table found in most books on statistics.) The value of .42 is far below the critical value and, thus, not in the rejection region. This result suggests that the null hypothesis of no difference cannot be rejected.

It is instructive to explain why the statistical evaluation of this hypothesis may contradict the observation that mediation did indeed produce higher-quality ratings. The reason is that the ratings within each condition are dispersed. Further, variation within conditions is more problematic for small numbers of observations within those conditions. A larger difference between condition means (the numerator) would be needed to overcome variation within the conditions (denominator) as the number of observations or ratings decrease. In this example, the variation within conditions must be around 2 for a mean difference of 4 units on the rating scale to be significant.

The ideal distribution of scores for this example is the following:

Group A (With Mediation)	Group B (Without Mediation)
Ratings	Ratings
8	4
8	4
8	4
8	4
Mean = 8	Mean = 4

This outcome shows no variation within either condition. The t ratio is 4/0, producing a t value of infinity, which is, of course, in the farthest possible reaches or tails of the sampling distribution. This result would lead to strong rejection of the null hypothesis, even for a very small n.

These examples illustrate the importance of variation and the number of observations. Any difference between means for conditions is evaluated in relation to variation: Much (or little) variation reduces (or increases) support for an alternative hypothesis. These are key factors in the evaluation of experimental hypotheses.

The same logic applies to comparisons among three or more conditions. However, the statistical tests used to evaluate these comparisons are different. These procedures will be illustrated in the sections to follow on measurement issues.

Summary. This brief section contains many ideas about the discipline of inferential statistics. My intention is not to repeat the detailed discussion of this topic found in many texts on statistics. Rather, I wanted to convey the essential ideas as succinctly as is possible. These ideas include: (a) the probability distribution, (b) the sampling distribution as a type of probability distribution which is the basis for inferential statistics, (c) the rejection region as values in the tails of sampling distributions, and (d) the statistical ratio as a comparison between condition means and variation within those conditions. These four ideas provide the researcher with the tools to evaluate hypotheses about CA&R processes. The stage is now set to move on to other aspects of statistical analysis.

Measurement and Statistical Power: Two-Group Designs

The mediation example given above is based on an assumption that scores (dependent variable) are numbers on an interval scale that ranges from 0 to 12. This means that the size of the interval between any two numbers—such as 2 and 3—is the same as the size between any two other numbers—such as 8 and 9. This assumption is essential for performing the arithmetic operations of adding, subtracting, multiplying, and dividing. Ruled measurements of physical objects, including height and weight, satisfy this assumption. Measures of time or speed to dispute settlement also satisfy the assumption. For many other measures, social-science researchers have constructed *equal-appearing* interval scales. This procedure was developed originally by Thurstone and Chave (1929), whose scale of attitudes toward war (ranging from favorable to unfavorable) is analogized to a 12-inch ruler. A related procedure for measuring attitudes was devised by Likert (1932). His five-step scale, ranging from strongly agree to strongly disagree, is widely used in social science. Another popular scale, devised to measure the meaning of concepts, is the seven-step semantic differential scale (Osgood, Suci, & Tannenbaum, 1957). (For a good overview of attitude scaling, see Secord & Backman, 1964, ch. 3.)

These measures have the advantage of permitting an investigator to use the more powerful parametric statistical tests for analysis. They have the disadvantage of possibly creating a false sense of confidence in the precision with which social science variables can be measured and can thus be misleading. Many investigators simply assume that the use of a Likert scale renders the data as having interval properties. The issue of interest is a trade-off between measurement precision and statistical power.

In most statistics textbooks, measurement precision is discussed in terms of scaling assumptions. The distinction made among nominal, ordinal, interval, and ratio scales captures the difference between categories, ranking, and interval scaling with or without a zero point. These scales progress from weaker to stronger levels of measurement. More powerful statistical tests can be used when the dependent variables (e.g., speed to settlement, perceptions of conflict) are measured on interval or ratio scales. Power refers to the sensitivity of a test in detecting differences between experimental groups (e.g., different kinds of third-party interventions) when they exist. Statisticians refer to this as the probability of committing a Type I or Type II error: Type I errors are made when the null hypothesis of no difference between conditions is *rejected* falsely; Type II errors occur when the null hypothesis is *accepted* falsely. These errors are less likely to be made when the stronger parametric tests (e.g., *t* test, ANOVA, regression) are used to evaluate hypotheses. They are more likely to occur when the somewhat weaker nonparametric tests are used. Hence, the dilemma for the social scientist: He or she is tempted to make the assumptions that permit analyses with parametric tests while realizing that many variables cannot be measured with sufficient precision to permit use of these tests. The equal-appearing interval scale discussed above is an invention that satisfies the temptation. But the question is, how much is gained by using parametric tests of statistical significance? Is it worth risking being misled by measurement devices in order to benefit from the sensitivity of the more powerful tests? This issue may be easier to understand with a computational example. (The interested reader should consult Chapter 2 in Siegel & Castellan [1988] for more on measurement issues in relation to choice of statistical test.)

A parametric statistical test provides a strong basis for inference from samples to populations. This is because it specifies the distribution of responses in the population from which a research sample is drawn. It also assumes that the scores being analyzed are measured on at least an interval scale. More information about the sample is provided by the interval-level data. The *t* test, illustrated above in the section on statistical ratios, is a parametric test designed to compare two groups. A nonparametric test does not provide specific information about the form of the distribution from which the sample is drawn. Thus, it is a weaker basis for making inferences to a population. It is based on fewer assumptions and is applied appropriately to data measured in an ordinal or nominal scale. The Wilcoxon-Mann-Whitney test is the ordinal-level counterpart to the *t* test. The chi-square is the popular nominal-level test that can be used to evaluate two or more groups.

Application and comparison of these techniques are demonstrated with the same data used to illustrate the idea of a statistical ratio.

Recall that the calculation based on the mediation example resulted in a t ratio of .42. This value has a probability of occurring more than 30% of the time in the random sampling distribution for the statistic. It is, therefore, not significant. What would happen, however, if a different statistical test was used to evaluate the difference between the mediation and non-mediation conditions? Suppose that the ratings were considered as ranked rather than interval data. In this case, a non-parametric statistical test would have to be used. The appropriate test is the Mann-Whitney U test for comparing two groups. This is also referred to as the Wilcoxon-Mann-Whitney test, W_x (see Siegel & Castellan, 1988, section 6.4). A first step is to order the ratings by rank, from the lowest score (rank of 1) to the highest score (rank of 8), as follows:

Group A (With Mediator)		Group B (Without Mediator)	
Rating	*Rank*	*Rating*	*Rank*
12	8	8	6
10	7	6	4.5
6	4.5	2	2
4	3	0	1
Sums of Ranks	22.5	Sums of Ranks	13.5

Note that tied scores—the two ratings of 6—are assigned the average rank in the sequence, in this case between 4 and 5, or 4.5. The calculations are performed on the ranks that are regarded as an interval scale. For this test, a simple formula produces a ratio whose value can be evaluated in terms of the sampling distribution. The formula is

$$U = n_1 n_2 + \frac{n_1(n_1 + 1)}{2} - R_1 \tag{1}$$

where n_1 is the number of observations in Group A, n_2 is the number of observations in Group B, and R is the higher of the two sums of ranks. The result is a U value of 3.5. This value is likely to occur between 10% and 17% of the time by chance. It is, therefore, not significant. Notice that this conclusion is the same as that obtained from the t test calculation. However, a difference is that the probability of rejecting the null hypothesis of no difference between the groups is lower.

The difference between ordinal- and interval-scaled data can be illustrated. Suppose that Group B's scores were as follows: 9, 6, 3, 1. This distribution would result in the same ranking of scores and, thus, produce the same U value. However, the intervals between the scores are now different: They are no longer separated by the same interval of 2 as shown in the box above. The mean for the new Group B is now 4.75 (compared to 4), and the standard deviation is 3.50 (compared to 3.65). The t ratio is 1.01, which is significant at approximately the .17 level. (As noted above, a critical value of t needed for significance is 1.94.) It is important to recognize that this probability value is considerably lower than that obtained from the original data ($p < .35$ vs. $p < .17$). It is also very close to the probability obtained by the rank-order Mann-Whitney statistic. The reduced probability occurs despite a smaller difference between the means (4 vs. 3.25). It is due to the difference in standard deviations (3.65 vs. 3.50), which reflect the variance in the scores or the intervals. Thus, the interval makes a difference. Two sets of identical rank-ordered data produce the same ratio and probability level with ordinal statistical tests, irrespective of the intervals. If, however, the intervals differ for the two data sets (and, thus, the standard deviations are different), that difference will influence the result obtained from interval-level statistical tests.

Now suppose that the data were considered as nominal rather than either interval or ordinal. In this case, the number of settlements that resulted in each group would be examined as follows:

	Settled	*Unsettled*	*Sums*
Group A (Mediation)	3 (2)	1 (2)	4
Group B (No Mediation)	1 (2)	3 (2)	4
Sums	4	4	8

This configuration can be evaluated with the nominal scale statistic, chi-square. The calculations are quite simple. First, the differences between the expected and obtained values (in parenthesis) are taken. Second, each difference is squared. Third, the squared difference is divided by the expected value. Fourth, the resulting ratios are summed. The summed value is chi-square. The formula is:

$$\chi^2 = \sum_{i=1}^{k} \frac{(O_i - E_i)^2}{E_i} \qquad (2)$$

where O is the observed value and E is the expected value. This is a goodness-of-fit test. It asks about the extent to which the observed scores deviate from a chance distribution, in this case no difference between the scores. The calculation results in a χ^2 of 2. A value of this size occurs less than 20% of the time by chance according to the sampling distribution of the χ^2 statistic. It is, therefore, not significant. This conclusion corresponds to that reached on the basis of the interval and ordinal scale analyses reported above. The probability is similar to that obtained with the Mann-Whitney U test (namely, below 20%) and is lower than that obtained with the t-test (that is, above 30%).

What then is to be concluded from a comparison of the three statistical analyses performed on the same data?

1. Insofar as the same general conclusion was reached, the analyses reinforce each other.

2. The conclusion is bolstered by the stronger support obtained from the parametric t-test than from the nonparametric tests. The chance of making a Type I error—rejecting the null hypothesis when it should be accepted—is reduced with the more powerful parametric test. Although not significant, the lower probabilities obtained with the two nonparametric tests suggest a stronger difference between the conditions than may be warranted by more-precisely scaled data.

3. Each of the tests may be appropriate depending on assumptions made about the data. If measurement precision is an issue, then the choice is to use the nonparametric tests. This is the trade-off between measurement and power of the statistical test: Type I errors are less likely when parametric tests are used on interval data; results of parametric tests run on non-scaled ordinal data are likely to be misleading. When in doubt, I suggest presenting results from all the tests. If they lead to different conclusions, then this becomes a topic for discussion in the research report.

The examples given in this section consisted of a comparison of two groups. Many experimental designs are comparisons among three or more groups. These designs present the same sorts of trade-offs between measurement and statistical power. The discussion turns now to examples of these problems.

Measurement and Power: Three-Group Designs

The same issue exists with regard to designs that compare more than two conditions. Data collected from these designs are analyzed typically with the ANOVA. Before delving into the details of analysis with the parametric and nonparametric versions of ANOVA, a word is in order about the technique.

The early development of it is credited to the statistician R. A. Fisher. He had this to say about it:

> ... (T)he analysis of variance, which may perhaps be called a statistical method, because that term is a very ambiguous one—is not a mathematical theorem, but rather a convenient method of arranging the arithmetic. Just as in arithmetic textbooks . . . we were given rules for arranging how to find the greatest common measure, and how to work out a sum in practice, and were drilled in the arrangement and order in which we were to put the figures down, so with the analysis of variance; its one claim to attention lies in its convenience. (Fisher, 1934, p. 52)

It is also a powerful method for detecting differences between experimental groups. These features were recognized early by agricultural researchers who applied the technique to problems in soil science and botany. It spread widely across a variety of experimental disciplines, particularly to problems in psychological research.

In essence, the technique consists of calculating a ratio that compares two types of variation, between groups (in the nominator) and within groups (in the denominator). As with the *t*-test, the object for the experimental researcher is to increase the numerator—the between-groups term—in relation to the denominator—the within-groups term; the higher the ratio, the more likely the result is not a chance occurrence. The sampling distribution of this ratio, referred to as an F distribution, takes the form of a curve skewed to the left with the rejection region (or critical ratios) in the right tail as shown in Figure 4.2 below. The calculations are illustrated by adding a third group to the mediation–no mediation comparison developed above. This

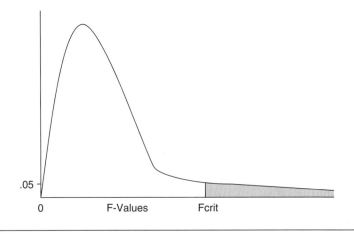

Figure 4.2   Sampling Distribution for the *F* Ratio

group can be referred to as facilitation, a less direct and more disputant-involved form of third-party intervention than mediation.

When a rating scale that ranges from 0 (*poor process*) to 16 (*excellent process*) is used, the following scores are obtained for the three groups. (Notice that the same scores are used for Groups A and B for ease of comparison with the two-group design.)

Group A (Mediation)	Group B (No Mediation)	Group C (Facilitation)
12	8	16
10	6	14
6	2	10
4	0	8
Sum: 32; Mean: 8	Sum: 16; Mean: 4	Sum: 48; Mean: 12

The calculations are intended to produce two variation terms, a between-groups variation and a within-groups variation. These are two parts of the total variation—referred to as a sum of squares (SS)—in the data across groups: Total SS = Between-groups SS + Within-groups SS. They are easy arithmetic calculations, as follows.

1. Obtain the total variation by squaring each of the 12 scores and subtracting the squared sum of the scores (96) divided by the total N (12). This produces a value of 248.

2. Calculate a between-groups variation term by squaring the sum of the scores in each group, dividing each of these squared sums by the group n (4), and subtracting the squared sum of the scores (96) divided by the total N (12). The result is 128.

3. Obtain a within-groups term by calculating the sum of each group's squared scores, subtracting the square of the group sum (32, 16, or 48) divided by the group n.

4. The within-groups term is the sum of these calculations. However, there is a much easier way of getting the within-groups term: Simply subtract the total sum of squares from the between-groups sum of squares (248 − 128 = 120).

It is evident that ANOVA is a "convenient method for arranging the arithmetic" (Fisher, 1934, p. 52). The calculations can be summarized in a sources-of-variation table, as follows.

Table 4.1   A Source Table for the Analysis of Variance

Sources	SS	df	MS	F	p
Between groups	128	2	64	4.80	< .05
Within groups	120	9	13.33		
Total	248	11			

In Table 4.1 SS is the sum of squares, *df* is the degrees of freedom, MS is the mean square, *F* is the statistical ratio, and *p* is the probability level for the *F* value. These terms are calculated as follows.

a. The total degrees of freedom is obtained by subtracting 1 from the total *N* of 12. The between-groups *df* is obtained by subtracting the number of groups (3) by 1. And the within-groups *df* is obtained by subtracting the number of groups (3) from the total *N* (12).[1]

b. The mean square is obtained by simply dividing the SS by the *df.*

c. The *F* value is then obtained by dividing the between-groups MS by the within-groups MS.

d. The probability of obtaining a ratio of this size (4.80) is ascertained by locating it in the sampling distribution of the *F* statistic. The mechanics consist of finding the critical value of *F* (at the .05 level) for 2 and 9 *df.* That value is 4.26. Because 4.80 is higher, the null hypothesis of no difference among the conditions is rejected.

We now know that when a facilitation group is added to the experiment, the ratings differ significantly. However, this is not the whole story. The ANOVA detection of differences among the three groups does not reveal specifically what accounts for the differences. For this, more detailed information is necessary to compare each of the three pairs of groups (A vs. B, A vs. C, and B vs. C). This is accomplished by another procedure, referred to as *multiple comparisons.* There are several different kinds of multiple comparisons, each known by the name of its inventor. For our purposes, the procedures are quite similar, and each produces an evaluation of where the significant differences are found. (The interested reader can refer to any of a large number of textbooks that concentrate on experimental design; a particularly lucid source is Edwards, 1960, chap. 10.) Application of the Duncan multiple-range test shows that the key difference is between the facilitation group (C) and the no-mediation group (B); differences between Groups A and B and between Groups B and C are not significant. Thus, we learn that, unlike mediation, facilitation produces a better process than the control group, even when each group is limited to just four ratings.[2]

These results are meaningful if the investigator is confident that the ratings were made on an interval scale. If, on the other hand, he or she is more confident that the ratings take the form of an ordinal scale, then the group differences should be evaluated with a nonparametric statistical test. The Kruskal-Wallis one-way ANOVA performs this function with rank-ordered data. The calculations are made on the ranks, which are as follows.

Similar to the Wilcoxon-Mann-Whitney test discussed above, the scores are ranked consecutively from lowest to highest (see Table 4.2 below). Tied scores receive the average rank. The calculations involve simple arithmetic: The only information needed for the formula is the number of ratings in each group (4), the total number of ratings (12), and the average of the ranks within (6.5, 3.5, and 9.5, respectively) and across the groups (6.5). The formula is shown in Siegel and Castellan (1988, Section 8.3). The result of the calculations is 7.84. A value as large as this is located in the rejection region of the sampling distribution for the statistic (see Siegel and Castellan, 1988, Table O; the critical value at the .01 level is 7.66). It is likely to occur only one time in 100 by chance alone. Thus, the null hypothesis of no differences between the conditions is rejected.

This result supports the finding obtained with the parametric F ratio and is even somewhat stronger (.01 vs. .05 levels of significance). A multiple comparison among the groups shows that the key difference is between the facilitation (C) and no-mediation (B) groups. (For procedures used to perform a multiple comparison on ranked data, see Siegel & Castellan, 1988, Section 8.3.3.) Thus, the nonparametric finding supports the result obtained with the parametric analysis shown above. (Another nonparametric statistic suitable for ranked data is the Friedman two-way analysis of variance by ranks. This test is used for matched samples such as when an experimental subject is exposed to all the treatments. This is the idea of a repeated measure discussed in the section below. The

Table 4.2   Calculations for Kruskal-Wallis One-Way ANOVA

Group A (Mediation)		Group B (No Mediation)		Group C (Facilitation)	
Rating	Rank	Rating	Rank	Rating	Rank
12	10	8	6.5	16	12
10	8.5	6	4.5	14	11
6	4.5	2	2	10	8.5
4	3	0	1	8	6.5
Sum of Ranks: 26		14		38	

Friedman test assigns the ranks within subjects across the conditions, rather than across all the subjects as in the Kruskal-Wallis test. For details, see Siegel & Castellan, 1988, section 7.2.)

Most researchers perform calculations of this sort with a computer program. Perhaps the most popular software package for statistical analysis is the Statistical Package for the Social Sciences (SPSS). Thus, it would be helpful to review the steps needed to perform the calculations presented above. These are presented for the one-way ANOVA and the Kruskal-Wallis tests in the box to follow.

Calculating One-Way ANOVA With SPSS

The most important requirement for using SPSS is to understand your data and how they should be entered into your file. The independent and dependent variables are *process type* and *process rating*. The process-type variable is a "dummy" variable designed to create break points for the ANOVA and Kruskal-Wallis tests. Each of the groups should be given a numeric value (1 to 3 works fine), and for ease of analyzing your results, you should assign textual values to each number by using the *value* field of the variable. Values for process rating are the numeric rankings shown above and should be all entered into the same variable column. The result should have each case represented by two numeric values, one for the process type and one for process rating (i.e., a rating value of 1 and a type value of 12 for the first case).

When the data are arranged in this fashion, you can run the one-way ANOVA by selecting **Analyze, Compare Means, One-Way ANOVA.** Move the Process Rating variable into the Dependent List and Process Type into the Factor window. A number of additional tests can be run by pressing the **Post-Hoc** button and selecting from a list of available tests. Do this and select the **Duncan** test. Press **Continue** and then **OK** to run the test.

The output should resemble these two tables:

ANOVA

Process Rating

	Sum of Squares	df	Mean Square	F	Sig.
Between groups	128.000	2	64.000	4.800	.038
Within groups	120.000	9	13.333		
Total	248.000	11			

Process Rating

Duncan[a]

		Subset for alpha = .05	
Process type	N	1	2
No mediation (Group B)	4	4.00	
Mediation (Group A)	4	8.00	8.00
Facilitation (Group C)	4		12.00
Sig.		.156	.156

Means for groups in homogeneous subsets are displayed.

a. Uses harmonic mean sample size = 4.000.

Additionally, with SPSS it is possible to exclude each of the groups by removing the cases from the variables and running an ANOVA on the reduced set of two groups. The results of these analyses show that only the comparison of no mediation (Group B) with facilitation (Group C) gives a significant result of .021 with an F of 9.6.

Kruskal-Wallis

In SPSS 11.0, the Kruskal-Wallis test is listed under nonparametric tests. Select **Analyze, Nonparametric Tests, K Independent Samples**. Move the Process Rating variable into the Test Variable List and Process Type into the Grouping Variable window. You will need to select a range by pressing the **Define Range** button below the Grouping Variable button. Because your variable ranges only from 1 to 3, use these values. There are two tests available for the K Independent Samples; select **Kruskal-Wallis** rather than Means and press **OK**.

The output will consist of a table of mean ranks and a table of test statistics.

Now suppose that the investigator is uncomfortable with the assumption that the ratings can be ranked. An alternative would be to arrange the data in categories. As in the example of the two-group comparison, the groups can be compared in terms of the outcome, as settlements and non-settlements. The data may take the form shown in Table 4.3.

This 3×2 cross-tabulation table can be evaluated by chi-square. As in the example of the 2×2 table above, the squared difference between each of the obtained and expected (in parentheses) frequencies divided by the expected

Table 4.3   Calculations for 3 × 2 Chi-Square

	Group A (Mediation)	Group B (No Mediation)	Group C (Facilitation)	Sum
Settled	1 (1.33)	0 (1.33)	3 (1.33)	4
Unsettled	3 (2.67)	4 (2.67)	1 (2.67)	8
Sum	4	4	4	12

frequency are summed. When this is done, a chi-square of 5.25 results. A value this large is likely to be obtained by chance about 8 times in 100. It is smaller than the critical value of 5.99, which would be significant at the .05 level with 2 degrees of freedom. Thus, the null hypothesis of no difference is not rejected, although the results are clearly in the direction of more settlements for the facilitation condition. This borderline significant finding generally supports the results obtained for the process ratings data. However, the effects on process appear stronger than on outcomes. But the jury is out on a final decision until more dispute ratings and outcomes are analyzed.

The chi-square result can also be expressed as a correlation, showing the strength of association between the two variables—third-party type and settlement. The Cramer coefficient, designated as C, is calculated as the square root of the chi-square value (5.25) divided by the number of ratings (12). The result of these calculations is a value of .66. A correlation of this magnitude suggests a strong relationship between the variables. However, the significance of the relationship can be evaluated by consulting the value of chi-square, in this case 5.25. Siegel and Castellan (1988) note that the chi-square distribution is a good approximation of the sampling distribution of C and provides a considerably less complex procedure for ascertaining significance. Because the chi-square value computed above is not significant, we also conclude that the Cramer coefficient does not differ significantly from zero. This result is no doubt due to the small number of disputes used in the example. Thus, the size of the coefficient can be misleading. (The interested reader is encouraged to consult Siegel & Castellan, 1988, Section 9.1 for a detailed discussion of this coefficient.)

Factorial Designs

The one-way ANOVA, discussed in the previous section, concentrates on one variable (third-party technique) with two or more levels (with a mediator, without a mediator, with facilitation). Many experiments are designed to investigate the influence of two or more variables on one or more dependent variables (process ratings, outcomes). With two or more variables (e.g., mediation and group representation), each with two or more levels (with or without mediation; group vs. self representation), a "treatment" consists of a combination of levels (e.g., mediation with group representation) for each variable. As Edwards (1960) stated, "When the treatments consist of all possible different combinations of one level from each factor, and we have an equal number of observations for each treatment, the experiment is described as a *complete factorial experiment with equal replications*" (p. 175). A defining feature of the factorial design is that the independent variables are orthogonal, or uncorrelated. All possible combinations of the levels of the variables are represented in the design. This configuration allows a researcher to assess the influence of each independent variable (on a dependent variable) separately as well as the effects of the variables in combination. The separate assessments are referred to as *main effects*. The combined assessments are referred to as *interactions*. These features distinguish the factorial design from the one-way ANOVA: In the latter, only one main effect (and no interactions) is assessed. An example can help to increase the reader's understanding of the concept and mechanics of factorial designs.

Suppose that we were interested in exploring the effects of mediation and group representation on various indicators of dispute resolution. Three hypotheses are suggested, as follows: (a) Mediation facilitates dispute resolution, (b) group representation hinders dispute resolution, and (c) mediation facilitates resolution better for self than for group representatives. Hypotheses (a) and (b) posit main effects; hypothesis (c) suggests an interaction. These hypotheses can be evaluated with a two-variable factorial design referred to as a 2 × 2 design. Each variable has two levels, mediation versus no mediation and group versus self-representation.

This design takes the following form.

	With Mediation	*Without Mediation*
Group representation	$N = 10$	$N = 10$
Self-representation	$N = 10$	$N = 10$

It is a complete factorial design with an equal number of replications (10) in each cell, defined as a combination of the variable levels. Each of the 40 pairs of disputants is randomly assigned to one of the four cells. A pair is given only one of the four combinations of conditions (group representation with mediation, group representation without mediation, self-representation with mediation, or self-representation without mediation). Data are collected on three dependent variables: process ratings, time to resolution, and outcomes. Relationships between the independent and dependent variables are analyzed with ANOVA.

For the 2×2 design, the between-groups variation is partitioned into three components, the mediation and representation main effects and the interaction between these variables. These are also referred to as components of variation. The within-groups variation is calculated across the four cells or 40 disputant pairs.

The source of variation table takes the form shown in Table 4.4. The sums of squares (SS) are calculated for each source of variation following the procedures described above in the discussion of the one-way ANOVA. These terms are then used to calculate the mean square (MS), which are the bases for the F ratios. Note that we evaluate three effects in this design, two main effects (A and B) and an interaction (A $\times$ B). The total degrees of freedom (df) is $N - 1$ $(40 - 1 = 39)$. This total is divided into four parts; the two main effects (number of levels [2 minus 1]), the interaction $(df$ for A $\times df$ for B), and the within-groups term (total df minus the sum of the df for the other sources of variation).

Significant main effects are indicated by F ratios located in the rejection region of the sampling distribution. They would support hypotheses (a) and

Table 4.4   Source Table for a 2×2 ANOVA Design

Source of Variation	df	Sums of Squares (SS)	Mean Square (MS)	F
Mediation (A)	1		$\dfrac{SS\,(A)}{df}$	$\dfrac{MS\,(A)}{MS\,(within)}$
Representation (B)	1		$\dfrac{SS\,(B)}{df}$	$\dfrac{MS\,(B)}{MS\,(within)}$
Mediation $\times$ Representation (A $\times$ B)	1		$\dfrac{SS\,(AB)}{df}$	$\dfrac{MS\,(AB)}{MS\,(within)}$
Within groups	36			
Total	39			

(b) and can be illustrated with hypothetical data on the dependent variable, time to resolution. Suppose that the following average times were obtained for each cell.

	No Mediation	Mediation	Row Averages
Group representation	30 minutes	20 minutes	25 minutes
Self-representation	25 minutes	15 minutes	20 minutes
Column averages	27 minutes	17 minutes	

Note: Minutes = means.

This set of average times can be depicted in the form of a graph. The four averages are arranged in terms of the independent (mediation, representation) and dependent (time to settlement) variables in Figure 4.3.

Main effects are indicated in the figure by the parallel diagonal lines. (The points are connected with lines for ease of interpretation. Bar graphs are actually a more accurate way of depicting differences among the points.) The distance between the lines is the difference between the average times for the group (25 minutes) and self-representation (20 minutes) conditions.

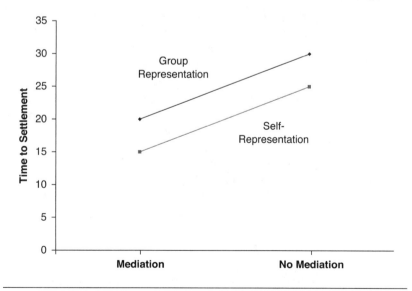

Figure 4.3   Main Effects for Representation and Mediation

The distance between the points for the mediation (average of 17 minutes) and no-mediation (average of 27 minutes) conditions is indicated by the slope of the diagonal lines. Significant F ratios (below the .05 level) for each of these differences would provide evidence for the representation and mediation main effects. This configuration of average times does not result in an interaction.

Plots and statistics for factorial ANOVA designs can be obtained with SPSS. The procedure for obtaining the two-way plot illustrated in Figure 4.3 and the source table for main effects and interactions is described in the box to follow.

Factorial ANOVA With SPSS

The most important aspect in using SPSS to calculate a factorial ANOVA is to enter your data properly. For this example, you will need to create three variables for resolution time (dependent variable), type of representation (independent variable) and type of process (independent variable). For type of representation (hereafter termed *group*), assign a numerical value of 1 to self-representation and 2 to group representation. For process, assign a numerical value of 1 to mediation and 2 to no mediation.

To enter data on resolution time in the SPSS spreadsheet, type all 40 numbers (10 for each of 4 combinations of conditions) in the first column. A series of 10 numbers for Group 1 (self-representation) and Process 1 (mediation) is followed by 10 numbers for Group 1 (self-representation) and Process 2 (no mediation) and so on for Group 2 (group representation) and Process 1 (mediation) and then Group 2 (group representation) and Process 2 (no mediation). In this example, enter the time to resolution for each negotiating dyad in conditions 1 and 1; for example, 8 minutes, 12 minutes, 8 minutes, and so on for the remaining seven dyads in these conditions, followed by the time to resolution for each negotiating dyad in conditions 1 and 2; for example, 18 minutes, 22 minutes, 18 minutes, and so on for the remaining seven dyads in these conditions. Then enter the value, either 1 or 2, that corresponds to the group variable (self- or group representation) condition for each dyad. For example, next to 8, 12, 8, enter 1 for the self-representation condition. In the fourth column, enter 1 for the mediation condition. When you have completed your data entry, it should look as follows.

Data Entries

Row	Time (min.)	Group	Process
1	8	1	1
2	12	1	1
3	8	1	1
—			
—			
—			
10	20	1	1
11	18	1	2
12	22	1	2
13	18	1	2
—			
—			
—			
20	30	1	2
21	13	2	1
22	17	2	1
23	13	2	1
—			
—			
—			
30	25	2	1
31	23	2	2
32	27	2	2
33	23	2	2
—			
—			
—			
40	35	2	2

SPSS version 11.0 does not use the term *factorial ANOVA*. Instead, select Analyze, General Linear Model, and Univariate. Place Time in the Dependent Variable box. Then place Group and Process in the Fixed Factors box, where independent variables are to be entered. To obtain your plot, select the Plots button that appears on the same screen where you see the Dependent Variable and Fixed Factors boxes. Place Process in the Horizontal Axis box and Group in the Separate Lines box. Then press Add, Continue, and OK. The plot will be the same as that shown in Figure 4.3, indicating two main effects and no interaction.

SPSS also generates a table summarizing the ANOVA output as follows:

Tests of Between-Subjects Effects

Dependent Variable: Time

Source	Type III Sum of Squares	df	Mean Square	F	Sig.
Corrected model	1250.000	3	416.667	13.298	.000
Intercept	20250.000	1	20250.000	646.277	.000
Group	250.000	1	250.000	7.979	.008
Process	1000.000	1	1000.000	31.915	.000
Group * Process	2.200	1	2.200	.070	.98
Error	1128.000	36	31.333		
Total	22628.000	40			
Corrected total	2378.000	39			

* R squared = .526 (Adjusted R squared = .486).

The table shows that the main effects of group and process are significant at the levels of .008 and .000 (less than .001), respectively. It also indicates that there is no interaction effect, as shown by the significance level of .98 for the Group * Process source.

Suppose, however, that the configuration of average times for the conditions took the following form.

	No Mediation	Mediation	Row Averages
Group representation	Mean = 30 minutes	10 minutes	20 minutes
Self-representation	15 minutes	25 minutes	20 minutes
Column averages	22.5 minutes	17.5 minutes	

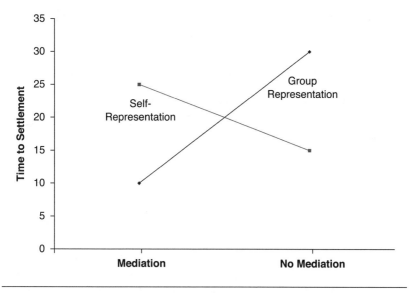

Figure 4.4   Interaction Between Representation and Mediation

This set of average times can also be depicted in the form of a graph, as shown in Figure 4.4. This figure shows a crossover interaction effect. The direction of difference between the average times for group and self-representation depends on whether the dispute is mediated: Group representatives take more time than self-representatives when the dispute is not mediated; self-representatives take more time than group representatives when the dispute is mediated. Put in another way, mediation worked better for group (10 minutes) than for self (25 minutes) representatives. Interactions are contingent effects. They indicate that the effects for one variable, such as representation, depend on the operation of another variable, such as mediation (see Fisher, 1997, for a discussion of contingency theory in CA&R). In this example, there are no main effects for either variable; the differences between the row averages (representation variable) and between the column averages (mediation variable) are not significant.

The factorial design can be extended to include more than two variables. The 2 × 2 × 2 configuration (three variables, each at two levels) is one of the most popular experimental designs. It was the design that I used for my doctoral dissertation on simulated collective bargaining (Druckman, 1967). It can be illustrated by adding a third variable to the problem shown above. A research question of interest is whether the effects of representation and mediation on the process and outcome of dispute settlement are contingent on the presence of observers.

The design may take the following form, with the number of dispute pairs and average times to settlement in the cells.

	Observers		No Observers	
	Group Rep	Self-Rep	Group Rep	Self-Rep
Mediation	$N = 10$	10	10	10
	Mean = 23 min.	15 min.	16 min.	20 min.
No mediation	$N = 10$	10	10	10
	Mean = 30 min.	20 min.	10 min.	22 min.

This design has eight cells. With 10 disputant pairs in each cell, the total number of pairs is 80 (or 160 individuals). Thus, by adding one variable to the 2 × 2 design, the number of pairs (and individuals) needed to complete the factorial (2^3) is doubled. In fact, each time a new factor is added, the number of replications needed is doubled (an increase of 100%). Adding another level to one of the variables (e.g., tape recorded without live observers) for a 2 × 2 × 3 design adds four more cells or a 50% increase (40 more pairs) in the number of replications needed.

The time-to-settlement data would be analyzed by ANOVA. The source table (with degrees of freedom) takes the form indicated in Table 4.5. As in the 2 × 2 problem discussed above, the sources of variation are components of a between-groups term (including the three main effects and the four interactions) and a within-groups or error term. The total degrees of freedom is the number of dispute pairs minus one. This number (79) is divided into the main effects (number of conditions minus one), interactions (product of the df for the conditions), and the within-groups variation term (total df minus the sum of the main effect and interaction df). The calculations are performed for the sum of squares (SS), mean square (MS), and F ratio in the same way as described above for the one-way ANOVA.

The time-to-settlement data, shown above, can be depicted graphically. For ease of interpretation, a bar graph depicting the three conditions (mediation, observers, and representation) is shown in Figure 4.5. These results show that the combination of no observers and group representation increases time to settlement when sessions are not mediated. This is a three-way (A × B × C) interaction. Main effects for mediation (A) and representation (B) occur only when observers are present. No effects occur when no observers are present. When no observers watch the settlement process, self-representatives take about as long to reach agreements as group representatives. Similarly,

Table 4.5   Source Table for a $2 \times 2 \times 2$ Factorial ANOVA Design

Source of Variation	df	SS	MS	F	p
Mediation (A)	1		$\dfrac{SS\ (A)}{df}$	$\dfrac{MS\ (A)}{MS\ (within)}$	
Representation (B)	1				
Observers (C)	1				
A × B	1				
A × C	1				
B × C	1				
A × B × C	1				
Within groups	72				
Total	79 $(N-1)$				

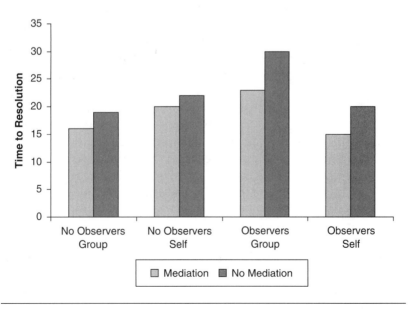

Figure 4.5   Three-Way Interaction for Mediation, Observers, and Representation

mediators do not decrease the time to settlement when no observers are present. They do, however, produce faster agreements when observers are present. This result partially supports findings on the difference between public and private negotiations: Public negotiations have been shown to reduce negotiators' flexibility and prolong the talks (Druckman & Druckman, 1996). Here, public negotiations have this effect for group representatives in non-mediated sessions. Of course, this finding is obtained only for the time measure. Additional insight into this relationship would be obtained from analyses of the process ratings data.

Repeated Measures and Other ANOVA Designs

The discussion in this section covers other types of ANOVA designs and analyses, including repeated measures designs, randomized blocks designs, analysis of covariance, Latin square designs, and meta analysis.

REPEATED MEASURES

The factorial designs discussed in the previous section are limited to a one-time assessment of the dependent variable (e.g., time to settlement). They do not take into account changes that may occur during the process of trying to settle disputes or reach negotiated agreements. Repeated measures taken on the experimental subject, which may be a person, a dyad, or larger group unit, are needed to assess change through the course of a process. They can be assessed in the context of factorial designs. Because the repeated measures are correlated, they are part of the within-groups variation term in the ANOVA design and included in the design along with the between-group variables. The way this is done can best be illustrated with examples of experiments on CA&R topics. Three published projects included repeated measures in the experimental design. One study, introduced in the section of Chapter 3 on simulation, focused on the flexibility of participants in a simulated conference on the regulation of gases contributing to the depletion of the ozone layer. The conference was conducted in four stages, which was the repeated measure. All participants made decisions about their positions on the issues in each of the stages: pre-negotiation planning, setting the stage, the give-and-take, and the endgame. The stages were embedded in one of three experimental conditions: a condition that encouraged flexible decision making, a condition that discouraged flexible decision making, and a condition that changed from encouraging inflexibility in the early stages to flexibility in the later stages. Each condition was defined by a scenario that incorporated several variables or aspects of negotiation hypothesized to increase or decrease flexibility.

The three conditions were the between-groups independent variable in the ANOVA design. The four stages were part of the within-group variation term in the analysis. This was a 3 × 4 experimental design defined by three experimental conditions (the flexibility variable) and four stages (the repeated measure). Questions of interest were as follows: (a) Do decisions about positions change during the course of the simulated conference? and (b) Do the effects of the experimental conditions vary by stage? The first question is addressed by assessing a main effect for the stage's variable. The second refers to a two-way interaction between stages and the conditions.

The effects of the conditions were evaluated on nine dependent variables, including the outcome, decisions on positions, strategy preference, and various perceptions of the situation. Results were reported for two samples of simulation participants, an environmental scientist sample and a sample of professional diplomats. Significant main effects for the experimental conditions occurred for many of the variables in both samples. Significant effects for stages occurred only for one of the perceptual variables for the scientist sample: the extent to which the conference was viewed as a win-lose contest or as a problem-solving debate. The interaction between stages and the experimental conditions occurred only for one perceptual variable in the scientist sample (win-lose vs. problem solving) and in the diplomat sample (satisfaction with the outcome). These findings indicate that the effects of the experimental variable generalize across the four stages. Decisions and perceptions change little as a function of stage; they change largely due to experimental condition. It does not mean, however, that the same variables influenced decisions in each of the stages. Further analyses—using a pair-comparison procedure—showed that different variables in the scenario had the strongest effects on decisions in each of the stages (for the details on these and other findings, see Druckman, 1993).

Another project was a study of the effects of being a group representative on children's bargaining behavior. Using a simple board game task, effects of a variety of variables, including aspects of the bargaining task, situation, and culture, were investigated. For purposes of illustrating the repeated-measures idea, I will describe only the initial studies reported in articles that appeared in journals in the early 1970s (Druckman, Solomon, & Zechmeister, 1972; Solomon & Druckman, 1972). The first experiment examined the effects of representative role and communication set on bargaining decisions. This was a 2 × 2 factorial design, representing a group versus self-representation and either justifying offers or persuading the other to accept proposed offers. Each bargaining dyad played three games, divided into a beginning, middle, and end phase. When game number and phases are included as variables, the research takes the form of a 2 × 2 × 3 × 3 design, with the last two variables being repeated measures (game and phase within games).

Significant main effects were obtained on many of the measures for the representative role variable: Group representatives were more competitive than self-representatives. A number of significant interactions with game number and phase were also obtained. The largest difference between group and self-representatives occurred in Game 1, with the group representatives rejecting more offers. Bargainers became more competitive as the game progressed through the phases, but at the same time became more accepting of each other's competitive moves, perhaps through a process of reciprocity. Further, the number of statements emphasizing values decreased from one phase to another. Other game and phase effects occurred in a second experiment that manipulated observers. Particularly interesting were the interaction effects with gender: Girls (but not boys) showed declining competitiveness in the observers-present condition but increasing competitiveness from one game to another in the no-observers condition.

Of more theoretical interest, perhaps, are the results of another experiment conducted with the board game bargaining task. This experiment was an attempt to evaluate competing hypotheses from Piaget's notions of distributive justice and from equity theory. The findings showed that children of different ages used different criteria for deciding on how resources should be distributed between a representative who either lost or won a prior bargaining contest. The equity-theory notion of rewarding players based on their performance (winners get more than losers) applied only to the youngest age group (7–9). The intermediate age group (10–12) used the principle of strict equality (winners and losers get the same), whereas the oldest group (13–15) distributed more resources to the losers than to the winners based upon an idea of compensation. When game phase was included as a repeated measure in the analysis, additional insights into the findings were obtained. The losing representative in the oldest group became increasingly competitive through the phases, with the largest difference (between the losing and winning players) occurring in the end phase. This behavior contrasted with the results obtained for the two younger groups: The winning representatives became increasingly competitive through the phases in the youngest group; the winning representative showed a jump in competitiveness from Phases 2 to 3 in the intermediate-age group. By including the repeated measure of phases in the analysis, it was possible to show differing patterns in the development of competitiveness leading to the outcomes.

The studies described above show how analyses of repeated measures contribute in important ways to interpretation and understanding of experimental variables. This was particularly the case in an analysis of data collected in an experiment on bilateral monopoly bargaining. A surprising finding was that opposing bargainers who were told that they had similar attitudes produced more deadlocks and needed more trails to reach agreements than dissimilar bargainers. However, the similar bargainers made larger concessions or were "softer" bargainers than the dissimilar pairs. This discrepancy between process and outcomes was difficult to understand: How could softer bargaining dyads produce more deadlocks than harder dyads? Internal condition phase analyses, comparing agreers with nonagreers, suggested an answer. The nonagreers were softer through the first three phases and tougher in the final phase than the agreers and the dissimilar-condition bargainers. They also changed their attraction ratings, with the opponent being rated less favorably on several scales than the agreers and bargainers in the dissimilar condition. Thus, the high average softness and large number of trails for bargainers in the similar condition were due largely to the bargaining behavior of the nonagreers in this condition. These bargainers reacted to the discrepancy between their relatively soft behavior in the first three phases compared to the tough behavior shown by their programmed opponent (see Druckman & Bonoma, 1976). This trend became the basis for a theory of bargaining referred to as *threshold adjustment.* Bargainers monitor their own and the other's moves through time; they react to any discrepancy by adjusting their moves to match the moves of the other. This pattern often leads to impasses. It became the basis for a theory of bargaining evaluated with a variety of international cases. The evaluations provided strong support for the theory (Druckman & Harris, 1990).

Conflict resolution processes are best analyzed with repeated-measures data. The objective of disputing actors is to monitor or produce change through time. Quantitative measures of change have been developed in their most sophisticated form with bargaining tasks. For example, in one study, changes across four phases were measured in concessions, bargaining postures, minimal goals, and predictive accuracy. Each of these types of changes was a repeated measure in an experimental design: The three independent variables and phases resulted in a 4 (programmed opponent bargaining strategy) × 2 (initial offer) × 2 (relative defensibility of positions) × 4 (phases) factorial design. The most interesting results were interactions between the conditions and phases. Different trends in concessions made in response to different opponent bargaining strategies were evaluated in terms of their shape. The within-groups variation term in a repeated-measures ANOVA can be partitioned into linear (straight line) and quadratic (curved line) components. The partitioning provides an evaluation of differences in the slopes of the trends. (Edwards, 1960, provides an excellent discussion of trend analysis in his Chapter 14.) The bargaining data showed a number of significant linear and quadratic trends in concessions (minimal goals, predictive accuracy) for the different opponent bargaining strategy conditions (see Druckman et al., 1972, p. 527). The related topic of time-series analysis will be discussed in Chapter 6 on case studies.

RANDOMIZED BLOCKS AND ANCOVA

It has been discovered that simple random assignment of subjects to experimental conditions may result in large variation among them on some dependent variables. If the treatment is not strong, these differences are likely to prevent significant effects from occurring. In more technical terms, the within-groups term is large relative to the between-groups term, resulting in a small F ratio. If, for example, a simulation were conducted with subjects from different countries, it is likely that there would be wide differences among them in reactions to a conflict scenario. Assigning them randomly to different third-party intervention conditions may not reduce the variation on the dependent variable, for example, their preferred approach for resolving the conflict.

An alternative design consists of grouping the subjects by country or region. Suppose that there are 25 subjects and five types of interventions. The subjects can be grouped roughly into five regions, considered as blocks in the design. Each person within a block is randomly assigned an intervention. This means that each of the five subjects receives one of the five interventions. This procedure is known as a randomized blocks ANOVA design. It emphasizes the feature of clustering, which serves to reduce the within-group variation. (Note that clustering serves the same function in survey research discussed in Chapter 5.) It takes the form indicated in Table 4.6.

Each of the regions has five subjects; each subject within a region is exposed to one of the five interventions. The ANOVA consists of three sources of variation, interventions (a between-groups term), regions or blocks, and a within-groups term. The within-groups term is actually the residual variation among subjects remaining after variation due to the intervention and regions are removed. The F ratio of interest is calculated as the intervention mean square divided by the residual within-groups mean square. When relatively homogeneous blocks are created, the design increases the chances that the F

Table 4.6   A Randomized Blocks Design

Region	Types of Intervention				
	Mediation	*Facilitation*	*Arbitration*	*Med/Arb*	*No 3rd Party*
North America					
South America					
Western Europe					
Eastern Europe					
Middle East					

ratio will be significant. (For more technical details on randomized block designs, the reader is encouraged to consult a statistics textbook that emphasizes the ANOVA.)

The randomized blocks eliminate the variation among regions from the within-groups variation term. There may, however, be other sources of variation that reduce the chances for obtaining significant treatment (interventions) effects. One of these sources may be the time when the intervention is given. Suppose reactions to interventions depend, at least to some extent, on when they are administered. If so, then, time of administration should also be removed from the within-groups term. This can be done with another type of randomized blocks design known as *Latin square*. It consists of a schedule of administering interventions by time period. Interventions are administered randomly within days and hours, as shown in the following table.

Table 4.7   A Latin Square Design

| | Hours | | | | |
Days	*1*	*2*	*3*	*4*	*5*
Monday	B	E	D	C	A
Tuesday	C	A	B	E	D
Wednesday	D	B	C	A	E
Thursday	E	C	A	D	B
Friday	A	D	E	B	C

Source: Edwards (1960, Table 15.1)

The letters correspond to the interventions (A is mediation, B is facilitation, C is arbitration, D is med/arb, and E is no third-party intervention). For this design, each intervention (letter) appears once in each row or column. This is a completely symmetric design; the number of rows equals the number of columns, which equals the number of treatments. The logistics involved in arranging the schedule may be complex, but it is worth the investment if time of administration is a factor that influences the effects of a particular intervention.

Another ANOVA procedure can be used when other supplementary measures are available for experimental subjects. These measures may not be used to group subjects into blocks but instead used as *covariates*. The analysis of covariance (ANCOVA) is a technique for controlling the effects of other variables that may be correlated with the dependent variable. For example, subjects' preferences for conflict management techniques are likely to influence their responses to the different forms of intervention. Information about those preferences, obtained prior to the experiment, can be useful. The information may take the form of responses to a questionnaire about preferences for alternative techniques. These responses would then be covariates in the ANOVA design. The analysis controls for the effects of this variable by removing the correlation between the pre-experimental preferences (X variable) and the dependent variable (Y) from the evaluation of the treatment (intervention) effects. This procedure provides a better estimation of the effects of the treatments on responses.

It is also possible to calculate the difference between the X and Y variables and use these scores in an ANOVA. This is often done with data gathered from subjects on the dependent variable prior to the experiment. The data are referred to as baseline estimates. For example, if the preferences assessed prior to the intervention experiment are re-assessed after the treatments, then a before-after difference can be calculated. The downside to administering a pre-tests is the possibility of a testing effect. This can be controlled by adding a no pre-test control, as in the Solomon four-group design discussed in Chapter 3. There are also some technical considerations that may lead to different results from the ANOVA (difference score) and ANCOVA (covariate) results (see Edwards, 1960, chap. 16 for the details).

META-ANALYSIS

All of these ANOVA procedures are intended to provide improved estimates of treatment effects. To this point, we have discussed effects in terms of tests of statistical significance. Another way of estimating the impacts of treatments on dependent variables is by calculating a ratio known as the *effect size.* This ratio provides a common metric for evaluating the impacts of similar independent variables from different studies and is used in meta-analyses. It converts the significance-test ratio obtained from analyzing a relationship between an independent and dependent variable (F, t, or chi-square) into a correlation coefficient (r). Wolf (1986) provides the ratios. An example is the effect size for an F ratio:

$$r = \sqrt{\frac{F}{F + df\,(\text{error})}} \tag{3}$$

When these effect sizes are aggregated or averaged across similar experiments, a researcher has information about the cumulative strength of the relationship between variables. For example, the average effect size calculated across 14 experiments that investigated the relationship between pre-negotiation experience (independent variable) and compromising behavior was .37. This is a stronger effect than was obtained across the nine experiments conducted to investigate the relationship between group representation and compromising behavior, which was .30. This procedure facilitates comparisons among a variety of independent variables within a research domain (other examples in bargaining include time pressure, opponent's strategy, and initial distance between positions). Although the technique has been criticized for combining studies that differ in at least as many ways as they are similar (the apples-and-oranges problem), it has been shown to be valuable in discovering factors that moderate relationships between variables and in suggesting new hypotheses for investigation. (Interesting examples of meta-analyses on CA&R topics are De Dreu et al., 2000, and Druckman, 1994a.)

Before embracing this approach as a panacea for the challenge of cumulation in research, students should be aware of the lively debate about the strengths and weaknesses of meta-analysis. The key issues in the debate can be summarized along with possible solutions.

1. *Logical conclusions cannot be drawn by comparing and aggregating studies that include different measuring techniques, definitions of variables, and subjects because they are too dissimilar.* This criticism is addressed by taking advantage of both the similarities and differences among the studies. Regarding similarities, further breakdowns within independent variable categories into relatively homogeneous sets of studies reduce the apples-and-oranges problem. An example is the separation of cognitive and interest conflict studies from the more general category of *type of conflict.* Regarding differences, analyses of *outlier* studies—unusually high or low effect sizes compared to other studies in the same category—have led to the discovery of new variables (see Druckman, 1994a).

2. *Results of meta-analyses are uninterpretable because findings from poorly designed studies are included along with those obtained in well-designed studies.* This problem can be avoided by establishing and adhering to quality control criteria. One widely used criterion is publication in a refereed journal. Although useful, it is not a guarantee of quality. Many meta-analyses I have read specify criteria for inclusion. These criteria usually require a second-tier review of the methodologies used by the authors. But, if the included studies can still be distinguished in terms of quality of design, then comparisons of effect sizes can be made.

3. *Published research is biased in favor of significant findings because nonsignificant results are rarely published; this in turn leads to biased meta-analysis results.* This problem has been recognized and addressed. The designation *file-drawer problem* refers to completed studies either not submitted for publication or rejected because of nonsignificant findings. Rosenthal (1984) has provided a computational procedure, referred to as the *fail-safe* N, that estimates the number of additional studies with nonsignificant results that would be needed to reverse a conclusion drawn from the published studies available and analyzed.

4. *Multiple results from the same study may bias the meta-analysis. Because these results are not independent, they either exaggerate or attenuate the effect sizes artificially.* This problem can be avoided by including only one effect size per included study. When several measures are calculated within a study, and these are known to be correlated, the meta-analyst can combine them into an index or choose one based either on conceptual criteria or randomly.

5. *Interaction effects are ignored at the expense of main effects.* It is the case that effect sizes are computed only for main effects or for a single variable at a time. However, like many of the techniques discussed in this book, meta-analysis can be used creatively. By comparing procedures used in the studies with the highest and lowest effect sizes (in a category), one can detect interactions or contingent effects. For example, I found that the weak overall effect size for visibility (presence or absence of an audience) of the bargaining process was due primarily to the studies that did not create strong face-saving pressures on the bargainers. When face-saving pressure is included in the experimental manipulation, the effect size increases substantially. The interaction is between visibility (audience present or absent) and face-saving pressures (high or low).

Meta-analysis is a labor-intensive activity. My own experience has led to the opinion that once may be enough. However, with the advent of computer programs to perform computations and research teams to divide the tasks, it becomes more manageable. A well-organized effort to analyze a body of literature has many rewards (see the section in Chapter 2 titled "The Literature Review"). One is that it encourages careful reading of studies within a research domain. Another is that it provides a perspective on a field that can come only from broad coverage of the published literature. A third is that it identifies gaps in understanding a topic, leading to suggestions for research agendas. And a fourth is that it is likely to result in a publication that has a reasonably long shelf life evidenced by frequent citations. Developing the synthetic skills needed for performing meta-analyses complements the analytical skills needed to perform original research in CA&R.

Summary

The variety of problems faced by the experimental researcher creates a need for a corresponding variety of analysis techniques. Many of these techniques are reviewed in this chapter. I start with statistical techniques used to evaluate two-group designs. This discussion highlights the trade-off between measurement precision and power to detect a difference between conditions. It is illustrated by analyses of the same data with three different statistical tests: *t* test, Wilcoxon Mann-Whitney test, and chi-square. The discussion then moves to analyses of three-group designs. Highlighted in this discussion is the analysis of variance. Third-party interventions are evaluated in one-way and factorial configurations. The one-way analysis techniques include both parametric and nonparametric ANOVA and multiple comparisons for isolating the pairs of conditions that are different. The factorial analyses call attention to the difference between main effects and interactions.

Many factorial designs are static in the sense of analyzing results obtained from a one-time assessment of a dependent variable. This limitation is addressed by ANOVA designs that include repeated measures. Prominent among repeated measures in CA&R are assessments of decisions made during phases of negotiation-conference interactions. These designs utilize more information from parties. Other ANOVA approaches control for information that would complicate interpretations of results. These include randomized blocks, Latin square, and analysis of covariance (ANCOVA).

The chapter concludes with a discussion of effect sizes. These ratios, which are correlation coefficients, are used in meta-analysis. Both strengths and limitations of this approach to the cumulation and comparison of experimental findings are presented.

Discussion Questions

This chapter surveyed a variety of methods for analyzing experimental data. The discussion was intended to increase your understanding of these techniques as well as your skills in using them to analyze data. The questions to follow provide a review of what has been learned. You may use them to ascertain how much you have learned. You may also choose to use them as bases for group discussions about the technical issues raised in the chapter.

1. What is the sampling distribution of a statistical test? Why is the rejection region of the sampling distribution important in making decisions about the impacts of experimental variables?

2. What are the parts—the numerator and denominator—of a statistical ratio? What is the relevance of the relative size of these parts in ascertaining statistical significance?

3. What is the power of a statistical test? What are the trade-offs between the way a dependent variable is measured and the statistical power of the test used to evaluate the relationship between the experimental treatments and the measured variables?

4. What considerations would you entertain in trying to decide whether to use a more powerful parametric or less powerful nonparametric statistical test to evaluate your data? State some of the advantages and disadvantages of each of the two types of statistical analyses.

5. Suppose that a statistically significant result was obtained with a non-parametric analysis but not with a parametric analysis of the same data. How would you reconcile the differences?

6. What is the difference between a two-group and a three- (or more) group design? What statistical tests are designed to evaluate two-group designs? What tests are appropriate for three or more group designs?

7. What is the meaning of the statement that "large-N experiments increase the chances for obtaining statistically significant results?"

8. What are some advantages of factorial designs? Distinguish between main effects and statistical interactions. Then, depict a two-way interaction graphically.

9. Repeated-measures ANOVA designs provide opportunities to analyze change in the context of alternative conditions. Of particular interest are possible interactions between the repeated measures and conditions. Give an example of how such interactions might provide valuable information about a conflict process.

10. Researchers in CA&R have begun to appreciate the value of meta-analytic techniques. What are some advantages? What are some limitations? What CA&R research topics would benefit from meta-analysis? Which topics are less likely to benefit and why?

Notes

1. The definition of *degrees of freedom* provided by Henkel (1976) is as follows:

The degrees of freedom reflect the number of values in a distribution which are free to vary after certain constraints have been removed—in other words, the degrees of freedom are the number of independent variables in the distribution. The constraints are the number of relations specified among the values. For example, we might impose the constraint that the sum of a set of values is fixed. In this case, for a sample of N values, only the first N − 1 of the values is independent, since the last value must be the difference between the fixed sum and the sum of the first N − 1 values . . . [however] the rationale for the degrees of freedom will vary from technique to technique. (p. 89)

2. The difference between the two extreme means (12 and 4) is significant. The multiple-range test evaluates the size of the differences between all pairs of means: in the example, 12 vs. 8, 12 vs. 4, and 8 vs. 4. The differences are compared to the *shortest significant ranges,* which are found in tables in many statistics textbooks. (These are based on calculations of the square root of the ANOVA error mean square.)

Note that these tests take into account the set of means and variances for all the conditions being compared by the one-way ANOVA. The *Student's t test* is not appropriate. It isolates each pair of means for comparison and thus removes them from the set being examined by ANOVA.

Part III

Designing and Conducting Surveys

The chapter in this part introduces the reader to the broad topic of survey research. Although this discussion is not intended as a substitute for books on the subject, it does provide the reader with information about many facets of this complex methodology with examples of problems from CA&R.[1] The chapter opens with an overview of the approach followed by general issues of research design. It then unfolds with more detailed treatments of technical issues concerning measuring, sampling, and data collection, concluding with a discussion of ethical considerations to be entertained in conducting and analyzing surveys. A useful comparison of the different survey modes—interview, mail, telephone, and Internet surveys—on a number of aspects of administration is shown in tabular form at the end of the chapter.

For many survey researchers, the most important contribution of the approach is in the area of sampling design and procedures. The key alternative designs are presented in this chapter. They include both probability (simple random, systematic, stratified, multi-stage, cluster) and non-probability samples (focus groups, purposive, and quota samples). For probability samples the issues of sample size, variability, and sampling fraction are important. These types of samples strengthen the external validity of research findings. For non-probability samples, issues of population representativeness are salient: A nonrandom representative sample can provide useful information for some problems and also contribute to external validity. These issues are discussed in some detail in the chapter. Of special interest for researchers in CA&R are the challenges of access to isolated minority groups, including various insurgencies (or spoilers) with a stake in the conflict, securing their identities, and obtaining information on sensitive matters. Issues that concern reaching these populations and question wording are also discussed in the chapter.

For many researchers, the choice between performing experiments and conducting surveys turns on a trade between internal and external validity. A key difference is between random assignment to experimental conditions and random sampling from a known population. The former reduces threats to internal validity; the latter reduces threats to external validity as discussed in Chapter 3. Both types of threats can be reduced when randomized experiments are embedded in surveys: Respondents drawn randomly from a population are assigned randomly to different conditions. The conditions may consist of exposing survey respondents to different conflict scenarios. Although this type of innovative design has not been used to explore CA&R problems to date, it has been implemented in a number of attitude surveys conducted by sociologists and political scientists (see Sniderman & Grob, 1996). It is an example of how multiple methods, used in a complementary and supporting fashion, can strengthen research designs.

Note

1. For useful general treatments of the many facets of survey research, the interested reader should consult Czaja and Blair (1995), Fowler (1995), Henry (1990), or Salant and Dillman (1994).

5

Survey Research

Scott Keeter

Overview

The survey is the most commonly used social research method for collecting data from individuals in a population of interest. Surveys are conducted by nearly every government in the world, by academic researchers, by nonprofit and nongovernmental organizations, by journalists, and by corporations and businesses. Much of what we know about the economic, physical, and social characteristics of the populations of the world is derived from survey data.

Perhaps the best-known survey in the United States is the U.S. census, mandated by the Constitution to gather information about the size of the population through an "actual enumeration" of every person every 10 years. The word *census* means a collection of data from all units in a population. But most surveys are not censuses. Rather, they entail some type of sampling in order to save time and money in the data collection process.

Surveys can be conducted in many different ways. An interviewer may ask the questions, either in person or by telephone, or the respondent may complete the survey by reading the questions in a paper questionnaire or on a computer screen and providing written or electronic responses. And there are other possibilities as well, including prerecorded questions administered to respondents, who answer via the touch-tone pad on their phones or on a computer screen. Some surveys use more than one data collection technique.

As with all social research, surveys raise important and difficult ethical questions as well. Good research takes ethical concerns seriously and attempts to minimize the time and effort required of respondents, to protect their privacy, and to ensure that the survey does no harm to those who participate.

This chapter will review the principles of good survey research in an effort to provide some of the knowledge needed to design and conduct effective surveys. Even if you do not conduct your own survey, an understanding of good survey practice will enable you to assess the quality of survey evidence used in others' research.

The discussion here will be organized around four critical aspects of the survey process. The first is the overall *research design,* which encompasses elements of the other three aspects. Key decisions in the overall research design include the question of whether to do a survey at all or to use some other type of data collection method, the choice of the population to study, the timing of the data collection, the choice of whether data collection is to be done at one point or at multiple points in time, and the nature and level of resources to be made available to the study.

The second aspect is *measurement,* or how the key variables of interest will actually be measured. In practical terms, what questions will be asked of the respondents? The third aspect of survey research is *sampling.* Unless a census is undertaken, choices must be made regarding who in the population will be selected for interviewing. How samples are drawn and implemented determines how well the data will represent the population of interest. The fourth aspect is *survey administration.* Choices must be made regarding the mode of data collection and how it will be implemented. For example, if the telephone is used to collect data, when will calls be made and how many attempts will be made to reach each sampled telephone number?

Although surveys are usually thought of as a type of *quantitative* research, they stand at an intersection between the qualitative and the quantitative, and the best surveys make use of key principles and methods from the major forms of qualitative work. Surveys can make a strong claim for reliability because of the relatively large number of cases in a typical survey (at least by comparison with the typical qualitative study), but reliable evidence is an insufficient base on which to make important decisions; the evidence must also be valid, and qualitative research is fundamentally concerned with validity.

Ultimately, the goal of a successful survey is to describe the population with a minimum of error. At each stage of the process, we must consider how to reduce error so as to maximize *both* reliability and validity. Achieving greater reliability and validity in surveys requires attention to a range of details in the design and implementation of a survey. With a finite amount of time and money, we are constantly faced with choices about how to allocate resources most effectively; greater effort placed on one aspect of the survey may mean less effort can be made in another aspect. Do we spend money enlarging the sample size (which would reduce sampling error and improve reliability), or do we spend the money on achieving a higher rate of response with a given sample? Do we spend more time testing our questionnaire before putting it into the field, or do we spend the time making sure that our sampling frame is clean and accurate? These are the trade-offs inherent in the complex process of survey research. The goal of this chapter is to help you make educated choices about your own survey and to be an informed consumer of surveys conducted by others.

Survey Research Design

After settling on a research topic, the first big choice in a project is how to collect the data. Is a survey the best way to obtain the needed data? Most of the major alternatives to a survey are covered in other chapters in this book. Surveys are complicated and costly, both for the researcher and for the respondents because of the time they require to complete. Some subjects simply are not amenable to survey research because respondents do not have the knowledge necessary to respond in a useful way or may not be willing to answer candidly.

Archives of Survey Data

Inter-university Consortium for Political and Social Research, University of Michigan. http://www.icpsr.umich.edu/

Roper Center for Public Opinion Research, University of Connecticut. http://ropercenter.uconn.edu

Central Archive for Empirical Social Research, University Cologne (Zentralarchiv für Empirische Sozialforschung, Cologne) http://www.gesis.org/en/za/index.htm

Pew Research Center for The People & The Press, Washington, D.C. http://people-press.org

U.S. Census Bureau, U.S. Dept. of Commerce. http://www.census.gov/

One consideration is that survey data regarding your topic may already exist and could be subjected to *secondary analysis* to answer the key research questions. An astounding quantity of excellent survey data can be found in several important *data archives* around the world (see box). Additionally, many researchers who have collected survey data for a particular purpose are willing to share the data after they have mined it for their needs. But often these surveys are not donated to archives, and finding them will require a little detective work. Even if you do decide to go forward with your own survey project, looking at other surveys on your topic can be extremely helpful. For example, U.S. census data can give you a good idea about the incidence of certain groups in the population, a concern you might have if you are targeting a relatively small minority of the population. Census data can also tell you where you are likely to find certain kinds of people, which might help you be more efficient in your sampling. And a review of other surveys on your topic can help you find survey measures that may be appropriate, along with data with which to make comparisons across populations or over time.

If you decide to conduct a survey, several important decisions loom. Many of these will be discussed in greater detail in the sections on measurement, sampling, and survey administration below. Assuming that you have a clear goal in mind for your research, some overarching questions include the following:

- How much money (or other comparable resource) do you have available for the survey?
- How much time do you have to complete it?
- Given the resources you have available—specifically, money and time—what is the appropriate scope of the study?
- How much data do you need to collect from each respondent? How many respondents do you need to interview?
- Is it essential or even feasible to use a probability sample? If not, can an acceptable non-probability sample be created?
- What mode of data collection should be employed? When is the best time to conduct the survey?
- Will this study be a one-shot data collection, or is it a longitudinal study with data collections at multiple points in time?

Advertising Slogan for a Survey Research Firm

We offer . . .

- Quality
- Speed
- Low Cost

Pick two.

Answering these questions, even if only tentatively, will help to set the general contours for the research. Answering them may illuminate basic tensions and tradeoffs among the elements. In almost every kind of research, there is an inherent tradeoff among quality, speed, and cost. Because the money available is almost always limited to some degree, decisions must be made about which aspects of the survey would benefit the most from greater investment and which would harm the study the least if corners were cut. One of the clearest examples of this tradeoff can be found in the choice of a sample size. The marginal cost of additional data collection is usually very high, so it is worth considering how the money that would otherwise be used for an expanded sample could be better used. If we settle upon the smallest possible sample that will satisfy the research needs, we might be able to increase the size of the questionnaire and measure more concepts of interest, or obtain better measures of concepts by using multiple measures. We might do more extensive pre-testing of the questionnaire to ensure that respondents understand the questions and can answer them. Or we might even use the savings to obtain a higher response rate and reduce the chance that nonresponse will introduce a serious bias into our results.

THE ELEMENT OF TIME

One key decision about your research design does not fit neatly into the other three aspects of the survey process but is logically prior to them—the timing and number of surveys. For many, if not most, research projects, it may not matter a great deal when the data are collected, and this decision is made largely by default. The data collection occurs whenever the researcher can assemble the necessary resources and logistical wherewithal to execute the study. But often the timing of the study is critical to the validity of the inferences we want to draw from it. Or, our population of interest may be more accessible to us, or more amenable to cooperating, at some times rather than others. Researchers in the United States often try to avoid conducting important surveys of the general public during the last two weeks of August or during the Christmas holidays, both traditionally times of vacations and travel. Surveys of schoolchildren conducted during the last week of the school year may not receive the careful attention from the students we would otherwise hope for. And, of course, researchers should respect the privacy of respondents by not conducting telephone surveys late in the evening or early in the morning. In general, researchers should consider the personal habits and schedules of those in the population and adjust the timing of the surveys accordingly.

Perhaps a more important element of timing pertains to knowledge, perceptions, or experiences we wish to measure with our survey. In general, the sooner we interview someone about an experience they recently have had, the more reliable their recall of the experience. At the same time, the full import of events may not be felt until later. Thus, the choice of when to conduct a survey depends on the research goals. Surveys about public response to the terrorist attacks in the United States on September 11, 2001, conducted within a few days of the event yielded different results from surveys conducted months later. If we are interested in assessing the long-term impact of the event, the latter surveys may be more valid because they will reflect the thinking of the public after considering the issue, discussing it with friends and family, and absorbing news coverage and commentary. But if we want to know exactly what people felt at the time, how they reacted emotionally, and how they followed news coverage of it, surveys conducted near the event provide better evidence.

Time is an important basis for comparison as well. Many surveys are conducted to measure change in opinions or experiences over time. For some phenomena, we try to draw inferences about change using a single survey by comparing people who are older and younger, using the assumption that the difference between them is an indication of the effect of aging, or changing financial or life cycle circumstances. Or, we compare people who have been married for different lengths of time, in an effort to gauge whether people and relationships change as time passes. Surveys used in this fashion are sometimes called *cross-sectional surveys*. But this is a relatively weak way to assess change; people in a single survey may differ for many other reasons besides their ages or how long they have been married.

In order to make better inferences about change, we need surveys taken at more than one point in time. The simplest design for a *longitudinal* study would use two surveys of the same population at different time points. Inferences about change over time are much stronger with this kind of design because we can make comparisons between similar people in the two surveys (e.g., lower income African Americans or older divorced women) and thus control for other possible reasons for differences between them. If similar groups in the two surveys are different, we can draw the inference that something happened in the interim to produce that change. If the amount of time between surveys is very large, normal aging and movement through the life cycle are also a plausible explanation for the changes we observe. One technique for examining this type of process is *cohort analysis,* in which we compare people from the same birth cohorts—that is, people who were born in the same year or set of years—at the two time points. A simple example will illustrate.

One of the more interesting attitudinal changes observed in the United States during the past three decades is the decline of interpersonal trust. According to standard measures that have been asked of survey respondents since the 1970s, the percentage of people who indicate that they believe others will take advantage of them has increased. In 1973, the large national General Social Survey (http://www.norc.uchicago.edu/projects/gensoc.asp) found 34% saying people would try to take advantage of them. By 2002, 40% felt this way. What has happened to social trust in the United States? Three general mechanisms could be at work, separately or together.

- *Aging effects:* Have people become less trusting as they grew older through a process of growing skepticism that came with greater maturity?
- *Period effects:* Did the social climate in the United States deteriorate so much that people lost faith in others as they experienced greater conflict, crime (and the depiction of crime on television), and disorder?
- *Cohort effects:* Did change occur because successive generations of young people came of age socialized to regard others with lower levels of trust, replacing older, more trusting cohorts who were dying out?

Table 5.1   Example of Cohort Analysis

Percent Who Say People Will Try to Take Advantage of You				
Birth Year	1973–1982	1983–1992	1993–2002	Total
< 1915	28	26	22	26
1915–1924	31	28	29	29
1925–1934	28	33	33	31
1935–1944	33	33	33	33
1945–1954	40	36	36	37
1955–1964	48	43	40	42
1965–1974		51	49	49
1975–			54	54

Source: General Social Survey.

Although there are many complexities to cohort analysis, and it is nearly impossible to definitively isolate the relative importance of each of the three mechanisms, we can gain considerable insight into what's going on by comparing successive cohorts across time. People aged 20–29 in 1973 were aged 30–39 in 1983. Even though the same individuals were not interviewed again, those who are ages 30–39 in the 1983 survey are a sample of the same people who were 20–29 in 1973. In 1993, this group would be 40–49. As the table shows, the evidence is very strong in support of a cohort effect. Each new generation of young people is less trusting than the one that came before it, but once into adulthood, the cohorts do not become less trusting as time passes. The overall level of trust goes down because of generational replacement; older cohorts, who are more trusting, leave and are replaced by younger ones, who are less trusting (see Table 5.1).

Measurement

During the 1980s, in the early days of survey research about the growing problem of AIDS in the United States, researchers were testing questions for a survey on sexual behavior. At one university survey center, a middle-aged woman was taking part in an in-depth interview that would help clarify how people understood the language and terminology to be used in the final survey questionnaire. A critical question was about sexual orientation. She was asked, "Are you heterosexual, homosexual, or bisexual?"

The woman thought about the question for a moment, and then replied, "Well, it's just me and my husband, so I guess we're bisexual." The researchers then knew that they needed to work on the question a little more before putting it into the field.

Creating and executing a successful survey entails a skillful combination of art and science. In no part of the survey process is the need for art greater than in measurement: the creation of the questions that respondents will be asked. This is not to say that measurement is uninformed by science; to the contrary, our ability to write clear, specific, comprehensible questions that people are able and willing to answer has been greatly enhanced by psychological theory and research as well as by rigorous experimentation (see Tourangeau, Rips, & Rasinski, 2001). Yet the fundamental task of communicating clearly remains a quintessential application of human sensitivity and judgment. Fortunately, even though few of us will have the good fortune to always write the perfect question, there are many habits we can develop that will help us improve our skills to write good ones.

The first principle of good question writing is to know what the heck you want to learn from respondents. While this may sound obvious, it is sometimes harder to put in practice than it seems. A typical research project has a clear idea of the general subject of interest and of many important elements of the subject. But surveys tend to be quite detailed in content, and the process of writing questions often founders because of a lack of clarity about what information is actually needed from respondents.

Several important points to be considered in this section are the following:

- Always ask yourself these questions before writing survey questions: Will respondents have the necessary *knowledge* and *cognitive skill* to understand the questions and to answer them? Will respondents be *willing* to answer the questions? Will they be willing to answer them *honestly?*
- Seek as much input and criticism about your draft questions and questionnaire as you can afford.
- Always allow adequate time and resources to test your questionnaire with typical respondents before putting the survey into the field.
- Put as much effort into planning the sequencing of questionnaire items as you put into the construction of the individual items themselves.

There are important differences between measures of *subjective* and *objective* phenomena. Attitudes and opinions fall into the category of subjective phenomena, while events, demographic characteristics, and physical conditions are objective phenomena. Both are important in most surveys, but each presents different challenges to good measurement.

Consider the audience for your research and, more generally, the purpose of the survey when writing specific questions that deal with the heart of your project. There is often a trade-off to be made between optimal measurement for statistical analysis versus ideal measurement for face validity and interpretability of the questions. For example, if you are building a statistical model to explain the extent of commitment to an ideology or a negotiating position and plan to use multiple regression analysis, you might choose to measure popularity through a "feeling thermometer" that gauges warm and cold feelings on a scale of 0 to 100, or through a set of familiar 10-point scales. The use of these quasi-continuous variables may produce greater variance in the dependent variable and distributions that better conform to the assumptions of regression and thus perform better in the statistical analysis. But if you are going to rely largely on cross-tabular analysis and are writing for a nonspecialist audience, a measure that uses commonly understood words and modifiers such as "strongly committed" or "somewhat committed" would be preferable. Nonspecialists will find it easier to understand that "60% of Muslims compared with only 35% of Christians are strongly committed" than "the position's mean thermometer rating among Muslims is 60 while it is only 35 among Christians."

OPEN AND CLOSED QUESTIONS

One of the most fundamental choices in drafting survey questions is whether to ask respondents to choose among alternative answers or to simply ask the question and let them respond in their own words. Most survey questions, especially for nonspecialist populations, are *close ended*, meaning that respondents are provided with a set of answer categories. For example:

Here are four problems facing our nation today. Please tell me which one is the most serious threat to our nation [READ RESPONSE OPTIONS]:

(1) terrorism
(2) poverty
(3) racial conflict
(4) AIDS and other diseases
(9) Don't know/No answer [DO NOT READ]

The alternative to a close-ended question is an *open-ended* question, which does not provide alternatives to the respondent:

What is the most serious problem facing our nation today?

(1) Answer given [RECORD VERBATIM]
(9) Don't know/No answer [DO NOT READ]

Both types of questions can provide valuable information, but there are distinct advantages and disadvantages to each. In exploratory research, we may not know a great deal about how respondents think about an issue or problem, and there is a danger that our close-ended questions may not include the proper response options or that we may impose a framework on them that is inappropriate to the way they perceive the issue. In this case, an open-ended question allows us to hear respondents talk about a problem in their own words, to see the range of ideas they bring to the question, and to better understand what they believe our question is asking. For the "most important problem" question, an open-ended question might show that something other than the four problems we list (the economy, for example) is actually more commonly mentioned. One way to put this advantage is to say that sometimes open-ended questions can have better validity than close-ended questions.

But there are disadvantages as well. As is often the case in research, greater validity of one sort often comes at the expense of reliability. Respondents vary greatly in their willingness and ability to express themselves verbally, which means that one respondent will give much more complete and insightful answers than another one—even when their underlying opinions may be the same. Because we would then code the two respondents differently (even though their basic opinion was the same), our measure would be unreliable.

Open-ended questions also impose a considerable burden on respondents. They require substantial cognitive effort, and too many of them may lead some respondents to refuse to continue the interview. They are also a burden for the researchers because effective use of the responses requires a lot of work to categorize and code them for analysis. The coding process itself is susceptible to inconsistencies. A large survey may require more than one person to code, and there are often differences between coders in how certain responses are categorized. This problem is another source of unreliability in the measurement process.

Yet open-ended questions are valuable if used strategically. For pilot or exploratory studies with relatively small samples, where the goal is to learn enough about the population to design a larger, more rigorous survey questionnaire, open-ended questions can be very helpful in gauging how respondents perceive an issue or problem. For the main data collection, open-ended questions as a follow-up to close-ended questions (e.g., "Why do you feel this way?") and for certain kinds of topics—the "most important problem" item, for example—can still be useful and can give the survey additional credibility with an audience because respondents were not "steered" toward a particular subset of issues. An important principle to keep in mind is that open-ended questions should be placed early in the questionnaire, so that later content does not suggest answers to respondents or remind them of issues that might not be especially salient to them. If the "most important problem" question follows a lengthy series of items about crime, you can bet that crime will be mentioned far more often than if it had been placed earlier in the survey. That said, surveys should *not* begin with open-ended questions because respondents find them somewhat intimidating. It is better to "warm up" the respondent with some relatively easy items before asking them to discuss an issue or problem in their own words.

The open-end format is also appropriate when the information sought is concrete and likely to be readily retrievable by the respondent. Examples include the following: "What was your age as of your last birthday?" "In what country were you born?" or "How many times in the past year did you consult with a mediator?" In each of these instances, you can record the responses and then code the answers into categories at a later date. Capturing the exact information gives you the option to categorize it in many different ways—including leaving it uncategorized—according to the purposes of your analysis. One caveat about this is that some kinds of concrete information may be too difficult to remember with the specificity necessary to give a single answer. For example, if we ask, "How many times in the past year did you and your spouse discuss money and family finances?" we may find that few people are able to provide a specific response. We would have better luck by determining whether they *ever* discuss money and finances and how often they typically do it within a shorter time frame, such as 1 month.

We often want to have the benefits of both the closed- and open-ended formats at the same time. Questions can be written that provide response options but also allow for the capture of responses from people who volunteer an alternative to the offered choices. Sometimes we use the open-ended format but *pre-code* a set of expected responses to make it easier for the interviewer to capture the answers and keep the interview flowing. For example, a list of important problems can be provided to the interviewer but not read to the respondents; if a respondent mentions the economy, the interviewer simply checks that category and moves on. If the respondent does not mention any of the problems on the pre-coded list, the interviewer records the answer verbatim.

As this discussion suggests, the best close-ended questions are ones that offer response options that accurately reflect the way respondents actually think about the issue or topic at hand. At a minimum, the options offered must be *exhaustive* and *mutually exclusive.* That is, the list provided should cover all of the possible answers, or at least include a provision for accepting "other" responses that are not included in the alternatives. (The alternatives are exhaustive of the possibilities.) And it should be clear to the respondent and to the interviewer that a logical answer can fit into only one of the possible alternatives offered. (The alternatives are mutually exclusive.)

The list of alternatives in a close-ended question should be relatively short—ideally, three or four—unless the list is likely to be familiar to the respondents.

Even with a short list, there is evidence that items appearing first or last in the list of response options may be favored because they are easier for respondents to remember (see McClendon, 1991). For this reason, it is often useful to rotate the order in which response options are presented to respondents.

ATTITUDES AND NON-ATTITUDES

In the 1980s, the Gallup Organization, one of the world's preeminent survey organizations, conducted a series of international surveys tapping public opinion on world political issues. The questionnaire for Germany had been finalized and transmitted to the German field house that would collect the data. When the survey was conducted and the data transmitted back to the United States, the Gallup president, Andrew Kohut, immediately saw that there were no "no opinion" responses recorded. He contacted the German field house and asked how they had obtained results with no missing data. "The questionnaire you sent us did not include a 'no opinion' category. So we made them answer," was the response. Normally, Kohut would personally conduct a final review of all questionnaires, but was unable to take a last look at this one, and assumed that the final version of the questionnaire would be reviewed by a project manager. Unfortunately, that review did not occur. No one caught the fact that the "no opinion" category was not explicitly included on the questionnaire. The German survey organization implemented the instrument exactly as written.

This affair illustrates two important points about survey research. One is that details matter, and attention to detail is critical in the success of such projects. Review by multiple participants can help ensure that errors do not slip by. The second point is that people will answer questions if asked to do so, even if they don't really have opinions on the subject at hand. We can think about the stereotype of the obedient German and laugh at the notion that *every* respondent would answer every question when prodded to do so, but the vast majority of respondents in any culture will provide a response if the interviewer insists. Thus, it is important to make sure that respondents are capable of answering the questions we write and that our interviewing procedures do not put undue pressure on people to offer an opinion if they have none (Smith, 1984).

The more practical question is whether to explicitly offer a "no opinion"—a "don't know (DK)"—response in the question itself or to simply leave it implied that a non-response is an acceptable alternative. Not surprisingly, extensive experimentation indicates that more people will choose "no opinion" when it is offered than when it is not—anywhere from an eighth to a third, depending on the topic (Converse & Presser, 1986). DK responses remove otherwise useful respondents from your multivariate analyses and reduce your sample size. This is because these responses are usually coded as missing data in such statistical procedures as regression and factor analysis. Studies show that the overall distribution of opinion (e.g., the ratio of approval versus disapproval) remains the same even when DK is not offered, and thus the substantive "bottom line" is not harmed. On the other side is the indisputable fact that many of the people who answer in the absence of an explicit DK are simply inventing a response on the spot. This response may not be entirely invalid because it appears that people use their values and whatever knowledge is available at the time to figure out a position on the question—and thus often come up with a response not unlike that of their better-informed or more opinionated brethren. But encouraging answers from those who have thought less about the issue undoubtedly introduces more random error into the data, depressing correlations and making it more difficult to detect causal relationships.

Another related question is whether to provide an explicit middle-of-the-road option to respondents when measuring opinion that falls along a continuum. Consider, for example, a survey of residents in a nation undergoing post-war reconstruction. Many decisions about a new political system may need to be made, and surveyors could ask respondents whether they approve or disapprove of each proposal. Should they be offered the option to say they "neither approve nor disapprove" of each one? Assuming that the topics being asked about are not entirely outside of the experience or knowledge of the population being surveyed, the best approach would be to omit the middle option and capture the extent of certainty or uncertainty through a measure of intensity. The "DK" response is available for respondents who simply cannot or do not want to offer an opinion. The measure of intensity can be built into the question or asked as a follow-up to the initial item.

Do you approve or disapprove of the provisional authority's proposal to shift ownership of the country's electricity generating plants to the private sector over the next 12 months?

If approve: Do you completely approve or mostly approve?
If disapprove: Do you completely disapprove or mostly disapprove?

(1) Completely approve
(2) Mostly approve
(3) Mostly disapprove
(4) Completely disapprove
(9) Don't know/refused

THE ACQUIESCENCE PROBLEM

Although the approve/disapprove format is useful when measuring judgments about leaders or specific proposals or options for future action, we must be on guard against a potential bias that results from a tendency of less educated or less informed respondents to agree with assertions or proposals offered to them in a survey. Experiments have revealed that the less educated—compared with the better educated—are more apt to acquiesce to the suggestions of the researchers, to agree rather than disagree to a statement presented in an agree/disagree format (see Schuman & Presser, 1996). Such a bias can result in drawing incorrect inferences; for example, one could mistakenly believe that certain proposals are more popular among poorer people than among wealthier ones. And by inflating support or agreement among a portion of the sample, the acquiescence phenomenon may inflate overall levels of apparent support. Although we do not find acquiescence bias in every instance, it is a common enough problem that we should use the forced-choice format when respondents are being asked to consider alternative proposals or values.

Acquiescence Bias

Agree/Disagree Format (October 1999)
> *The best way to ensure peace is through military strength (54% agree, 42% disagree)*

Forced-Choice Format (July–September 1999)
> *The best way to ensure peace is through military strength (33%)*
> *OR*
> *Diplomacy is the best way to ensure peace (53%)*

Source: U.S. surveys by Pew Research Center.

To illustrate what difference this format can make, and to highlight the difficult nature of trade-offs faced in survey research, consider the example of the Pew Research Center's longstanding series of questions tracking American values. These agree/disagree items have been asked of large national samples since 1987. In 1994, the center decided to add forced-choice versions of many of these core questions to its inventory of standard questions for use in its voter typologies. In the example shown in the box, far more people agreed with the assertion that "the best way to peace is through military strength" than were willing to choose this option when the alternative of diplomacy was available to them. (See also Druckman, 1970, for a discussion of the bias on reversed attitude scaled items.)

Because of the value of the time series using the agree/disagree format, the center has continued to use them. Even though they may not provide the most valid measure of the precise level of opinion, they remain valuable for tracing *changes* in opinion over time.

SOCIAL DESIRABILITY

The human tendency to present oneself in the best light (even if only to oneself!) constitutes a challenge to accurate survey measurement. Some of the content of contemporary surveys touches on sensitive topics about which people may not be motivated to reveal the full truth about their actions. When surveys have evoked inaccurate responses to questions about sensitive matters, we say they have been affected by *social desirability bias* (Druckman, 1970; Groves, 1989). Social desirability can lead respondents to understate behaviors they may be ashamed of or to overstate behaviors that are considered praiseworthy. Respondents may fail to report interpersonal conflict in the family or violent behavior on their part. They are likely to underestimate the amount of alcohol they consume and may falsely deny using illegal drugs. There is evidence that people overstate the extent of their charitable giving, churchgoing, and even the regularity with which they wash their hands after using the toilet. These biases do not affect all individuals in the same way. Men may overstate the number of sexual partners they have had, whereas women may understate the number. (For a provocative discussion of this issue, see Lewontin, 1995.)

Respondents are more apt to tell the truth if they believe that their responses will be kept confidential and that they will not be judged by the interviewer. This means that it is important to establish a high level of trust with respondents. Sponsorship of the survey by an organization known to and trusted by the respondent is helpful. Professional, serious, empathetic interviewers are critical. Highly sensitive questions should placed later in the interview, after the respondent has had a chance to become comfortable with the interview and to judge the seriousness of the research by reflecting on the other content of the questionnaire. It is also helpful to remind the respondent of the importance of thorough and complete answers.

Unfortunately, no magic tricks exist to solve the problem of social desirability bias, but a number of techniques have been employed and found useful in certain circumstances. When asking about socially desirable behaviors such as voting or churchgoing, use a preface that "normalizes" behavior that does not conform to the ideal. For example, a typical voter registration question in the United States might be prefaced by the following: "These days, many people are so busy they can't find time to register to vote, or move around so often they don't get a chance to reregister. . . Are you *now* registered to vote in your precinct or election district, or haven't you been able to register so far?"

A similar technique first asks if the respondent has "ever" engaged in a behavior (such as volunteering to help others in the community), then asks about activity within the past 12 months (or other shorter time frame). The "ever" question allows people to provide a socially desirable answer, reducing the pressure to overstate how recently they engaged in the behavior.

When asking for an estimate of the frequency with which an individual engages in socially undesirable behaviors (such as binge drinking), offer categories of response that include relatively high levels of the behavior. Respondents take their cues about what is normal from the alternatives offered. Consider the question, "On how many days in the past month did you have five or more drinks of alcohol?" This could be asked in open-ended format, allowing the respondent to provide a number. But given the tendency for some people to underestimate this behavior, it is better to offer a set of categories. Yet if the categories include a relatively low range (e.g., 0, 1–2, 3–4, 5 or more), people may gravitate to the lower end of the range. A better range might be 0, 1–2, 3–5, 6–9, 10 or more.

For certain kinds of highly sensitive questions, special methods can be employed. For questions about drug use or sexual behavior, researchers have had success in gaining better answers by allowing respondents to take part of the survey by sitting at a computer keyboard while listening to a recorded interviewer ask the questions through headphones. This method is known as audio-CASI (computer-assisted self-interviewing; see Tourangeau et al., 2001). Another method is the *list experiment*, in which respondents are randomly divided into two groups, each of which is read a short list of behaviors and asked how many—not which ones—they have engaged in. One group is given a list of four items (including common and non-sensitive items such as shopping today for an article of clothing), whereas the other gets the identical list plus an additional item—the item of interest to the researchers (e.g., struck a spouse or loved one in anger). The difference in the mean number of items is the proportion of respondents who engage in the behavior. Although the technique can yield a valid estimate of the incidence of particularly sensitive behaviors for the overall sample and for subgroups (e.g., men versus women), it cannot identify individuals who engage in the behavior.

ASSEMBLING QUESTIONNAIRES

Let us assume that you have constructed excellent questions for each of the concepts of interest in your survey. You now face the task of putting them together into a coherent and attractive questionnaire for administration. In many respects, this aspect of the measurement process is just as important as the design of the questions themselves. Reasonably good survey questions of concepts on which respondents have opinions or readily retrievable experiences can work well, even if flawed. But how questions are embedded within the context of other questions can have a substantial impact on results—even greater than changes in the wording or format of individual questions themselves. And how questionnaires look and sound to respondents can have a big impact on their willingness to undertake the survey or to finish it.

A detailed discussion of questionnaire composition and layout is beyond our scope here, but fortunately a fine resource exists in Dillman (2000). Most of the principles discussed are applicable to personal and telephone interviews as well.

A few key issues in questionnaire construction are worth reviewing. First, pay attention to the first question in the survey. This is particularly important in telephone interviews, where the first question arrives before a good rapport with the respondent can be established. Even in a self-administered survey where the respondents can "see beyond" the first question, we should be concerned about its impact on their willingness to continue with the interview. In general, the first question should be something that everyone in the sample can answer easily, but it should not be so dull or mundane as to suggest that the survey is going to be boring. Many political surveys begin with a question about presidential approval, or a judgment about the state of the nation. Others may begin with a question asking respondents to rate their community or state as a place to live. Never begin a survey with a sensitive demographic question such as family income—and do not begin with innocuous demographics either, because they are boring. If you need to ask demographics at the beginning of the survey in order to find respondents who meet a specific criterion for the sample, consider offering one or two substantive questions first, even if the responses to these are simply going to be "thrown away."

Demographic questions should be placed at the end of the survey unless they are needed to route respondents to certain questions (e.g., Catholics to questions about their opinion of how the church has handled the sexual abuse scandal among priests; mediators to questions about the way they implement their third-party role in a particular conflict). Some respondents resent being asked about age, race, and especially income, and many people find the full range of demographic questions to be somewhat intrusive.

Perhaps the most difficult choices in questionnaire construction arise over the sequencing of the substantive questions. Despite our best efforts to write clear questions, the context in which they are asked is often very important in how they are interpreted by respondents. The dilemma of choosing an appropriate context is a classic issue of validity. Is it better to measure approval of the mediator at the beginning of the survey, before asking about a variety of issues that bear upon judgments of his or her performance? Or is it better to ask a series of questions about different issues to get the respondent immersed into the political soup and then to ask about the job a particular mediator is doing? Arguably, the latter approach would yield a more thoughtful, considered response, akin to what we might achieve after a discussion with a friend over dinner or in a bar. We could even say that this is a more valid measure of opinion. But a question about a mediator's performance asked at the beginning of the survey will certainly yield a more reliable measure over time. Unless we precede the question with the exact same series of questions in successive surveys—questions about approach, about empathy, about advice given, about personal qualities, and so forth—we cannot be confident that the context was the same from one survey to the next.

Sampling

Sampling is a critical aspect of survey research, but the subject is relevant to nearly all scientific inquiry and not just to surveys. The principles that underlie survey sampling are the same as those at work in fields such as agriculture, business, accounting, biology, and the law. A solid understanding of sampling can be useful in all sorts of human endeavors, including CA&R.

Our lives entail the taking of one sample after another. The people we meet, the food we eat, the places in which we live and visit, and the ideas we encounter represent small samples of all of the people, food, places, and ideas that could be experienced. At a gut level, we understand this, and also realize that our samples of reality are *biased* in important ways. The people we know are a lot more like us socially, financially, and culturally, than a true cross section of the world's population. Similarly, the ideas we encounter are a combination of things available to us in the physical, social, educational, and media environment. From these settings and sources, we exert some control over what we see and hear, but we recognize the limitations on the breadth of what is available to us.

Similarly, survey research typically gathers data from a sample of a population of interest. We use samples for many reasons: We do not have time to gather data from everyone; we do not have the money to pay for data collection from the entire population; we do not want to ask everyone in the population to take the time to give us information, either out of respect for their limited resources of time or, sometimes, because we do not want the entire population exposed to our work.

The critical question for sampling is how well the sample we obtain will resemble the population in which we are interested. The sample is a *model of the population*. As with any model, it should be as similar to the population as is possible. Achieving this can be very difficult and costly, and we rarely achieve perfection. Fortunately, the laws of probability are our good friend in this endeavor.

If we set out consciously to gather a sample of Americans that represents the general public in every possible respect, we might assemble a list of all of the attributes we want to ensure are properly reflected in the sample. This list could include state of residence, type of housing, race and ethnicity, sex, and age. Or it might include parental and marital status, experience with drugs and alcohol, automobile ownership, preference in pets, psychological dispositions to anger and violence, and physical fitness. We could continue to list characteristics, including anything of specific relevance to our research project, and would eventually collapse in exhaustion. It seems apparent that a conscious effort to make a sample representative is bound to fail, simply because we cannot anticipate every attribute that may be relevant. It is also bound to fail because we have no way to characterize people according to these attributes until we have actually interviewed them, so these cannot be used as a basis of selecting people in the first place. Even if we did know the attributes, we would still have to have a way to select a few people from among the many who shared attributes we wanted represented. This process might inevitably introduce biases, in which we picked people who were the easiest to find, or most willing to be interviewed, or most attractive.

The best solution is a selection method that is essentially blind to people's attributes, that ignores such characteristics in favor of a neutral selection process that allows each person in a population to have an equal—or more properly, a *known*—chance to be selected, *regardless of their attributes*. This general approach is known as *probability sampling,* also often called *random sampling.* For some types of research probability, sampling may simply be impossible or too costly to conduct. In such cases, we may have no alternative to *non-probability sampling.* Although non-probability samples are much less desirable, when properly designed they can yield useful information and are widely used in certain situations—especially those relevant to conflict. Examples include respondents in war zones, dialogue workshop participants, and peacekeepers returning from missions.

PROBABILITY SAMPLING

The great virtue of probability sampling is that it permits us to compute an estimate of the accuracy of the sample. Without probability sampling, there is no way to gauge the degree to which the sample actually matches the population. But with it, we can state the likelihood that our results are within a specific margin of the true value for the population. Such estimates of precision are critical for decision making under conditions of uncertainty where the cost of action (or inaction) may be very high. For example, manufacturers often sample products coming off an assembly line to assess the quality of the manufacturing process. If occasional defects are discovered, it is important to be able to estimate exactly how common they are because stopping production and addressing the problem may be extremely costly. Probability sampling of items on the line can allow the decision makers to make a precise estimate of how common the problem is within a given range. In other words, they can estimate how many total units will be defective out of the total number produced. With this information, a decision can made as to whether stopping the line and fixing the problem is worth the cost.

Probability sampling entails several steps.

The first step is to decide how precise the estimates need to be—that is, how much uncertainty about the findings can be tolerated. This decision affects the size of the sample needed, and can also affect decisions about how the sample will actually be drawn.

The second step is to specify exactly what population you wish to represent. This sounds obvious, but in practice it can be difficult. If you want to represent "the general public of the United States," does this include people who do not speak English? (If so, you will need to make provisions to have your questionnaire translated into many languages and to hire interviewers who are fluent in those languages.) Does it include people without telephones? (If so, you cannot collect all of your data with a telephone survey.)

The third step is to assemble a list of the population, also called a *list frame* or just *sampling frame*. Sometimes a list is simply unavailable, and often a list will have serious problems. Take one commonly used list: the telephone directory. People in the population will be missing from the list (e.g., people with unlisted numbers do not appear in the telephone directory), others will appear more than once (e.g., people with more than one telephone number may appear in the directory more than once), and still others appear in the list but are no longer in the population (e.g., people who moved away will still be in the book until an updated directory is printed). For professional populations, such as the Society for Professionals in Dispute Resolution (SPIDR), printed directories or lists of members may be relatively complete and up-to-date, providing an excellent list frame. This list was used by Birkhoff (2001) to study mediators' perspectives on power. She mailed a survey to each of the 500 SPIDR members categorized as trained mediators; because these members defined the population of professional dispute resolution mediators, a sampling frame was not used. Although only 184 mediators returned the survey (about 37%), this "sample" was shown to represent the population on various demographic variables. In general, the completeness of list frames varies considerably from population to population.

The final step is to actually draw the sample and attempt to contact the sampled individuals. There are many methods for doing this, which are discussed below.

How Large Should the Sample Be?

Because one of the great benefits of sampling relative to taking a census is the savings in time and money that a sample provides, deciding how big the sample should be has implications for both the accuracy of the study and the costs—with accuracy going up along with the costs. In general, a sample should be large enough to provide an acceptable degree of precision not only for estimates about the population as a whole, but also for important sub-groups that are represented in the sample (for example, racial minorities or the elderly). The precision of a sample is affected by three factors, which for most situations can be arrayed in order of importance, as follows:

- The size of the sample (very important)
- The variability of the population (important)
- The fraction of the population taken into the sample (usually not important)

Simply put, the precision of a probability sample increases as the size of the sample increases. So bigger is better, but as we shall see, there is a law of diminishing returns that makes it relatively straightforward to choose an optimal sample size because additional precision beyond a certain point can be very costly. But size is not the only factor; populations that have greater variation in the variables of interest to the study yield less precise estimates with a given sample size than do populations that are more homogeneous. And although it is usually of no consequence except in cases of very small populations, the proportion of the population actually included in the sample can affect the precision of the results. As logic would suggest, taking a bigger percentage of the population into the sample improves the precision, but—contrary to what common sense would tell us—for relatively large populations (say, several thousand and up), the sampling fraction has almost no impact on precision for samples of the size we are likely to be dealing with.

To explore these practical matters in greater detail, we need to take a side journey into the theory underlying probability sampling. Even though we are typically drawing only one sample from the population for our study, the easiest way to grasp the basics of sampling is to think about *many* samples drawn from the same population and not just one sample. The big question is how similar or different successive samples are likely to be. Ideally, we would like to know that repeated samples of the same size from the same population will yield results that are nearly identical every time, and that this result is close to what we would get if took a census and not just a sample. If so, it means that any given sample is likely to be a good model of the population. If samples vary a lot—if they are very different from each other even though we are using the same techniques in drawing them—then we will have less confidence that any given, single, sample we draw is going to be accurate.

Fortunately, we have control over how much samples are going to vary. The biggest factor under our control is the size of the sample. Consider the simple example of coin flipping. Coins have two sides: heads and tails; thus, the population value for heads or tails is .50. Our experience with flipping a coin tells us that occasionally we will get several heads in a row. But over a longer series of flips, the number of heads and tails will even out. We would not be surprised to get 7 heads (70%) in a sample of 10 flips, but how likely is it that we would get 70 heads in 100 flips? Unlikely. Or 700 in 1,000 flips? Very, very unlikely. Indeed, we can specify *exactly* how unlikely for each of these outcomes because the results of random samples are themselves distributed according to the normal curve, with a mean and a standard deviation just like any statistic. This distribution has a special name: *the sampling distribution,* which is the hypothetical distribution of the results of all of the possible samples of a given size drawn from the population. According to sampling theory, the mean for any given statistic plotted from all of the possible samples we could draw from a population will equal the population mean (in the same way that lots of coin flips eventually establish the fact that the coin has two faces that are equally likely to turn up), and the variability of this statistic is affected by—you guessed it—three things: the size of the samples we have been drawing, the variability of the variable we are estimating with the samples, and the sampling fraction. (See Chapter 4 for a discussion of the sampling distribution and the coin flipping example in the context of experimentation.)

A more thorough discussion of how to compute the standard error is beyond the scope of this chapter, but here are some useful tools that both illustrate the principles described above and provide a basis for making decisions about sample size. First, Figure 5.1 plots the relationship between sample size and sampling error of a proportion for samples ranging from 10 cases all the way up to 4,000 cases. This graph "cheats" by changing the scale along the x-axis (twice), but this manipulation helps to show visually why most survey samples tend to fall within a narrow range of sizes.

Take a moment to orient yourself with Figure 5.1. The margin of error is plotted on the y-axis, and the sample size is plotted on the x-axis. A given point on the line tells us the expected error margin for a sample of a given size; for example, the expected error for a sample of 100 cases is plus or minus 10 points. As you can see, the amount of error drops rapidly as samples increase through the range of 10 to about 50, then the curve flattens out. When the x-axis scale changes from tens to hundreds beginning at 100, another dip occurs, with expected error declining from 10 points down to about 7 points. So adding 100 cases to your sample of 100 improves the precision of the sample by 3 points, about the same as adding 10 cases to a sample of 20 or 30. After the drop from 100 to 200 cases, the curve again flattens out, with each additional increment of 100 cases improving the accuracy of the sample, but by smaller and smaller amounts. Between 1,000 and 2,000 cases, we see another decline in the margin of error (slightly less than 1 point), but after that, even adding an extra 1,000 cases makes only a marginal difference.

The practical implication of the relationship depicted here is that samples need not be much larger than about 1,000 to provide a reasonably precise estimate of the population. Adding more cases can be very expensive

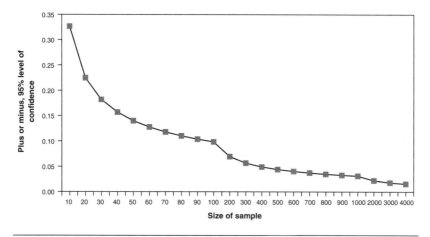

Figure 5.1   Sampling Size and Sampling Error

but does not yield much in the way of additional precision. At the other end of the chart, it is clear that additional cases with small samples can make a lot of difference in the sampling error. One caveat—mentioned earlier—is that we are ordinarily not interested only in the overall sample estimates for the population as a whole. We are often interested in subgroups in the population as well, such as foreign-born residents. If such a group represents 10% of the population, we can anticipate obtaining interviews with 100 of them (assuming they are just as accessible and amenable to being interviewed as native residents). Thus, although the overall margin of error for the sample of 1,000 will be plus or minus approximately 3 percentage points, the margin for the foreign-born residents will be plus or minus 10 percentage points. If we need a more precise estimate for this group, we will have to obtain a larger sample of the overall population, or we will have to employ some other method to increase the number of foreign-born residents in the survey (for example, by drawing a larger portion of our sample in cities than in small towns and rural areas).

Figure 5.2 shows how the amount of variation in the characteristic we are trying to measure can affect the amount of sampling error. The top line shows the sampling error for a survey question in which the responses divide evenly: 50% give one answer, 50% give another, for example, whether the respondent is male or female. This is the highest level of variation that a proportion can achieve. The bottom line on the graph shows the sampling error for a question in which 5% of respondents give one answer, and 95% give a different answer, for example, that there is or is not an extremist living in the household. This variable is almost a constant. Nearly everyone gives the same answer; only a few

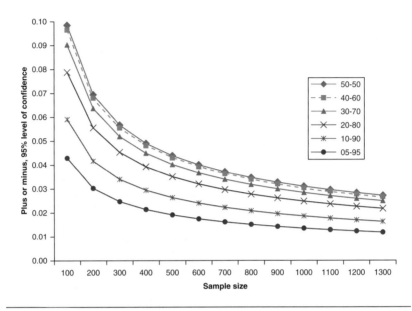

Figure 5.2   Effect of the Variability of the Variable of Interest on Sampling Error

people report living with someone prone to extreme violence. As Figure 5.2 shows, the sampling error is much smaller for a question with little variability than for one that varies a lot.

Figure 5.3 illustrates how little difference the sampling fraction makes. Only when the sample is a significant portion of the population, for example, 50%, can we see a clear improvement in the sampling error. As the chart shows, a sample of 500 taken from a population of 1,000 will have a sampling error of plus or minus approximately 3 percentage points. The same size sample from a population of 5,000—a sampling fraction of 1/10—has a sampling error of plus or minus 4.2 percentage points.

Types of Probability Samples

There are many different ways to create a probability sample, and the choice of approach depends on several factors: whether a good list frame is available, the mode of the data collection (telephone, mail, Internet, personal interviews), whether or not additional interviews with certain kinds of people are needed, and so forth.

The somewhat misleadingly named *simple random sampling (SRS)* requires a list frame, wherein the elements are numbered and then selected

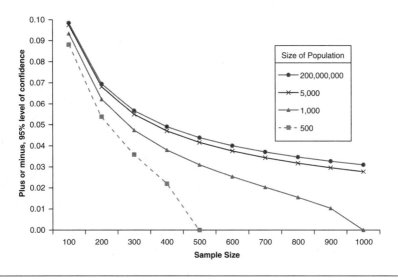

Figure 5.3   Sample Size and the Sampling Fraction

randomly using a computer process or a random-number table. This method is akin to selecting ping pong balls with lottery numbers, or drawing names or numbers out of a hat, though neither of these common approaches may be truly random. In practice, SRS is often complicated to implement because it requires a list and can be cumbersome if the list is large. A more common method is *systematic sampling,* which entails the selection of every *n*th element of a list. For example, if we need a sample of 100 college students taken from a telephone directory containing 10,000 names, we could simply choose a random number between 1 and 100, count from the beginning of the directory to the student whose name fell at that point in the list, and then select every 100th name in the directory after that. Systematic sampling is also used in situations where no list is available, such as in intercept surveys of voters leaving polling places (also known as *exit polls*). Researchers will estimate the expected number of voters at a precinct during the day (e.g., 200) and then divide that figure by the number of interviews they need at the location (e.g., 10) to determine the *sampling interval* needed (200/10 = 20). The interviewer will then attempt to conduct an interview with every 20th voter.

Often our list frame will contain information about the people in the population, information that can be used to improve the accuracy of the sample or to help us target certain groups of special interest. This information makes it possible to sort people into groups or strata, from which random samples can be drawn. This is called *stratified random sampling.* For example, a list of college students may include class standing. With this information, we could ensure that the sample we draw matches the population on this characteristic: the correct percentage of freshmen, sophomores, and so on. Or if we were particularly interested in freshmen and wanted to make sure we had enough interviews with them to provide good estimates of their views and experiences (i.e., a low margin of error), we could oversample them, taking a higher percentage of freshmen into our sample than would occur by chance.

Lest stratified sampling sound like the hypothetical purposive sampling we described (and rejected) at the beginning of this section, they are not the same thing. Sorting the population into strata and then sampling randomly from within the strata cannot damage the representativeness of the sample; in fact, it can actually improve the statistical accuracy of the sample because it removes one source of variation between the population and the sample. The sample is now guaranteed to match the characteristic on which we stratify. Nor does over-sampling necessarily damage the sample. However, it is necessary to statistically adjust the results when oversampling has occurred.

Recall that the strict definition of a probability sample is one in which every object in the population has a *known* chance of selection, not necessarily an *equal* chance. Consider a study of racial conflict and cooperation in an American university. We hypothesize that freshmen are apt to experience higher levels of conflict but also more experiences with cooperation because they are more likely to be placed in living situations with a diverse population. Let us say that we decide to take twice as many freshmen into our sample as there should be, based on their actual percentage in the student body. (For example, if freshmen are 25% of the student body, we might decide to make our sample 50% freshmen because we want to make sure we have enough interviews with them to do detailed analysis.) When we use our survey findings to report on the opinions and experiences of the entire student population, our results will be biased in favor of the freshman experience because there are twice as many freshmen in the sample as is appropriate. For example, we might estimate rates of racial conflict that are much too high for the overall student population. But we can use *weighting* to adjust the results so that freshmen interviews account for only 25% of the total—in other words, count each freshman interview as half of an interview. Computer programs for survey data analysis have the capability to make these adjustments; all we need to do is tell the computer what weight to assign to cases for a given type of respondent. The bottom line is that stratified sampling—even with oversampling—is still probability sampling.

Most of the examples of samples discussed thus far entail a single stage: We have a list and choose people from the list. But many samples entail *multistage sampling*. Multistage samples are commonly used when no list frame exists or it would be impractical to construct one for the whole population.

Objects in the population may belong to categories or groups that can be sampled at the first stage. At the second or a subsequent stage, it may be more feasible to construct a list or to use some type of systematic sampling. A couple of examples will illustrate the concept.

Exit polls of voters are multistage samples. At the first stage, a sample of precincts from all of the available precincts in a jurisdiction is drawn. Because some precincts are larger than others, it may be necessary to give some precincts a better chance of being selected than others. If ping pong balls were labeled with precinct names and used to conduct the random selection, we could give bigger precincts a higher chance of selection by including more ping pong balls with their names. We can also stratify precincts according to past voting history to make sure that a politically diverse and representative mix of precincts is included in the final sample.

When we have a sample of precincts, the second-stage sampling occurs when interviewers go to the precincts on election day and conduct a systematic sampling of voters. The resulting sample meets the fundamental test of probability sampling: Every object (every voter) in the population had a chance to be included in the survey (because any precinct *could* have been selected at the first stage, and any voter in selected precincts could have been intercepted by an interviewer); moreover, we can compute the probability that any given voter would be selected if we know how many voters live in each of the precincts in the population and what fraction of voters we sampled within each of the selected precincts.

Another kind of multistage sample can be very expensive to implement but provides the best opportunity to achieve a truly representative sample of an entire population. *Area probability sampling* is employed in face-to-face surveys for which no list frame of the population is available and there is a desire to reach people regardless of whether they have a telephone or not. At the first stage, geographic areas (such as counties) are enumerated and sampled, usually taking into account the size of the population living in them (as with exit polling, jurisdictions with larger populations may have a larger chance of being selected). At a second stage, the selected counties might be subdivided further, for example, by city blocks, and a sample of these divisions taken. At a third stage, all of the housing units in the selected divisions will be listed and a sample of housing units drawn. At a fourth stage, the residents of each sampled housing unit will be enumerated, and a sample of one adult in each household will be selected for an interview. Area probability sampling is employed to obtain probability samples in most developing nations, because many, if not most, households lack telephone service. Although travel costs can be high, low labor costs make it more feasible to use personal interviewers. The presence of an interviewer is useful because literacy levels are often low.

Virtually all multistage sampling involves *cluster sampling* as well, in which more than one respondent is interviewed within the second or subsequent stages of the sample. This is usually a practical necessity, as it is much more efficient to obtain multiple interviews at a single voting precinct than it would be to send an interviewer to a precinct and interview only one voter. Travel costs may be very great for area probability samples, so many households within a sampled community may be chosen for interviews.

Clustering in multistage samples does have a slight negative impact on the precision of the samples, relative to a non-clustered sample with the same number of interviews. This occurs because objects within a cluster (e.g., children within a selected classroom, voters in a selected precinct) are likely to be more similar to each other than would be a set of randomly selected children or voters from all of the possible classrooms or voting precincts in the population. Put another way, cluster samples will be slightly more internally homogeneous than non-clustered samples. But cluster samples are still probability samples because we are able to specify the probability of selection for any individual in the population.

Practical Sampling

Often a list for a population of interest will be available, though sometimes it may require a good bit of detective work to locate and obtain. Privacy concerns usually make it difficult to obtain lists of the general public, such as college student directories, driver's license records, or auto registration lists. But lists of professionals and other elite populations are often available from state or local governments or from nonprofit organizations. Most states have regulatory agencies that license or certify professionals (such as nurses, lawyers, EMTs, mediators, and the like), and these lists may be relatively up-to-date and available for purchase. States or localities may also have lists of businesses or employers, and "yellow page" directories can also provide a reasonably complete list of certain kinds of businesses. Professional and trade associations may have mailing lists of members for sale, and voter registration lists are available for purchase in most states.

Several companies exist for the purpose of creating and selling survey samples. These companies design *random digit dialing* samples for telephone interviewing, but they also may have specialized samples of businesses, professionals, individuals with particular consumer or lifestyle interests, and the like. Many specialized samples do not qualify as probability samples, but some do. Two respected companies in the sampling business are Survey Sampling International of Fairfield, Connecticut (http://www.surveysampling.com), and Genesys Sampling Systems of Fort Washington, Pennsylvania (http://www. m-s-g.com/genesys/genesyshme.htm).

Sometimes, however, no commercial sample or obvious source for a list frame exists, and a certain amount of ingenuity is needed to construct one or come up with an acceptable alternative approach to creating a probability sample. Multistage sampling is often an option but can introduce a good deal of complexity into the statistical analysis. Most university departments of mathematics or statistics have specialists who can help with this type of problem, but the planning necessary to create a multistage sample is best done by someone who is familiar with the population of interest and the topic at hand—typically that would be you, the researcher!

Consider the prospect of interviewing homeless people about their experiences with violence on the streets. Believe it or not, obtaining probability samples of homeless people is possible. But the researcher's knowledge of the habits of the homeless—where they tend to stay, when they move to shelters and when they do not, and so on—is essential in creating a practical plan. The parts of a city known to be occupied by the homeless can be divided into sectors and a sample of sectors chosen. A specific day for the survey can be designated and interviewers dispatched to the sampled locations to search for the homeless. Every homeless person encountered would be counted and a sample of them selected systematically for interviewing. All shelters that are open at the time of the survey—or a sample of them—would also be visited, an enumeration made of the occupants, and a sample of them interviewed. Although difficult to plan and implement, such a sample design could yield a probability sample of homeless people because all locations in the city likely to have homeless residents had a chance of inclusion. The more accurate the researcher's familiarity with the population and its habits, the more successful the study would be.

NON-PROBABILITY SAMPLING

The discussion of sampling will conclude with a few words about non-probability samples. For some purposes in survey research, it may not be essential or even feasible to have a probability sample. But as with everything in life, some non-probability samples are better than others.

In general, exploratory research may be an appropriate setting for non-probability sampling. Typically, there is an interest in gathering in-depth data from a relatively small number of cases, and although such research is relevant only to the extent that it can be generalized to the population of interest (otherwise, why do it?), there would be no effort to generalize the findings to a broader population using numerical data and estimates of sampling error. In-depth interviews with people to explore key concepts for a survey are often conducted with individuals chosen purposefully to represent a range of perspectives. Focus groups conducted with small numbers of participants to help in crafting language for survey questions are usually conducted with non-probability samples of individuals who are located near the facility in which the group will meet. Focus groups are widely used in CA&R research to provide data difficult to collect by other means. Often the participants are experts or individuals who have firsthand experience in situations of interest. They can provide estimates of the internal stability of a regime and the potential for a coup, the activities of terrorist organizations, evidence about progress toward democratic institutions, and judgments about the success of peacekeeping missions.

More systematic research is also conducted with non-probability samples. A great deal of consumer behavior research uses *quota sampling,* often through intercept surveys in shopping malls. Interviewers are instructed to intercept shoppers more or less randomly who pass by a certain point in a mall and invite them to participate. The interviewers are asked to interview a specified number of people who fit each of a set of different categories (e.g., by age, race, gender). Quotas for each type of person are established (based upon judgments about the population of interest, which may be the consumers of a particular product), and the interviewer tries to fill the quotas by selectively intercepting individuals who appear to match the categories. Unlike probability sampling, quota sampling usually allows the interviewer to use his or her discretion in approaching and intercepting individuals for interviews. Although quota samples do not provide any basis for estimating sampling error—or indeed any kind of gauge of representativeness—they are relied upon for billions of dollars of business and marketing decisions worldwide, to get views from selected individuals living in war zones regarding the prospects for peace, and are often accepted in courts of law as credible evidence in legal disputes.

Data Collection

A useful survey entails not only developing a good questionnaire and a valid sampling plan, but success in actually interviewing the sampled individuals. One of the first decisions in a survey design is how the data will be collected. The choices of a data collection method and its implementation are key elements in the survey process. The four principal modes of data collection are as follows:

Personal interviewing, in which an interviewer interacts face-to-face with a respondent. Sometimes this interaction may also involve the use of a written questionnaire or a computer, with the respondent completing certain parts of the interview on paper or on the computer.

Telephone interviewing, in which an interviewer interacts over the telephone with a respondent. There are also telephone surveys using recorded interviewers that ask the respondent to answer by keying responses on the telephone touch-tone keypad, but we do not consider these to be true telephone interviews. They are more akin to self-administered surveys.

Printed self-administered interviewing, in which respondents complete a printed questionnaire that has been provided to them through the mail, by personal delivery (such as a drop-off at home), by an employer, or in a group setting.

Internet interviewing, in which respondents complete a survey on a Web site or in an e-mail message.

Often the decision regarding survey mode is driven almost entirely by monetary considerations. Graduate students conducting large-scale surveys without grant funding may find it impossible to use personal interviewing or even telephone interviewing because of the costs involved. Even well-funded entities find that they cannot afford personal interviewing for most projects.

But money is not the only consideration relevant to the choice of survey mode. This decision usually entails the balancing of a number of considerations and trade-offs. The population of interest may be more amenable to one type of mode than another. (For example, people with low levels of education may lack the skills to handle printed questionnaires; some elite populations may be inaccessible by telephone.) Certain kinds of survey content may require a specific mode (the need for detailed information about particular negotiations would point to printed questionnaires that can be completed after records are consulted). Some populations cannot be reached by certain modes. (About 5% of U.S. households do not have home telephones; perhaps one quarter do not have access to the Internet; an increasing number of young people have a cell phone but no land line.)

ADMINISTRATION OF THE SAMPLE

A sample is only as good as its implementation. That is, a good sampling plan, executed with a good sampling frame, may yield a terrible set of interviews if administered in such as way as to result in serious biases. For example, if a mail survey of the general public in a community obtains a high rate of response from upper-middle-class residents but almost no response from lower-income residents, we would say that it obtained a biased sample. The results are certainly not going to be representative of the larger community. The infamous *Literary Digest* straw poll of presidential voting intentions in 1936 is a good example of the problem. The sample for the poll was itself biased, in that it was drawn from lists of automobile owners, households with telephones, and magazine subscribers. In the midst of the Great Depression, this sample was certainly skewed toward upper-income citizens.

But the sample itself was not the most important reason the poll predicted that President Franklin Roosevelt would be defeated for reelection. The problem was that voters who disliked Roosevelt were more motivated to respond than were those who planned to vote for him. The poll drew about 2 million responses—a huge number by the standard of any contemporary poll—but a very low rate of response. Thus, a bias toward the Republican candidate was introduced, and the poll failed to predict the outcome of the election. If the *Literary Digest* had prodded non-respondents to participate, this bias might have been avoided. The magazine went out of business shortly after publishing these results.

We frequently encounter online polls at Web sites we visit. These polls invite us to register our opinions, and it is entertaining to take these polls and compare our results to the totals registered on the site. But these polls cannot be generalized to any known population and are essentially meaningless as gauges of public sentiment. Because any visitor to the site (and *only* visitors) can take the poll—and can take it numerous times—such polls are subject to serious biases. America Online posted online polls asking people what should happen to President Clinton after his affair with a White House intern was revealed. A majority said Clinton should resign, and the site tallied over 100,000 "votes." But valid public opinion polls representing the American public at the same time showed big majorities opposing impeachment or resignation. Those who visited the AOL site and were motivated to take the poll were more hostile toward the president than those who did not do this, so the poll was biased.

Much has been made about declining response rates in the United States and elsewhere. It is true that response rates are lower now than even 6 years ago. Well-designed telephone surveys by major media organizations typically obtain response rates in the range of 25% to 40%. And concern about response rates in any given survey is not misplaced. But implementation of a good probability sample in such as way as to minimize the possibility of bias in the obtained responses is more important than achieving some kind of mythic target response rate.

Personal Interviewing

For many purposes, personal interviews are ideal. A skillful interviewer approaching a potential respondent in person is more likely to solicit cooperation than a telephone interviewer or an approach via mail or e-mail. The rapport that a good interviewer can establish with a respondent makes it possible for personal interviews to be much longer than is possible in other modes (1-to 1½-hour interviews are common), and in-person interviews can yield significant benefits in terms of item non-response (people are more willing to answer questions) and in respondent comprehension of the questions. Respondents appear to take personal interviews more seriously than other kinds of interviews and to put more effort into providing the requested information.

Personal interviewing is very costly, chiefly because of the travel time required. Unlike telephone interviewing, where many interviewers are working in a common location and are able to efficiently conduct a large number of interviews, personal interviewers must travel to the sampled locations, find the respondents at home, and secure their cooperation. Not surprisingly, much of their time is wasted in travel and unsuccessful efforts to contact respondents. This is similar to the problem of subjects not appearing for a scheduled session of an experiment.

Mail Surveys

Self-administered questionnaires delivered by mail probably constitute the most common type of survey in the United States. Despite their reputation as a "method of last resort," the mail survey can achieve high response rates and in many situations is the method of choice (see Fox, Crask, & Kim, 1988). Certainly mail surveys can be inexpensive to mount and are popular with students, nonprofit organizations, and others who want to conduct an affordable survey.

Successful mail surveys require a significant degree of skill and attention to detail, however. The first element is a good questionnaire, discussed earlier. The self-administered questionnaire must be easy to comprehend and complete ("user-friendly") and not so long or intimidating as to turn off respondents.

Equally important is how the survey is presented and what effort is made to convince the respondent of the importance of the research. Donald Dillman is the acknowledged expert of self-administered surveys. In the 1970s, he assembled a set of principles for good survey practice under the rubric of the "Total Design Method," which has evolved into the "Tailored Design Method" (see Dillman, 2000). Underlying his approach is the notion of the social exchange, in which the researcher communicates to the respondent the seriousness of the enterprise and the social benefits and rewards he or she would receive in exchange for the effort involved in responding to the survey.

In practical terms, this means that mail surveys must appear professional and personal to the respondent. Essential elements of the design would include

- First-class postage—stamps preferred—on the envelope delivering the survey to the respondent. Self-addressed stamped envelope included for return of the questionnaire
- Personalization of the address (no letters to "occupant")
- A personalized cover letter to the respondent, explaining the value and purpose of the study, how the data will be used, who is conducting it, and how to get further information about it. The letter is signed by the researcher (preferably with ball point pen)

- Questionnaire is in booklet format, with an attractive cover, no questions on the inside cover, plenty of margin space, relatively large type, room for comments on the back cover
- Carefully timed follow-up mailings, including a reminder postcard 1 week after the initial mailing, a second questionnaire and new cover letter to non-respondents 2 weeks after that, and additional mailings a few weeks later (perhaps using express mail or overnight delivery to convey the seriousness of the enterprise)

Fortunately, modern computer technology, desktop publishing, and mail-merge programs make it possible for almost anyone to generate professional looking surveys, cover letters, and envelopes. It is easier than ever to mount a high-quality mail survey. Depending on the population, properly designed mail surveys can achieve response rates comparable to telephone surveys and, for certain populations, may be the only way to gain access.

Telephone Surveys

The telephone remains the most common mode of survey administration for most large-scale surveys in industrialized nations. In addition to the United States, it is feasible to conduct national population surveys by telephone in Great Britain, Germany, France, Japan, the Netherlands, all of the Scandinavian countries, Belgium, Italy, and Spain. The telephone is much less feasible as a data collection tool in the less-developed countries that are often the focus of research in CA&R. In these countries, the personal interview is often the preferred mode of data collection.

Telephone administration has an advantage over other modes in terms of speed and quality control. A large national telephone survey can feasibly be conducted in 2 to 3 nights, and acceptable samples may be gathered in a single night if certain caveats are accepted. Telephone interviewers typically work in a centralized facility where their work can be monitored to ensure that all questions are being asked in a standardized way with appropriate probes and follow-ups. Productivity in these facilities is usually very high.

Long surveys may be problematic on the telephone, though some telephone surveys extend to 40 minutes or longer. Additionally, respondents with hearing problems or limited formal education may find telephone surveys challenging because of the absence of visual and emotional cues that help people understand the content of interpersonal communication.

The greatest concern about telephone surveys today pertains to declining rates of response. Many factors are contributing to this problem. The public encounters a growing number of telemarketers and solicitations for non-profit organizations. Concerns about crime such as identity theft, credit card fraud, or burglary lead people to be less willing to give out information about themselves on the telephone. Growing numbers of households have call screening devices such as answering machines, caller ID, and call blocking. The result is that response rates have declined over the past three decades, with perhaps an acceleration of the decline in the past 6 years as new technologies for call screening have become available.

We have a great deal of evidence that declining response rates have not yet damaged the ability of telephone surveys to provide valid data about the U.S. public. Telephone surveys conducted at the time of national elections still yield accurate forecasts of how the public will actually vote in the elections. Experiments comparing well-designed surveys with higher and lower rates of response find little difference in the substantive conclusions they draw (see Keeter, Miller, Kohut, Groves, & Presser, 2000).

Internet Surveys

Online surveys are a welcome innovation in the survey world. The Internet makes it possible for anyone with access worldwide to receive a solicitation and complete a questionnaire online in very short order. As with telephone or computer-assisted personal interviewing (CAPI), online questionnaires can be dynamic and contingent, skipping and branching according to the responses given. Unlike the telephone survey, they can provide the respondent with visual materials.

It is not yet clear whether data quality with online surveys will be better or worse than in other modes. Online surveys are like all self-administered surveys in that we can expect higher levels of item non-response—there is no interviewer present to urge respondents to answer. But there is also evidence that respondents take the interview more seriously and expend more cognitive energy in online surveys than in telephone surveys.

The chief concern about online surveys is how to get the sample to complete the survey. In some situations, this is relatively easy. Employee surveys are often conducted online. Employees are contacted at work by e-mail or through a mailing and asked to go to a Web site and complete the survey. If Web access is provided at the work site, everyone will be able to access the survey, and we can expect high rates of response. Even outside the work setting, Internet surveys of professionals who are interested in the survey tend to yield high response rates. College students are also apt to complete online surveys. But if respondents are not intrinsically motivated to respond, it may be essential to reach them through mail, telephone, or personal contact to urge them to go to the Web site and complete the interview. Because of spam and the very impersonal nature of e-mail, it has tended to be a less effective recruitment tool for online surveys. (For an example of an online survey of negotiation experiences, see Druckman, Ramberg, & Harris, 2002.)

Multimode Surveys

Sometimes the most successful surveys involve more than one mode of contact and data collection. Some surveys provide respondents with a choice of how to respond, for example, to be interviewed by telephone or to go to a Web site and complete the questionnaire. Multimode surveys present special challenges and can be more costly than single-mode studies, and there is often a question about the comparability of data collected in different modes. (For example, we expect somewhat greater item non-response in self-administered surveys.) But for certain populations such as professionals, offering a choice of mode may help you achieve a better response rate. And for populations that may be missed entirely by one mode—for example, people without telephones, people in less-developed nations where telephone coverage is incomplete—a survey that needs to represent the entire population may need to consider using multiple modes.

SUMMARY OF ADVANTAGES AND DISADVANTAGES OF DIFFERENT SURVEY MODES

A summary of important considerations in choosing a survey mode is presented in Table 5.2. Cost is almost always a critical concern and may override other considerations, but many of the other criteria shown in the table are important to the choice of mode as well.

PRE-TESTING SURVEYS

The final topic we discuss in planning a survey is not at all the least important—the *pre-test,* or preliminary test. Compared with many other kinds of research, survey research uniquely benefits from real-world testing of questionnaires and survey administration techniques. Regardless of how carefully we try to craft questionnaires to capture how people feel and think about a topic, we can never anticipate all of the ways in which our words can be misunderstood, misconstrued, or simply offend or bore a respondent. Nor can we fully anticipate how responsive a population will be to our request for cooperation, unless we are replicating a well-known methodology such as an RDD (random digit dialing) telephone survey.

For these reasons, preliminary testing of the questionnaire (and, where necessary, the data collection process itself) is essential to success in the survey process. Pre-tests typically consist of administering the draft questionnaire to a small sample of respondents drawn from the same population and in the same way as is planned for the real study. A small part of the RDD sample is used for the pre-test, and 15–25 interviews may be conducted. Often the pre-test is administered by the most experienced interviewers on the staff, because they can do a good job with an unfamiliar questionnaire and can provide useful feedback on questions that do not work or on problematic sequencing of questions.

Table 5.2   Survey Modes

	Personal Interviewing	*Mail Surveys*	*Telephone Surveys*	*Internet Surveys*
Cost	Very high	Low to moderate	Moderate to high	Low to moderate
Accessibility to population of interest	Very high	High	High, except for non-telephone households	Moderate; 25% of individuals in the U.S. have no Internet access
Length of data collection	Lengthy	Lengthy	Fast	Moderate to lengthy, depending on respondent motivation
Infrastructure and staffing needed to administer	Substantial	Minimal	Substantial	Minimal to moderate
Level of questionnaire complexity	High	Moderate (depending on population)	Moderate	Moderate
Maximum length of survey	Long	Moderate	Moderate to long	Moderate
Response rates	Moderate to high	Low to moderate	Low to moderate	Very low to moderate
Respondent cognitive skills needed	Low	High	Low to moderate	High
Ease of use of open-ended questions	Easy	Difficult	Easy to moderate	Difficult
Use of graphics or other visual aids	Yes, including video and animation	Yes, static graphics only	No	Yes, including video and animation
Item nonresponse	Low	Moderate to high	Low	Moderate to high
Control over order of items answered	Complete	Low	Complete	Depends on implementation
Ability to control who responds	High	Low	High	Low

In almost all surveys, we create draft questionnaires that are simply too long, due to the "nice to know" problem ("it would nice to know if. . . ."). The pre-test can tell us how long the survey actually runs and helps us focus on how to pare it down to a manageable length.

Perhaps the most important value of pre-tests is to identify questions that respondents do not understand, or struggle with, or do not try to answer accurately. The principal investigators should listen to the pre-tests—most interviewing facilities have the capability to allow the unobtrusive monitoring of the telephone calls—and the talk with the supervisor and the interviewers about the experience of administering the new questionnaire. Experienced interviewers often have good suggestions about how to reword questions, and simply hearing respondents as they wrestle with questions often yields insights about how to reframe a query.

Another useful role for pre-tests is to assess a data collection method. With RDD surveys of the general public using organizations that have conducted many such studies, we can make reliable estimates of response rates. But when conducting surveys of specialized populations—either by telephone, mail, or in person—we often do not know what to expect. This uncertainty is problematic, as we may not know important parameters, such as how many questionnaires to mail out in order to achieve a certain sample size. If time permits, a pre-test of the survey mode with the selected population can provide insight about the amenability of the population to the survey. If we get an especially low response rate from the test, we can consider alterations to the design such as including a monetary incentive, using a prenotification letter prior to calling or sending the survey, or other similar techniques.

Pre-testing is a broad topic that encompasses even more complex methods than we have described here. But any study will benefit from even a simple pre-test, and often more than one attempt is useful.

Ethics

Ethical concerns in research are discussed in Chapter 1, but a few points are worth repeating in the context of surveys. The first is that your survey should do no harm. Most surveys are unlikely to harm anyone, but certain topics— especially in CA&R—are highly sensitive and can cause distress. Respondents in such surveys should understand that they are free to skip questions that are upsetting to them. What is more important, researchers must consider whether the questions being asked pose any risk to the respondents. For example, public health researchers may want to know whether a respondent has been the victim of domestic violence, but such questions asked in a telephone survey may pose a risk to the respondent. An abusive (and suspicious) spouse or partner might be listening to the interview.

A second concern is that responses must be kept confidential. This means that identifying information that could connect a respondent with an interview must be kept hidden and, as soon as possible, destroyed. Identifying information (such as a telephone number) may be needed so that interviews can be verified, but after a reasonable time period, these links should be deleted. Most surveys are subject to subpoenas by courts of law, but if the information linking the surveys with specific respondents has been destroyed, the subpoena cannot result in the identification of individual respondents and the disclosure of confidential responses.

A third ethical concern about surveys is that they take the time of respondents on behalf of your research, and this contribution of time should be respected and not wasted. A 10-minute survey with 1,000 respondents represents the equivalent of a month of full-time work (8-hour days times 5 days per week) contributed by volunteers to your research. Although these individuals may derive psychological benefits from participating in the research, they have nevertheless contributed a finite and valuable resource to it. It is our obligation to use this time wisely and carefully.

Conclusions

For professionals in CA&R, the ability to describe and analyze the experiences and perspectives of larger populations—those who have lived through wars and other violent conflicts, mediators in all types of settings, people who are currently dealing with conflict in their work lives, and so forth—is often essential to achieving their goals. The sample survey is a primary tool for providing this description and analysis.

Surveys can provide credible evidence when they draw from representative samples of the population of interest and when they measure concepts of interest in a valid and reliable way. This chapter has focused on how these objectives can be met. An important theme has been the trade-offs we must make throughout the survey process. Especially in the field of conflict analysis and resolution, conditions are often not optimal for survey research. Probability sampling may be difficult or impossible. Political considerations or restrictions may limit the questions we can ask, or we may be asking about topics that are highly sensitive to respondents. This does not mean that surveys should not be conducted, but we must be aware of the problems and adapt our methods to meet these challenges.

The sample survey is a critical tool for giving voice to the silent, for empowering the powerless, for offsetting the advantage that the articulate and well connected have in the world of politics and public affairs. The difficulties of conducting surveys notwithstanding, it is a critical tool for ensuring that all sides in a conflict can be heard and considered.

Discussion Questions

In this chapter, we have covered many aspects of survey research, including issues of design, questionnaire construction, sampling, and administration. You should review this material before embarking on a survey. The following discussion questions are intended to help with the review process. They cover the various parts of the chapter.

1. For what types of research projects are surveys an appropriate mode of data collection? When would surveys be inappropriate?

2. Hundreds of thousands of survey questions exist in archives, providing valuable comparisons with other populations and other times in history. What considerations should be used to decide between a question from an archive and one that might be tailored for a specific research situation?

3. Discuss the practical implications of the humorous advertising slogan that tells potential survey researchers to choose two options among quality, speed, and price.

4. For what topics in conflict analysis and resolution would open-ended survey questions be most useful? For each topic you suggest, draft one or two close-ended questions that would address the same subject matter.

5. Describe how you would go about creating a sample of mediators for a survey. What lists, if any, could you use? What proportion of the population of mediators would these lists cover? What kinds of mediators would be omitted from such a sample?

6. If you were conducting a survey of the general public about experiences with conflict in daily life, how would you draw the sample? Would an RDD sample suffice, or should certain groups in the population be over-sampled? If so, how would you do this?

7. Probability samples offer the ability to estimate the accuracy of a survey. For what kinds of research in the field of conflict resolution is this ability important for the credibility of the results? How does a researcher resolve the tradeoffs between the higher costs of probability samples and the benefits of greater reliability of the results?

8. For surveys of U.S. peacekeepers recently returned from conflict regions, what survey mode would be most appropriate? What mode is most appropriate for people experiencing serious conflict in their work lives?

9. Describe the steps you would take to ensure that your survey would not exacerbate the anxiety felt by refugees from a conflict region.

10. A government official demands an explanation of why you are spending thousands of dollars on survey research, drawn from funds intended to assist people in war-torn regions of a nation of interest. Aside from your specific research interests, what general justification for survey research in conflict regions can you offer?

Part IV

Doing Case-Based Research

This part is introduced by an overview of the case study method. It sets the stage for our discussion in this and the next chapter of single and comparative case study research.

The Case Study Method: An Overview

Case-based research, like experimental research, is conducted in a variety of ways. Unlike experiments, however, the approach is not guided by an overarching paradigm or set of assumptions (see the opening section to Chapter 3). The key unifying theme is that of a bound process that can be documented in time and/or space. This idea covers both the relatively loosely bound cases that are often the subject of ethnographies as well as the more tightly bound cases that are used as units of analysis in comparative studies.

Loosely bound case studies are often performed in an inductive-emic tradition that allows for inventiveness at all stages of the research. Tightly bound case studies, conducted in an etic tradition, proceed from a research design that specifies in advance the data collection and analysis procedures; however, the design is rarely as structured as experimental designs. For both types of case studies—and those that are in between—the task of documentation provides the data needed for analysis. The data may consist of notes from unstructured conversations, diaries, tape-recorded discussions held in negotiation or mediation sessions, or a recording of events that occur in defined time periods such as hours, days, or weeks. Any of these kinds of data can be analyzed in a variety of ways, and both qualitative and quantitative techniques are used in case study research. Topics of case research design and analysis are discussed in this and the next chapter. The discussion is organized by a framework that distinguishes among the various approaches.

The case study approaches shown in the box proceed from focusing on a smaller to a larger number of cases. The analytical case study includes both ethnographies, discussed in the next part of the book (Chapter 8), and analyses that use single cases to demonstrate theoretical propositions discussed in Chapter 6. A difference between these approaches is an in-depth treatment of a case (culture, organization, or group), on the one hand, and a focus on those aspects of a case relevant to the theory, on the other. The enhanced case study is an attempt to provide a theoretical structure for the collection of qualitative data. It does this without forfeiting a key advantage of qualitative research, which is the collection of a vast amount of qualitative information, often rich in contextual detail. The analytical structure focuses attention on those aspects of cases that address theoretical issues. They also show how qualitative information can be used to evaluate a specific theory or hypothesis.

Going even further, the chapters in this part show how more observations can be collected on a dependent variable (time series) and how the same variable can be observed in different contexts (focused comparison, aggregate data analysis). This strategy for doing case-based research is similar to the approach taken to qualitative research by King et al. (1994). Both their book and this one encourage efforts to perform multiple-method research, including observing and analyzing the operation of several variables (independent and dependent) across contexts.

The other three approaches shown in the box are explicitly comparative. Time-series analyses are comparisons of data points (events, moves, pronouncements) taken through the course of a defined period of time. Focused case studies compare a small number of similar cases matched on all but a few variables. Aggregate studies compare a large number of different cases, usually as a cross section (time is not a variable) but sometimes also longitudinally (time is a variable). Time-series and aggregate studies typically use statistical methods of analysis, whereas focused case comparisons are usually qualitative analyses. There are a number of other differences among the approaches, and these are shown in the table. Time-series analyses provide a detailed charting of change in events or processes. Focused comparisons address issues of causation and often include both process and context in the analysis. Sophisticated modeling and statistical generalization are advantages of the large-N aggregate analyses. Each of the approaches is relevant to particular types of research problems and constrained by the availability of appropriate data. Together, they illuminate the advantages of combining qualitative and quantitative approaches in seeking answers to research questions. These advantages are heralded by King et al. (1995), who note that "to combine both types of data productively, researchers need to understand the fundamental logic of inference and the more specific rules and procedures that follow from an explication of this logic" (p. 475). Design and analysis issues relevant to these approaches are discussed in some detail in Chapters 6 and 7. Because the four case study approaches are considered as a set, the discussion questions are combined and presented together at the end of Chapter 7.

Features of Four Methodological Approaches

Features	Analytical (Enhanced) Case Study	Time-Series Case Study	Focused Case Comparisons	Aggregate Case Comparisons
Number of cases	One	Usually one	Usually 2–4	Large # (>10)
Unit of analysis	Whole case	Events	Whole cases	Events, moves
Qualitative or quantitative analysis	Qualitative	Quantitative	Qualitative	Quantitative
Causal analysis	Difficult	Lagged correlations	Careful matching of cases	Correlation, path models
Generality	Limited	Limited	Limited	Relatively wide
Case penetration	Thick	Relatively thin	Can be thick	Thin
Process analysis	Detailed	Detailed	Detailed if process tracing	Limited
Role of context	Emphasized	Usually de-emphasized	Can be emphasized	Usually de-emphasized
Consequences of outcomes	Long term	Data points can be extended through time	Sometimes monitored	Infrequently monitored
Applications	Frequent, broad	Moderate, limited	Moderate, limited	Infrequent
Stage of inquiry	Usually early	Can be early or later	Usually later	Later

Source: Druckman (2002a, p. 23).

6

Enhanced-Case and Time-Series Analyses

Theory and the Case Study

A substantial amount of case study research is descriptive. Unfolding processes and events are documented in order to provide readers with a record of what happened at particular periods during the conflict. An example of a public archive of case studies in international affairs and conflict resolution is the Pew Case Studies in International Affairs assembled by Georgetown University's Institute for the Study of Diplomacy (see the 1999 Compendium or go to http://cfdev.georgetown.edu/sfs/programs/isd/). This archive of more than 250 cases has been used for many of the analyses discussed in this chapter. These sorts of descriptions of conflicts can be regarded as "data" for various kinds of theoretical investigations. Some of the studies reviewed in this chapter consist of evaluations of theories; others use the case material to illuminate a particular theoretical perspective. In this section, I discuss the latter type of analysis, which is referred to as an enhanced case study. See the box in Part IV's introduction for a list of enhanced case study features.

The *enhanced case study* is both interpretive and analytical. By viewing the case through the lens of an interpretive framework or particular concepts, the researcher provides a broader understanding of what happened. The case then serves as an example of the application of those concepts. Generally, two approaches have been used. One consists of using a multidimensional framework (such as those illustrated in the Chapter 2 section "Constructing Frameworks") as a lens through which a case is understood. Another uses a few key concepts as the basis for interpreting a case. Because many more examples of the latter strategy can be found in the literature, that strategy receives more attention in this section of the chapter.

An example of a framework-driven analysis is the computer-assisted tool referred to as "Negotiator Assistant" (Druckman et al., 2002). This project has been conducted in a series of steps, bringing systematic research, in the form of strenuous reliability and validity evaluations, to bear on case analyses. As well, the example considers the usefulness of the approach.

This framework, consisting of questions about five aspects of negotiation, was devised originally to diagnose cases in terms of the flexibility of negotiating parties. Diagnostic validity was demonstrated by the results of comparisons between computer-generated diagnoses and the actual outcomes obtained in nine historical cases. The framework was recently expanded to include questions (or variables) about many other conditions and processes of negotiation, and is now organized into 10 sections: (1) questions about topics and issues discussed, (2) the international environment, (3) the domestic environment, (4) the negotiating situation, (5) the negotiators' cultures, (6) the delegations, (7) negotiation strategies and tactics, (8) negotiating alternatives, (9) the negotiators, and (10) negotiation outcomes.

Much effort has been expended in assessing the reliability of these questions. This is done by comparing the answers given to each question by two case experts who code the same historical cases independently. Cases have included the SALT talks, the Panama Canal negotiations, NAFTA, a Canada-U.S. negotiation over acid rain, the partial nuclear test ban negotiations, and the talks over mutual and balanced force reductions. As a result of these applications, many of the framework's questions have been discarded, altered, or re-conceptualized.

The refined framework is being evaluated further for validation and usefulness. Two validation questions are

- How well does the framework distinguish among different types of actual cases?
- Which variables or questions in the framework are more or less important?

Two usefulness questions are

- Does the framework contribute to negotiating effectiveness in terms of better outcomes and more positive turning points?
- Is the framework a useful tool for international negotiators in the context of everyday delegation activities?

These questions are addressed with many of the analytical techniques discussed in this book, including simulations, which are discussed in earlier chapters, and comparative case analyses, discussed in the chapters to come.

As noted above, most of the applications of this methodology have not attempted to apply this sort of complex framework to cases. Nor have they used a systematic approach to evaluate the fit between framework concepts and cases. Rather, they have concentrated on applying a few key theoretical concepts in a more interpretive tradition. A number of examples from the published literature can be drawn on to provide an understanding of the way enhanced case studies have been performed to date.

A stream of studies on various types of negotiations among nations, published mostly in the 1970s, provide examples of this approach. Young's (1968) study of the post–World War II record of negotiation between the United States and the People's Republic of China showed that contrasting bargaining styles, referred to as adversarial versus convergent, influenced both the process and outcomes of those extended talks. Bonham's (1971) case/simulation study of disarmament talks illuminated the constraints imposed by issue incompatibility on progress. Similarly, Newhouse's (1973) discussion of SALT I emphasized size and ranking of issues as well as bureaucratic structural factors as impediments to reaching agreements. Underdal's (1973) study of the European Community deliberations showed a relationship between structural characteristics of the community and goal attainment in negotiation. Midgaard's (1974) study of pelagic whaling disputes uncovered a relationship between long- and short-term interests and bargaining strategies. Haskel's (1974) research on the Scandinavian market negotiations highlighted the role of power symmetries and asymmetries in the process of regional negotiations. Campbell's (1976) analysis of the 1954 Trieste talks made a compelling argument about the importance of secrecy for effective third-party intervention. Winham's (1977) analysis of the Kennedy round of trade talks showed that the likelihood of an agreement may depend on the complexity of the issues. And, Hopmann and Walcott's (1977) analyses of arms-control negotiations made evident the way that stress and goal rigidity can influence flexibility and outcomes.

More recently, Druckman and his colleagues (1991) proposed the concept of turning points to depict how the talks on intermediate nuclear forces, conducted in the late 1980s, unfolded. This concept was used also by Tomlin (1989) to describe the events, during pre-negotiation phases, leading to the North American Free Trade talks, and Cameron and Tomlin (2000) viewed the activities leading to agreement in the NAFTA process, which took place in the 1990s, in terms of turning points. Another attempt to superimpose concepts on a case is illustrated by Druckman and Green's (1995) study of a negotiation between the Philippines' Aquino regime and the National Democratic Front (NDF). The authors described the process in terms of a set of linked propositions concerning the interplay between values and interests. The "interplay" called attention to dynamics in terms of cycles of polarized and de-polarized values that influenced the intensity of the larger conflict between the parties. (This study is discussed below in more detail.)

More ambitious attempts to understand cases through the lens of theory are the books edited by Rubin (1981) on Kissinger's shuttle diplomacy in the

Middle East, by Zartman (1994) on multilateral negotiation, and by Cohen and Westbrook (2000) on ancient diplomacy. Each of these projects brought diverse theoretical perspectives to a particular historical case. The authors of the chapters in these edited books interpreted the same case from such perspectives as game theory, social psychology, coalition theory, organizational theory, and international relations.

This set of studies highlights aspects of issues—their size, complexity, type, and preference structure—types of goals as short or long term and goal rigidity or flexibility, power symmetries and asymmetries, approaches to negotiation, process dynamics, structural influences, events that increase or decrease stress, and factors in the situation that influence the process. These are elements of a larger framework devised originally by Sawyer and Guetzkow (1965) and discussed in the Chapter 2 section "Constructing Frameworks." They are examples of variables in each of the boxes shown earlier in Figure 2.2: preconditions, background factors, processes, conditions, and outcomes. The studies cited above illustrate how some of these variables operate in particular cases. They do not, however, provide evidence for hypothesized relationships between different parts of the framework. Nor do they provide an evaluation of an entire framework as illustrated with the Negotiator Assistant study mentioned earlier.

The theory-driven case study has both strengths and weaknesses. Strengths include establishing a broader theoretical relevance for cases, demonstrating applicability or robustness of theoretical concepts, and providing a basis for comparison with other cases. This is done, for example, by assessing the impact of varying degrees of issue complexity or incompatibility (in several cases) on outcomes. One weakness is opportunistic evaluation of the theoretical concepts. A single case cannot be used to verify a relationship between variables. Another is failure to eliminate counterfactual explanations due to missing control groups. This applies more generally to single case studies. A third is the difficulty in separating the concepts from the case. The case itself influences the choice of concepts. Other weaknesses include difficulty in reproducing the case and the problem of overlooking other contributions to the way a process unfolded or an outcome occurred. The decision to employ only a few concepts limits the interpretive value of the exercise. On balance, however, the enhanced case study can make useful contributions, especially if it is considered to be a source of insights or hypotheses to be evaluated in the more systematic ways discussed in the sections to follow.

An example of an enhanced case study sheds light on how the approach may be implemented. My 1995 study with Green shows how theory may enhance understanding of a case's unfolding chronological path. The case of negotiations between the Philippines regime and the insurgent movement, the NDF, was analyzed in terms of the concepts of ripeness and formula. Ripeness was used to help understand how the parties decided to come to the negotiating table. Formula was used to provide an understanding of the negotiating process itself. With regard to getting to the table, we defined ripeness in terms of a process in which the parties monitor changes in the balance of power between them. We suggested that they do this by assessing changes in relative power and legitimacy. Ripeness is then defined as the intersection between judgments of relative power (as increasing, constant, or decreasing for each party compared to the other) and relative legitimacy (as increasing, constant, or decreasing). For example, a decision to negotiate by the insurgent group is made when their power is increasing and legitimacy is constant or where legitimacy is increasing and power is constant; the regime is willing to negotiate when its legitimacy is growing and its power is either increasing or decreasing. (See Table 12-1 in Druckman & Green [1995] for the various combinations leading to decisions to come to or back away from the negotiating table.)

The process of negotiating in this case is also understood in terms of a few concepts from the theoretical literatures on negotiation and the sociology of conflict. Propositions about the way values and interests interact through the course of a conflict resolution process were woven through the chronology of the case. Activities early in the talks illuminated the conflict-intensifying effects of contrasting values (or ideologies) on the process (Proposition 1 from Druckman & Zechmeister, 1973). As the talks developed, differences within each party surfaced. The differences—moderates and extremists—reduced the polarization and intensity of the conflict between the parties on the divisive issues (Proposition 2 from Druckman & Zechmeister, 1973). Midway through the talks, a Philippines' senator introduced a broad set of principles on which both parties could agree (Proposition 3). This was a formula that had the promise of guiding the parties through the tough bargaining over details to follow. Its vagueness backfired. It did not address fundamental differences, which turned out to frustrate attempts to reach agreements on detailed issues. This then led to an erosion of the "alliance of moderates" on both sides. Through time and repeated encounters, the parties became polarized, which served, in turn, to increase the intensity of the conflict (Proposition 4; this is the third proposition in Druckman & Zechmeister, 1973). The talks broke down, and the conflict between the regime and the NDF escalated.

This case demonstrates a cyclical pattern of intensified and reduced conflict, culminating in an impasse due to within-party convergence toward extreme positions described by the fourth proposition. The impasse was sustained, leading to further violence. The violence was eventually reduced through attrition caused by repeated military confrontations. The possibility of shared interests, referred to also as *cross-cutting interests*, between the parties was not realized. (Note here the fourth proposition in Druckman & Zechmeister, 1973, which postulates a de-escalation due to cross-cutting interests; the process in this case did not complete the cyclical pattern.) Together, the set of propositions captured the dynamic interplay between values and interests in this case of disappointed expectations on both sides for a negotiated settlement.

This study also illustrates the value of case chronologies. Chronologies provide important information for the theory-based analysis. Although the analysis may not be performed chronologically, the ordering of events in time is useful. Among other things, a listing of events by time period (weeks, months) enables the analyst to detect variation in the concepts: for example, changes in bargaining styles inferred from decisions and proposals, increasing or decreasing polarization on issues inferred from differences in tabled offers or demands, or at which time in the course of events power differences influence decisions. Thus, an early task for the case analyst is to develop a chronology of events. This task also serves to bound the case by defining a beginning, middle, and end, which is particularly useful for analyses of phases and phase transitions. Less clear in this exercise are decisions concerning the amount of detail needed and the most relevant time unit to use. These decisions depend on whether the analyst intends to perform a broad interpretive study (Cameron & Tomlin, 2000; Haskel, 1974; e.g., Young, 1968) or a probe of relations among variables that define the concepts (e.g., Bonham, 1971; Hopmann & Walcott, 1977), The Druckman-Green analysis combines both interpretive and relational approaches.

This approach to doing research has become quite popular in recent years. More enhanced case study papers are being presented at the meetings of the International Association for Conflict Management, and at the Academy of Management (Conflict Management section). They have also been presented at the First International Biennial Conference on Negotiation held in Paris in December, 2003. Examples are the papers presented by Crump (2003) and Bottom (2003). Crump used the case of a sale of a U.S. Major League baseball team to a Japanese investor group. These multiparty negotiations took place over a 6-month period in 1992. His analysis illuminates a relationship between issue re-framing and interorganizational unity and disunity in both distributive and integrative negotiations. It also identified techniques that can be used to enhance interorganizational unity, infuse disunity in an opponent, or protect against techniques that would create disunity in one's own organization.

Bottom (2003) examined the case of the 1919 Paris Peace Conference to compare alternative hypotheses about rationality. He discovered that two of the hypotheses (referred to as semi-strong and strongly bounded behavioral conceptions of rationality) accounted for the structure of the treaty. However, only the behavioral hypothesis seemed to account for the failure in treaty implementation and the evolution of the Allied policy of appeasement. Both these studies illustrate the research strategy of superimposing concepts or theories on cases. Both analyses shed insight on the particular cases used, increased the value of the concepts chosen, and provided ideas for further case and laboratory investigations.

I now conclude the discussion of theory-based case studies. The reader would gain appreciation for the approach by examining the references cited in this section. These are a sampling of the kinds of cases and concepts used by conflict analysts. Better yet, try performing an enhanced case study: First, select a CA&R case to analyze; then, develop a chronology of the case; third, decide on the concepts that are relevant to the events that transpire; and, finally, reach conclusions that provide new insights into the case. Even though the analysis may be performed "to perfection," do not brag about the explanatory value of the exercise. Bragging rights will come with the kinds of systematic time-series analyses discussed in the sections to follow and the multiple case analyses taken up in the next chapter.

Time-Series Designs and Analyses

The features of time-series designs are listed in the second column of the box shown in the part introduction. The time series usually consists of a sequence of events accumulated over a relatively long period of time. The data are similar in many ways to repeated measures in experimental designs, discussed in Chapter 4: Both involve providing data points for analyzing trends within subjects or cases. Both analyze these trends for changes, patterns, and shapes. But there are also some differences. One difference is the focus on events rather than responses or moves made by subjects in experiments. Another difference is the case context within which the real-world events occur rather than an experimental environment in which subjects perform structured tasks. Repeated measurements are usually data collected as part of an experimental design; the data are analyzed as part of the error-term component of ANOVA (see the Chapter 4 section "Repeated Measures"). Time-series data are usually collected through the course of a defined period of time, often corresponding to a chronology of an activity such as negotiation or the duration of a war; the data are typically analyzed with regression or correlational statistics, taking into account the correlations among the data points themselves.

Several types of time-series designs will be discussed in the subsections to follow, including examples of both quantitative and qualitative analyses. Although calculation routines are provided for some of the more popular techniques, the discussion emphasizes CA&R examples. For the step-by-step calculations on a variety of time-series techniques, see the chapters on forecasting in Frei and Ruloff (1989). The first subsection shows how time-series data can be used for post-diction. The second subsection illustrates how forecasts are done with regression techniques, including the concepts of least squares and the techniques of partial and multiple correlation. A third subsection presents the idea of interrupted time-series analysis followed by a discussion of Bayesian approaches to analysis. The next major section provides examples of several qualitative time-series analyses of conflict processes.

POST-DICTING EVENTS WITH TIME-SERIES DATA

When an analyst is interested in predicting known outcomes in completed or historical cases, he or she is doing *post-diction*, which is sometimes referred to as *retro-diction*. This type of analysis is performed for several reasons. One is that an investigator is interested in learning about the antecedents of particular events, such as crises. Another is that an analyst desires to re-create a path of events leading to an outcome. And a third reason is to evaluate the plausibility of alternative explanations or theories about the occurrence of an event. For each of these reasons, it is advantageous to know—or to have control over—the outcome. The question of interest is, what process or pattern unfolded prior to the event of interest? This question can be addressed from either an inductive or a deductive perspective. An example of each approach to post-diction—on the same research issue—is presented. Coincidentally, these examples come from back-to-back articles in the same 1986 issue of the *Journal of Conflict Resolution.*

A negotiation occurred in 1975 between the governments of Spain and the United States to renew the base rights granted by Spain to the United States during the previous 5-year period. These talks were regarded by U.S. policymakers as routine. Previous agreements provided the framework for the terms of a new agreement. However, the negotiation process defied these expectations. It was not at all smooth. Spain's demands were extraordinary—including a demand to be admitted to NATO—and the U.S. delegation was not prepared for them. A bilateral agreement was reached in 1976, a year and a half after the talks began. The impasse during this period was punctuated with several crises, including walkouts by the delegations. Three research questions were asked: (1) Was there a pattern in the events that preceded the crises? (2) How were the impasses resolved? and (3) Was there a pattern in the events that occurred following impasse resolution? Time-series analysis was used to address the first and third questions.

Statements made by both delegations during the sessions were coded into categories reflecting hard and soft negotiating rhetoric. The categories were from a coding system known as bargaining process analysis (BPA). Designed originally by Walcott and Hopmann (1978), the BPA is intended to facilitate analyses of verbal behavior in international negotiation. Ratios indicating the percentage of the total statements made by a delegation during a session (total of 22) within a round (total of 10) were calculated and summed for an aggregate score for each delegation by session. The aggregate scores were then plotted in two dimensions, percent hard (vertical dimension) and sessions (horizontal dimension). The resulting trends provided a time series for each delegation. By placing each of the six crisis sessions on the graph, it was possible to analyze patterns of verbal behavior before and after the event.

Correlational analyses revealed a distinct pattern of behavior before and after the crises. (Note that computations of correlation coefficients are presented in the next section.) Succinctly stated, the pattern took the form of a gap between the delegations in a percent-hard index during the session before the crisis. The gap was closed by the *softer* delegation. It increased the number of hard statements, matching the *harder* delegation, resulting in mutual hardness and an impasse. This pattern became known as comparative responsiveness and formed the basis for further research with multiple cases to be discussed below. It was discovered inductively in a case study not guided by hypotheses. (The study also investigated the way these crises were resolved and the patterns of behavior that followed resolution; see Druckman, 1986, for details.)

A companion study reported by Stoll and McAndrew (1986) investigated patterns of responsiveness through 10 years (1969–1979) of talks between the Soviet Union and the United States on strategic arms limitations (SALT). Performed with a deductive approach, these investigators evaluated the fit of three alternative models of reciprocity, referred to as directional, trend, and comparative reciprocity. Each of these models predicts the reactions to concessions made by the other negotiating team. The *directional model* specifies that negotiators will either match (a concession for a concession) or mismatch (a retraction in response to a concession) the other's move. The *trend model* indicates that negotiators will either increase or decrease their concession in response to a previous increase or decrease by their opponent. The *comparative model* predicts that negotiators will increase or decrease their concessions in response to a higher or lower concession made by the opponent in the previous round.

Several time series were used to evaluate these models. They included the round-by-round moves made by the Soviet and U.S. delegations during SALT I (November 1969–May 1972), at Vladivostok (June 1972–November 1974), in SALT II (January 1977–June 1979), and across the entire set of rounds from 1969 to 1979. The results showed that the comparative model provided the best fit to the concession data. In technical terms: The highest correlations between the expected and actual responses from one round to the next occurred for the comparative model in five of the eight analyses (four data sets for each national delegation). These results are consistent with those obtained in the base-rights study. A key difference between the studies, however, is between an inductive discovery (Druckman, 1986) and a deductive evaluation of alternative models (Stoll & McAndrew, 1986).

The deductive time-series work was extended to an evaluation of additional models with more cases of international negotiation. In this study, 10 models of reciprocity were evaluated with time series of round-by-round moves in seven negotiations. The directional model was compared to five versions of the trend and four versions of the comparative model: The five trend models consisted of different lags (varying in terms of the number of previous rounds included) and weightings for more recent and more distant rounds; the four comparative models consisted of different combinations of the comparative and trend models. The negotiation cases varied in terms of the length of the time series from 8 rounds (the Mutual and Balanced Force Reductions between NATO and the Warsaw Pact) to 22 rounds (post-war disarmament talks between the Soviet Union and the United States). The actual moves made by the delegations from one round to the next were correlated with the moves made in the same or earlier rounds by the opposing delegation. The data used for the calculations of correlations were specified by each model: For example, response to the immediately previous concession for the directional model, an increase or decrease in concession from $t - 2$ (two rounds earlier) to $t - 1$ (one round earlier), is correlated with the change in the other's concession from $t - 1$ to t for the trend model.

Goodness of fit for the various models was evaluated by the relative size of the correlations. The strongest correlations occurred for the comparative model (9 of 14 correlations were significant). Thus, the comparative model produced a better fit to the data than the 9 alternatives, including the various combinations of comparative and trend models. These time-series findings corroborate and attest to the generality of the results obtained in the 1986 studies described above. They tell us that professional negotiators are attentive to each other and react to any difference that exists between the moves made by their own and the other delegation. For most of the negotiating delegations in this sample, the reactions follow a comparison of moves made in the immediately previous round (see Druckman & Harris, 1990, for details).

FORECASTING WITH REGRESSION TECHNIQUES

The analysis of variance, discussed in Chapter 4, is based on a linear model that posits a causal relationship between an independent (X) and a dependent (Y) variable. This relationship takes the form of

$$Y = f(X) \tag{1}$$

The function specifies how values of X can be used to calculate values of Y. For ANOVA, the X values are categorical. They are the manipulated conditions of the experiment. The ANOVA calculations show whether the Y variables, measured on either an ordinal or interval scale, are related causally to the manipulated X variables, created by the experimenter. For many problems, however, both the X and Y variables are measured on scales. If the relationship between these variables is assumed to be linear, then values of Y can be calculated from knowledge of values of X according to the following equation:

$$Y = a + b \cdot X \qquad (2)$$

The a and b terms define the function, which, in this case, is linear. This is known as a *regression equation*, where a is the intercept and b is the slope of a straight line. If a and b are known, then for any values of the independent variable X, the corresponding values of Y can be calculated. These calculations can be illustrated with data assembled from moves made during eight rounds of an international multilateral negotiation.

The question of interest is whether concessions made by one team in a particular round could be used to predict the other team's concessions in the same or in a future round. To answer this question, it is necessary to ascertain whether there is a relationship between the concessions made by the two delegations, X and Y, from one round to the next. This can be done by assembling a record of concessions made by both teams over the course of several rounds. The record takes the form shown in Table 6.1 (the higher score indicates a larger number of concessions).

All the data needed to calculate the slope (b) and the intercept (a) are provided by these concession scores. The arithmetic consists simply of taking sums of the columns (ΣX, ΣY), squares of the scores (X^2, Y^2), summing the squared scores (ΣX^2, ΣY^2), calculating cross products ($X \cdot Y$), and summing the cross products ($\Sigma X \cdot Y$). The results of these calculations are plugged into the following equation for the slope (predicting Y values from X values).

$$\beta = N \Sigma X Y - (\Sigma X) \cdot (\Sigma Y) / N \Sigma X^2 - (\Sigma X)^2 \qquad (3)$$

In this equation, the numerator is a covariation term (X and Y scores vary together), whereas the denominator is a variation term (variation among the X scores). The calculations result in a slope of 1.09. A similar equation can be written from the other direction, predicting team X's scores from knowledge of team Y's scores. Those calculations result in a slope of .54.

Table 6.1   Concession Scores by Round

Round	Team X	Team Y
1	6	11
2	7	15
3	8	9
4	9	13
5	12	23
6	13	18
7	13	15
8	16	22

The other calculation is the intercept (a). With b already calculated, it is simply a matter of inserting the means for the X and Y columns of data and inserting them into the following formula:

$$a = Y - b \cdot X \tag{4}$$

The intercept for predicting Y from X is 4.3 (a=15.8 − 1.09 [10.5]). The intercept for predicting X from Y is 1.97 (a=10.5 − .54.[15.8]). We now have all the information needed for the regression equation. This is where the fun begins. First, we can draw the line represented by the equation. This is known as the least squares: It is the best fit for the XY points, minimizing the squared distances between the points and the line. Then, we can use the equation to predict one team's concessions from knowledge about the other's concessions. Let us do both.

Only three items of information are needed to draw the least squares line, the means for each team's concession data and the calculated intercept. The line is drawn through the intersection of the means (in this case, 15.8 and 10.5) and the point on the Y-axis that is the calculated intercept score (in this case, 4.3). The XY scores for the eight rounds are shown in relation to the line in Figure 6.1. The slope (1.09 in this case) determines the amount of change in Y for each unit change in X. To see how this works algebraically, we can plug the values of a and b into the regression equation. If the X value is set at 6 (concession in Round 1), then the value of Y is calculated as follows:

$$
\begin{aligned}
& Y = a \text{ (intercept)} + b \text{ (slope)} \cdot X \text{ (Round 1 concession} \\
& \qquad \text{score for team } X) \\
& Y = 4.3 + 1.09 \cdot (6) \\
& Y = 10.84
\end{aligned}
\tag{5}
$$

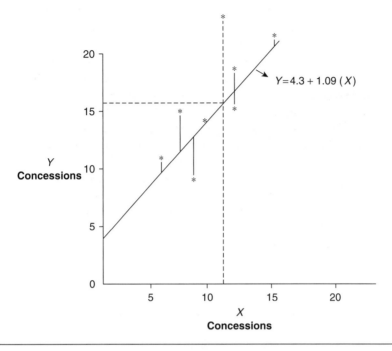

$Y = 4.3 + 1.09\ (X)$

Figure 6.1   Least Squares Line From X to Y

Thus, it can be seen that Y's concession in Round 1 (11) is predicted rather accurately from the information used in the regression equation, only off by a small rounding error of .16. Of course, the same procedures are used for predicting concession scores of team X from information about team Y's scores. If the Y value is set at 11 (concession in Round 1), then the value of X is calculated as follows:

$$X = a\ (\text{intercept}) + b\ (\text{slope}) \cdot Y\ (\text{Round 1 concession score for } Y)$$
$$X = 1.97 + .54\ (11) \tag{6}$$
$$X = 7.91$$

Because X's actual concession score is 6, our prediction is off by 1.91. We did better in the other direction, predicting Y from X.

For most research analysts, regression statistics and least squares plots are obtained with the Statistical Package for the Social Sciences (SPSS). The mechanics for producing these outcomes are shown in the box to follow.

Regression With SPSS

The example in the text consists of two variables, concessions by team X and concessions by team Y. Select **Analyze, Regression, Linear.** Concessions by team Y are referred to as the Dependent Variable (DV) and concessions by team X are the Independent Variable (IV). Of course, the labeling of variables would go in the other direction if team Y's concessions (IV) are used to predict team X's concessions (DV). You may enter more than one independent variable to obtain a multiple regression. To obtain a plot similar to the one we generated by hand (but expressed as cumulative probabilities rather than concession scores), select the **Plots** button and check the box next to **Normal Probability Plot.** Press **Continue,** then **OK.**

The output is as follows.

ANOVA[a]

Model	Sum or Squares	df	Mean Square	F	Sig.
1. Regression	102.744	1	102.744	8.713	.026[b]
Residual	70.756	6	11.793		
Total	173.500	7			

a. Dependent Variable: Concessions Y.
b. Predictors: (Constant), Concessions X.

Coefficients[a]

Model	Unstandardized Coefficients		Standardized Coefficients	t	Sig.
	B	Std. Error	Beta		
1. (Constant)	4.273	4.073		1.049	.335
Concessions X	1.093	.370	.770	2.952	.026

a. Dependent Variable: Concessions Y.

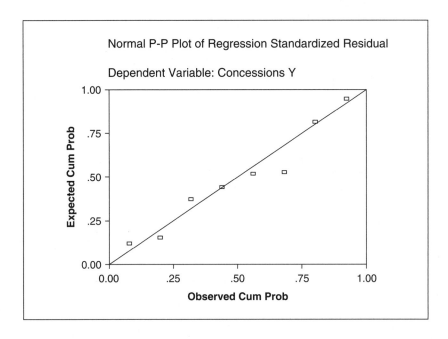

The least squares lines can be used also to calculate the correlation coefficient between X and Y. The correlation is derived from the regression equations; unlike regression, it does not specify direction. It is defined trigonometrically as the cosine of the angle created by the intersection of the least squares lines drawn in both directions (from Y to X and from X to Y). The angle is shown in Figure 6.2.

The correlation is also defined algebraically as the square root of the product of the two betas (from Y to X and from X to Y) as follows:

$$r \text{ (correlation coefficient)} = \sqrt{b_{yx} \cdot b_{xy}}$$

$$r = \sqrt{.54 \cdot 1.09}$$

$$r = \sqrt{.59}$$ (7)

$$r = .77$$

This is a strong correlation, which is significant at the .01 level; with only eight data points, a large correlation is needed for statistical significance. It indicates that the concession scores for team X co-vary with the concession scores for team Y. The higher the correlation, the more likely it is that one team's scores can be predicted from the other team's scores. Thus, the prediction problem, which is addressed by regression, is closely related to the covariation problem, which is addressed by correlation. The regression equation can

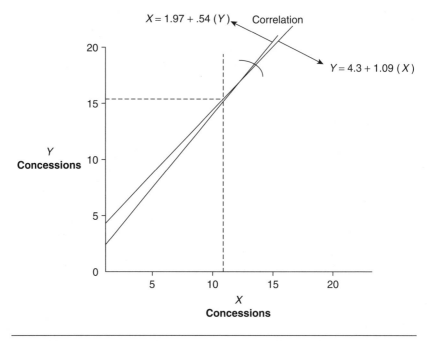

Figure 6.2   Two Least Square Lines From *X* to *Y* and *Y* to *X*

be used to predict the likely concession to be made by team *Y* (e.g., the other team) in Round 9 when a concession of a certain size is made by team *X* (e.g., our team) in that round. The correlation coefficient provides information about the percent of variation in one team's scores accounted for by the other team's scores: This is calculated as the square of the coefficient, which is, in this case, 59%; it is referred to as the *coefficient of determination.* The correlation coefficient can also be calculated by a formula similar to that used for computing beta. The numerator is the same (covariation of *X* and *Y*); the denominator includes the variation terms for both the *X* and *Y* variables. This calculation produces the same result—$r = .77$—as obtained by the square root of the product of the betas shown above. (See also Druckman, 1997a, for visual depictions of bivariate correlations.)

   Suppose that we were interested in knowing whether moves made by one team in the previous round influenced what the other team will do in the next round of negotiation. Often, in negotiation, responses made by one team to another's moves are delayed. When a team decides to "table a proposal," it encourages the other side to reflect on its merits and come back with a response at a later time. These delayed moves and countermoves can be captured by statistical analysis in the form of a lagged correlation: Concessions

Table 6.2   Lagged Concession Scores by Round

Round	Team X	Round	Team Y
1	6	2	15
2	7	3	9
3	8	4	13
4	9	5	23
5	12	6	18
6	13	7	15
7	13	8	22

made by team X in a previous round are correlated with those made by team Y in the next round, as shown in Table 6.2.

Note that team X's scores from Rounds 1 through 7 are correlated with team Y's scores from Rounds 2 through 8. The number of data points is reduced from 8 to 7; concessions made by team Y in Round 1 and those made by team X in Round 8 are excluded from the analysis. The calculation results in a correlation of .50, which is significant at the .125 level. (Because the lagged correlation is directional, it is evaluated with a one-tailed probability level.) The smaller, non-significant correlation indicates that the teams had a stronger influence on concessions made in the same rather than the next round. The time lag highlighted by this analysis suggests that team X's previous moves had some influence on team Y's later moves. The problem with this inference, however, is that other possible influences on team Y's moves are not controlled, leaving open alternative explanations for significant correlations. This is a difference between case-based times-series analysis discussed in this section and experimental designs discussed in Chapters 3 and 4. By addressing threats to internal validity, the experimental designs provide an investigator with more confidence (than the case study) in inferring causation.

A question may arise about whether the concession scores are measured on an interval scale. It may be more appropriate to describe a difference between scores as indicating more or fewer concessions than to assume that we can ascertain precisely the size of the difference between them. The ordering assumption does not preclude statistical analysis; it indicates a preference for nonparametric techniques. These techniques can be used to calculate a correlation between concessions made by teams X and Y. The calculations are performed on ranks with the formula for the well-known Spearman rank-order

Table 6.3   Ranked Concession Scores for Teams X and Y

Team X	Rank	Team Y	Rank	d_i	d_i^2
6	1	11	2	1	1
7	2	15	4.5	2.5	6.25
8	3	9	1	2	4
9	4	13	3	1	1
12	5	23	8	3	9
13	6.5	18	6	.5	.25
13	6.5	15	4.5	2	4

correlation coefficient, indicated by the symbol r_s. It entails converting the scores to ranks from lowest to highest, as shown in Table 6.3.

Note that scores are ranked for each team separately, and the average rank is used for tied scores (i.e., 4.5, 6.5). The calculations simply involve taking the differences between the ranks and adding the sum of those differences. This is a "back of the envelope" calculation done as follows:

$$r_s = 1 - 6 \sum_{i=1}^{N} \frac{d_i^2}{N^3 - N} \tag{8}$$

$$r_s = 1 - 6 \, (26.5)/8^3 - 8$$
$$r_s = 1 - 159/504$$
$$r_s = .684$$

A correlation this large with an N of 8 is significant at the .05 level. Although significant, this correlation is somewhat smaller than the .77 Pearson coefficient, which is significant at the .01 level. The Spearman lagged correlation—calculated between Rounds 1–7 for team X and 2–8 for team Y—is only .52, which, based on an N of 7 observations, is significant only at the .12 level (one-tailed). Thus, similar to the results obtained from the parametric analysis, each team's concessions influences the other's concession behavior more in the same than in the next round of negotiation.

The box to follow shows how three types of correlations are computed with SPSS. The example uses data collected from negotiators representing countries in the Organization for Security and Cooperation in Europe (OSCE) (Sandole, 1998). The correlations—Gamma, Spearman, and Pearson—are also compared.

Calculating Correlations With SPSS

SPSS bivariate correlation calculation routines are illustrated with an example of data collected from OSCE negotiators. After entering the data, select **Analyze, Correlation, Bivariate**. Move as many variables as you wish to test into the **Variables** box. For this analysis, choose the **Pearson** and **Spearman** boxes and evaluate the significance in either direction by selecting a **Two-Tailed** test (i.e., direction is not specified in advance). We also suggest that the **Flag Significant Correlations** box be checked. Press **OK** to receive your output as follows, first for Pearson and then for Spearman correlations.

Correlations

		Ethnic conflicts pose the major threat	NATO can play an effective role in responding to ethnic conflicts	NATO should have been used earlier in Bosnia	NATO peacekeeping should reflect post–cold war realities
Ethnic conflicts pose the major threat	Pearson Correlation	1.000	−.242	.006	−.259
	Sig. (two-tailed)		.084	.965	.064
	N	52	52	52	52
NATO can play an effective role in responding to ethnic conflicts	Pearson Correlation	−.242	1.000	.370**	.259
	Sig. (two-tailed)	.084		.007	.064
	N	52	52	52	52
NATO should have been used earlier in Bosnia	Pearson Correlation	.006	.370**	1.000	.002
	Sig. (two-tailed)	.965	.007		.987
	N	52	52	52	52
NATO peacekeeping should reflect post–cold war realities	Pearson Correlation	−.259	.259	.002	1.000
	Sig. (two-tailed)	.064	.064	.987	
	N	52	52	52	52

** Correlation is significant at the .01 level (two-tailed).

Correlations

		Ethnic conflicts pose the major threat	NATO can play an effective role in responding to ethnic conflicts	NATO should have been used eariler in Bosnia	NATO peacekeeping should reflect post–cold war realities
Ethnic conflicts pose the major threat	Spearman correlation	1.000	−.239	.035	−.272
	Sig. (two-tailed)		.088	.805	.051
	N	52	52	52	52
NATO can play an effective role in responding to ethnic conflicts	Spearman correlation	−.239	1.000	.295*	.125
	Sig. (two-tailed)	.088		.033	.378
	N	52	52	52	52
NATO should have been used earlier in Bosnia	Spearman correlation	.035	.295*	1.000	−.142
	Sig. (two-tailed)	.805	.033		.317
	N	52	52	52	52
NATO peacekeeping should reflect post–cold war realities	Spearman correlation	−.272	.125	−.142	1.000
	Sig. (two-tailed)	.051	.378	.317	
	N	52	52	52	52

* Correlation is significant at the .05 level (two-tailed).

The tables show mirror images of the top right and bottom left, bisected by the perfect correlation of each variable with itself.

For categorical data, a Gamma coefficient can be calculated. For this procedure, a decision must be made about which variables to place in the rows and which in the columns. For purposes of illustration, the Gamma is run on the significant correlation shown above. Select **Analyze, Descriptive Statistics, Crosstabs.** Question 2 is placed the **Rows** box, and Question 3 is in the **Columns** box. Then select the **Statistics** button and choose the **Correlations** and **Gamma** boxes. Press **Continue** and **OK**. The following output compares Gamma with Spearman and Pearson correlations.

Crosstab

Count

		NATO should have been used earlier in Bosnia				
		2.00	3.00	4.00	5.00	Total
NATO can play an	2.00	1		1		2
effective role in	2.50	1				1
responding to	3.00		1	1		2
ethnic conflicts	3.50				1	1
	4.00	2	7	18	4	31
	5.00		3	6	6	15
Total		4	11	26	11	52

Symmetric Measures

Measurement Scale	Type of Correlation	Value	Asymp. Std. Error[a]	Approx. T[b]	Approx. Sig.
Categorical by categorical	Gamma correlation	.416	.192	1.989	.047
Ordinal by ordinal	Spearman correlation	.295	.141	2.187	.033[c]
Interval by interval	Pearson correlation	.370	.139	2.820	.007[c]
N of valid cases		52			

a. Not assuming the null hypothesis.

b. Using the asymptotic standard error assuming the null hypothesis.

c. Based on normal approximation.

Multiple Regression and Correlation

As we noted just above, an analysis of the relationship between two variables in nonexperimental or field settings is problematic. Other sources of influence on these variables are not controlled. In the concession-making example, these sources may include effects on a party's moves from internal policies, constituents' interests, or external events. Adding these influences extends the analysis from a single-variable (the other party's concessions) to a four-variable problem (concessions, policy, constituents, events). The information contributed by these sources enables an analyst to assess the importance of concessions relative to other possible influences. Multiple regression facilitates this sort of assessment. The regression equation is extended to include beta weights for each of the variables as follows:

$$Y = a + b_1 X_1 + b_2 X_2 + b_3 X_3 + b_4 X_4 + e \qquad (9)$$

where Y, the dependent variable, is team Y's concessions, and X_1, X_2, X_3, and X_4 are the sources of influence or independent variables, namely, team X's concessions, team Y's policy, team Y's constituents, and events. The parameters b_1, b_2, b_3, and b_4 are called partial regression coefficients; a is the intercept; and e is the error term.

The regression model is additive. This means that each independent variable (X) contributes an independent source of variation to the dependent variable (Y). In other words, the independent variables X_1, X_2, X_3, and X_4 are uncorrelated. This assumption is satisfied in the experimental factorial designs discussed in the Chapter 4 section "Factorial Designs": The variables are orthogonal, which means independent or uncorrelated. It is rarely satisfied with case study time-series data. In our example, it is unlikely that internal policy is uncorrelated with constituents' interests. This problem is referred to as multicollinearity. At issue is the seriousness of the problem. There are two schools of thought about this problem. One school claims it can be serious (e.g., Cohen, 1968), the other that it is not (e.g., Achen, 1982).

For those who regard this as a serious problem, two solutions have been proposed. Both are attempts to reduce the number of independent variables in the regression equation: One is a statistical procedure known as *stepwise regression,* which eliminates correlated (or redundant) variation by focusing only on the increment in variance explained, not upon the beta coefficients. In describing the procedure, Cohen (1968) states that "since what is added is independent of what is already provided for *(by other variables),* this is a general device for partitioning R into orthogonal *(independent)* portions" (p. 435). An example of application is provided by Krause, Druckman, Rozelle, and Mahoney (1975) in the context of coalition formation. Using stepwise regression procedures, these analysts showed the increment in variance accounted for in decisions by a subjective weighting variable (subjects' estimates of the relative importance of ideology and interests) over and above that accounted for by the values for group ideology and interests assigned by the experiment. Another "solution" consists of combining the correlated variables into an index. Critics of these "solutions" have claimed that they eliminate information that contributes to explanation and prediction: The correlations among the independent variables are rarely high enough to justify excluding some of them from the equation. There is usually more unexplained than explained variance in a relationship between any two variables, and this adds information to the model.

Regarding the question, "What should I do about multicollinearity?" Achen (1982) suggests,

> But multicollinearity violates no regression assumptions. Unbiased, consistent estimates will occur, and their standard errors will be correctly estimated. The only effect of multicollinearity is to make it hard to get coefficient estimates (*beta weights*) with small standard error. But having a small number of observations also has that effect, as does having independent variables with small variances. (In fact, at a theoretical level, multicollinearity, few observations, and small variances on the independent variables are essentially all the same problem.) (p. 82)

Like many other statistical decisions, there is no rule of thumb for providing guidance to the analyst about what to do with correlated variables. My own practice is that elimination of variables from the regression equation depends on the extent to which the correlations between them approach 1. Very strong correlations between independent variables, for example, above .75, suggest that the analyst is using two indicators to measure the same construct. For example, if internal policy and constituents' interests are both indicators of domestic pressures on negotiating delegations, the prudent decision is either to eliminate one of the variables or, perhaps, to combine them into an index. In other cases, when the correlation is below .75, for example, it would seem wiser to include both variables in the equation. But empirical analysis is not the only basis for inclusion or exclusion of variables. Variable specification is also a theoretical problem. Advanced theoretical development on a CA&R topic such as negotiation should guide decisions that are made about variables before the analysis is conducted (see also Lewis-Beck, 1980, for more on how to deal with the multicollinearity problem).

It is a relief to know that a certain amount of multicollinearity does not render regression analysis hopeless. Indeed, if this were the case, regression would rarely be used for analyzing nonexperimental data. However, these problems can be put aside if we are less interested in assessing directionality. Many interesting analytical questions can be addressed with correlation methods. For example, the relative strength of relationships among the variables hypothesized to influence team Y's changes in concessions—changes in the other's concessions, policy changes, changes in constituents' interests, and changes in events— can be estimated. To do this, it is first necessary to calculate all the bivariate correlations among the five change variables. This would produce 10 correlations arranged in a 5×5 matrix, as shown in Table 6.4.

Table 6.4   A 5 × 5 Correlation Matrix

	Y's Concessions	X's Concessions	Policy Changes	Constituents' Interests	External Events
Y's concessions		.60	.34	.42	.62
X's concessions			−.12	−.30	.57
Policy changes				.74	.48
Constituents' interests					.24
External events					

Correlations along the diagonal are all 1.00. The bottom half of this matrix merely repeats these correlations. It can be seen that team Y's concessions are related most strongly to changes in external events (.62). Team X's concessions also correlate strongly with events (.57), and policy changes within Y's nation or organization correlate strongly with changes in Y's constituents' interests (.74). But are these results sufficient to provide an interpretation of influences on team Y's concessions? The answer is that they are not sufficient. It is conceivable that the correlation between team X and team Y concessions is influenced also by external events: Both concession change scores correlate strongly with events (.57 and .62, respectively). Thus, it would be necessary to control the influence of events on both concession scores. This is done with partial correlations.

Partial Correlation

This calculation produces a correlation between team Y (variable 1) and X (2) concessions, controlling for the correlation of these concessions with external events (referred to here as variable 3). All the information for this calculation is contained in the correlation matrix above. The formula is as follows:

$$r_{12\cdot3} = \frac{r_{12}-(r_{13})\,(r_{23})}{\sqrt{1-r_{13}^2}\,\sqrt{1-r_{23}^2}} \qquad (10)$$

The numerator of this formula consists of a subtraction of the correlations of each variable (Y and X concessions) with the control variable (events) from the correlation between X and Y concessions. The denominator essentially removes the contribution of the control variable (3) to both Y (1) and X (2) concessions. The partial coefficient is usually lower than the non-partial correlation, which is .60. Let us see what happens when we plug the coefficients into the formula.

$$r_{12 \cdot 3} = .60 - (.62)\ (.57) \big/ \sqrt{1 - .38}\ \sqrt{1 - .33}$$
$$r_{12 \cdot 3} = .39 \tag{11}$$

Indeed, the correlation is dramatically reduced when external events are controlled, from .60 to .39. This is because the events variable correlates strongly with both team X and team Y concessions. It would have been misleading to conclude that the teams' concessions were highly correlated. The correlation is inflated due to the relationship of concessions with a third variable, changing external events. Partial correlations can be calculated also for the other variables in the matrix, policy change and constituents' interests. These variables are less strongly correlated with concessions and, in fact, show an inverse relationship with team X's concessions. Thus, the partials are unlikely to reduce the correlation between team X and Y concessions by much and may even increase its value. (Partials can actually be larger than the non-partial coefficient when the control variable is not related to one of the other variables or related to them in opposite directions, as in this case.) Higher-order partials that control for several variables simultaneously—such as policy, constituencies, and events—can also be calculated (see Blalock, 1960, for the formulae and other applications). Now that you know how it is done, use the correlations in the matrix to calculate other partials. Then use the various analyses to draw conclusions about the relationship between team X and Y concessions. An SPSS procedure for calculating partial correlations is described in the box.

To calculate partial correlations using the data described above, select **Analyze, Correlate, Partial**. Move two or more variables whose correlation is of interest into the **Variables** box. For instance, in the example shown in this section, move team Y (variable 1) and team X (variable 2) into the Variables box. Then move one or more control variables, or the variables to be kept constant, into the **Controlling for** box. In the present example, move external events (variable 3) into the Controlling for box. Before you press **OK**, makes sure to click on the **Two-tailed** and **Display actual significance level** options. The result of this calculation is a simple two-by-two table, where the partial coefficient between variables 1 and 2 controlling for variable 3 is shown with corresponding levels of significance and the Ns.

Blalock provides a clear exposition of how causation may be inferred from correlations (see Section 19.3 in his 1960 textbook). Drawing on Simon's

(1954) argument, he shows that if certain assumptions are met, it is possible to infer causation, at least in the three-variable case. One assumption is that at least some of the possible causal relationships among the variables do not hold. This means that we can logically assume that, for example, team Y's concessions is the dependent variable and, thus, cannot cause either policy changes or external events. Another assumption is that all other variables influencing Y's concessions are uncorrelated with all other variables affecting policy changes and external events. So, although, we can admit that there are other uncontrolled variables such as team X's concessions and constituents' interests, these variables are assumed to have a random effect on the three variables of interest. In other words, we do not assume, as in the ideal experiment, that all relevant variables have been controlled. We recognize correlations among these variables, as shown in the matrix above, but assume that they do not disturb the pattern of relationships among Y's concessions, policy changes, and events.

Partial correlation helps to control for these "disturbances," bolstering the argument for causal relations in the three-variable case. The challenge of inferring causation for systems of four or more variables is larger. It is more difficult to meet the assumptions. It is also difficult to amass the number of cases needed to overcome inaccuracies due to sampling error. Although problems remain in attempts to use correlation analyses to infer causal relations—these analyses are not substitutes for control group experiments—the student would benefit from reading Blalock's (1960) insightful discussion of the issues.

Multiple Correlation

The partial correlation removes variation contributed by a third or fourth variable to the relationship between two other variables. To use an opposite idea, add variation contributed by a third or fourth variable to a bivariate (two variable) relationship. This is done with the multiple correlation coefficient. The following formula is used to calculate the proportion of variation contributed to team Y concessions (variable 1) by team X concessions (2) and external events (3).

$$R^2_{1 \cdot 23} = r^2_{12} + r^2_{13 \cdot 2}\,(1 - r^2_{12}) \tag{12}$$

where $R^2_{1 \cdot 23}$ is the proportion of variation in 1 contributed by 2 and 3 together, r^2_{12} is the proportion of variation in 1 explained by 2 alone, $r^2_{13 \cdot 2}$ is the additional proportion explained by 3 controlling for 2, and $1 - r^2_{12}$ is the proportion unexplained by 2. All of these coefficients have already been calculated. They can easily be plugged into the formula as follows:

$$R^2_{1 \cdot 23} = (.60)^2 + (.41)^2 \times [1 - (.60)^2] \tag{13}$$

The result of these calculations is .47. This means that 47% of the variation in Y's concessions is explained by the combination of X's concessions and events. The square root of R^2 is comparable to the bivariate (also referred to as zero-order correlations) and partial correlations calculated above. In this case, it is .69. Note that it is only somewhat larger than the three zero-order coefficients, which are .62, .60, and .57. This happens when the set of variables is highly correlated: There is little new variation contributed by adding correlated variables as in this case. When the zero-order correlations are low, the multiple correlation is likely to be much larger than any of them: The multiple correlation reaches its maximum value when all the bivariate correlations in the set are zero.

These analyses can be further complicated by combining the ideas of partial and multiple correlations. Formulae have been developed that add variation contributed by some variables (e.g., policy changes and events) while controlling for other variables (e.g., team X concessions and constituents' interests). A stronger case can be made for causation, however, when the partial-multiple is performed on lagged correlations.

These techniques can be used to detect relationships among actors in highly interdependent interactive systems such as multilateral negotiations. An example of this sort of analysis is an attempt to parse out influences from pairs of nations responding to each other's moves in a negotiation conducted in the 1970s over conventional forces in Europe. Coded transcripts of discussions held among five nations over the course of eight rounds provided the data, which consisted of indices of hard or soft posturing. Bivariate correlations among all pairs of national delegations were arranged in a 5×5 matrix. These correlations were then used to calculate various combinations of multiple (combined effects of several nations' behavior on another nation's responses) and partial (effects of one nation's behavior on another, controlling for the behavior displayed by other nations) correlations.

The calculations allowed us to gauge more precisely the influence between any pair or trio of nations, controlling for the effects of any other nation or nations in the talks. One result indicated that the behavior of the leader of one bloc had a stronger impact on the behavior of the other bloc leader in the next round when the influence of a key bloc ally was removed. The ally attenuated the lagged correlation between the bloc leaders; a bivariate correlation of .47 increased to .63 when the ally's influence was controlled statistically. These analyses allow the researcher to infer causation (lagged correlations) and to reduce spuriousness of relationships between variables (partial correlation). For more details on this study, see Druckman (2002a).

INTERRUPTED TIME-SERIES ANALYSIS

The variables used in the correlational analyses above are measured as changes over time: as changes in concessions, policies, interests, and events. The computations illustrate the use of correlational techniques, including ways of attempting to infer causation. Another way of thinking about some of these variables is as decisions or events that occur at a particular juncture in a sequence of moves made by the parties. For example, an external event may occur abruptly at the beginning of a middle round of the talks. Assuming that the event is attended to by the parties, it interrupts the course of the negotiation. The question of interest is, what impact does the event have on the negotiation process? It is answered by comparing the trend of concessions prior to the event with those that occurred following it. This comparison is similar to the before-and-after designs discussed in Chapter 3. It is evaluated with significance tests rather than with correlational techniques. A data set of events collected during a 6-year period of the conflict between Armenia and Azerbaijan over the territory known as Nagorno Karabakh provides a CA&R example of the way an interrupted time-series design is implemented.

The case provides an opportunity to examine whether various attempts to mediate a serious conflict were effective. Hypotheses about timing and readiness were examined by the investigators. A total of 3,856 events spread over the 6-year period were coded on a scale ranging from most peaceful ($+3$) to most violent (-3). Average monthly scores were calculated for analyses of trends before and after each of six attempts to mediate the conflict. In addition, the impact of another event, intensive warfare occurring between April 1993 and February 1994, was examined: by comparing the average violence scores 6 months before and 6 months after the event. Thus, seven types of "interruptions" or interventions were analyzed: six mediations and the military combat. This approach to analysis is more similar to experimentation than to modeling or regression.

Regarding both the mediations and combat as "treatments," similar to independent variables, the conflicting parties' behavior is compared from before to after the treatments. The data set then consists of dependent variables evaluated in a sequence of before-and-after quasi-experimental designs without control groups (see Cook & Campbell, 1979). Because the mediations and combat are treatments rather than dependent variables, neither the mediators' behavior nor the combat casualties during the period of warfare were included in the events data set. Significance tests were used to assess the changes from before to after an intervention (mediation, combat) in a manner similar to the way data would be analyzed from a laboratory experiment. A difference, however, is that it is easier to establish control groups in laboratory than in field experiments.

The results showed that changes in violent behavior, assessed by the various before-to-after comparisons, occurred only as a result of the combat. None of the six mediations was effective in changing the parties' behavior. The mediators did not create opportunities for settlements by reducing the violence and bringing about the conditions for a ceasefire. On the other hand, the combat did provide the condition for reduced violence and a ceasefire agreement. De-escalation was preceded by escalation to the point of a mutually hurting stalemate (Zartman, 2000). Reasons for this outcome are discussed by Mooradian and Druckman (1999).

Although this study provided insights into a question that has both theoretical and practical implications, it is a relatively weak experimental design. The differences found between the mediated interventions and the combat suggest that the latter had a stronger impact on violent behavior than the former. It does not suggest that escalation (combat) *causes* de-escalation (reduced violence). A causal interpretation of these findings would be more plausible if a comparable case without the interruptions (mediations, combat) was included in the design; specifically, if de-escalation occurs in a time series that includes combat but does not occur in a similar time series that does not include combat. By limiting the analysis to the single case of Nagorno Karabakh, these sorts of inferences are unwarranted. By extending the analysis to another case, they become more plausible. This extension can be made by performing a focused case comparison. The features of this approach are shown in the table in Part IV's introduction, and discussed in a later section of this chapter.

The idea that interruptions are treatments suggests that they have certain characteristics. These include being relatively abrupt, although not necessarily sudden, relevant to an ongoing process, attended to by the parties involved in the process, and hypothesized to have an impact on that process. Other kinds of interruptions of interest to CA&R researchers include worker strikes, government or company collapse, a natural disaster such as an earthquake, the insertion of a peacekeeping force, a summit conference among national leaders, an influx of foreign economic aid, or an entirely new insight into the source of a conflict. Perhaps you can suggest other examples of interruptions that are hypothesized to have an impact on an ongoing series of events or on a conflict resolution process.

BAYESIAN INFERENCE

Another type of time-series analysis, invented by Reverend Thomas Bayes in the 18th century, is based on assumptions about how the past and the present can be used to estimate probabilities about the occurrence of events. Bayes's theory of probability is described in an essay published posthumously in a 1764 issue of the *Philosophical Transactions of the Royal Society of London*. (This article is reprinted in Pearson & Kendall, 1970, pp. 131–153.) It was sent to the Royal Society by Richard Price, who wrote,

> I now send you an essay which I have found among the papers of our deceased friend Mr. Bayes, and which, in my opinion, has great merit. . . . In an introduction which he has writ to this Essay, he says, that his design at first in thinking on the subject of it was, to find out a method by which we might judge concerning the probability that an event has to happen, in given circumstances, upon supposition that we know nothing concerning it but that, under the same circumstances, it has happened a certain number of times, and failed a certain other number of times. (For more on Bayes, consult the information at http://www.history.mcs.st-andrews.ac.uk/history/Mathematicians/Bayes.html.)

The analysis consists of evaluating alternative hypotheses about the occurrence (H_i) or non-occurrence (H_j) of an event, for example, whether or not a coup will occur within a defined period such as 1 year. The first estimates consist of *initial probabilities* that a coup will ($P[H_i]$) or will not occur ($P[H_j]$). These probabilities can be estimated from statistics on coups that have occurred in the country over the last 30 years. The next estimate is referred to as a *conditional probability* and consists of the chances that an event (coup or no coup) will occur if a *particular symptom* is present ($P[EH_i]$). Examples of symptoms related to coups, which are listed in Frei and Ruloff (1989), are cabinet reshuffling (.4 that coup will occur, .3 that it will not occur if there is reshuffling), call for free elections (.6 that a coup will occur, .5 that it will not occur), and purges (.1 and .8, respectively). The estimates for symptoms often come from experts or from expert panels. When the conditional probabilities are taken into account, a *revised initial probability* results ($P[H_iE]$), as calculated by the following formula:

$$P(H_iE) = \frac{P(H_i) \cdot P(EH_i)}{\Sigma\,[P(H_i) \cdot P(EH_i)]} \tag{14}$$

where $P(H_i)$ is the initial probability of the hypothesis H_i, $P(EH_i)$ is the probability that E is a symptom of the event hypothesized to occur, and $P(H_iE)$ is the revised initial probability $P(H_i)$ under consideration of E.

By inserting the initial (.25, .75) and conditional probabilities for reshuffling (.4, .3) into this formula and performing the calculations, the result is .31 that a coup will occur in the next year and .69 that it will not occur. Note that the initial probability for a coup, based on past evidence, increases somewhat when the symptom of reshuffling is taken into account (from .25 to .31). What results emerge when each of the other symptoms, free elections and purges, are included as conditional probabilities?

An example more closely related to CA&R is the chance that a peace agreement will hold through time. Suppose that past experience suggests that peace agreements have held for at least 5 years in one third of the cases examined; thus, $p(H_i)$ is .33 and $p(H_j)$ is .67. Suppose also that an expert panel decided that there are five factors that affect the longevity of agreements. They assigned conditional probabilities to the factors as follows: spoilers (.1 supporting H_i; .6 supporting H_j), schisms within the parties (.2 and .4), regime continuity (.5 and .3), international pressure (.7 and .2), and availability of arms (.2 and .5). The effect of the symptom referred to as spoilers is to reduce the chances of sustaining the agreement from .33 (initial probability) to .08 (revised probability). The effect of the symptom referred to as international pressure is to increase longevity from .33 to .63. When the conditional probabilities of all five symptoms are combined in the formula, the revised probability is .30, roughly the same as the initial probability of .33; apparently the symptoms are offsetting with two favoring longevity—regime continuity and international pressure—and three jeopardizing the agreement—spoilers, schisms, and availability of arms. These are easy calculations. Try estimating the revised probabilities with each of the other symptoms: schisms, regime continuity, and availability of arms.

Bayesian analysis may be understood as an alternative to regression for forecasting events. The beta weights that are derived from a regression analysis are estimates of the relative importance of variables—which may be symptoms in a Bayesian analysis—in predicting a dependent variable (an event in Bayesian terms). When used for forecasting, the regression equation is a linear extrapolation of past trends, considered as the initial probabilities or "priors" in a Bayesian analysis. Unlike regression, Bayesian forecasts are updated probabilities for events that take both past (initial probabilities or "priors") and present (conditional probabilities of symptoms) into account. The updating can be continuous as a result of monitoring situations on a regular basis. Expert judgments can also be refined as new information becomes available. Regression is backward-looking in the sense of relying on a past that cannot be changed, although memories of the past are often adjusted. Bayesian analysis is an attempt to capture present events or processes, focusing attention on changes that have implications for forecasts. CA&R researchers would benefit considerably from this form of diagnostic analysis.

Systematic Expert Judgment

The conditional probabilities in Bayesian analysis are estimated usually by experts. They are asked to identify the symptoms associated with certain events and to answer the following question: What is the probability that each of certain symptoms (e.g., international pressure) would occur, given that a particular event (peace agreement) takes place? The value of the analysis turns on the accuracy of these probability estimates. Thus, it is important to elicit judgments as systematically as possible from knowledgeable people. This means two things: The judging task is carefully structured, and the experts' perspectives or biases are known. A poorly structured, elicitation task introduces random or unpredictable error. Experts' biases introduce systematic or predictable error. These features of expert judgment are discussed in this section.

One rule of thumb according to Frei and Ruloff (1989) is that "several combined assessments promise better results than a single assessment" (p. 138). That said, it is essential to define what is meant by an expert. The intention is not to choose a random sample as in opinion polling, but rather to choose people who have demonstrated specialized knowledge about the subject area. They may be practitioners involved in making similar judgments—for example, about the stability of political regimes—or scholars who have a strong record of academic publications on the subject. In any large group of experts, there is likely to be variation in depth of knowledge about the topic. This can be handled by assigning weights of varying magnitude to the judgments. This is part of the structured task designed to elicit the needed information.

Other ways of structuring the task include the following steps:

1. Divide large questions such as judging the future stability of a country into smaller partial questions, such as judging the chances of nation-wide strikes or the size of wealth differentials.

2. Ask clear questions, preferably with multiple choices specified.

3. Collect the judgments in the form of responses to questionnaire items without protecting anonymity. (Experts should be identified for purposes of weighting and taking perspective biases into account.)

4. Present the results as panel-weighted averages and dispersions (variances or standard deviations).

5. Perform comparisons among the different types of experts, for different questions or judging tasks, and to assess different possible weighting schemes (sensitivity analyses).

This kind of task can be performed with either small or large samplings of experts responding to only a few or many questions. Which way to go depends on the importance of the project and on the availability of resources for implementing it. A larger sampling of people and questions is preferred when feasible. The large sampling serves two purposes, one at an exploratory stage of research, another at a later stage. It is useful to elicit a wide range of opinions early before a research design is set in stone. It is useful to push for a consensus when the judgments are used as data in a research design. This is often done by adding rounds of questioning with feedback, using the results of early rounds to formulate new questions to be used in later rounds. One popular version of this multiround procedure, known as Delphi analysis, is intended to produce consensual judgments used as data in the research projects. (For procedural details, see Frei & Ruloff, 1989, chap. 26; for an example of application in the context of research on political stability, see Druckman & Green, 1986; see also Green & Druckman, 1986, for an analysis of the sources of disagreement in expert panels.)

Despite the frequent use of expert-generated data in CA&R, international relations, and related fields, it is viewed with some degree of skepticism by many social scientists, especially when used as a substitute for "harder" data. Some of the reasons for this skepticism include the following biasing tendencies and task implementation shortcomings:

- A temptation by experts to weight the near term more strongly than the more distant future, leading to reduced confidence in long-term forecasts
- An urge to predict, especially when "don't know" responses are not an option in the questionnaire

- An urge to simplify complicated processes or situations
- The possibility of illusory expertise caused in part by the expert designation—they may feel compelled to offer uninformed opinions on some topics
- An optimism or pessimism bias encouraged by the feedback process where panelists classify themselves in one or the other "camp"
- Sloppy implementation of the judging task, which may occur when researchers try to "cut corners" on spending
- A temptation, perhaps subconscious, to manipulate the results, orienting the opinions in particular directions during feedback sessions
- An over-enthusiasm for the approach, over-selling its scientific value when recruiting participants and when presenting results to colleagues (see the cartoon below)

These shortcomings lead to both random and systematic errors of judgment. They can be addressed through careful information gathering about the experts and structuring of the task by the administrators. Reducing errors is important. But so too is acknowledging that people have opinions, often disagree even on interpretations of scientific results from well-executed experiments, and may indeed be reluctant to accept a group consensus as anything more than an average of varied judgments. Knowing this, and realizing that we do not seek anything approaching perfect accuracy, what can be done to increase the value of this sort of information?

Note: CALVIN AND HOBBES ©1992 Watterson. Reprinted with permission of Universal Press Syndicate. All rights reserved. Reprinted with permission.

First, it is important to realize that expert judgments are perceptions, not facts. This means that they provide useful information for comparison and for inferring meaning in a more qualitative sense. Second, it is important to develop an analytical strategy for processing the perceptual information. This refers to the sort of careful task structuring discussed above; it also refers to the way judgments—as consensus or dispersed—are interpreted in the context of an experimental, case study, or survey design. Third, it is probably better to use expert panels during the more exploratory phases of a research project. This is because the judgments can be used in flexible ways for exploring alternative design and analysis options; by so doing, the researcher avoids the need for obtaining consensual judgments or regarding them as "hard" data. Fourth, and perhaps most important, expert-generated judgments should be regarded as one of several sources of data in a multi-method research design. In addition to being compatible with the theme of this book, a multi-method approach takes the pressure off of any one kind of data collection or analysis procedure. This is advantageous for the "softer" forms of data, including those produced by expert panels. (Further discussion of the strengths and weaknesses of this and other types of data collections is found in the concluding chapter.)

A related methodology that relies less on experts is *focus group research.* This kind of data collection is similar to expert panels with regard to reducing both random and systematic errors: Random errors are addressed by the way the judgment tasks are structured; systematic errors are addressed by taking into account the perspectives brought to the table by the nonexpert members of the group. The use of nonexperts, however, is a feature that distinguishes focus groups from the kinds of panels we have discussed in this section. Many focus group studies are intended to gauge representative public opinion about products, candidates, or issues. For this reason, it is important not to rely only on specialists for the judgments. This feature renders focus groups more similar to survey research discussed in Chapter 5: Purposive sampling designs are more common than random sampling.

Focus groups are becoming increasingly popular in CA&R, especially on topics that have received little attention in the literature. A focus group can contribute ideas that help an investigator sharpen his or her concepts as a preliminary stage preceding a survey or experiment: The group can suggest question wording for surveys or define independent or dependent variables for experiments. As well, the focus group participants may serve as informants about cultural or institutional influences on peace-making interventions or peace-building initiatives. Useful treatments of focus group methodologies can be found in Greenbaum (1997) and Fern (2001).

Qualitative Time-Series Analysis

Qualitative approaches can provide insight into patterns of interaction over time that are difficult to measure with precision. An example is Lepgold and Shambaugh's (1998) analysis of Sino-American relations from 1969 to 1997. These researchers attempted to explain the causes and consequences of reciprocal exchanges between these nations during this period. Their typology of four distinct patterns of exchanges was used to depict changes in the bilateral relationship. The types were defined in terms of expectations about time horizons and the degree to which national decision makers anticipate a reliable stream of benefits from the relationship. Various time periods within the three decades were depicted in terms of one of four cells: short or long time horizons and low or high expectations of benefits.

They showed that when American and Chinese perceptions of their time horizons and the likelihood of reliable streams of benefits diverged, the country that had a longer time horizon or perceived more benefits from the relationship was able to drag out negotiations until a preferable outcome had been achieved. These variables were also shown to influence bargaining strategies, for example, whether they engaged in specific reciprocity (exchanges are precisely matched in terms of equivalence or contingency), diffuse reciprocity (exchanges are not precisely matched), or a mixed strategy. The time series in this study consisted of the three decades of interactions between these governments. The analysis consisted of distinguishing periods within the time series in terms of the four-fold typology and related reciprocity strategies. It sheds light on the sources and consequences of various types of expectations by each party over time.

Leng's (1998) analysis of 12 recurring militarized crises between post–World War II rivals (United States and Soviet Union, India and Pakistan, Israel and Egypt) provides an example of a mixed qualitative-quantitative time-series design. The qualitative analyses consisted of characterizing each of four crises within each rivalry in terms of the dominant influence strategy used by the two nations. The strategies were bullying, reciprocating, trial and error, and stonewalling. For example, the four crises in the U.S.–Soviet relationship with corresponding strategies and outcomes were as follows: Berlin Blockade, 1948–1949 (Soviet bullying, United States reciprocating, leading to a U.S. victory); Berlin Wall, 1961 (Soviet bullying, United States reciprocating, leading to a stalemate); Cuban Missile, 1962 (Soviet trial and error, United States bullying, leading to a U.S. victory), and Middle East Alert, 1973 (Soviet trial and error, United States reciprocating, leading to a U.S. victory). The other two rivalries relied primarily on bullying strategies leading usually to wars or, in one crisis over Kashmir, stalemate. Based on these patterns, Leng concluded that reciprocating strategies are the most effective means of promoting cooperation in militarized crises.

Leng's findings are consistent with quantitative time-series analyses, calculated as weekly average hostility scores during the period of the crisis, also performed by the author on these three rivalries, as well as with the author's earlier findings based on a larger sample of crises occurring between 1816 and 1980 (Leng, 1993). These are particularly interesting findings in light of the selection of cases. They challenge a popular assumption that the most effective means of prevailing in interstate militarized disputes is through the use of escalating coercion. They also reinforce the value of combined analyses for bolstering confidence in findings obtained by only one approach.

PROCESS TRACING

A qualitative analogue to time-series analysis is known as *process tracing.* This is a technique that consists of searching an historical record of events for evidence about whether a postulated process did or did not occur. The record is usually, but not always, developed from bounded cases such as the periods of crisis used in Leng's analysis or from negotiation or mediation interactions. The analysis is facilitated when the choice of events is guided by a framework, as in Druckman's (2001) study of turning points.

In that study, a path of events that occurred in each case of negotiation was developed in terms of a three-part framework: precipitants, departures, and consequences. Precipitants are regarded as causes of changes in the negotiation process; they can be external or internal to the process. An example of an external precipitant in the talks over strategic arms limitations (SALT I) is when the Soviet Union's nuclear arsenal approached parity with the United States' own arsenal. Departures are changes that occur in the process; they may be relatively abrupt or non-abrupt and are regarded as turning points. In reaction to the Soviet nuclear arsenal development (precipitant), domestic pressure increased for a bilateral agreement to suspend further weapons development. This was a rather abrupt departure from a public that placed little pressure on the U.S. administration to seek an agreement. Consequences can be escalatory, leading away from agreements, or de-escalatory, leading toward agreements. The de-escalatory consequence of the departure in this case was that bilateral talks between these nations began, leading to a treaty in 1972. The path is depicted in the following form:

SALT I: external precipitant → abrupt departure → de-escalatory consequence

Another example of process tracing comes from the global environmental talks leading to the signing of the Montreal Protocol in 1987. The procedural or internal precipitant was a succession in the presidency of the conference from the United Kingdom to Belgium. This led to a departure in process, taking the form of European community support for a U.S. plan. The consequence was an agreement on banning the production of certain types of chlorofluorocarbons (CFCs). The path takes the following form:

Montreal Protocol: procedural precipitant → non-abrupt departure → de-escalatory consequence

These kinds of paths were constructed for each of 34 cases of international negotiation in three issue areas: security cases (13), trade cases (10), and political/environmental cases (11). For most cases, paths were constructed for early, middle, and late time periods in the talks; several turning points occurred in most cases. The case paths were then aggregated for each type of negotiation—security, trade, and political—resulting in a "typical" path.

A typical security cases path, which includes longer term consequences (at time $t + 1$), takes the following form:

Security cases: external precipitants $\rightarrow$ abrupt departure in the process $\rightarrow$ de-escalatory consequences at time $t \rightarrow$ de-escalatory consequences at time $t + 1$

Another application of process tracing comes from my research on situational levers of flexibility. Using experimental techniques, an attempt was made to identify the situational variables that had the strongest impact on flexibility in each of four stages of a simulated environmental conference on ozone depletion. Paired-comparison judgments made by the negotiators provided weights for each of several aspects of the situations manipulated in the experiment: The task consists of asking each judge to compare each variable with each of the other variables in terms of relative impact on flexible negotiating (see Guilford, 1954, chap. 7 for details). The paths consisted of the aspect (or variable) with the largest weight. Separate paths were constructed for the sessions that produced an agreement and those that concluded with an impasse.

An example of an agreement path is as follows:

Friendly relations (pre-negotiation stage) $\rightarrow$ peripheral location for the talks (setting-the-stage) $\rightarrow$ limited media coverage (bargaining stage) $\rightarrow$ limited media coverage (endgame stage)

An example of a stalemate path is as follows:

Being the delegation's primary representative (pre-negotiation stage) $\rightarrow$ central location for the talks (setting-the-stage) $\rightarrow$ wide media coverage (bargaining stage) $\rightarrow$ wide media coverage (endgame stage)

Note that the critical variables in these paths are location and media coverage. They appear in Stages 2, 3, and 4 of both paths. The variables identified in each stage influence a process toward an outcome. Together, these influences are considered to be trajectories (or levers) toward eventual agreement or stalemate (see Druckman, 1993; Druckman & Druckman, 1996, for details).

The process can be thought about as a kind of backward tracing from a particular event or outcome through a series of earlier decisions or events arranged chronologically. This can be done with documented cases by developing a chronology of events. Examples of chronologies can be found in the Pew Case Studies in international affairs (1999); a detailed chronology of a negotiation that occurred in 1986 between the Philippines' Aquino regime and an insurgent group is shown in Druckman and Green (1995). It can also be done with observational data by developing a category system for verbal statements and nonverbal behavior as these occur through the course of an interaction.

Carstarphen's (2003) analysis of a dialogue about racial prejudice provides an illustration. The dialogue occurs among a group of men from different backgrounds. It is presented in the well-known documentary film *The Color of*

Fear. She used these interactions to investigate shifts that occur at the individual, relational, and group levels of analysis. The focal event of interest was a shift in relationships at the group level. Moving backward from this outcome, she captured the unfolding group dynamics at each of several points of time. Those dynamics take the form of a path that culminates in the focal event. It takes the following form:

Lee Mun Wah's question to David (D): "What keeps you from believing?" → D's lack of understanding produces an impasse in the discussion → facilitator intervention → D reflects on his own experience and resistance to change → D's reframing → D's new self-awareness → D's acknowledgment of his own prejudices and that racism exists → other members' changed attitudes toward D → African American member acknowledges D's acknowledgment → group shift in D's relationship with the other members.

This path illuminates the group's reaction to a "deviant" member (David), the role played by the facilitator, change at both emotional and cognitive levels, and the role of acknowledgment in changing relationships within the group. It consists of sequential observations or a chain of events, including a conflict resolution intervention, that led to a particular outcome. It is a more complex, process-oriented time series of causation than many correlational analyses involving only a few variables. (For more discussion of the methodology of process tracing, see George & Bennett, 2004, and Stern & Druckman, 2000.)

Pruitt's (in press) analyses of the Northern Ireland peace process and the negotiations between Israel and the PLO in Oslo are other examples of *process tracing.* The tracing (referred to also as a *chain analysis*) is illustrated with the latter process. He traced the negotiation process through four stages by depicting a chain of communication among various official and unofficial actors. Stage I depicts the chain before the talks began as the mediator, Larson, got both sides to the table. It looks like this:

Arafat ← → Mediator ← → Israeli professors ← → Israeli diplomat

Stage II is the situation that developed during the first five sessions. The Israeli foreign minister, Peres, was added at one end of the chain, and the mediator was dropped in the middle. The mediator sat outside the meeting room ready to provide assistance without becoming involved in the discussions.

Arafat ← → PLO delegates ← → Israeli professors ← → Israeli diplomats ← → Israeli foreign minister

Stage III is the situation that developed in the last seven sessions, when Israeli diplomats took over from the professors, who stayed on as advisers.

Arafat ← → PLO delegates ← → Israeli diplomats ← → Israeli foreign minister ← → Rabin

Stage IV is a final telephone conversation between Arafat and Peres, in which the details of the agreement were hammered out. They did not, however, talk directly; interpreters conveyed the messages.

Arafat →   ← Israeli foreign minister ← → Rabin

The progression from Stages I to IV shows how intermediaries drop out of a chain as optimism grows. The progression from Stages I to III shows how unofficial (Track II) diplomacy, involving the mediator and professors, was replaced by official (Track I) diplomacy involving government officials on both sides.

The process tracings illustrated here have several features in common. Each depicts a linear process through chronological time. They all proceed toward an outcome that serves to conclude a process. And each involves a relatively small number of actors or parties. Of interest is the question, Can the technique be used to depict non-linear interactions among many actors in situations in which the process does not conclude with a single outcome? A CA&R example is the problem of coordination among different intervenors (or nongovernmental organizations) working to reduce conflict in the same region. Data collected by Allen Nan (1999) on the activities of many organizations operating in three former Soviet Republics make evident the difficulty of constructing paths to outcomes. For this problem, multiple paths involving various types of intervenors and interventions converged and diverged toward or away from reduced levels of conflict: There were too many actors, activities, and varieties of coordination and complementarity to discern a path proceeding from initial to end states. This sort of complexity is captured better by frameworks that show the interplay among the actors, activities, and processes, including recursive relationships between them (see, for example, Allen Nan, 1999, Figure 8.8.1). Both process tracing and framework construction are examples of ways to envision information to enhance understanding of social processes. (For more on envisioning complex information, see Tufte, 1990.)

Summary

It is time to catch our breath and review what we have learned before moving to the next chapter. We have covered a lot of techniques in this chapter, starting with several types of time-series designs. When a researcher is interested in explaining an historical outcome, he or she may analyze the course of events or processes leading to that outcome. The question of interest is whether the known outcome can be "predicted" from information about those processes. Another purpose served by these analyses is to evaluate alternative explanations for a process that occurred in historical cases. The availability of detailed information about the processes enables a researcher to code the events or moves made by the actors. Examples from correlational studies of negotiation show how these analyses are done. Regression techniques have also been used in forecasting studies. These techniques are based on the assumption that the future resembles the past sufficiently well to allow for extrapolation. The technical aspects of regression are based on the idea of least squares, which is the best-fitting line for a scatter of points plotted on two axes, x and y. The idea of correlation is shown to derive from least squares and is illustrated with data on concessions made by parties in an international negotiation. Problems that arise from correlated independent variables are addressed with partial correlation procedures, which are also useful for thinking about causal relations.

Time-series data are shown as well to be used in experimental evaluations of interventions. Impacts of interventions such as mediation can be assessed with before-and-after comparisons of trends. Although these are often weak designs, especially when implemented without control groups, they have the advantage of focusing an analyst's attention on events that can alter—or interrupt—a process in important ways. The process-altering features of particular events are also the focus of Bayesian analysis. This form of forecasting entails monitoring situations on a regular basis. It highlights the role played by indicators of key events such as coups, wars, or the unraveling of a peace agreement. Like regression, it takes the past into account. Like interrupted time series, it pays attention to key events. Unlike both of those approaches, however, Bayesian analysis revises probabilities based on past events with information from indicators or "symptoms" of a possible future event.

Data used in time-series designs are often collected from experts. Indeed, specialists are used to provide estimates for a wide variety of social science research problems, especially in areas where it is difficult to assemble the kind of data collected from experiments, surveys, or archival resources. For this reason, it is important to define clearly what is meant by an "expert" and to structure the data collection tasks with care. Ways to avoid or reduce the systematic and random errors that accompany expert judgments were discussed. In addition, the related methodology of focus groups was introduced. That approach relies more on representative than on expert judgment and is, thus, similar to public opinion polling as discussed in Chapter 5.

Alternatives to the precise coding needed to perform the quantitative analyses of time-series data are qualitative approaches. These approaches are particularly useful for analyzing complex interactions among many parties or settings where detailed information is not available. Theoretically inspired typologies or frameworks replace coding systems as analytical tools. They have been shown to distinguish among patterns of exchange between nations, bargaining and influence strategies, and the kinds of events and decisions that precede turning points or shifts in group processes as well as the consequences of those changes. When it is feasible to depict events in the form of a traced path in chronological time, these approaches suggest causal processes involving many more elements than is usually measured by correlation analyses. It would seem that the advantages of qualitative time-series analysis complement those of the quantitative techniques (a useful resource for computer analysis of qualitative data is Weitzman & Miles, 1995).

Now it is your turn. Devise a CA&R time-series problem that can be analyzed with several of the techniques discussed in this chapter. How about trying your hand at forecasting an event—of your choosing—that can alter a process (Bayesian techniques), evaluating its impact on that process (interrupted time series), and then devising a path of the events and decisions that led to its occurrence or to an outcome that emanated from it (process tracing)? What is to be concluded about the likelihood that the event will occur, its impact on a process, and the way it emerged from a sequence of prior events? Other challenges are presented by discussion questions on these topics collected at the end of the next chapter.

7

Comparative
Case Study Approaches

This chapter focuses on the comparative case study approaches referred to in the Part IV introduction table titled "Features of Four Methodological Approaches" as *focused case comparisons* and *aggregate case comparisons*. These approaches are designed to compare different cases that may share some features or characteristics. The chapter begins with a discussion of a small number of similar or different cases.

Focused Case Comparisons

Research on a small number of cases is preferred when the problem is difficult to analyze with a large number of cases. Examples of such problems include (a) explorations of aggregate systems-like units, referred to also as *holistic systems* (b) deep probes into cultural practices or behaviors and (c) problems seeking causal explanations of variation between closely matched units of analysis. In this section, special attention is given to the methods used for exploring the kinds of problems posed by the third example. The features of this approach are shown in the third column of the Part IV introduction table titled "Features of Four Methodological Approaches."

Another enhancement to the traditional case study is the structured, focused case comparison, which I will refer to in this section as the focused comparison. Similar to the enhanced case study discussion in Chapter 6, the focused comparison approach uses theory or concepts to guide case selection and description. Unlike the enhanced case study, this approach includes case comparisons that emphasize matching of cases. These features of focused comparisons contribute to theory and cumulation in research. Recent applications to problems in CA&R promote the value of the approach to the field. Several of these applications are described in this section following a discussion of the history and procedures for implementing the approach.

The focused comparison is an attempt to impose the logic of experimentation on a small number of cases (see Chapter 3). This logic was developed by John Stewart Mill, who, in his book *A System of Logic* (1843), distinguished between the method of difference and the method of concomitant variation. The method of difference, which is referred to by Faure (1994) as the Most Similar Systems Design (MSSD), applies when only a few cases are available for analysis. The method of concomitant variation is used in the context of a large number of cases that can be analyzed with statistical methods such as the partial correlation (see Chapter 6). Lijphart (1975) compares these methods as follows:

> [the] method of testing hypothesized empirical relationships among variables on the basis of the same logic that guides the statistical method, but in which the cases are reflected in such a way as to maximize the variance of the independent variables and to minimize the variance of the control variables. (p. 164)

Although the logic of the methods is similar, MSSD relies on case selection of a small number of similar cases, whereas the method of concomitant variation relies on representative sampling of different cases. The idea of matching is central to MSSD. Cases are chosen because they are similar in most respects. The cases differ on only one or a few independent variables. The difficulty, of course, is deciding which variables to explore and which cases to choose for the exploration. The idea of representative sampling, as in survey research, increases variation in the independent variables, creating a Most Different Systems Design (MDSD). But the MDSD approach can also be used with a small number of cases in order to examine "typical" cases with contrasting profiles of variables. These issues are discussed further in this section, as we focus attention primarily on the small-*n* MSSD approach. (See also Faure, 1994, for an interesting discussion of the way these approaches address problems in the field of comparative politics; for further applications of both the MSSD and MDSD approaches in this field, see Pennings, Keman, & Kleinnijenhuis, 1999, chap. 3.)

PROCEDURES

George (1979) developed procedures for conducting a focused-comparison (MSSD) study. He discussed the procedures in the framework of three phases. Phase I, design, consists of five tasks, as follows.

Task 1. Specify the research problem by identifying the class of events on which the study will focus, searching for existing theory that bears on the events, and singling out aspects of the existing theory for exploration.

Task 2. Specify the variables—independent, intervening, and dependent—that enter into the controlled comparison of cases.

Task 3. Select appropriate cases for the controlled comparison. Further, the universe from which the cases are to be selected should be well defined such that the cases to be compared come from the same class or universe of cases.

Task 4. Consider how to discover causal relations between various outcomes and configurations of independent and intervening variables.

Task 5. Formulate the questions to be asked of each case in the controlled comparison (the data requirements).

The second phase involves the implementation of the case studies. Each case is examined from the standpoint of the data requirements or questions developed in Task 5 of the first phase. The challenge for the investigator is to develop a plausible causal interpretation consistent with the available data. Plausibility "is enhanced to the extent that alternative explanations are considered and found to be less consistent with the data" (George, 1979, pp. 57–58). The criteria for judging plausibility differ from the statistical methods discussed in earlier sections. They are based on standards of historical scholarship and are subject to reassessment when new historical material becomes available. Thus, implications of focused-comparison studies for theory development are provisional. They depend on the plausibility of explanations for outcomes obtained in particular cases.

The third phase consists of developing the theoretical implications of the case studies. The analyses performed in the second phase are intended to address, refine, or elaborate the theory articulated in the first phase. However, it is unlikely that these analyses will provide a clear confirmation or invalidation of the theory. This is due both to the formulation of the theory—few CA&R theories are formulated precisely enough to permit rigorous testing—and to the limited number of cases evaluated. Yet, even with these limitations, focused comparisons can identify various causal patterns that may occur for the events of interest. The key is the differences among the cases. Insofar as the cases differ only on a few variables, the plausibility of particular causal patterns is strengthened. As in laboratory experiments, differences in patterns (or on dependent variables) can be attributed to these differences (in independent or intervening variables). According to George (1979), these implications contribute to contingent generalizations, which are the discriminating explanations sought in many of our analyses of conflict. These implications may become clearer with a few examples of studies using the approach.

EXAMPLES OF FOCUSED-COMPARISON STUDIES

One of the more interesting uses of the focused-comparison approach is Putnam's (1993) comparison of two Italian regions. He compared the legislative system of a northern and a southern Italian province in terms of 12 indicators of performance: cabinet stability, budget promptness information services, quality of reform legislation, legislative innovation, day care centers, and so on. The two regions were similar in most aspects of their political systems. They differed, however, in terms of economic development, with the north outpacing the south. They were also found to differ on the development of a civic culture, which is indicated by such activities as newspaper readership, association membership, and preference voting (choosing between voting for parties or individuals). These two differences were the independent variables in the focused comparison.

He found that the two regions differed on many of the performance indicators, which were the dependent variables. If, as Putnam (1993) argued, the differences between these regions are limited to economic and civic development, then either or both of these independent variables could be used as an explanation. Using partial correlation and other methods of control, he discovered that civic culture was the better explanation: When levels of civic culture were controlled, economic development made little difference in performance. Searching for an interpretation of these findings, he showed how the civic cultures of these regions developed differently over the course of a century. For example, the north had always been an independent entity, enabling them to build what he calls "social capital," whereas the south was colonized.

The limited number of cases used in this study makes it vulnerable to plausible alternative explanations for the findings. Indeed, Tarrow (1996) suggested that state development, which refers to political institutions, precedes and is concomitant with the development of a civic culture. He thought that this is a better explanation for Putnam's (1993) findings. Thus, we have contending explanations, each one considered to be a major factor in political performance: culture, economics, and institutional structure. With regard to this study, the analysts agree that economic development is not a strong explanation for the findings but disagree on the relative importance of culture and structure.

Three studies illustrate the use of focused comparison in different arenas: discretionary influence over selection and promotion in political and military institutions, coordination among conflict-resolving organizations in the former Soviet Union, and conditions that influence base-rights negotiation processes.

The research issue in the selection and promotion study was the extent to which regime (or presidential) ideological preferences influenced promotions at the top levels of the Brazilian military and cabinet. A first analysis focused on cabinet-minister appointments. Four regimes, in office from 1967 to 1985, were the matched "cases." It was argued that these regimes were similar in most respects but differed on policy preferences: The sharpest policy discontinuity occurred between the Geisel (1974–1978) and Figueiredo (1978–1985) regimes. Hypotheses specified relationships between regime preferences and background characteristics of cabinet members. Examples of background variables included U.S. experience, international positions, and technical experience. Results showed that a smaller set of the background variables discriminated among the regimes as expected by the hypotheses. The distinction between the Figueiredo and Geisel regimes was particularly clear with 83% of the cases classified correctly by the discriminant analysis. (See Klecka, 1980, for technical details; see the box below for a brief description.) The strongest discriminating variables were U.S. experience and urban versus rural background: Figueiredo ministers had more U.S. experience and urban backgrounds.

The aim of *discriminant analysis* is to ascertain whether it is possible to distinguish statistically between two or more groups in the sense of being able to tell them apart. For example, we may want to know whether very violent cultures can be distinguished from moderately violent, and non-violent cultures on the basis of a set of behaviors or characteristics (e.g., schisms, crime rates, frequency of intergroup conflict, preparations for warfare, marketplace economies). By weighting and combining a set of measured behaviors or characteristics in a linear fashion, the technique identifies one or more dimensions on which violent cultures are clustered at one end, non-violent cultures at the other, and, perhaps, moderately violent cultures in between. The technique contains features of both the analysis of variance (see Chapter 4) and correlational analysis (see Chapter 6). Like ANOVA, it discriminates among the conditions of an independent variable. The classification function shown in Table 7.1 illustrates this feature. Like correlation, it assesses relationships among the measured variables. An object of the analysis is to discover the smallest subset of variables that effectively discriminates between the cultures or groups.

Table 7.1 shows that, based only on information about four background variables (urban-rural, U.S. experience, professional clubs, and international positions), 83% (34 of 41) of the cabinet ministers were placed in the correct regime. Similar discriminations were obtained in two other analyses.

Of the 316 generals on active duty during each of the regimes examined in the study, 54 received political appointments. The research question of interest was how a president decides who from among a list of eligibles will receive

Table 7.1   Classification Results for Predicted and Actual Regime

		Predicted Regime	
Actual Regime	*No. of Cases*	*Figueiredo*	*Geisel*
Figueiredo	22	18	4
Geisel	19	3	16

Source: Druckman and Vaurio (1983).

appointments and what criteria distinguish between the two samples, appointees and non-appointees. The analyses consisted of age-cohort comparisons. Each of the 54 political appointees was matched with a non-appointee according to regime or promotion to current grade level, year of last promotion, and age. This procedure was designed to control for as many variables as possible, other than the critical factors being compared. It was intended to make the two samples as much alike as possible, much more alike than if they had been selected independently. Thus, this qualifies as a focused comparison. Using matched-pairs *t* tests, appointees and those eligible for appointment were compared for each of three types of regimes, nationalist-military, civilian, and internationalist-military. These regimes were quite similar except for worldviews. The strongest results were obtained for the nationalist-military regimes: Appointees in these types of regimes had less U.S. experience and fewer technical courses than the matched sample of non-appointed eligibles.

A third analysis examined criteria used by the different regimes for selecting top-level general-officers. Very good discriminations were found for a set of eight background factors: 84% of the generals were classified correctly by regime; 77% of generals were correctly classified by types of regime (civilian, internationalist, nationalist). The internationalist regimes of Branco and Geisel used U.S. experience, technical courses, and academic distinctions as criteria for promotion. They also promoted candidates more quickly than presidents of other regimes. The civilian regimes emphasized foreign medals and de-emphasized courses taken in Brazil and military courses in general. Presidential preferences were reflected more in the later than in the early years of a regime's tenure.

All of these results make evident the importance of regime ideology as the critical factor in decisions. Confidence in this conclusion comes from the careful matching of cases and regimes (focused-comparison designs) and from the analysis techniques that provided precise distinctions among the variables (discriminant analysis, matched-pair *t* tests, partial correlations; see Druckman & Vaurio, 1983, for more details).

A qualitative focused comparison is illustrated by Allen Nan's (1999) study of coordination among conflict-resolving organizations. She examined the work being done by nongovernmental organizations (NGOs) in three former Soviet republics, Abkhazia, South Ossetia, and Transdniestria. The research focuses attention on processes of complementarity and coordination among these organizations. Of special interest in this study was whether the differences among the three cases influenced these processes. Because very similar cases were chosen, the differences were limited to only a few dimensions. The cases were matched on types of parties, interests, time, and power. One of these dimensions, or independent variables, was the long-term unofficial facilitated joint analysis among negotiators (LUFJAAN, referred to also as Track 1½ diplomacy). This occurred in two of the three cases; Abkhazia was the exception. The cases also differed on the key dependent variable, progress toward a cease fire; unlike the other cases, Abkhazia made little progress. Thus, a relationship was inferred between LUFJAAN and reduction of violence.

A third focused comparison consisted of an analysis of three cases of base-rights talks with the United States—Greece, the Philippines, and Spain. These cases had many similarities. Each of the countries negotiated with the United States; the power asymmetries were similar; the sovereignty versus security issue was central in all the cases, as was the legacy of relationships with the United States; and logistics, grants, and time period issues were almost identical. A key difference, however, was the political cultures of these host countries. These cultures seemed to have less impact on negotiation processes and outcomes than the common factors. All the cases contributed to lessons about base-rights negotiation processes. Particularly useful lessons were developed about delegations, procedures, tactics, and the use of language.

This study is an application of the focused-comparison methodology geared toward developing broader insights by combining similar cases. The decision to combine the cases followed an assessment of the role played by political cultures in negotiation. When the independent variable (in this case, cultures) has negligible effects on the dependent variables (in this case, process), then it is feasible to perform analyses that combine the data collected from similar cases (see Druckman, 1990).

MOST DIFFERENT SYSTEMS DESIGNS

The other method discussed by Faure (1994) as well as by Pennings et al. (1999), and proposed originally by Mill (1843), is a comparative design that emphasizes differences rather than similarities among cases. As mentioned earlier, this is referred to as the Most Different Systems Design (MDSD) method. For large-N designs, this is the method of concomitant variation:

Correlations are computed between variables measured on many different cases. For small-n studies, this is the opposite of the focused-comparison approach: Cases are selected because they differ on many variables except for the variable or process of interest. For example, an investigation into the relationship between negotiation processes and outcomes may select cases that differ on a variety of contextual and cultural factors but used similar negotiation processes. An example of such a comparison is the peace processes conducted in Mozambique and in the Ecuador-Peru conflict. The investigator then determines whether the relationship between process (held constant) and outcome (free to vary) is the same for these cases. If both pairs of cases show the same relationship between process and outcome, this would be a robust test of the hypothesis. A stronger evaluation of the hypothesis would combine the most similar (focused comparison) and most different systems designs. A most similar comparison may be between the matched historical cases of Nagorno Karabakh and the conflict between the Republic of Georgia and South Ossetia. If the same relationship between process and outcome is found for the focused comparison—the finding occurs in both controlled and non-controlled comparisons—the investigator has confidence in the generality of this finding.

The MDSD approach has been used also to evaluate exemplar cases for typology development. An exemplar is a case chosen to represent a particular type of conflict resolution process. Weiss's (2002) study of mediator sequencing strategies illustrates this approach. Each of the three sequencing strategies examined was represented by a case: Mozambique (gradualism), El Salvador (boulder in the road), and Angola (committee approach). Content analysis of the negotiation processes confirmed the approach used and identified a number of factors that discriminated among them, for example, type of most contentious issue, type of reasoning, trust building, and ripeness in the process. These differences were then used to construct profiles of indicators for the three strategies.

Another project compared the peace processes in Nagorno Karabakh with Mozambique, two very different cases. The former is an example of a cease fire with no improvement in the relationship between the parties; the latter is an example of an agreement that led to social and political change. This difference is referred to also as negative (Karabakh) and positive (Mozambique) peace (see Galtung, 1969, for this distinction). The analyses included process coding for the relative incidence of competitive and cooperative behavior as well as a description of the post-negotiation conditions in the two cases. Contrasting profiles showed a difference between the exemplar cases, one that highlighted the consequences of settlements, the other the consequences of resolutions. (See Druckman & Lyons, 2004, for details of the study; see also Druckman, 2002c, for more on the distinction between settlements and resolutions.)

Aggregate Case Comparisons

Another approach to case study research is the analysis of a large number of dis-similar cases in an aggregate comparison study, also known as the method of concomitant variation. With their emphasis on external validity, these studies are designed to generate findings that have wider relevance than the small-n focused-comparison study. (See the fourth column of the table in the intro-duction to this part for a listing of the key features of this approach.) Their wider relevance is derived from attempts to explain or to identify the sources of variation among the different (MDSD) cases. We are distinguishing between methods on the basis of the focus of the variation in the cases (MDSD) or in the variables (MSSD).

Large-N studies are preferred when (a) the investigation deals with smaller units such as individuals or small groups as in negotiation simulations or events accumulated across cases, (b) the purpose of the investigation is to eval-uate theoretical propositions about social behavior, and (c) the researcher seeks causal explanations for variation between cases that are difficult to match on most variables. Aggregate comparisons are in the etic tradition of comparative research (see Chapter 1). The logic of MDSD applies to both comparisons between a small number of different cases and a large number of different cases (see Faure, 1994). The large number of cases increases the scope of the com-parison and permits the use of statistical techniques for evaluating relation-ships. We are trading insights about a sampled universe for insights about any case within that universe. For example, we can do research aimed at learning about types of cultures, such as individualist versus collectivist, or at learning about a particular culture such as the Amish. The former investigation is in the etic tradition of research; the latter is in the emic tradition.

The use of statistical techniques for large-N case studies turns on two issues. One issue concerns the basis for comparison. The same questions should be asked, and the same content codes should be used for each case. Similar in some ways to the analytical case study method discussed in the Chapter 6 sec-tion titled "Theory and the Case Study," this method consists of providing the same lens through which the diverse cases are viewed. Another issue concerns sampling. It is important to define a universe of cases from which a sample is drawn for coding and analysis. The universe might consist of all documented cases of international mediation available in archival sources, or all cases of a particular type, such as third-party intervention in inter-governmental talks on security issues. When a population of cases is defined in this way, inferences can be drawn, and powerful statistical techniques can be used to reach robust con-clusions. (See Bercovitch & Langley, 1993, for an example of the way sampling is done in a study of international mediation.)

There are many examples of comparative case research in international relations (IR). Considerably fewer attempts have been made to accumulate cases on domestic issues: The effort to assemble 20 case transcripts for analyses of divorce mediation is an example of what can be done in this domain (Donohue, 1991). Analyses of the IR databases appear frequently in the journal of the International Studies Association (the *International Studies Quarterly*), in the journal of the Peace Science Society (the *Journal of Conflict Resolution*), or in the *Journal of Peace Research*, a journal of the International Peace Research Institute in Oslo, Norway. These sources can be consulted for applications of the methodology in various domains of IR. Most applications are rooted in the tradition of cross-sectional events data, which began with McClelland's (1976) World Events Interaction Survey. Highlighting indices of competitive and cooperative behavior, this survey provides coded data relevant to international CA&R issues. It has stimulated numerous studies over the course of more than two decades.

Perhaps the most extensive quantitative analyses of mediation is the work by Bercovitch and his associates (Bercovitch & Houston, 1996; Bercovitch & Langely, 1993). These investigators assembled a data set of many disparate cases on mediation—295 conflicts between 1945 and 1995—to evaluate hypotheses with statistical tests. Theoretically inspired hypotheses have also been evaluated with more limited data sets focused on fewer cases over time (Ayres, 1997; Carment & Rowlands, 1998; Goldstein & Pevehouse, 1997; Mooradian & Druckman, 1999). Further advances have been made by automating the coding process with computer programs that create events data from machine-readable text. The recent study reported by Schrodt and Gerner (2004) demonstrates how a particular computer program, referred to as the Kansas Event Data System (KEDS), is used to evaluate process-related hypotheses about mediation. They examined the time delay in the effects of mediation on the level of violence over time. A technically sophisticated analysis of this sort produces a complex, contingent finding: A reduction in violence was associated with mediation combined with conflictual action directed toward both antagonists plus cooperative action directed toward the weaker party.

Another source of data for large-N analyses is ethnographies (see the next chapter). An example is the Human Relations Area files, an indexed collection of ethnographic texts assembled and updated by a group at Yale University and deposited at many university libraries. These files were used for a cross-cultural study of resource unpredictability, mistrust, and war by Ember and Ember (1992). They used the information to code warfare and resource problems across 186 societies. A series of multivariate analyses produced path coefficients (causal models) showing that fears of others and of nature were the strongest predictors of war in this sample. More generally, fear of the future rather than current problems of scarcity appears to be the primary motive for going to war. Another study, outside of CA&R, also demonstrates the value of ethnographic reports for performing large-N (correlation and regression) analyses. Hodson, Welsh, Rieble, Jamison, and Creighton (1993) analyzed

90 cases assembled from 79 separate ethnographies to explore hypotheses about relationships among worker solidarity, autonomy, and participation. They found that autonomy or independence in the workplace had no effect on worker solidarity, but participation in work groups had a positive effect on at least one aspect of solidarity. These results question the idea that increased worker autonomy may undermine solidarity. It may be that workers can have autonomy without forfeiting solidarity, and both are needed to protect workers from abusive management practices.

Analyses of problems of violence have been approached in other ways. An early example is the systematic statistical analyses of a large number of cases performed by Bloomfield and Beattie (1971) to distinguish among cases in terms of their similarities and differences. They developed a computerized model, referred to as CASCON, for depicting and comparing international cases. In its initial version, CASCON consisted of 482 factors divided into three phases of crisis. Fourteen cases were coded in terms of whether each factor tended toward or away from violence. Although valuable for descriptive analyses of particular cases, the research was not useful for making inferences about samples of cases drawn from a population. In addition to the lack of a sampling frame, the study measured too many factors on too few cases: Similar to the use of replications in experiments, there must be many more cases than variables, usually a ratio of at least 3 cases to each variable. My reply to a question about an appropriate number of cases is that it depends on the number of variables being measured. What counts is the ratio, not the absolute number.

Other attempts to distinguish cases suffer from the same problem. These studies provide useful taxonomies that serve as guides for analysis (Druckman & Iaquinta, 1974; Frederiksen, 1971; Sells, 1966) or profiles that distinguish different kinds of exemplar cases as discussed earlier (e.g., Druckman & Lyons, 2004). They do not provide findings that serve to confirm or disconfirm the distinctions made among the relatively small number of cases used. Confirmatory evidence is provided by studies that adhere to the coding and sampling considerations mentioned above. These considerations are implemented in a series of steps.

The first step is to define research questions that can be addressed with comparative data sets. The second step is to construct a framework to serve as a structure for addressing these questions. Third, the analyst should translate the various parts of the framework into variables that can be coded with case material. The fourth step is to define a universe of cases from which analysis samples would be taken. The cases chosen should represent a larger set of cases in terms of domain or issue area and should be documented sufficiently to allow for reliable coding of variables. The fifth step is to develop an analysis plan that may include appropriate statistical techniques. And sixth, the analyst should interpret the results in terms of their implications for the research questions and framework. The implications should apply broadly over the subject domain represented by the sampled cases. This is perhaps the primary advantage of large-N comparative analyses of diverse cases.

Our evaluation of a framework of types of international negotiations provides an example of how these steps are implemented. The research question asked was: Could cases be distinguished in terms of the categories of the framework of negotiating objectives proposed by Iklé (1964)? The framework provides five categories of objectives: negotiations intended to re-distribute resources, those intended to extend the previous terms of an agreement, those designed to normalize relations between nations following conflict, talks intended to generate innovative approaches or institutions, and those that serve purposes other than reaching agreement (referred to as "side effects" negotiations). Each of these objectives is defined by Iklé in terms of its main characteristics. These characteristics were used to categorize the sampled cases prior to analysis. Each case was coded in terms of 16 categories derived from the Sawyer-Guetzkow (1965) framework of negotiation (shown in Chapter 2): six codes on parties, two on issues, two on timing, two on process, two on the negotiating environment, and two on outcomes.

The 30 sampled cases were drawn randomly within clusters from a universe of 176 cases listed in the 1993 catalog of the Pew Case Studies in International Affairs. (The sample consisted of 17% of the case studies.) The cluster sampling method was designed to increase the representativeness of the sample in terms of region and type of issue. The cases are distributed fairly evenly across the regions of the world: Africa (5), the Americas (7), Asia (5), Europe (4), the Middle East (4), and other (5). The sampling of issue types was proportionate to the distribution in the universe of cases: 16 trade cases, 9 security cases, 4 on environmental issues, and 1 on hostage negotiations. (The ratio of 61 trade to 37 security cases in the population is comparable to the 16:9 ratio of cases in the sample.) The case documentation was adequate for analysis. Each case is coherently and uniformly organized, concise, and readable. Many of them use primary sources such as interviews with the participants as their source of information. They are more descriptive of *what* happened than analytic about *why* it happened, and the set shows considerable diversity in topic and geographical region. As materials for research, they provide information that is useful for coding in terms of an investigator's conceptual framework.

The analysis plan consisted of several parts. First, the 30 cases were categorized in terms of Iklé's (1964) five objectives: innovation (8), redistribution (10), extension (5), normalization (5), and side effects (2). Each case was coded in terms of the 16 categories from the Sawyer-Guetzkow (1965) framework. (The ratio of cases to variables was 2:1.) A smaller sample of the cases was used to assess the extent to which coders, working independently, agreed on their judgments. For most categories, agreement exceeded 90%. Cases were assigned randomly to each of four coders. Several statistical tests were used. Two of the techniques were computed directly on the coded data—correlations and discriminant analysis. Three other techniques were derivative in the sense of being computed on the correlations (multidimensional scaling; see the box below for a brief description of this technique) or on the location of cases in the obtained multidimensional space (significance tests, cluster analysis). All of these analyses addressed the following questions: How alike are the cases? Can they be distinguished in terms of Iklé's negotiation types?

Multidimensional scaling (MDS) is a class of techniques that analyze distances among a set of objects. The objective of the analysis is to indicate similarities or differences among the objects. The output of the analysis consists of a map or configuration of locations for the objects that can be, for example, cities, nations, linguistic units, adjectives, political candidates, types of peacekeeping missions, or cases of negotiation or mediation. Distances among these objects are understood in terms of spatial dimensions that, when limited to two, take the form of a vertical and horizontal axis. The dimensions are thought to reflect a "hidden structure" in the data, and often make the data easier to comprehend. As in cluster and factor analysis, MDS reduces the data, which may consist of correlations among ordinal or nominal variables, to a coordinate system thought to capture the complexity of relationships among the variables. Data sets vary in terms of the number of dimensions that account for the variation in the objects. A measure of goodness of fit, referred to as "stress," provides a guideline for ascertaining the number of dimensions needed. However, there is a trade-off between variance accounted for and interpretability: Adding dimensions may account for more of the variation in the data but may also be largely uninterpretable (Kruskal & Wish, 1990).

I have found MDS to be a useful approach in research on international negotiation as described in this section as well as in studies of peacekeeping (Diehl, Druckman, & Wall, 1998). The study on peacekeeping showed the value of rotating the axes orthogonally (both axes move together without altering the point of intersection or origin) for improving the interpretation of the dimensions, which were type of process and type of party. Another study on a different topic also illustrates this point. In his study of conflict over online privacy, Leizerov (2001) identified two MDS dimensions referred to as "building trust" and "complying with rules." However, when the axes were rotated, he was able to distinguish among types of industries in terms of their compliance with the rules of the institutional system. These findings called attention to various cleavages among types of companies within the Internet industry with implications for Internet users and for federal compliance policies.

The results showed that the cases were clearly distinguished in terms of the categories of negotiating objectives. The multidimensional scaling (MDS) solution produced distinct clusters of cases organized by negotiation type: going from left to right in the MDS plot, innovation cases, redistribution cases, extension cases, cases illustrating side effects, and normalization cases (see Figure 1 in Druckman et al., 1999). Support for this finding was also obtained from the discriminant analysis: 21 of 27 cases were classified correctly based only on coded information (see Table 3 in Druckman et al., 1999). These are impressive results. They support Iklé's (1964) claim of five distinct objectives. In addition, a sixth objective was identified as multilateral regime talks. These were negotiations popular in the 1980s, two decades after Iklé wrote his book. The four cases in this category were outliers in the sense that they did not fit into any of the categories. We examined them closely and concluded that they had a key feature in common: Each was a negotiation about establishing regional regimes on security, trade, or environmental issues.

The question of whether the cases could be distinguished in terms of their objectives (based on the a priori classifications) was answered. But the answer does not satisfy the sixth step in large-N analyses, which refers to developing implications for the framework or theory and, perhaps, for practice as well. Implications for the framework were developed by constructing profiles of the cases within each of the categories. This was done by examining the codes assigned to each case for all 16 categories. The codes were then combined for the cases within a type of negotiation (6 cases of innovation, 10 cases of redistribution, and so on) to obtain the most popular or consensus code. For example, the consensus code for number of parties was bilateral for innovation talks, small multilateral for extension talks, and large multilateral for the other categories. This process produced distinct profiles for each type of negotiation. Redistribution cases were characterized by bargaining processes over many issues, with frequent breakdowns leading to compromise outcomes. The innovation cases were mostly bilateral talks over a few issues between parties with long-term relationships; the process had few breakdowns, leading to comprehensive agreements when agreements were reached. The multilateral regime cases were characterized by a large number of parties with a mixed bargaining and problem-solving process and few breakdowns, leading to compromise outcomes.

These profiles extend the 1964 typology by delineating many features of the different kinds of negotiations. The clusters from MDS may be regarded as "islands" of theory helpful for developing middle-range theories of negotiation, to borrow a metaphor used by Guetzkow (1957). For the practitioner, the profiles provide a basis for projecting likely patterns of negotiating behavior in both contemporaneous and future cases. These contributions to CA&R result from the six-step plan for implementing a large-N comparative research design. Now it is your turn. Apply the six-step plan to a problem of your choosing, not by actually carrying out the research, which you might do in the future, but by developing a proposal on another CA&R topic that follows the sequence used in the negotiation study.

Data collected from many cases can also be analyzed with qualitative methods. Typical or modal patterns, consensual decisions, and aggregated frequencies or percentages are in this tradition. The profiles constructed for the different types of negotiations in the study discussed just above are examples of modal patterns. The most frequent category across the cases within each type was chosen as the "typical" characteristic: For example, most cases in the innovation and side-effects negotiations dealt with few issues; most cases in the redistribution, multilateral regime, and normalization negotiations considered many issues, and the extension cases discussed a moderate number of issues.

Delphi panels and many focus groups are designed to generate consensual decisions from the panelists. For example, an expert panel may be asked to propose indicators of progress toward democracy. Panelists are given descriptions of political activities and institutions in a dozen countries located in different regions. From these descriptions, each of the panelists offers three key indicators of progress for each case. The nominated indicators are announced, discussed, and reconsidered in a next round of judgments. Discussion continues through several rounds of judgments until the panel agrees on the "best" set. Of course, the consensual indicators are likely to differ from case to case. This is useful information for regional or cultural assessments of democracy. The case indicators can, however, also be aggregated for a modal set. Both types of data, case-by-case and modal indicators, would then be used in cross-national studies designed to assess relationships among the various indicators and other aspects of the societies in the sample. (For more on expert panel and focus group techniques, see the Chapter 6 section "Systematic Expert Judgment," as well as Frei & Ruloff, 1989, and Fern, 2001.)

Studies using process-tracing techniques may also seek to generate an aggregate process from multiple cases. An example is the study on turning points discussed in the Chapter 6 section "Process Tracing." Aggregate traces were constructed at two levels, within a case and across the cases within an issue area. On the first level, a process tracing was devised for each of the several turning points judged to have occurred in each case. A case aggregate trace consisted of the type of precipitant (external, substantive, procedural), departure (abrupt, non-abrupt), and consequence (escalatory, de-escalatory) that occurred in more than 50% of the turning points. On the second level, a summary process trace depicted the primary precipitant, type of departure, and consequence for each of the three issue areas, security cases (13), political cases (11), and trade cases (10). The most frequently occurring precipitant (e.g., external for the security cases), departure (e.g., abrupt for the political cases), and consequence (e.g., de-escalation for the trade cases) was included in the summary path. For the political cases, substantive and procedural precipitants occurred an equal number of times; in several of these cases, both types of precipitants appeared. This study provides an example of using a framework as a lens through which one can view processes that occur in many cases of negotiation. It is a large-N counterpart to the enhanced single-case study discussed in the Chapter 6 section "Theory and Case Study." It also provides another illustration of the way qualitative methods can be used for analysis of many cases.[1] This discussion concludes this part of the book on case study research.

Discussion Questions

The questions to follow cover the topics treated in this and the previous chapter. These chapters have covered various ways of doing enhanced and comparative case study research. All the approaches share the ideas of theory relevance and analytical coherence. The single-case study and the small-n case comparison are enhanced by the theoretical questions addressed and by the insights derived from systematic analysis. The generality of those insights can be judged from the results of large-N comparative studies. Moving back and forth among these methods, and between qualitative and quantitative analyses, would strengthen the contribution made by the research. Developing competence in the use of these methods expands the tool kit of the CA&R researcher. The broad coverage of these chapters suggests many discussion questions—the proverbial 20 (+ 2) questions that encompass "all you ever wanted to know about the comparative method but were afraid to ask!" You may want to use them as a basis for class discussion and review before moving on to the next chapter on ethnographic research.

1. What are some strengths and some weaknesses of the theory-driven case study approach to research in CA&R?

2. Show how a case study can be used to demonstrate the value of theoretical concepts: What steps would be taken in performing an enhanced case study?

3. What is the value, and some limitations, of post-diction or retrospective case studies?

4. Time-series analyses can be performed inductively or deductively: What are some differences between these approaches to research? Give examples.

5. Define the parts of the formula for linear regression. What are some functions served by performing regression analysis?

6. What is the relationship between regression and correlation? Describe the relationship between these statistics in both trigonometric and algebraic terms.

7. How can causal relationships among variables be inferred from correlational analyses? Describe how partial and lagged correlations can be used in developing a causal model.

8. What does an interruption mean in time-series designs? Give examples of interruptions in CA&R and describe how their impact would be evaluated.

9. Give an example of a CA&R problem that can be addressed by Bayesian techniques.

10. Unlike regression analysis, Bayesian techniques do not rely exclusively on the past for making projections into the future. What are some advantages of this approach to analysis? What are some limitations of the way that assessments of probabilities of symptoms are made?

11. What steps would you take to improve the value of judgments from expert panels?

12. Process tracing is considered to be a qualitative analogue to quantitative time series. Describe an unfolding peace (or conflict resolution) process that you are familiar with in terms of a path from early to later events.

13. Compare the Most Similar Systems Design (MSSD) with the Most Different Systems Design (MDSD). How do these case study approaches complement one another?

14. What are the criteria that you would use in matching cases for a focused-comparison design? What are the independent variables, controls, and dependent variables in your study?

15. How do small-n and large-N comparative studies complement each other? What are the internal and external validity trade-offs for these two approaches to case study research?

16. Suppose that the cases chosen for a small-n focused comparison study were also included in the sample of cases used for analysis of a complementary large-N study. What are some problems in using the same cases for both parts (small-n and large-N) of a research design?

17. How might you address the impacts of culture on a conflict-resolving process with a large-N design?

18. When might a small-n research design be preferred over a large-N comparative analysis? Similarly, when would a large-N analysis be preferred?

19. A value of large-N comparative studies is that the data can be analyzed with techniques of statistical inference. However, while necessary, a large sample of cases is not sufficient for the use of these techniques. What other criteria must be satisfied?

20. Describe the steps that you would take to construct a large-N data set on a topic in domestic conflict analysis and resolution.

21. Several examples were used to illustrate qualitative analyses of multiple cases. What are some other examples? How can qualitative analysis, such as with expert panels, be used as part of a quantitative study?

22. Devise four research questions: First, design a question best suited for an enhanced case study. Second, devise a question that can be explored with matched cases. Third, come up with a question that can be investigated with either time-series or interrupted time-series designs. And, fourth, devise a question for which large-N comparative research would be most appropriate. What are some differences among these questions? Which questions might be explored with two or more of these methodologies?

Note

1. A useful resource for qualitative data analysis software is http://www.scolari.com/. This Web page provides detailed descriptions of several packages that assist with data collection, coding, and analysis of textual or narrative material. A particularly popular application is QSR NUD*IST Vivo. Additional Web sites and citations are provided in Chapter 8, note 1.

Part V

Writing Ethnographies

The ethnographic approach to research is the primary example of investigations in an emic tradition and may be regarded as being somewhat less abstract or more inductive than the theory-driven comparative studies discussed in the previous part. (See Chapter 1 for the emic-etic and abstract-concrete distinctions.) This approach has been developed and refined by anthropologists and is becoming increasingly popular as a way of studying conflict. For these reasons, I decided to devote an entire chapter to a discussion of this research tradition, with applications to CA&R problems. The chapter is authored by Linda J. Seligmann, who also provides sources for computer analysis of the sort of data often collected by ethnographers.

Although not regarded as a comparative method, ethnographic research is implicitly comparative, as Seligmann points out. The approach provides both an illustrative "test" of a theory and a "data point" for later comparative analyses with other cases. Many ethnographies can be viewed as single case studies in the framework of many others. Moreover, the descriptive case study literature (which includes ethnographies) provides the social scientist with additional information that can be brought to bear on a problem (King et al., 1995). This experience also helps researchers to get to know their topic in more subjective and intimate terms. For example, in planning an experimental study on the use of threats in negotiation, it may be useful first to study the way threats are used and reacted to over time in a particular cultural setting.

It is noted that first-person references are frequently used in this chapter. This is because, unlike the case study approaches discussed in the previous part, the researcher is the primary "technique" for data collection and analysis; thus, the investigator is the central figure in the research process. He or she is the interpreter of the stories told by informants, which often reveal processes of constructive or destructive conflicts among groups within the bounded space and time of the investigation. Because the interpretation is critical, it must be validated for authenticity. This is often done by sharing written or oral interpretations with the informants ("storytellers") and may be regarded as a test of validity in a more phenomenological or subjective tradition of research. (See Senehi, 2002, for a discussion of the role of storytelling in peace research; see also Firth, 1994, for linguistic analyses of negotiating activity in the workplace.) The chapter concludes with a set of guidelines for performing and writing ethnographies, followed by discussion questions for review.

8

Ethnographic Methods

Linda J. Seligmann

I n the last two decades of the 20th century, recognition developed in disciplines other than anthropology of the usefulness of ethnographic methods, as well as a simultaneous critique of them. Yet few of the individuals in these fields (English, conflict analysis and resolution [including mediation], and cultural studies, to name a few) have ever actually done field research relying on ethnographic methods. This chapter explains what ethnographic methods are, how to implement them, and the kinds of insights they produce. In describing the philosophical underpinnings of ethnography and specific kinds of methods that ethnographers rely upon in field research, this chapter also addresses major ethical dilemmas or challenges that may face researchers using these methods. The chapter includes suggestions for the reader on how to record or catalog and analyze data that have been gathered through ethnographic means. The final section summarizes what the principal ethnographic methods are and how to operationalize them.

What Is Ethnography?

Ethnography, a term coined by anthropologists, constitutes a written account of a particular culture. At the same time, ethnographic methods contribute directly to the nature of the written account that is produced. Hence, in understanding the place of ethnography for students and practitioners of conflict resolution, it is important to consider the construction of both process and product. It is best to begin by delineating a few general characteristics of ethnography.

Ethnography is implicitly comparative. That is, in understanding the specificity of a particular situation—how a bureaucracy is organized or the meaning of "democracy" and how it is operationalized in a region—one's understanding necessarily draws on a comparison with how bureaucracies are organized or principles of democracy operationalized in other regions, and one's own experience of those phenomena. One of the most paradoxical dimensions of ethnography and ethnographic methods is that, often, the glimmering of the value of one's own culture is through interaction with, and knowledge of, more than one culture. This initial comparison may lead to a reaction in which one first reaches the conclusion that one's culture is undoubtedly superior and perhaps the only culture they would consider civilized. This very common attitude is referred to as *ethnocentrism*. The difference between this kind of comparison and the kind of work that field researchers undertake is that field researchers consciously reject ethnocentrism to embrace the assumption of *cultural relativism*. They begin with the premise that there is a rationale or logic to each society's or culture's values, beliefs, and practices; that no one way is better than or superior to another; and that the goal, then, is to strive to understand each culture's logic and rationale.

A caveat is in order here. Cultural relativism is not the same as moral relativism. Moral relativism is a value-laden move from understanding a particular cultural rationale or logic to embracing any and all social practices and beliefs without regard for any kind of moral standard. The paradox here is one that both policymakers and ethnographers alike continue to wrestle with: Is it possible to arrive at a universal standard of morals or human rights, or are people bound by their own cultural values in judging the morality or immorality of social behavior? My own position, which emerges from posing this very question, is that cultural considerations lead to variable and distinctive apprehensions and uses of so-called "universal" moral standards and legal codes. In turn, the on-the-ground interpretations of such standards and codes, usually emanating from the West, may have an impact on the standards and codes in question, eventually allowing for a workable accommodation. I would argue that the process itself constitutes a working toward a universal standard of morals and human rights.

Another general characteristic of ethnography relates to both the methods and theories that field workers use. What ethnographers do best is arrive at middle-range grounded theories that are poised between inductive and deductive theories. They do not randomly collect all and every bit of empirical data and describe them; neither do they begin with general hypotheses and test them, as discussed in Chapter 3 on experiments. Instead, they engage in theoretically informed practice, and they often rely on both qualitative and quantitative methods. For reasons that will become clearer below, they assume that despite the best efforts to be systematic and exhaustive, all empirical data are partial. Ethnographers apprehend and interpret data that are frequently inaccessible through other methodological means and that complement data collected through surveys, experiments, or other techniques.

To give one example, when I began to research the causes of violence in Peru's civil war (1980–1992) between the Shining Path guerrilla movement members and sympathizers, and the military and paramilitary, I was aware of many theories of conflict and explanations of the causes of social violence. Examples are class conflict and control over resources, relative deprivation, how the control by the state over valuable resources may pit groups and individuals against each other as they struggle to gain access to those resources, religious fundamentalism, and colonialism and the carving up of territory into illogical entities as sources of ethnic conflict. I carried these theories with me as I explored, on the ground, the mutual perceptions among Quechua-speaking peoples who were members of civil society, the members of and intellectual vanguard of the Shining Path movement, and the government apparatus at different levels that constituted "the state." I then reflected on the data I gathered through a wide range of means in the light of different theories and arrived at conclusions that took account both of general arguments and specific data. Another way of putting this is that ethnographers are most skilled at understanding rather than predicting behavior (see Chapter 1 on the distinction between explanation and understanding). That understanding, at its best, is quite different from simple empirical description. Though it may not solve conflicts, it sheds light on them. Accounts of causes and processes that ethnographers offer are fine-grained in a way that is difficult to achieve through surveys and experiments. Such accounts may permit greater insight into a particular conflict and allow policymakers to consider a wider range of discourse, modes of interaction, and policies in seeking to reduce conflict through mediation, consensus, cease-fires, and the like.

Why Do Ethnography?

In this section, I would like to address some questions about the production of ethnography. First, why do ethnography? What does it offer that other kinds of methods do not? Experienced field researchers are able to put their finger not only on structural causes of behavior, but also on how meaning systems and symbols contribute to the making and enactment of those structures. Household dynamics or conflict are as much informed by symbolic systems— where different kinds of spaces, inside and out, private and public, female and male, are located and the symbolic powers attributed to them, for example— as by structural conditions, such as economic inequality or systems of political power at work in people's daily lives. The meaning or symbols associated with structures of inequality give those structures a life of their own. Without an awareness of this dynamic, policymakers and ethnographers alike may not fully comprehend the discourse invoked by differing parties or the actions they take, especially in conditions of conflict. Field researchers also learn to be acutely aware of what is "public" and what is "hidden." Skilled ethnographers are able to grasp simultaneously that which they can document empirically, count, or precisely apprehend, in conjunction with what they symbolize and represent. These dimensions of social life are often taken for granted or impossible to specify for any number of reasons, including fear and terror.

Ethnographic methods avoid generalization and reductionism. A number of contributors to Nordstrom and Martin's (1992) volume make these points. For example, Dumont (1992), in describing the reaction of peasants to threats of violence exercised by the Philippine state—through martial law, family planning, and the widespread screening of *The Killing Fields*—found that they "responded . . . neither with enthusiasm or rebellion but with increased passivity, cynicisms, and witticisms. . . . A solid grasp on current events and the institutional analysis of sociopolitical structures are, indeed, necessary to explain, or better to interpret, the occurrence of violence. Yet . . . this remains insufficient because violence is represented, manifested, and manipulated on many different levels and in many difference arenas, and because violence is informed and constructed by a variety of factors that transcend the hic et nunc of its occurrence."

The skilled ethnographer, attentive to how social structure and daily life are interwoven, may generate new concepts, and their interpretations may serve as the basis for others to do the same. This latter point is, perhaps, the most difficult for an ethnographer to achieve. Ethical debate surrounds how conditions of violence or conflict are "captured" or cast as one possible moment and thereby become a powerful representation and medium for how those who read or hear of these accounts view a particular people or conflict (see Avruch, 2003; Nordstrom & Martin, 1992). This consideration is not one with a resolution or a methodological solution, but rather remains a cautionary concern that should always cause ethnographers to reflect on each step of the process that constitutes their work, including the product itself.

Finally, and not least important, both the process and the product should be accessible and available to the subjects of the field-worker's research so that they, too, may generate new concepts, interpretations, and practices. For example, in a study of an extraordinary, complex irrigation system, dating at least from Inca times, we discovered that part of the system had been abandoned and the district was rife with conflicts over water rights (Seligmann & Bunker, 1994). Given the need for water, we attempted to find out why a critical part of the system had been in disrepair for so long. In the course of our research, we found that (a) two nongovernmental agencies were competing with each other to improve the district's irrigation system, (b) neither knew of the other's work, and (c) the district's inhabitants were "milking them" for all they were worth in order to get as many resources as possible from them. Our queries and research stimulated change.

First, people became more self-conscious about the environmental knowledge they had and their loss of such knowledge. Myths abounded about the construction and destruction of the canal system, but what became evident was that a loss of political power; a transformation in land tenure patterns mingling private, collective, and household lands allocated to families who had fulfilled their obligations to their community; a loss of environmental knowledge; and a limit on labor capacity conspired to prevent district members from repairing the canal system. The two NGOs began to collaborate rather than compete with each other, and district members became anxious about the future and what would happen if the entire canal system collapsed. Five years later, although land tenure problems still existed, the canal system had been not only repaired but also expanded, and district members exhibited a notable pride in their understanding of their waterworks, climatic conditions, and the environment through which it traversed.

A second example of the generative capacity of ethnography is less straightforward. In my book (Seligmann, 1995), I concluded with an analysis of the many suggestions that district members themselves had offered over "what was to be done" to improve their district, and I argued that the Quechua people of Peru should be given the rights and responsibilities of citizens, at the very least. More specifically, I enumerated (relying on their insights) the kinds of rights they felt they lacked as citizens, including health and education, basic communications infrastructure, and political representation at the departmental and national levels. None of this was surprising, yet they had suffered from the repeated broken promises made by state personnel and politicians, and this helped to explain why some among them found the Shining Path movement a satisfying revolutionary alternative.

Ironically, the next democratically elected president, Alberto Fujimori, decided to implement many of these citizenship rights, making services and infrastructure available to rural communities throughout the Andes. It was truly an odd sensation to return to the district and find that many of my recommendations had been implemented. With a sinking feeling, I had to agree that while these changes had made some constructive difference, they had eventually taken a strange turn in the road. Fujimori's agenda had been one of gathering greater and greater power to himself as a dictatorial populist, eliminating the equivalent of a parliament (the Constituent Assembly) and the judiciary. Yet he had received the full support of the district because of the services he extended to it. Eventually, he fled the country in disgrace, embroiled in multiple schemes of corruption and a blatant disregard for due process.

My point is that ethnography never stands alone. Entwined in structures, actions, policies, and meanings that emanate from multiple sources and are constantly interpreted and acted upon, the most ethnographers can do is to go as deeply and widely as possible and awaken each day recognizing that the familiar and new are sometimes difficult to distinguish. They should deliberately rely on multiple methodologies, recognizing that findings are always in part an artifact of method, move from what they sense to what they note down with exhaustive care, and be alert to their own biases and history as they create a narrative text that can be shared with and used by others (for more on the construction of narratives, see Chapter 10).

The Logic of Ethnography

Given these general definitional characteristics of ethnography, what kinds of methods do field-workers use to conduct their research? Ethnographic methods require skills that must be developed and honed. Clearly, the more one does field research, the easier it is to perform. However, it is useful to provide some guidelines as to what to avoid and what to make sure one takes account of in doing fieldwork. In order to understand why field-workers use the kinds of methods I will describe below, it is worth considering what they want to avoid and what they want to make sure they consider.

Many novice field-workers think that they should do their utmost to collect objective data. In contrast, an experienced field-worker has learned that data will never be wholly objective. They are influenced by the presence of the field-worker. This reality is called *the observer's paradox*. When humans study other humans in a social context, they affect the research environment. One of the ways that this reality becomes immediately apparent is that people, in the presence of a stranger who has come "to study" or to learn from them, engage in what is called *impression management*. We are all familiar with this practice. When strangers or newcomers ask us questions, we tend to do two things initially: (a) We give them ideal answers, which do not necessarily conform to our own practices, and (b) we engage in acting and behaving in ways that are different from how we would behave if they were not in our presence. For example, if someone asks us about traffic lights, we dutifully tell that person what we do when the light is green, yellow, or red. Yet, the more the person watches drivers in action, the more he or she will come to realize that these rules are norms that may guide action but are not equivalent to behavior. It is not that the rules do not matter, but rather we must try to understand that gray area between rules and action, norms and practice. These two conditions lead to fundamentals of field research, the most important of which is called *participant-observation*.

PARTICIPANT-OBSERVATION

Participant-observation is the hallmark of ethnographic field research. It consists of simultaneously *participating* in as many of the activities as possible at a particular site or in a particular setting, *observing* what is transpiring, and *interpreting* what the researcher has participated in and observed (Becker & Geer, 1960). Participant-observation allows for a field researcher to learn from the act of participation itself; the field researcher gradually comes to be a more familiar fixture in people's lives; they, in turn, will subsequently be more likely to abandon impression management; and the field researcher will learn more and more about that gray area between ideals and practices. Usually, field researchers use participant-observation over a long, rather than a short, period of time, sometimes spending months and years at a particular research site. Field researchers have found that a long duration of time and on-the-ground interaction with subjects allow for more depth and breadth in their research findings. The term coined for this kind of approach to ethnographic research is the *case study*. In addition to enhancing naturalized interactions in the field, case studies often illuminate major patterns, trends, comparisons, and contrasts with other cases. (Comparative case studies were discussed in Chapter 7.)

At the same time, ethnographers have recognized that there are some significant weaknesses to this practice, namely that they tend to perceive their own site as a kind of closed community with boundaries, and they may fail to take account of the larger picture, confining themselves instead to a bird's-eye view of things. Since the 1980s, ethnographers have begun to revise the way they do participant-observation in order to account for events and processes that take place in a wider field. They have been moving toward multi-sited field research (Marcus, 1998).

Multi-sited field research is interpreted in many different ways. I find two definitions useful. The first is that the field researcher, for example, actually investigates the place of powerful men in oil-rich Texas and the place of powerful men in pig-rich New Guinea and she tries to discern the similarities and differences in the ways that hierarchy and gender are constructed and what doing research in one setting can tell us, not only about research in the other setting, but also about the researcher herself (Marcus, 1998). The second definition is that the field researcher, recognizing that the context for what occurs at a particular research site may include other research sites, attempts to conduct research in multiple locations (Gupta & Ferguson, 1997). If I want to understand the impact of agrarian reform on Peru's rural inhabitants, I would need to do research on the history of land tenure and labor relation, the power structure, and economic stratification in a particular agrarian district. But I would also interview lawyers responsible for crafting, implementing, and litigating cases related to the agrarian reform law in the departmental and national capitals,

NGOs, government personnel, officials in the military, and other national and international bodies that may have played a role in agrarian reform.

Additionally, I might need to compare multiple districts in order to understand why agrarian reform was more successful in one case than another. Only then would I be able to make sense of what was happening in a particular district. A shorthand way to state this is that systems of power and flows of information, products, and knowledge are very far flung, and field researchers need to follow and study these trajectories. However, one person alone doing field research can find this to be a daunting challenge. Teams can undertake this kind of multi-sited field research in a more effective fashion.

Two other aspects of participant observation allow researchers to be sensitive to the subjective nature of their research: interpretation and reflexivity. As field researchers work and, especially, as they analyze and write up their research, they assume that, to a greater or lesser degree, there is an interpretive dimension to their findings and analysis. They will therefore need to reflect on and be explicit about how their own biases, life experiences, status and power, and character shape their findings and interpretations. Although they cannot eliminate them, they can acknowledge their impact, alerting readers to problems of overemphasis, or alternatively, gaps, in their ethnographic accounts (see Clifford & Marcus, 1986).

CHOOSING A FIELD SITE

One of the most pressing questions that field researchers must address is where they will do their fieldwork. How should they choose a site? What kind of preparation do they need before they begin their work? Picking a site is not a random selection process. How a research problem is defined, or the questions that interest an ethnographer, may constrain considerably where they do their research. If one wants to understand how experiences of civil war affect the ways that civil society subsequently participates in government or decision making, then, obviously, one will go to sites where that has been the case. It is critical to try to learn to speak the language in order to avoid relying heavily on translators. Many field-workers use interpreters or translators, but it is much better if they themselves speak the language. Translators occupy a particular social niche in their own society and, in spite of themselves, the ways they rephrase questions and the responses they receive may bias one's research considerably. On the other hand, if researchers feel they have facility in the language, they may find it useful to work with a translator, especially if they collaborate in training the translator to ask value-neutral questions.

It is unwise to pick a site where the likelihood is high that ethnographers will not be permitted to pursue their research. Ethnographers will want to do background research on the site they have selected before going there. In fact, if they are also attempting to obtain funding for their research, they may want to spend several weeks or months at the site doing preliminary research before writing their proposal. They will then be in a stronger position to write a credible proposal. They will also want to familiarize themselves with others who have worked in the region. Others may provide introductions and contacts, and they may have suggestions as to where the best place for research might be found. This appears fairly straightforward, but it turns out to be a more hazard-prone process than one might imagine. Political instability may prevail, preventing ethnographers from pursuing their original plans, or their project may simply seem problematic to government officials who are in a position to permit them to do their research. Villagers themselves may oppose a research project that an ethnographer is proposing. Therefore, it is critical that ethnographers have a backup plan, another research site they could go to instead.

OBTAINING PERMISSION

Once ethnographers have picked a site, an even greater challenge looms before them. It is one thing for government officials to stamp a visa and for an educational institution or place of employment to provide ethnographers with a letter of introduction containing a gold seal. It is quite another to gain the informal yet critical permission to do research from the leaders or authorities in the region where ethnographers plan to work. How do ethnographers go about doing this? They must first introduce themselves. In my field research in the Quechua-speaking highlands of southern Peru, I introduced myself to the local district authorities, who represented a number of smaller units, and asked them what I needed to do in order to obtain permission to work there. They told me to make a presentation at a general assembly. All the elected leaders of the different villages constituting the district attended the assembly and discussed my proposal. I made my presentation in Quechua, and I tried as best I could to explain who I was, why I was interested in this particular research, and what I thought we might learn from each other through the research process. The ambience was tense, especially because this particular research stint took place in the middle of the worst brutality of Peru's civil war in a region that had been directly affected by it. After the presentation, the room was unusually still. Finally, the president of one of the more powerful communities stood up and endorsed my project. Others followed suit.

It is also important to make sure that ethnographers introduce themselves to local police or military authorities. In my case, the local police were required by the Peruvian government to document my presence. One of the most frightening moments in my research took place when the local police refused to record my name and the identification numbers of my passport and visa, asking, "If you are doing 'clean' research, why do you care?" This mattered, because had I disappeared, there would have been no written record of my presence. To counterbalance that unnerving experience was another experience, less frightening for me than for the people with whom I was working. In the district I had chosen for my field research in southern Peru, prior to my arrival, a cell of guerrillas from the Shining Path movement had blown up the tractor that the cooperative had depended on to farm over 300 hectares of relatively flat land. Subsequently, a force similar to the Green Beret ("sinchis") had entered the district, and people's nerves were frayed.

I arrived with the intention of interviewing village members about issues surrounding land tenure, labor relations, and political organization. It was apparent that cooperative members did not want to talk to me. They reasoned that I might be connected with the Shining Path in some way. It was only when one man, who was a political representative of the cooperative, endorsed me that more cooperative members took the risk of engaging in conversation with me. Indeed, it was a risk for them, especially had Shining Path members within the district decided that they were betraying the cause, which included an attitude of anti-imperialism or anti-Americanism.

TRUST AND RAPPORT

Perhaps the most difficult thing for field-workers to comprehend is that they cannot simply walk into an existing and ongoing social organization with its own structure, momentum, and history and expect to be accepted. Establishing trust and rapport requires ethnographers to be aware of imbalances in power, both economic and political, between themselves and their informants, and to seek ground on which parity or the possibility of reciprocity, which is a mutual exchange of goods, services, or knowledge, may prevail. A few things helped me find paths I could take and ties I could forge with people.

I attempted to behave with genuine humility. I assumed that my knowledge of their lives was at best that of a young child's, and I was not averse to occupying the role of child, student, apprentice, and, sometimes, fool. I was less keen about losing control through drinking but, in fact, drinking was one mechanism that villagers used among themselves for multiple purposes, one of which was to challenge their drinking companions to let down their guard, lose control, and assume that trust would prevail.

I also did not try to offer official explanations of what I was doing. As awkward as it was, I tried to convey to others what my interests were and to conduct myself respectfully. This demeanor allowed us to struggle together through misunderstandings and mistakes with a degree of good humor and an eye toward building rapport. I cannot stress how important it is to assume that among the people with whom ethnographers work, there will always be some who have a genuine interest in their work. Assuming this parity—a mutual interest in the exchange of knowledge—has a significant bearing on how people view the differences in power between ethnographers and them, a subject I will discuss at greater length toward the end of this chapter.

Not all cultures value reciprocity, and the rules of reciprocity differ from one society to the next, but the third effort I made was to pay close attention to reciprocal practices and to emulate them. For example, in many cultures, the norm is to offer visitors, even strangers, food. The consequences of refusing a meal simply because one has just eaten are greater than one might imagine. It is remembered and circulated within the community as an indicator of disrespect and thoughtlessness. Likewise, if a community member visits the ethnographer, he or she should be prepared to offer food and drink to that member. These small actions build on each other and create the conditions for either trust and rapport or disrespect and rejection. Furthermore, once this trust and rapport begin to build, it usually becomes possible over time to be more honest about why one does not want to eat three meals, one after another, in the course of making multiple visits to different households in one day. A recognition of and respect for different cultural mores begins to emerge and takes the place of either suspicion, on the one hand, or a rigid adherence to custom, on the other.

Making Sense of Other Worlds

When field-workers have been allowed to "set up business," even more challenges await them, in particular, figuring out the order and kinds of data to gather. They have very different ideas about what constitutes intrusive research, and this depends partly upon the history of the research site in question. For example, in the Andean highlands, it would be wholly inappropriate to enter a village and map it; collect census data, including details about ethnic affiliation, gender, and age stratification; take photographs of villagers and the village; or conduct formal household interviews about land tenure patterns. Many times in the past, these were exactly the kind of practices that colonial or national officials engaged in, leading to further loss of land or relocation of villagers. People are likely to shut down or lie. Many chroniclers of invasion and conquest who had their origins in native communities have pointed this out in their narratives. More recently, I was doing field research in a community where several young bureaucrats from a nongovernmental agency appeared and began interviewing households about their land holdings. I happened to be present at one of these interviews and had visited the family's lands many times. The response they gave the young man doing the interviews contrasted sharply with their actual land holdings, which were much greater.

My recommendation instead is that ethnographers should spend most of their initial time going to work with people, as long as people are willing to tolerate their presence and, in some cases, permit them to help out. In conditions where people do not tolerate the presence of an ethnographer or when the very presence of one creates divisiveness, it may be impossible to pursue research at that site, and one would be better off going elsewhere. In the past, some ethnographers (e.g., Chagnon, 1968; Evans-Pritchard, 1976), recognizing that individuals or groups were vying with one another for higher status or were jealous of one another, would court one group in order to elicit competing narratives from another group that initially had been reluctant to talk to them. Usually, however, the ethnographer's presence is tolerated, however reluctantly initially.

There are any number of questions that ethnographers can ask that will be connected to learning about and understanding the work process itself that are not threatening, deepen rapport, and allow ethnographers to begin to learn things of significance; for example, who works where, how people are related to one another, how they work together or not, how their time is allocated during the day, and the organization of the division of labor, which is linked to other interesting demographic questions about age and gender differences as well as stratification. Ethnographers can continue to build rapport and a knowledge base by using some of the following themes and settings that are usually nonthreatening, or at least far less threatening than a series of questions that may seem pointed, prying, or irrational.

More than the other methodologies discussed in this book, ethnography is an attempt to build context for apprehending the structure, history, organization, and practices of a community that may or may not be different from their own. Ethnographers could ask people about their life histories. This opens windows onto major events that have transpired during the course of their lives, the history of their community, and other people who have played roles in their lives. In turn, informants may move on to explain, from their vantage point, some of these major events. Similarly, ethnographers can use as talking points any number of items of material culture, from farming utensils to typewriters and cooking pots. They can spend a day with someone. They can pay attention to body movements and the organization of space and time. If ethnographers have photos or drawings, they can ask people to explain their content or talk about them. Children's drawings are especially interesting in revealing aspects of socialization processes and worldviews, as well as key transformative events that may be unfolding.

Two things usually happen as a result of beginning in this way. One thing leads to another. The people ethnographers become close to will introduce them to other people—a snowball effect—and gradually, they will be able not only to expand the questions they ask, but also, simultaneously, to focus on topics of interest to them and their specific research project. In short, they will begin to move from participant-observation in a random-like manner to a more systematic informal series of interviews. They might also then begin to embark on unobtrusive research, mapping out the region, charting the connections among people including kinship relationships, figuring out where people live and the kinds of housing they live in, as well as the activities they engage in and with whom. This is by no means a linear process. Rather, it requires ethnographers to tack back and forth constantly among multiple modes of engagement. As they do, patterns may gradually emerge in what people say and do. As those patterns become familiar, ethnographers can then begin to search for pattern variation and what might cause them.

INFORMANTS

Along with participating in people's daily activities, another practice, and perhaps the most common one that permits field-workers to begin to become integrated into a field site, is to ally themselves with individuals whom Agar calls "professional stranger handlers" (Agar, 1996, p. 135). These are the famous "informants" of so many ethnographies who have stood in for entire villages. These stranger handlers are unusual, yet they are the primary gateway for many field-workers into their research, and it is almost inevitable that ethnographers will work with one or more of them. They themselves may exist on the margins of their community, because they come from somewhere else and have had to learn the rules and practices of their new home, because they have an intellectual curiosity and want to learn as much as possible about the world in which they find themselves, or because of their personality, a physical defect, or some other quality, they have been marginalized by members of their own community.

Informants are often mediators and straddlers, located both inside and outside of their communities, and come closest to mimicking the kind of participant-observation of the field-worker. A cautionary note is in order, however. Their very positioning means they offer the field researcher unique insights, but it is important not to ally oneself too closely with them because of how they may be viewed by other people and to obtain as wide a range of perspectives and interviews as possible. Qualitative research demands this kind of care in order to avoid reductionism or overgeneralization. In the past, many anthropologists relied solely upon these informants, and instead of making it clear to readers that this was the case, they generalized, assuming that such informants stood for all members of the community. In addition to being a poor research practice, it also led to a notable flatness in many ethnographies, a lack of nuance and variation among the perspectives, experiences, sentiments, and practices of different community members.

ASKING QUESTIONS

Two other important methodological challenges are (a) how to ask questions and conduct informal and, eventually, formal interviews and (b) how to take and use field notes or data. Experienced researchers have been taught and have learned over time to ask questions neutrally, to avoid leading questions, and not to embed responses in the questions themselves. This is more difficult than it might seem. Translators have not been trained to do this; using leading questions is the easiest way for many of them to complete their work, and they are often irritated by the failure of research subjects to understand what they are asking or why. They may also be embarrassed or feel ashamed that their fellow villagers are not responding or understanding "properly" what is being asked of them. They then take the easiest route, that is, answering the questions themselves that they ask of their subjects or subtly embedding the answer they prefer in the question itself.

Ethnographers try to figure out the best way for people to make sense of their interests and questions. They can do this by paraphrasing and reframing questions and re-asking them in as many ways as possible. Field-workers also try to move from one question to another smoothly, avoiding abrupt transitions, "going with the flow," even though it may not be where they want to go. It is surprising where people will lead field researchers, and it is often eye-opening and intriguing.

Finally, once a degree of comfort is reached in dialogue, ethnographers may then break one of the cardinal rules of many other methodological approaches. They may deliberately ask leading questions either to confirm a conjecture or hunch or to have it challenged. It can be a form of very effective validity testing, but it is useful only after a fairly long period of fieldwork has already taken place (see Agar, 1996).

The questions ethnographers ask may fall flat for any number of reasons. In my case, people never answered blatant questions about guerrilla members of the Shining Path, for example, and any references they made to unsettling individuals or events were always by way of using the catch-all terms, "terrorista," "subversivo," or "abigeo" (cattle rustler). I found it necessary to describe, go around, depersonalize and generalize, and use links and juxtaposition to get at who was who and what was what. As I engaged villagers in conversation, I would ask as neutrally as possible about changes in general in a region, how villages were organized, the relationships between different political units, or about what their children were doing, their education, and where they were living. I would ask about who people were, sometimes including those who I thought were sympathizers to one party or another. I would juxtapose nostalgia for the past to the present and to changes in the making for the future in an effort to tease out what had brought about the changes themselves. People were in far too much danger to be specific, and the memory of violence in some cases was too raw and grief filled to risk being recalled. It has been observed that once a civil war has subsided, there is widespread social fear that even talking about the past could cause a resurgence of violence (Nordstrom, 1992; Suárez-Orozco, 1992).

In many cases, responses to exploitation, terror, and violence take the form of subtle but collectively shared resistance—through foot-dragging, sabotage, and different kinds of aesthetic expressions (Scott, 1985, 1992; Sluka, 1992). In addition, terror traumatizes. Indeed, one of the purposes of terror is to silence or to create an ambience of pervasive paranoia. A larger question, of course, emerges: Is it possible for a community to heal without a way to talk about, enact, or act upon the horror of the past?

A few other pointers are to listen well and pay as much attention to silence as to what people say. Silence is telling, but telling too much is also telling. People will often repeat and emphasize particular events or sequences because of the role they played in them, the impression the event has made on them, or because they are well aware that the event, actions, and people associated with it are controversial and subject to multiple interpretations. Use good timing. At first, field researchers may not know what good timing means, but if they pay attention, they will begin to observe people's irritation and impatience with them if their timing is off.

More complex but informal kinds of interviewing and participant-observation may involve studying how existing organizations work, both from the top down and from the bottom up. Field researchers should always remember that organizations are composed of people, so that to understand structure and process, they will need to "map out" organizations in multiple ways. They should map the formal structure, but also create other maps by talking to the people within the organization, as well as those that in one way or another are connected with it (Agar, 1996). I found this to be especially important in my work on the implementation and impact of one of the most radical agrarian reforms in Latin America. The construct of "the state" fell away, replaced by a far more contradictory, complex, and multifaceted organization, in the course of my conversations with lawyers who were part of the leftist military junta in Peru responsible for implementing the reform. I learned about their life histories and their connection with the central government, different political parties, and the litigations in the countryside in which they participated. I also talked to both the landed estate owners and Quechua peasants who were taking their cases to these lawyers and were parties to the litigations in question.

Whatever methods ethnographers use, they must get permission from informants. Ethnographers must ensure that people understand the uses to which data, narratives, and photographs might be put in the future and in what fora. Ethnographers are first and foremost responsible to the human subjects of their research. Some may want to speak but will want you to refer to them by using pseudonyms. Others may very much want to be heard in their own voice, but ethnographers must make it clear how this could conceivably endanger them, if that is indeed the case. This is a very complex domain, and human subjects review boards have become more conscientious and stringent in enforcing ethics codes. Optimally, ethnographers attempt to obtain permission in writing. Although the 1993 American Anthropological Association Ethical Code (http://www.aaanet.org/committees/ethics/ethcode.htm) does not require written permission, verbal permission is necessary and, most important, there must be credible evidence that the person or persons with whom ethnographers work understand what is meant by "permission."

NAÏVETÉ AND IDEALISM

Another cautionary note seems appropriate here. As a young field-worker doing my first research, I allied myself passionately with the plight of the Quechua peasants and the exploitation and abuse they had suffered since at least the time of the Spanish Conquest in 1532. When I did my crusading fieldwork, I made it clear to the people in the village that I was far more interested in talking, eating, and working with them than with petty bureaucrats, teachers, storekeepers, or landed estate owners. My fieldwork did not go very well, though I loved what I was doing and I thought of it as a "romantic experience." After several years more of study and reading, reflection, and more fieldwork, it became obvious to me how biased and distorted my research had been.

First and foremost, people, rather than trusting me, distrusted me, because of how explicitly I rejected interaction with other members of their society, with whom they themselves interacted. Second, there was no way I was able to arrive at a thoughtful understanding or explanation of what was taking place, either in the present or past, without a good understanding of the positions, beliefs, and practices of the individuals I had rejected so vehemently. I never made that mistake again, though at times I was extremely uncomfortable speaking with some individuals because of their notoriety. It provided me with a complex and nuanced portrayal of the causes and dynamics of conflict and permitted me to calculate when a situation was so dangerous that I should extricate myself from it.

Avruch (2003) offers an analysis of the need for ethnographers, especially when they are engaged in conflict resolution, to reach a balance between "experience-near" and "experience-distant" ways of understanding culture. For example, in an "experience-near" view of culture, if one becomes too allied with the down-trodden or oppressed, or wedded to explanations that consider cultural differences as one of the principal causes of that oppression, one may be blind to how the discourse of cultural differences itself is implicated in exacerbating conflict. On the other hand, "experience-distant" ways of understanding culture—more or less ignoring the role of culture, reducing it to attitudes, or assuming that it is far less important than structures of inequality themselves or the presence or absence of institutions or processes that are assumed to be universal—will inevitably lead to a superficial understanding of conflict and its causes. In his words:

Analysis aims to get at culture as an experience-distant idea—*and this includes plumbing the experience-near aspects of it.* In contrast, culturalism is a politico-moral stance, a statement about "identity politics mobilized at the level" of the ethnic group or nation-state (Appadurai, 1996, p. 15). Over-valuing culture . . . can result in a practitioner's understanding of and approach to a dispute or conflict that proves harmful to some of the parties because it will:

- Mask or efface underlying structural issues such as gender, class, ethnic discrimination, or racism, in favor of attention to individuating or communication-biased issues such as "communicational styles."
- Reify culture as an agent capable of action on its own terms.
- Essentialize culture toward a single and unified expression.
- Homogenize all group members toward invariant behavioral stereotypes.
- Risk replacing older, 19th-century notions of essentialized racial differences with 21st-century ideas of cultural ones.

We have gained nothing—on the contrary, promulgated much harm—if we embrace the cultural turn and end up replacing racism as a way of dealing with diversity with a culturalism enlisted for the same ends (Avruch, 2003, pp. 366–367).

There is no perfect solution to this conundrum. Good ethnographic research entails using both experience-near and experience-distant approaches to different social sectors, and it requires attention to history. Good ethnographic research and analysis may consist of "messy" methodology in order to avoid overgeneralization, reductionist approaches, or simply a tedious descriptive reiteration of what is readily apparent.

PAYMENTS

Ethnographers should not ask too many questions and not too many of the same questions. They should not forget that people already have their day mapped out—they have plans and things to do—and here is a stranger, taking their time and their labor away. On the other hand, some people may find the presence of a stranger stimulating, entertaining, and challenging. Nevertheless, some field researchers think it appropriate to pay informants for their time. Others think this is a terrible ethical practice because it is akin to bribery. My view is that if people work, then it is only reasonable that they be paid for the time they take from their work and that a rate be gauged to the value of wage labor (if it exists) in that society.

I found another solution to my ethical concerns about monetary payments. The solution allowed me to begin to use photography as a means of documentation. People were excited about receiving a photo of themselves or their family in exchange for conducting an interview with me. Obviously, if ethnographers are in a setting where photos are not rare, then they will have to think about other avenues that might serve as alternatives to payment with money.

SAMPLING

As field-workers move toward more formal interviews, they will be faced with even more concerns. Who should they interview? Should they use random samples? In that context, what could constitute a random sample? In the abstract, formal methods for obtaining a well-balanced interview database seem logical and reasonable. In the field, they are often absurd because it is difficult to get people to cooperate with conforming to the structure of an ideal sample (see Chapter 5 on Survey Research). Nevertheless, there are some qualitative modes of sampling that are effective (see Agar, 1996, for more details on these kinds of sampling methods).

One is to interview individuals who seem to be willing and cooperative as informants. This is referred to as *opportunistic* sampling. These individuals would include the ethnographer's initial "stranger handlers." Another is to interview individuals who have a direct bearing on one's research topic. This is referred to as *judgmental* sampling. A third is to use *stratified* samples that reflect the ethnographer's general impressions of stratification along different lines, be they in terms of land holdings, ethnicity, age, or power. The strata can be compared. This is similar to using focus groups. A fourth is to deliberately interview people who seem different from those the ethnographer has already interviewed, for purposes of gaining a sense of comparison and attempting to ascertain what those differences may be attributed to. Finally, ethnographers should pay close attention to how people in a particular site group themselves and others and their explanations of why they are grouped that way. Novice researchers often tend to superimpose their own grouping devices on already existing groups and fail to take into account the potential significance of existing clusters.

RECORDING DATA FOR ANALYSIS

How do ethnographers move from the collection of data to interpreting that data? What are the best ways for recording data for purposes of analysis? It is overwhelming to consider just how much one may absorb in a few hours of field research and intimidating to figure out which data are important, which are not, what are missing, and whether or not data are being manipulated. Where are the gaps? What does the ethnographer need to do next? Ethnographers should try to write down everything and should not trust their memory.

Most ethnographers carry a notebook with them, and people become accustomed to seeing them with their notebook. In fact, in my experience, the situation became so comfortable that they would often tell me to take out my notebook and write down certain things that I had not thought were important. When I reached a level of comfort with people, it was then possible for me to tape conversations, microfilm archival material, and use photography or other kinds of visual media as means of recording data. Gathering data through different kinds of media and across many strata offer multiple perspectives on the same phenomenon. It is similar to the "Rashamon" effect in which individuals who witness the same event have remarkably different narratives and interpretations of it. These variant narratives allow ethnographers to piece together things in a way that would be more superficial were they to rely on one informant or one kind of medium. Furthermore, they may find significant correlations or clusters in the similarity of narratives and the respective characteristics or profiles of the individuals providing the narratives. Finally, this method almost always raises new questions and avenues for inquiry.

Taking Notes

How ethnographers record their notes requires careful thinking, not only for purposes of protecting informants, but also for purposes of analysis. How ethnographers record data shapes their analysis of the data. Sanjek (1990) provides an excellent discussion of the challenges of recording and analyzing field notes. Ethnographers may want to use some kind of code for people's names. This is particularly important when they are working in situations of conflict and may need to protect the identities of individuals in the event that their data are confiscated by authorities. Film or taped data are more dangerous than written data and may be of more value to multiple parties who are at odds with one another. This became dramatically apparent to me in one field situation when the municipal authorities, police, and the individuals whose livelihoods were being threatened by expulsion from their workplace wanted access to my film and tapes. In the end, I was simply lucky that the mob of workers surrounded me and literally "pushed" me into a taxi. The authorities did not attempt to follow my taxi but, unfortunately, it became close to impossible for me to pursue further interviews with political leaders representing any of the parties involved.

TAKING NOTE WHILE TAKING NOTES

In organizing notes, ethnographers should follow some critical procedures. First, they should write them up as quickly as possible. Exhausted as they may be, they should prepare their notes. They need to think about whether they want to have several different formats. In my case, I used, more or less, three simultaneous formats. One consisted of entries, day by day, with each entry specifying keywords or categories, the individuals involved, the date, and the narrative text. I incorporated into that set of entries my own sentiments or opinions as well, something that some field researchers leave out: I thought it important to be able to reflect on the relationship between my sentiments or reactions at the moment and the data themselves. The second set was in the form of key categories alone, with entries subsumed under the categories. The third was a general chronology that took account of events happening in a wider setting; newspaper, radio, and television reports; political events; and regional considerations. I also used separate databases for archival resources I consulted at the local, municipal, and national levels and incorporated keywords or categories. I kept a detailed record of the photos and slides I was taking, and attempted to cross-reference them with my written notes. Subsequently, I was able to look at my list of keywords, modify or consolidate them, and use them as a means of selecting all related data. The same was true of dates or specific individuals.

The software program I adapted for this purpose is called *Citation*, but there are many others, such as *Ethnoscape*.[1] One caveat is in order here, however. What I liked about *Citation* was that it did not organize the keywords hierarchically. Ethnoscape does and can lock a user into a framework that may be inappropriate and blind you to important dimensions of your fieldwork data. In other words, it may overdetermine interpretation, which then becomes an artifact of the software program. At the same time, I found that the software program I used was flexible enough that it served me very well as a powerful tool, allowing me a comparative, multifaceted view of a large body of varied data through time. It also allowed me to shift the locus of my data in any number of ways.

When ethnographers have written up their notes—and we are very lucky to be able to use notebook computers now rather than portable typewriters with carbon paper—they should reread them. This is one of the most important parts of note taking. In the course of rereading, I always write notes in the margins indicating connections with prior observations or notes, insights that were not yet necessarily substantiated, and queries for further follow-up. It is in the re-reading that ethnographers find relationality—where there are gaps, what seems odd, what explains or brings to light contradictions, and surprises. These are the "aha" moments. Agar (1996) calls them "rich points," though he is referring more to the process of participant-observation itself rather than reflexivity with respect to notes. For Agar, rich points are key moments when ethnographers realize that they do not understand something, when things finally fall into place, or when something unexpected happens. These moments challenge the assumptions and implicit theories of the ethnographer about the way the world works. They are the primary reason for revising assumptions and hypotheses, whether these are stated in formal or informal terms.

EMIC AND ETIC ANALYSES

In a broader and more philosophical sense, these rich points are the link between two methodological and philosophical positions that have entered the anthropological lexicon—the emic and the etic, which were discussed in Chapter 1. As we noted there, the emic refers to the "insider's" point of view; the etic, the "outsider's." Yet this is too simplistic. The assumption of ethnographers who use methods to uncover the "emic" perspective is that they are attempting to approximate as closely as possible the experiences, values, belief systems, and practices of members of a particular culture, even though they cannot duplicate them. The assumption of those who claim to be using the "etic" perspective is that whatever people say, do, or believe, one can arrive at another analysis that explains those same phenomena using a more analytical and functionalist framework. A good example might be that the Yanomami engage in conflict, warfare, and killing among themselves for religious reasons or to avenge the death of a member of their immediate group. Yet M. Harris (1994) or Chagnon (1968) might argue that conflict and warfare take place as a consequence of competition for women, regardless of what the Yanomami themselves might say. And Ferguson (1995) might offer another explanation, arguing that it is the result of the introduction of new commodities and weapons.

Are emic and etic analyses essentially dichotomous, as suggested by the table in the Chapter 1 section "Etic and Emic Approaches"? Great debate surrounds this question. I would argue that they are not, that "rich points" not only illuminate one's own data, but they also offer a bridge between "emic" and "etic" approaches. In a way, emic and etic approaches also entail differences in the scope and locus of data and the kind of lens one is using—fish eye, telephoto, single lens reflex, the use of a satellite, or videotape. Are the data longitudinal or do they form a constellation of a single moment? Close-up or overarching? Furthermore, whether or not a single etic argument may allow for generalization, which may be very satisfying to policymakers and those interested in systematic comparison, ultimately, it may not be useful in actually understanding behavior or implementing policy in cases where attempts are being made to forge peace.

A final observation about the duality of emic and etic confronts the entire enterprise of undertaking field research. The strength of fieldwork lies in using a range of methods in order to collect data, interpret, and then translate them in such a way that they create a text that is comprehensible to others. These bridging activities of interpretation and translation, which lie at the heart of ethnography, demonstrate that it is possible to move between the emic and etic. As Avruch (2003) suggests, these activities are not only desirable, but necessary as well, if one is to avoid accounting for all observations in terms of cultural differences or to avoid being too insensitive to the role that culture plays in social conflict. Part of the skill and success of ethnography depends on the kinds of bridges that are built.

FIELDWORK OVER TIME

We usually think of rich points as taking place during a single stint of field research. In the case of those who are students or practitioners of conflict resolution, it may be unrealistic to think about longitudinal research when conditions are too volatile or efforts are being made to deal in an immediate way, through negotiation or mediation, with conflict. I would nevertheless argue that longitudinal research would probably enhance the success of these moments. There is no question that illuminating questions and insights emerge from doing research in the same region over many years, returning periodically. No matter how meticulous and conscientious ethnographers are about taking field notes, it is almost inevitable that they will not be able to track all the connections they need to make going forward. Evidence one encounters going forward into a situation makes a different kind of sense than evidence that one reviews looking backward, as in the retrospective case studies discussed in Chapters 6 and 7. It is only when looking backward that ethnographers realize a "plot" has unfolded or that they are missing key data that would either confirm or disconfirm their hunch about something important. Sometimes it is precisely what lurks in the margins that they have ignored or discounted as being trivial.

Similarly, that which becomes most familiar is often overlooked, yet may turn out to be exceedingly important. There is a remarkable tension between first-time field research and returning to the field. First-time field researchers experience exuberance, culture shock, anxiety, and the excitement of encountering everything as new, different, exotic, and stimulating to the senses. They are hyperaware, but fairly ignorant about history and the context in which these sensory delights, curiosities, or nightmares are unfolding.

Longitudinal research deepens familiarity between ethnographers and the people with whom they are working, and relationships become more nuanced and, generally, less strained. Notions of complex identities and a growing understanding of people's shared life experiences—deaths, births, weddings—unfold. Increased trust and better language skills permit for a more articulate expression of thoughts and sentiments. As a result, ethnographers are able to more accurately track change or the lack thereof. But longitudinal research is a double-edged sword. At the same time that relationships become routinized, this also means that the field situation becomes almost entirely expected and, therefore, the field-worker no longer notices or observes in a heightened fashion what is happening around him or her. Heightened observational powers are difficult to maintain when things become too comfortable.

It was pointed out to me that without a longitudinal perspective, field researchers may not realize the impact of social variables, such as age, on interactions.[2] For example, in many societies, youth are not permitted access to certain kinds of knowledge whereas elders are. Over the course of many years, the kind of knowledge shared by an informant with the ethnographer will differ as the ethnographer ages but returns periodically to his field site. As a young field researcher, there are certain things one is not allowed to know. As an elder, there are things one is introduced to, yet others that pass him by entirely because he should not have to be bothered with such matters. This varies from culture to culture. By doing longitudinal research, I also felt myself fortunate to be able to see better whether or not my hypotheses were borne out through time.

The Ethnographer's Tool Kit

Ethnographers, like any tool-making creatures, rely on tried and true methods in forging their tool kit. They have learned these methods, passed down and revised from one generation to the next of ethnographers. A skilled ethnographer uses these methods, but always mixes in a good dose of experience, insight, creativity, improvisation, and serendipity. These ingredients cannot be measured in a recipe. Nevertheless, each time an ethnographer embarks on field research, whether it is the first or fiftieth time, he or she should keep in mind the following advice.

• Excellence in participant-observation—consciously shedding ethnocentrism, cultivating cultural relativism, speaking and understanding the native language; listening well, not being intrusive, being alert to their own biases, and participating in people's daily lives—allows ethnographers to meet and interview the widest range of individuals and participate in the greatest number of activities at their field site.

• In interviewing subjects, ethnographers should try to move from key informants to a wider range of individuals; begin informal interviews with topics that do not appear to be threatening and that are of interest to people; in both formal and informal interviews, use different kinds of sampling; be sure to ask questions initially in an open-ended manner; be sensitive to the time people have taken from their daily work; and be conscious of the problems of relying on a translator or interpreter.

• In doing field research, ethnographers should recognize that their field site is not bounded, but rather affected by people, information, products, and political and economic processes from afar, and they should strive to work toward multi-sited research. They should also attempt to specify how the site itself may have an impact on processes or interactions that take place elsewhere.

• Ethnographers will always perform a tightrope act, illuminating the place of meanings, symbols, discourse, and representations in social dynamics, and also paying close attention to history in order to be attuned to how these symbolic representations and meanings become the vehicle for fortifying or justifying sociopolitical and economic structures of power. This balancing act builds bridges between emic and etic approaches to ethnographic analysis.

• The way ethnographers record their data and analyze them requires reflection and interpretation. Data and their interpretation are always partial. Taking field notes requires ethnographers to be disciplined in recording as exhaustively as possible each day's events. Ethnographers may want to consider using a software program to organize their notes. Making two or three sets of field notes is useful. One may incorporate the ethnographer's sentiments, reactions, and opinions; another may be chronological; a third might be arranged according to key topics. In taking field notes, ethnographers should always recognize possible connections and questions, using them to map out future directions of research.

• Ethnographic methods have an ethical component. Ethnographers should be familiar with the American Anthropological Association code of ethics and protect the subjects with whom they are doing research. They should behave with integrity, be respectful of their informants, and be sure to obtain proper permission to do field research. They should do their best to explain to subjects what their research is about and with whom they will be sharing their data and analysis. They should be careful about how they identify individuals and places in recording data.

These methods hardly constitute a complete tool kit, but they should allow a novice ethnographer considerable headway in making sense of other worlds and communicating that understanding to larger communities of professionals and nonprofessionals.

Discussion Questions

In this chapter, you have learned about the way an experienced field-worker prepares, collects, and records information; analyzes the information; and writes ethnographic interpretations. There are many lessons in this wide-ranging discussion for the student to learn. To help with the learning, we have written a number of discussion questions. Review them and reflect on whether you are now ready to conduct an ethnographic analysis of conflict within or between cultures and, then, write your results or interpretations for a dissertation or publication.

1. What is ethnography? What are the principal methods that an ethnographer uses and how do they differ from the other research methods described thus far in this book?

2. What impact does the use of these methods have on the kind of data that the researcher gathers?

3. What do you think is gained from aiming to understand rather than explain practices, beliefs, and values?

4. What are some disadvantages of using ethnographic methods?

5. Why do many ethnographers assume that all knowledge is partial?

6. What is multi-sited research and how does it differ from a more traditional case study?

7. What are some of the best ways to begin to establish rapport and reciprocity with research interlocutors or informants? What are some actions and behaviors to avoid in order not to alienate people?

8. What are some pitfalls that ethnographers should be aware of in conducting interviews?

9. What are some of the ways an ethnographer could deal with imbalances in economic and political power between him or her and the people with whom he or she is working?

10. What kinds of things should an ethnographer keep in mind in recording the data that he or she gathers for purposes of analysis? What are rich points and why are they important?

11. What do you think is the relationship between emic and etic methods or interpretations (see also Chapter 1)?

12. What do you think are the ethical considerations one should keep in mind in doing and writing an ethnography?

Notes

1. Useful resources for determining appropriate software programs to use in note recording and qualitative data analysis are Fetterman (1998), Fischer (1994), and

Weitzman and Miles (1995). Web site sources include the following: *Hyperresearch*, http://www.researchware.com/ or http://www.scolari.com/; *Ethnograph*, http://www.qualisResearch.com/ or http://www.scolari.com/; and *Citation*, http://www.citationonline.net/. Another Internet site, "Computer Programs Used in Ethnography and Ethnographic Data Analysis," linked to the American Anthropological Association Web site, also offers a range of resources. It can be found at http://www.stanford.edu/~davidf/ethnography.html.

2. Peter Black, personal communication.

Part VI

Analyzing Documents

Texts and Process Analysis

I n this part, we discuss one of the more popular approaches to the analysis of conflict. A considerable amount of information available to analysts comes from archival or textual sources. These include interview protocols, accounts of conflict processes provided by participant observers, descriptions of historical cases, speeches, policy documents, autobiographies, transcripts of discussions or conversations, and a variety of other kinds of publicly deposited documents. They also include real-time coding of ongoing interactions between parties to a conflict. These materials are valuable to the conflict analyst to the extent that they provide a window into the evolution and settlement of conflicts. They can be analyzed from at least two broad epistemological perspectives, one rooted primarily in positivism, the other in constructivism (see Chapter 1). A difference between the approaches is their respective focus on either behavior (largely etic) or subjective (emic) accounts. However, both approaches share the goal of searching for meaning in the form of speaker or writer intentions or worldviews.

Chapter 9 is a discussion of content analysis. This usually refers to the analysis of available text, but it applies also to analyses of ongoing conversations that are part of a conflict-resolving process. The discussion contains a mix of conceptual and practical issues. The prospective content analyst should know about the technical decisions that must be made in order to do an analysis: For example, a decision about the unit of text to be coded, the categories to be used, conducting reliability checks, and ways of combining codes for analysis.

The checklist of tasks, provided in the Chapter 9 section "Technical Issues for the Content Analyst," should help to organize a project as well as to remind the analyst that this is a time-consuming activity. The value of putting in the effort turns on the contributions made by content analysis studies. A sampling of these contributions is presented in the section on applications. These include both analyses of processes in experiments and case studies. The chapter then moves on to consider other complex forms of content analysis.

Chapter 10 is a discussion of one complex form of transcript analysis, which uses information from interviews or available text. This is the increasingly popular approach known as narrative analysis. As discussed by Linda Johnston, this approach is particularly sensitive to how language is used in different social contexts and emphasizes the vantage point of the speaker or actor. It also amplifies the role played by philosophical perspectives in doing research. Its placement here is intended to convey the idea that narrative analysis connects the analysis of oral and written communications, which is the theme of this part, with the active or involved subject idea highlighted in our discussion of action research in the next part of the book. The connections are made in the opening section of the chapter. The chapter concludes with an example of application to the tobacco conflict in the United States, which illustrates how the coding of a narrative is done. This example also conveys the storytelling feature of a narrative. This feature is seen by Senehi (2002) as playing an important role in the analysis and resolution of social conflict. Winslade and Monk (2000) regard it as a mediation tool for uncovering key relational issues that prevent disputants from addressing the conflict directly. And the contributors to Firth's (1994) collection of essays on negotiation highlight the linguistic aspects of negotiating discourses in the workplace. The stories and discourses can be generated within the framework of an action research project, and this is also discussed in Chapter 12.

Both chapters in this part end with a set of questions for discussion and review.

9

Content Analysis

Content analysis techniques help to organize the material systematically for both time-series and comparative analyses. There are, however, a variety of approaches that fall under the content analysis rubric. They range from simple mechanical word counts to broad-gauged interpretations of themes. Many of them are introduced in this chapter following an overview of the general approach and discussion of the technical issues surrounding its implementation.

Overview of the Approach

A general definition of content analysis is provided by Holsti (1969) as "any technique for making inferences by objectively and systematically identifying specified characteristics of messages" (p. 14). It is a flexible approach to analysis that can be applied to a wide variety of written or oral communications, allowing analysts to compare the content of communication across a variety of settings. A useful distinction that is relevant to CA&R is made between text and interaction process analysis. Texts are written documents that describe activities that have taken place in the past. There is little urgency in making coding decisions because the text can be read and reread at the convenience of the analyst. Process analysis usually consists of on-the-spot coding of statements made during interactions. This tradition can be traced to a coding system developed by Bales (1950) to capture processes in small problem-solving groups. Unlike text analysis, there is time urgency as coders must make decisions in conjunction with the ongoing conversations. Often, the coding decisions are made unobtrusively, behind one-way mirrors; sometimes they are made by observers positioned off to the side of the group. In either location, coders have limited time to reflect on or correct their decisions. Althoughaccuracy may be a problem, on-the-spot coding can enrich interpretations by taking expressions, especially affect, and the interaction context into account. Transcriptions of the conversations are limited to what has been said. Both of these types of content analysis are discussed in this chapter.

Both types of analysis can be performed for purposes of description or inference. Analyses that address questions of *what was said, who said it, and to whom it was said* describe the interaction. This is similar to a blow-by-blow account of a boxing match, capturing the moment-by-moment actions and re-actions. These codings are useful for charting trends in a process over time. Analyses that address questions of *why something was said, how it was said, and with what effect* provide interpretation. They are inferences about speakers' intentions and impacts that confer meaning on the interactions. For example, words used by negotiators to qualify a statement about their position on an issue may indicate their commitment to that position (how it was said). The reaction of the other negotiator is gauged by his or her statements, indicating attempts to abandon further discussion on that issue, further reinforce their own commitment to their position, or to offer a compromise or willingness to accept the other's proposal (with what effect). Relationships between communications made within the negotiation and underlying intentions may be corroborated by statements made by the negotiators in interviews or other settings outside the talks (why it was said). These inferences are made in the context of a research design that "ensures that the data gathering, analysis, and interpretation are integrated" (Holsti, 1969, p. 27). Content analysis codes are particularly relevant in the various time-series designs discussed in Chapter 6.

An important issue for content analysis is the validity of inferences made from the coding. This issue can be understood in terms of trade-offs between coding accuracy (reliability) and the meaning of the coding categories (validity). Agreement is usually easier to obtain with the descriptive categories addressing the questions *what, who,* and *to whom*. For example, a concession made in a laboratory experiment may be defined as the difference in offers made at time t and at $t + 1$. This coding of concessions is routine. Less agreement is likely to occur when concessions must be inferred from suggestions, exploratory proposals, and packages that combine several offers, as in many complex, real-world negotiations. In this case, coding is an interpretive exercise done with categories designed to capture these elements as they appear in negotiators' statements. The room for interpretation afforded by these categories is likely to reduce inter-coder agreement. It may, however, enhance the validity of the inferences made in attempting to answer the questions *why, how, and with what effect*. In an attempt to capture the richness of a concept such as concessions, a content analyst must rely on his or her understanding of the negotiation process, which includes the various ways concessions are expressed in statements and moves made through time. Because validity—referred to also as construct validity—depends on this sort of understanding, it is not surprising that inter-coder agreement is reduced.

The trade-off between reliability and validity is a consideration in decisions about whether to develop original content analysis systems or to adopt categories used by others in related applications. Original systems favor validity; adapted systems emphasize reliability. The emic research tradition, which was discussed in Chapters 1 and 8, prefers original categories. Reasons given for this preference are that the categories should be constructed to capture the essence of the phenomenon (e.g., a certain type of negotiation or mediation process), the categories are not independent of the data at hand, and comparison is not the purpose of analysis. In this tradition, validity refers to meaning defined in the context of single cases. Reliability suffers to the extent that specialized knowledge is needed to code the case materials.

The etic research tradition, discussed also in the earlier chapters, favors standard categories. This preference is based on the assumption that coding categories are independent of the data and on the desire for comparing different cases. In this tradition, validity refers to the accuracy of comparisons and to the generalizability of results. Reliability is strengthened to the extent that specialized knowledge is not needed to apply the categories to textual or process material. However, conflict analysts' preference for original categories has led to a plethora of content analysis systems in CA&R. One implication of this preference has been limited comparative research on topics in this field.

Pit against the many advantages of content analysis are arguments made against its use. Four criticisms have been made: (1) the codes miss nuances and innuendos that are the essence of conversation and interaction; (2) the exclusive focus on what is said misses other aspects of the process; (3) the analysis is limited by the material available in archives or by the access permitted; and (4) the analysis is restricted to micro-level interactions and, as a result, misses the broader structural context in which those interactions occur. Although these may indeed be criticisms leveled at a particular application of the methodology, they should not be considered as arguments against this general approach to analysis of text or process.

With regard to the first criticism, it is the case that any content analysis system can be fine-tuned to detect subtle aspects of processes. The history of the bargaining process analysis (BPA) system illustrates the way a system evolves with experience and developments in the conceptual literature of negotiation: The expansion of the initial system, from 13 to 33 categories, reflects a growing sensitivity to aspects of negotiated interactions largely ignored in the earlier literature on bargaining (see Harris, 1996). Regarding the second criticism, it is the case that verbal statements are the primary material for the content analyst; however, a system need not be limited to this material. Indeed, process analysis systems include the coding of emotion and nonverbal behavior evident to the analyst who observes (and codes) on-the-spot interactions. On the third criticism, limited material may indeed restrict an analysis. This is, however, a problem of sampling rather than a problem of the methodology. Small unrepresentative texts or data sets can have dire implications for inference, whether the research consists of surveys, cases, or textual material. Similarly, the matter of focusing on micro-level interactions is not a criticism of content or process analysis. The insights provided by the analysis at that level must be bolstered by complementary analyses of events that occur in the larger context within which those interactions occur. The adequacy of any analysis depends on its comprehensiveness. Research designs that include content analysis vary in terms of this criterion.

Some critics of the approach claim that it "atomizes" the content of communications. In their search for broad themes that capture meaning, these critics overlook the fact that the methodology does not preclude the emergence of contextual meanings. The issue concerns the way the technique is used. The unit of analysis could be the word or sentence, on the one hand, or a large chunk of text on the other. What is usually of greater interest to the CA&R researcher is the developing sequence of actions within a conflict resolution process over some period of time that can be followed with the tools of content analysis. We turn now to a discussion of those tools, which include the technical decisions facing an analyst keen on exploring a particular research problem.

Technical Issues for the Content Analyst

Like other research methodologies, content analysis consists of technical procedures that require the analyst to make decisions. A first decision concerns the material to be coded. For many CA&R researchers, the material is often conversations intended to settle or resolve disputes. The conversations can be video- or audiotaped for later analysis; or, they can be observed at the moment they are taking place. An important question is whether the available material or opportunities for observation cover the entire process. If so, then the analysis can capture the various stages through which the process evolves. If not, then the analyst must consider the implications of doing an analysis without the missing material. Questions asked include: Is the available material sufficient to describe the settlement process? Is the material sufficient to draw inferences about factors that influence that process? Can other methods, such as interviews, be used to recover some or most of the missing information? Another problem occurs when there is simply too much material to code, given the available resources. When this happens, it is necessary to develop a sampling plan. Sampling considerations are the same as those entertained for survey research discussed in Chapter 5. A premium is placed on some form of random sampling. When sampling is done carefully, an analyst can be confident that the coded material represents the larger extended process within which the sampled material is embedded.

A second decision concerns the unit of coding. For content analysts, this refers to the size of the unit and how it will be counted. The unit can range from single words or sentences to large sections of text (or process), including single speaker units, dyadic (or group) speaker units, issue discussions, timed units such as sessions, or even thematic discussions that span issues. This decision turns on the appropriate unit of meaning as defined by the purpose of the project. For example, a question about how often various issues are raised in a mediated dispute is answered by simply counting the number of times they are mentioned. If, however, an analyst wants to know how disputants conceive of relationships among two or more issues, a speaker unit (complete statements made by speakers) is appropriate. If the question is about differences between disputants on the issues, the dyadic unit (statement and reply) is preferred. And if the project is typological in the sense of classifying and comparing different kinds of mediated disputes, larger thematic units would be desired. In this case, a transcript would be coded for the relative prevalence of, for example, distributive or problem-solving themes.

Decisions about unit size also include reliability-validity trade-offs. Generally, the smaller the unit, the more reliably it is likely to be coded. The larger the unit, the better the chance of capturing connected themes and conversational context. To the extent that the broader context (or frame) is indeed captured, validity is enhanced. Validity is also improved when the range or scope of variations in a concept is reflected in the coding categories. The difference between a coding system that distinguishes between positive and negative affect versus a system that allows for gradations along a continuum of emotional expression is a case in point.

A third decision concerns the way the codes are used in analysis. This is known as the aggregation-disaggregation issue. The coding unit, which emphasizes meaning, may not be the unit of analysis, which emphasizes patterns and relationships. For example, the frequency of threats used in a negotiation may be regarded as one of several indicators of tough posturing. Others include commitments, accusations, attacks, warnings, and ultimatums. By combining these categories, an analyst can develop an index of "toughness." Similarly, promises, accommodations, acceptances, and arguments that support the other's positions would indicate soft posturing. The combination of these categories forms an index of "softness." Various ratios of the difference between these indices (corrected for by the total number of statements) can be constructed for charting trends in verbal behavior, including periods where escalation or de-escalation occurred. One advantage of aggregating codes in this way is efficiency: The analysis focuses on one rather than many variables. Another is that the general concept of toughness has currency in the bargaining literature, making it useful for comparative analysis. A disadvantage of aggregation is that distinctions among types of tough and soft behavior are lost, which is a critique leveled at the methodology. Of course, by coding the various components of these concepts (the unit of meaning), an analyst can perform both aggregated and disaggregated analyses of the trends.

Other kinds of aggregation decisions include time periods and speaker units. Micro coding units such as minute-by-minute (or sentence-by-sentence) remarks may mask larger patterns in the data. As with language codes, the key is to identify a meaningful time unit. These are often framed by the way meetings or workshops are organized, for example, conference agenda topics, negotiating rounds, problem-solving stages, sections of speeches, or months of activities. These organizing units are the aggregated data points in time-series or process-tracing analyses of unfolding interactions. Although statements (or words) are usually coded by individual speakers, the effective unit for some processes is the dyad, team, or delegation. This is especially the case in the highly interactive situations characteristic of most conflict resolution encounters, including negotiation, mediation, facilitation, and workshops. It is less the case for analyses of speeches made by national leaders or communications sent and received outside of conference settings. This decision has consequences for statistical analyses. The validity of inferential statistics depends on satisfying the assumption of independence between units of analysis.

Aggregation decisions also have implications for comparative research in the etic tradition. The moment-by-moment analyses performed in some content analysis studies contribute to deeper probes of interactions. They may pose problems for making comparisons between situations or cases. Comparability is actually helped by settling on aggregated units such as indexes of competitiveness (toughness) or cooperation (softness). These more abstract concepts transcend specific situations and, thus, contribute to research that seeks to uncover generalizable processes or patterns. The concepts reflect larger themes, aggregated from the micro-codings, that have currency in various settings. In research on problem-solving workshops, the substantive issues discussed have meaning primarily in terms of the history and development of a particular dispute. Thus, coding categories that deal with substance are less useful for comparisons among different workshops. On the other hand, categories that capture aspects of the interactions, such as indicators of cohesion or dissension, are more useful for comparison. The various adaptations of interaction process analysis (Bales, 1950) consist of these sorts of general categories. Many useful analyses of negotiation have included both substantive and process categories in the coding systems (see Druckman, 2002a, for a review).

A guiding list for performing a content analysis is provided in the box on pp. 264–265. Like any research technique, content analysis is implemented in the context of a research design. Thus, the first two points in the list deal with issues of design and hypothesis formulation. The next three points refer to the construction of the content analysis system. A conceptual framework serves to connect the system's categories with the theoretical literature: For example, the BPA system combines work done on strategic bargaining (Schelling, 1960) with work on social interactions in small groups (Bales, 1950). The categories are attempts to operationalize the concepts: For example, BPA strategic concepts are represented by categories such as demands, commitments, threats, and promises; interactive categories include agreements and disagreements, questions and answers, as well as positive and negative affect. Coding rules are defined in terms of the definitions of the categories: For examples, threats are defined as predicting negative consequences if another does not behave in a stated manner.

Points 6, 7, and 8 focus on the textual material to be coded. Often the available relevant material is either too voluminous or insufficient for analysis. When there is simply too much material, as in transcripts or memoranda from a multi-year dialogue or negotiation process, it is necessary to sample. Various random sampling designs, comparable to those used in survey research (see Chapter 5), can be used: For example, stratified sampling would ensure that each time period or process stage (strata) is represented in the analysis. The next decision is the unit of analysis. As discussed above, the content analyst must weigh the advantages and disadvantages of smaller and larger units of analysis, and this decision may be different for conversational as compared to textual material.

The next six points (9–14 in the checklist) refer to the coding process. First, a sample of the material is coded by at least two independent coders. Reliability of the categories depends on the extent to which the coders agree on the assignments to categories. Agreement is indicated when they assign the same unit (sentence, speaker unit) to the same category (a threat). These results provide guidance to the analyst with regard to common meanings and ease of application. Some revision of the categories or their definitions may improve the coding system, but these new categories should also be assessed for reliability. The next steps include recruiting and training two or more coders as well as preparing the forms to be used in the final coding process. Criteria for selecting coders include distance from the project and its hypotheses, experience in coding, and acceptable training results. Because coding decisions are not right or wrong answers, there is no criterion of accuracy. However, coders can indicate the extent to which they are confident in their decisions. They can also discuss the reasons for their decisions, especially when differences between the coders emerge.

When all coding decisions have been made, the data are ready to be analyzed. There are many ways to analyze the coded data, ranging from detailed time series to broadly interpretive narratives. A first decision is whether the coding categories should be combined into a larger unit such as strategic or substantive behavior. This decision is based on the way the research problem is conceptualized (Points 1–3). For example, an analyst interested in the influence of strategy on joint decisions may simply combine all the separate kinds of strategic codes into one index. The advantage of coding different kinds of strategic behavior (such as threats and promises) enables the analyst to distinguish among the kinds of strategies used. Thus, both aggregated and disaggregated analyses can be performed. Of course, there are several ways to combine categories. Implications of different aggregation decisions can be developed from sensitivity analyses, which consist of comparing results from the same analyses performed with different aggregations. When the aggregation decision has been made, allowing for the possibility of no aggregation of categories, the researcher is ready to perform analyses.

If the text or process data are coded in a chronological order, then a variety of time-series and process-tracing analyses are appropriate. If time is not important, then cross-sectional correlations or thematic interpretations are relevant. Further, when other types of data are available, these can be correlated with the content or process codes. For example, events data provide an opportunity to explore the effects of outside activities on a small-group problem-solving process. Perceptual data provide an opportunity to compare the actors' (or parties') views with their coded statements. All of these analyses are understood in the context of the research design and hypotheses formulated before the content analysis system is constructed. The analyses or, more broadly, the content analysis experience, also provides lessons for the category system, leading perhaps to renovations before the next applications are contemplated.

Content Analysis Checklist

1. Construct a research design to guide the study.

2. Formulate research questions or hypotheses to be evaluated by the analysis.

3. Develop a conceptual framework for the content analysis system.

4. Define the categories in the system.

5. Develop coding rules for the categories; these are considered to be operational definitions.

6. Identify a universe of (usually verbal) material about which inferences will be made; this may include collecting original data.

7. Design a sampling frame (some form of random sampling) for selecting the material to be coded (from the universe).

8. Decide on a unit of analysis: decide among grammatical, speaker, or thematic units.

9. Perform reliability analyses with independent coders on a sample of the material.

10. Pretest the coding rules for ease of application; assess face validity.

11. Revise the categories and coding rules based on the reliability analysis and pretests.

12. Recruit coders who are unaware of the research design or hypotheses.

13. Train the coders to criteria of confidence and reliability.

14. Prepare the final coding forms and code the selected material.

15. Aggregate the data for analysis by relevant categories.

16. Perform sensitivity analyses to compare results with different aggregations of categories and speaker units.

17. Perform statistical or other (qualitative) analyses on the aggregated data.

18. Correlate the coded variables with other data collected for the study (events, decisions, perceptions).

19. Interpret the results of analyses, develop implications for research questions, and make inferences to the universe from which the sampled materials were drawn.

20. Prepare a report including lessons learned for the research problem and for the content analysis system.

Content Analysis Applications

In this section, several content analysis applications to CA&R problems are discussed. Many of the applications are analyses of negotiations and, thus, illustrate process coding. However, the distinction, made earlier, between process and textual analysis is often blurred. Conversations during negotiation or mediation sessions are infrequently coded on the spot. More often, they are transcribed and coded from a text of the back-and-forth discussions. As a result, certain aspects of the process are missed: for example, nonverbal expressions and side conversations. Although the focus is on the interaction process, and this is a primary data collection, it shares some features with secondary analyses of texts, such as distance from the experience itself. But, as noted above, losses in validity are compensated for to some extent by gains in coding accuracy. The examples to follow illuminate this hybrid form of content analysis. Like any technique, the value of content analysis is judged by the contributions made to knowledge. Some contributions are illustrated in this section. I begin with recent applications of the bargaining process analysis system.

EXPANDING THE CODING SYSTEM

A revised version of the BPA was developed to take into account problem-solving behavior. These changes reflected a trend in the negotiation literature away from an emphasis on competitive bargaining and compromise to cooperative problem-solving and integrative agreements (Hopmann, 1995). The revised system, which expanded the number of categories from 13 to 33, increases the validity of process analysis by taking a larger variety of negotiating behavior into account. The system has been further enhanced by merging its categories with those developed in a parallel project by Lebedeva (1991). Her system adds the feature of negotiating phases, which are distinguished as classification, discussion, and coordination. The frequency of different coded behavior varies across these phases. Most of her categories appear during the initial phase (stressing points in common, stressing differences) and the final phase (identifying areas of agreement, rejecting a proposal, escalating demands). However, her category of "revealing positions" occurs mostly during the middle phase, along with a variety of BPA categories. By merging the two systems, categories of negotiating behavior can be divided into early, middle, and late phases of the talks. By adding topic codes, the system would also enable an analyst to chart trends by issue area within and between phases.

The combined system was used to evaluate a well-known hypothesis about behavior in small problem-solving groups. Referred to as the *phase-movement hypothesis* (Bales & Strodtbeck, 1951), it claims that an increasing number of both positive reactions (stressing points in common) and negative reactions (stressing differences) will occur from the first to the middle to the final stages of actions. Similarly, an increasing trend of controlling behaviors (making suggestions) is expected to occur while a decreasing trend of orientation acts (questions and answers) is expected. And most evaluative statements occur in the middle phase. Landsberger's (1955) analysis of 12 collective bargaining sessions showed that the trends in behavior followed these hypothesized patterns. The hypothesis about positive and negative reactions was only partially supported by the results of coded simulation transcripts: Support was obtained for positive but not for negative reactions.

COMPARING SIMULATED WITH HISTORICAL NEGOTIATIONS

The combined system was also used to compare the transcripts of simulated and real-world diplomats discussing similar issues. The key difference was that real-world negotiators displayed considerably more strategic maneuvering with accompanying affect (as inferred from the text) than the student role players in the simulations. Overall, the diplomats showed harder rhetoric—more statements stressing differences were made—than did the simulated negotiators, who showed more statements stressing similarities. Eighty percent of the simulation codes were in the categories of initiations, questions, and answers. The diplomats' codes were more evenly distributed across the categories of the two systems.

The BPA system was used to evaluate hypotheses in the context of an historical negotiation that took place in Lausanne just after WWI. Content analysis of the actual transcripts and those developed from a simulation of the negotiation provided an opportunity to ascertain differences and similarities between the settings. Several similarities were discovered. The enhanced competitiveness (on BPA categories) of the Turkish delegates in a coalition (compared to being a single party facing a coalition) was reproduced in the simulation. Similarly, the Greek delegates were more competitive as a member of a coalition facing a single party in both the actual conference and in the simulation. With regard to the incidence of disagreements (coded by BPA categories), the Greeks, but not the Turkish delegates, showed similar results in the simulated and real-world settings. Such similarities of process as these would seem to provide strong evidence for the impact of coalition membership on negotiating behavior. Being a member of a coalition increased the frequency of competitive statements (but not disagreements) made by the diplomats in the 1920s and by the student role players in the 1990s. These findings also strengthen the case for convergent validity of the simulation (see Beriker & Druckman, 1996, for details; see also the Chapter 3 section "Simulation Designs").

The BPA categories have been used also in modeling analyses. The evaluation of alternative models of reciprocity by Druckman and Harris (1990), discussed in Chapter 6 in the section "Time-Series Designs and Analyses," was extended back in time in analyses of the Lausanne talks. Using four indices of the BPA system (two versions of hard-soft behavior, agree-disagree, and positive-negative affect), Beriker and Druckman (1991) compared the goodness of fit of three models: directional (tit-for-tat), trend (evaluating past trends in response), and cooperative (evaluating similarity of response in the previous move) reciprocity. Confirming the earlier results, more significant correlations were obtained for the comparative model, which emphasizes perceived fairness, than for the trend and directional models. These results demonstrate that the same pattern that characterizes modern negotiators' behavior depicted the way that diplomats responded to each other in a much earlier historical period.

The BPA categories were used as well in a more complicated modeling analysis. The aim was to discover patterns of response in a multilateral negotiation.

Through the use of various combinations of correlations, both multiple (combined effects of several delegations' behavior on others' responses) and partial (effects of one nation's behavior on another, controlling for the behavior displayed by other delegations), we could gauge more precisely the influence between any pair or trio of national delegations, controlling for other interactions that took place in the talks. We discovered, for example, that the statements made by the lead delegation in one bloc influenced the statements made by the other bloc's leader in the next round when the influence of a key ally in the former bloc was removed: The lagged correlation between the bloc leaders was reduced when the ally's moves were included in the analysis.

The importance of these sorts of analyses of BPA data is that they parse out influences between pairs of nations in highly interdependent interactive systems like multilateral negotiations. They allow an analyst both to infer causation, through the use of lagged correlations, and to reduce the spuriousness of relationships, by using partial correlations (see the Chapter 6 section "Time-Series Designs and Analyses" for a discussion of these correlation techniques).

As I mentioned at the beginning of this section, the value of content analysis is realized by the importance of the findings it has produced. By this criterion, the BPA, as one kind of system, is quite valuable. Four of my research projects, discussed earlier, attest to its value. The first project I did with BPA was an analysis of a base-rights negotiation between Spain and the United States. Statements were coded, according to BPA categories, over time, producing trends of hard and soft posturing through the rounds. More detailed analyses of the trends revealed patterns identified as crises (a breakdown in the tasks) and turning points (events or decisions signaling progress) (Druckman, 1986). Patterns of coded statements were also discovered in a BPA analysis of a multilateral negotiation that took place in the 1980s. The patterns revealed areas in which compromise was feasible and the tactical behavior of the delegations. This information was useful in delegation planning for future rounds (see Druckman & Hopmann, 1989). The patterns discovered in the base-rights study were evaluated in the context of other negotiations. They were shown to depict the way negotiators responded to each other in seven cases (Druckman & Harris, 1990). Added to the insights produced by these BPA studies are the analyses performed on the Lausanne peace talks documents. Those analyses showed that agreements were more likely to occur when equally weak parties negotiate.

More recently, Ozcelik (2004) used the BPA system to compare negotiating processes in a simulated negotiation over ozone regime issues with actual climate change talks that took place within the Conference of Parties, the main arm of the UN Framework Convention of Climate Change. He found similar differences between asymmetrical and symmetrical power configurations in the simulation and case. Asymmetrical negotiating coalitions were less competitive and agreed more often than symmetrical coalitions. The stronger parties did not push through an agreement that benefited them more than the weaker parties within the coalition: Both the strong and weak members of the asymmetrical coalitions were satisfied with the agreements. These studies illustrate the value of this coding system for performing comparative research.

APPLICATIONS OF OTHER CONTENT ANALYSIS APPROACHES

Simulations

Process findings obtained in the simulation study by Druckman, Broome, and Korper (1988) provide another example of the value of content analysis. Analyses of outcomes did not distinguish between the fractionation and facilitation conditions: Recall the difference between Fisher's idea of fractionating issues and Burton's idea of discussing value differences. However, the analysis of the statements made during bargaining proved telling. Facilitation bargainers directed more statements toward joint rather than self-interests, agreed more often, and made fewer statements indicating dominance than those in the fractionation condition. Along with other results on process, these findings made the difference between a minor and substantial study suitable for the peer-review journal that published it.

A follow-up study by Druckman and Broome (1991), appearing a few years later in the same journal, added more interesting process findings. Their coding system consisted essentially of two categories: orientation as competitive, neutral, or cooperative and appeal as self, joint, or other. Interestingly, simulation role players in a low-liking condition expressed more cooperation and appealed more to joint interests than those in the contrasting high-liking condition, who appealed more to self-interests. This unexpected finding was interpreted as an example of ingratiating tactics used to persuade a difficult, recalcitrant opponent to compromise. The representative who disliked his or her opponent used appeals to mutual interests and a cooperative orientation to convince the other to reach an agreement; the representative who liked his or her opponent had less need to use these tactics and consequently adopted a more neutral posture, neither competitive nor cooperative.

Field Experiment

In their field experiment on mediation, McGillicuddy et al. (1987) developed a verbal content analysis system for coding both disputant behavior (26 categories) and mediator behavior (28 categories). As noted in Chapter 3, this study showed strong effects of the experimental conditions (mediation, mediator/arbitrator [med/arb] same, and med/arb different) on process indicators but not on the types of settlements obtained. The most striking differences were found between the med/arb same condition (the same person who was a mediator becomes an arbitrator) and the other two conditions. Although disputants were generally more cooperative and less hostile in this condition, the mediators used more heavy-pressure tactics, especially in the later phases of the interaction. This was done presumably in order to get an agreement before they turned into arbitrators. This did not happen (no difference among the conditions in outcomes). Apparently, disputants expected a fair decision from the mediator in his or her new role as arbitrator. Like the simulation studies reviewed just above, this experiment illustrates the value of process analysis. The coding systems reveal patterns that would be masked by focusing only on the outcomes of mediation.

Elaborate Coding Systems

More elaborate process analysis systems have been developed for coding bargaining behavior. The Neu and Graham (1994) system consists of 26 behaviors in the categories of content variables (self-disclosures, commitments), linguistic structure variables (hedges, use of *we* and the presumptive *you*), and paralanguage variables (pauses, volume changes, pitch, laughter). The paralanguage variables are rarely included in other process analysis systems, including BPA. Although significant relationships were found between certain aggregate behaviors (garrulousness, instrumental behavior) and outcomes (profits, satisfaction), the process codes were not related to self-report questions about similar behaviors. These discrepancies suggest that negotiators have difficulty recalling their own behavior even when asked immediately after the bargaining session.[1] In the sprit of multi-method research, it would be advantageous to include both types of measures. Behavior codes indicate what and how something was said; the questions designed to appraise one's own negotiating experience indicate attitudes.

A similar system of 21 categories was used by Roemer, Garb, Neu, and Graham (1999) to compare within-group Russian and American bargaining behavior on such types of statements as questions, information, commitments, conditions (threats, promises), consistency appeals, psychological tools (rewards and punishments), and garrulous behavior. They found similar patterns for the two groups: Most statements were made in the information exchange category, and both sides made frequent use of commitments, commands or requests, and promises. These similarities contrast with earlier analyses of differences between Soviet and American behavior (Druckman & Hopmann, 1989). Perhaps they reflect the changes that resulted from the end of the cold war. However, there were some differences, notably in the category of instrumental behaviors. The American bargainers put greater emphasis on promises and threats than the Russians did. The Russians emphasized commands, requests, and consistency appeals more than the Americans did. Whether Russians and Americans behave in these ways when negotiating with each other, rather than only with their own compatriots, remains to be discovered.

Another elaborate coding system combines categories used in several earlier systems. It was designed to record behavior as it occurred in court-appointed mediation sessions held at the Washington, D.C., small claims court. Mediators and disputants took part in a field experiment on the effects of furniture configuration in the mediation room on the mediation process. Half the sessions were assigned randomly to a chairs-without-tables configuration; the other half of the trios (two disputants, one mediator) discussed the issues behind tables. Another variable—an emphasis on own or joint orientation to the dispute—was included for a 2×2 factorial design. In addition to outcomes, various aspects of the discussions were coded on-the-spot. These included codes from BPA (agreements/disagreements, accommodations and commitments, offers and demands, promises and threats), the system used by Lebedeva (1991) (recognize common, recognize own), the interaction process analysis system (positive and negative emotions), and other categories suitable to the situation (caucusing, non-caucusing with the mediator). Various indices (e.g., offers divided by offers + demands; offers divided by minutes) and aggregations (e.g., similar to the hard-soft posturing distinction in BPA) were constructed.

Across the board, few of these coded variables were influenced by the conditions. The results did suggest some interesting explanations, however. One highlights the difficulty of getting significant effects for experimental conditions in non-replication field experiments. Many different types of disputes are likely to increase the within-condition error variance. Another explanation is that the disputants paid more attention to the mediator than to the other party, reducing the impact of the arrangement of space between the parties. A third is that the high (real-world) emotion aroused in the disputants reduced their reaction to visual cues in the room. This is known as the emotional flooding hypothesis. And a fourth explanation is that an apparent strong desire to win prevented the disputants from forming a positive relationship with each other as expected in the chairs-configuration condition. These explanations are the basis for new experiments, which is a benefit of research that can put a smiling face on negative results.

Coding Texts in Real Time

Another kind of content analysis study explored the relationship between peace processes and post-settlement relations in two cases, the 1994 negotiations over Nagorno Karabakh and the 1991–1992 talks to end the civil war in Mozambique. Statements were coded in four categories from texts describing the negotiations. The categories included an emphasis on relative power or absolute gains, emphasis on positions or interests, distributive or integrative bargaining, and concession exchange versus information exchange. One finding obtained from the aggregate codes was that the Karabakh negotiators were very competitive (an overall average, across the four categories, of –2 on a scale ranging from +3 as most cooperative to –3 as most competitive with 0 as a middle point). The Mozambican negotiators engaged in a process described as mixed motive, consisting of both competitive bargaining and cooperative problem solving (an overall average of 0 on the aggregated scale). The Karabakh process resulted in a limited cease-fire, which perpetuated the conflictual relationship between the parties. The Mozambican process resulted in a cessation of hostilities, a restructuring of the military, and political elections. This outcome led to improved relations among the previously warring parties in the post-settlement period. The content analysis data were instrumental in demonstrating this connection between process and societal change (see Druckman & Lyons, 2004).

Coding Hostage Negotiation

Donohue and Roberto (1993) coded the transcripts of 10 actual hostage negotiations to evaluate a perspective referred to as *negotiated order theory* (Strauss, 1978). The analysis consisted of several steps. First, each speaker utterance was divided into thought units that represent complete ideas (an independent clause with a subject and an object). Second, the units were coded in terms of dimensions of spatial (expressions of increased or decreased affiliation) and implicit (specification of the subject and object of the thought unit indicating inter-dependence) immediacy. Third, the immediacy codes were translated into the relational phases, as follows:

- High spatial, high implicit = moving toward
- High spatial, low implicit = moving with
- Low spatial, high implicit = moving against
- Low spatial, low implicit = moving away

In the fourth step, these relational properties were translated into several possible phase patterns or relational contexts. The patterns reflect a distinction between an emphasis on one or another relational property (toward, with, against, away), a sequential combination of the properties, or no particular emphasis, referred to as a null phase. Rules for defining the boundaries of phases were implemented by a computer program. This is a good example of how theories of interaction processes can be operationalized and evaluated with systematic procedures. The study also produced interesting results.

The analyses were designed to discover relational patterns across the 10 cases. Despite the diversity of the cases, parties tended to stick to a particular relational pattern once it was established. These patterns were usually either the "with-toward" or "away-against" combinations. The former pattern indicates high affiliation (spatial immediacy) with alternating inter-dependence (implicit immediacy). The latter pattern reflects low affiliation with alternating inter-dependence. Thus, the affiliation dimension was dominant in establishing a pattern for this type of highly charged, intense negotiation. This study demonstrated relatively stable patterns across the cases that "cycled around the inter-dependence relational dimension while holding steady on the affiliation parameter" (Donohue & Roberto, 1993, p. 195). Together with other findings, the research provides support for the assumptions of negotiated order theory. It is a good example of how content analysis techniques can be developed to capture several dimensions of interaction in a dynamic environment. The emphasis on phase transitions is also relevant to the work on process tracing and turning points discussed in Chapter 7. Whether these patterns are similar to those likely to occur in other kinds of negotiations awaits further research.

Coding Rule Use

Earlier research, also from the field of communication, focused on rule use in negotiation. Based on the assumption that bargaining is governed by a set of communication rules (e.g., Cushman, 1977), Donohue (1981) developed an elaborate category system for coding interaction processes in distributive negotiations. His categories were intended to capture the way negotiators use rules as well as to distinguish between winners and losers in competitive bargaining. Two groups of rules were formulated, a set of cueing rules and a set of responding rules: The distinction is that the former is not construed in relation to a prior utterance while the latter is. Each of these types of rules is divided further into the categories of attacking, defending, and regressing tactics. Experimental data were analyzed to explore the relationship between the cue and response codes. Using Markov chain procedures (see Chapter 3), Donohue showed how each cueing rule was related to each response cue: Examples are that the optimal response to a discrediting attack is a strong defense (rule CR1 in Donohue, 1981), that denying fault is necessary to sustain a user's position (rule CR4), that concessions are perhaps the most clear indication that the users' expected outcomes have been reduced (rule CR6), and that the failure to address a statement requiring a response gives tacit concession to the point being attacked (rule RR6).

The results largely supported the expectation that the outcome of negotiation was structured by the set of rules. In particular, the use of these rules distinguished between winners and losers in the competitive negotiation. They approached the situation differently: Winners made more offers and stuck to them while rejecting the losers' concessions, thereby gaining even greater concessions. Losers gave more conditional support while winners gave more outright rejections in response to almost every cue. A larger implication of these findings is that reciprocity (cooperation in response to cooperation) may not work well in distributive bargaining situations: Cooperativeness gave the other an opportunity to become more confrontational and less conciliatory. Winners used greater firmness more consistently.

We have, however, learned in more recent years that toughness may produce sub-optimal outcomes for the "winner" (see Druckman, 2003, for a review). Further, we have learned about strategies for changing competitive perceptions or for converting distributive into integrative situations (e.g., Conlon, Carnevale, & Ross, 1994). In Donohue's terms, the rule structure may be different in less competitive or more integrative situations; as well, the rules may change as perceptions of the situation change. Little is known about these different rule structures, and the pioneering content analyses performed in this study may continue to open avenues for further research that builds on the model.

This work on rule use concludes the chapter on content analysis. Let us now review the topic with the help of a set of discussion questions.

Discussion Questions

In this chapter, we have discussed many kinds of content analysis systems. These range from mechanical coding of words from texts to on-the-spot coding of live interactions. Each of these systems provides a window into the flow of ongoing dialogue and conversations. A key issue is whether microscopic (small units of analysis, such as words or sentences) or thematic (larger chunks of text) approaches better capture the meaning intended in the verbal material. One issue raised by this distinction is the trade-off between reliability and validity: The former may be enhanced by coding smaller units, the latter may be stronger for thematic coding. A number of other research issues surface for the content analyst. Many of these are similar to those raised by other methods—for example, sampling, coding rules, aggregation. They are, however, defined by the material available to the content analyst, for example, defining a universe of text, translating words into coding categories, and combining codes into larger categories to facilitate analysis. Now that you have read about these and related matters, we are now ready to review what has been learned.

1. Describe some differences between the analysis of text (content analysis) and of live interactions (process analysis).

2. Why is the distinction between descriptive and inferential analyses important? Give examples of each kind of system in conflict analysis.

3. Describe the trade-off between accuracy of coding (reliability) and the meaning of the codes (validity) in content analysis. What are the features of a reliable system? What features define a more valid system?

4. What are some arguments that emphasize the strengths of content analysis? What might be some weaknesses and how can these be addressed by the analyst?

5. Apply the checklist of tasks to a project that you are contemplating carrying out. How long would it take to complete? What is needed in terms of resources?

6. What are some advantages of using content analysis to compare two or more groups, organizations, or cultures? What are some of the technical issues that arise in making such comparisons?

7. Give examples of how content analysis data can be used to explain the relationship between process and outcome in negotiation and related conflict research.

8. What are some of the problems likely to be encountered in the use of content analysis for comparing different cultures?

9. Give examples of interesting findings obtained from the analysis of text of transcripts in conflict research. How might these findings stimulate further research?

10. The bargaining process analysis (BPA) system has evolved with new ways of thinking about negotiation processes. What are these developments and how has the system been adjusted to take them into account?

11. The earlier research on rule use in negotiation shows how content analysis addresses theoretical issues. Now it is your turn: Develop a couple of examples of other theoretical frameworks (or hypotheses derived from them) that would benefit from the systematic analysis of texts or process.

Note

1. A procedure that does not rely on recall consists of asking subjects to react to a videotape of their bargaining session. Interesting results were obtained with this procedure in an experiment by Olekalns and Smith (2003). Subjects in that study were asked to identify turning points in the ongoing exchanges of offers and demands.

10

Narrative Analysis

Linda M. Johnston

M oving from content analysis to narrative analysis is stepping over a methodological line. The same is true when moving from narrative analysis to action research, which is discussed in the next chapter. These moves require the researcher to change the paradigm in which he or she operates. Like content analysis, the study of narratives is a flexible approach that can be used with both written and oral communications, and in a variety of settings. Like content analysis, narrative analysis also addresses questions about what was said, who said it, and to whom it was said. Like content analysis, decisions have to be made early concerning the technical procedures for completing the analysis.

Narrative analysis parts ways with content analysis at this point; it goes deeper into the causes, explanations, and effects of the spoken word. It has the following features: (1) addresses nuances and innuendos, (2) focuses on what is said, as well as why, and with what effect it is said, (3) assembles a data set that can become larger at any time, (4) tellers of the narratives are the experts of their own stories, (5) an analysis can be as fine-tuned as needed for the research agenda at hand, (6) emotion and non-verbal behavior can be included as part of the analysis, and (7) allows for broad or thematic understandings of the conflict processes that capture not only what is said, but the meaning behind it.

Action research, on the other hand, starts with a real-life problem that is usually community based. Action researchers take seriously the shortcomings of traditional research methods and take into account the contributions of post-modernist, feminist, and critical theory (Stringer, 1999). In action research, like narrative analysis, the subjects are active participants in the process. Also like narrative analysis, the methods used in action research are interpretive and reflective, and there is an implied practical outcome to the research. Both of these methods may also encompass several disciplines.

The criticisms of narrative analysis are as follows: (1) it relies on interpretation both by the parties and the researcher or practitioner, (2) new information can be added, thereby forcing a continuing analysis, (3) validity is applicable only within the certain narrative (that narrative is true for that person), and (4) reliability usually lies only within the specialized knowledge of the one person telling the story.

The study of narratives began historically with the study of languages and later in terms of poetics and semantics. Recent years have seen an increased interest in narratives, especially emerging from post-modernist and feminist literature. At the same time, the work of analyzing narratives and discourse has become easier due to the development of computer software to aid in the transcribing, analyzing, and coding of vast amounts of qualitative data. The connections between narrative theory and practice are just beginning to be made in conflict analysis and resolution (e.g., Senehi, 2002). The study of protracted, seemingly unresolvable conflicts requires an in-depth method of research and analysis. These "stories" about conflicts reflect how people see a dispute, that is, their version of reality. Because the story of one participant in a conflict situation often contradicts or opposes another participant's in the same conflict, the task of the researcher as well as the practitioner is to untangle the truth from the fiction, the real from the imagined, and to locate those places in the tales that are congruent, perhaps in agreement, and overlapping. This process of untangling hopefully allows the third party to bring the disputants to a place where they could at least hear and understand the other person's story. This is similar to what Winslade and Monk (2000) refer to as the deconstructive phase in mediation, where the third party asks "questions that will open up space for reconsideration of the conflict-saturated story" (p. 78).

Overview of the Approach

The current work on narratives falls into two general categories: first, research methods and tools for analysis and, second, theories about what narratives can and do tell us about people and situations in conflict. There have been many contributions to the understanding of the use of narratives for comprehending varying perspectives in a conflict situation. These contributions lead the researcher to several considerations that need to be examined in order to proceed with the analysis.

The first consideration has to do with the worldview model in two senses, for the study of the narrative itself and to serve as a window for studying a person's approach to the conflict. The first use of worldview has to do with the studying of the narratives. Cortazzi (1993) presented several models for studying them: sociological (the social context of the telling of the story), socio-linguistic (the ways in which stories arise), psychological (the process of understanding, recalling, and summarizing stories), and anthropological (how the structure, function, and performance of stories vary across cultures). The researcher must choose a model that both fits the needs of the research project and that he or she is comfortable using. Although each of these approaches tells about a particular aspect of the narrative, it may be necessary to develop an interdisciplinary approach, especially when working in a field like conflict resolution. It is very seldom that conflicts can be understood from a single model.

The second use of worldview has to do with the orientation of the person in the conflict. Antaki (1988), who focused his research on everyday talk as a window into a person's worldview, has "two observations about explanations— that they have the power to challenge social realities, and that they seem to be implicated in changes in people's behavior" (p. 1). Explanations occur in the public domain, explaining the event and the person's place in it, and in the private domain, which reflects, for all practical purposes, the person's worldview. The latter is the personal account of the reasons why things happen the way that they do, the individual's feelings about what happened, and that individual's behavior as influenced by the event.

The second consideration has to do with how much attention is to be paid to voice and position in the conflict. Genette (1980) stresses the need to look at the context of the story in terms of whether it is being told in the first, second, or third person. Voice can also include the position of the speaker; the teller of the story has two choices as far as position to the narrator, that is, the story can be told by one of the characters or by someone from outside the story. The implications for the analysis for the theory of voice are that those that hear the narrative also take part in the writing and rewriting of it. A possible corollary to that would be that narratives can and do have audiences that are not always the intended ones. Another implication for CA&R is that the researcher can tell how closely the storyteller sees himself or herself to the conflict by the tense of the voice he or she uses in telling the story. The positioning by the storyteller can also aid the researcher in determining who to interview and the necessary content of the interview.

The third consideration has to do with timing. Genette (1980) talks about the party's perception of timing, that is whether the story is told in past, present, or future tense. Another consideration of timing is, whether or not the story that is told is a single narrating event, a story told about the same topic or incident over time, or different stories over time. In order to analyze this, he suggests that the researcher look at the order, duration, and frequency of the narrative. Greene (1986) discusses plotting sequences and how the organization of memories as schemas guides the interpretation of events, utterances, and written texts. The tools that she offers are similar to a popular model used in conflict analysis referred to as SPITCEROW (Sources, Parties, Issues, Tactics, Changed,

Enlarged, Roles, Outcome, Winner), which emphasizes the story, setting, theme, plot, episode, attempt, resolution, and goal. An implication of this for CA&R would be that the researcher is able to examine the party's version of the timing of the dispute by studying the tense of the verbs used by the storyteller.

Another theoretical angle for studying narratives is to examine the temporal associations of and within stories. Toolan (1988) gives an outline of the factors to look for when studying text and time, such as the order in which things are told; the duration of the text, summary, and scene; the frequency with which a single story incident is told; and how long after the incident took place the story was told. Historical knowledge that is presented as stories told about history through the eyes of one person is only as real as the teller's perception of them. Historical knowledge and narrative truth can be very different entities depending on who is telling the story and the amount of time that has elapsed between the actual event and its telling. Stories tend to be retold so that the timing is appropriate.

A fourth consideration has to do with the importance of the organization of the story. Riessman (1993) presents an example of how someone organizes his or her story and shows that the parts of the story are organized by their function. Bell (1988) illustrates the abstract thinking, the orientation to time and place, the complicating action of how that person sees the conflict evolving, and the resolution or finalization of the story. This process allows the researcher to show how stories move through time, are indicative of the individual's ongoing experience, and illustrate the teller's image of himself or herself in history, that is, the difference between "I did this" and "This happened to me." These truths for the teller do not reveal the past as it actually was, but they do tell the researcher truths about the person's experience through his or her own interpretation of the events. The researcher can then determine whether the person sees himself or herself as an active agent in the conflict, an innocent bystander, or someone who could be seen only as a victim of the circumstances of the conflict. Each of these orientations to the world influences our interpretation and shapes the meanings we derive from our experiences, that is, how we tell the story about the conflict.

Another aspect of orientation to a conflict is explored by Martin (1986). He discusses that "like Janus, the reader is always looking backward as well as forward, actively restructuring the past in light of each new bit of information" (p. 127). This is particularly interesting for conflict narratives because, according to Martin, "We read events forward (the beginning will cause the end) and meaning backward (the end, once known, causes us to identify its beginning)" (p. 127). For stories told about historical events, it would be naive to assume that there is one true interpretation of those events. When talking about the historical events of a conflict, the researcher can never expect for the one and only truth to be spelled out, if indeed any truth is revealed at all. The most that can be relied upon is, first, the fact that the teller of the story believes his or her story to be true and, second, that the actual facts of what happened may never be known for certain. Martin acknowledges the importance of looking at three other factors in the study of narratives: temporality, causality, and human interest, studying whether or not these fit together in the story and understanding that they may be socially constructed.

Other analysts have claimed that deep narrative structures are really patterns of meaning, not action. These cannot be explained within the rules of the society, but they are about the rules of the society. Brown and Yule (1983) posit that there are two types of language: transactional, which serves in the expression content or substance, and interactional, which is involved in expressing social relations and personal attitudes. The latter is especially important in understanding the underlying issues in a conflict. The authors also discuss schemata as being the organizational "background knowledge which leads us to expect or predict aspects in our interpretation of discourse" (p. 248). The assumption here is that background knowledge is shared by others and that we assume that others are using the same information and schema for interpreting the same events. This is not always the case when studying the narratives of conflicts, especially cross-cultural ones. This assumption can lead third parties into problems with the analysis. People orient their stories around those rules that tell them both about the conflict itself and the rules of the society that help them understand the conflict; this is partly due to the next consideration, which is culture.

A fifth consideration has to do with the sensitivity to culture. Swearingen (1990) points out that in different cultural contexts, there are distinctions between say and mean, text and interpretation, truth and falsehood, logic and poetry, and history and fiction. These cultural meanings may not be clear when studying narratives outside of your own culture. Scheub (1975) posits this cultural piece in yet another way, in terms of experience. Stories must be understood by the audience in terms of their common experience, the societal norms, and the external reality. Listeners must be able to relate the story to something in their past experience and the cultural norms they are accustomed to.

Duranti (1988) also offers a cross-cultural perspective to the understanding of discourse, and in particular, speech events. He demonstrates how discourse is part of the narrator's cultural construction of reality and how the very definitions of speaker and hearer may be culturally defined. Therefore, he concludes that discourse analysts must take the perspectives of the tellers of and participants in the narrative. All narratives and discourse are situated within a particular culture and must be understood within that specific context. For the same reason, it should not be assumed that a particular speech community is homogeneous, that variations might occur within that community in spite of the obvious cultural ties. White (1980) adds, "Far from being a problem, the narrative might well be considered a solution to a problem of general human concern, namely the problem of how to translate knowing into telling, the problem of fashioning human experience into a form assimilable to structures of meaning that are generally human rather than culture-specific" (p. 1). The lack of sensitivity to a specific culture should not stop the researcher from studying the narratives of that particular culture, but should rather raise a cautionary note in terms of understanding and interpreting narratives from cultures not familiar to the researcher.

A sixth consideration has to do with the method of eliciting a narrative. When the researcher asks broad-based, open-ended questions, respondents do not feel that their story is suppressed by attempting to limit their responses to "relevant" answers to narrowly specified questions. In other words, the interviewee is not kept to "a point" but rather is allowed to tell his or her entire story. The focus is kept on the person-centered feature of the account. There needs to be a balance between what the researcher wants to ask about and what the interviewee wants to talk about; the balance will dictate what is important in the interview. Mishler (1986) illustrates how the interviewee and the interviewer construct meaning together during the interview in an interactional context. In narrative analysis, researchers are not out to validate the accurateness of the person's story, but rather to discover the meaning of it. Just as in conflict analysis, it is not so much the accuracy of the "facts" presented, but the person's perception of the facts and his or her reaction to them that is most useful. These meanings are grounded within the particular conflict. It is the responsibility of the researcher to elicit and construct meaning during the interview process or to triangulate the intended meaning with the interviewee after the fact. This is done by asking carefully constructed questions and then listening closely to the answers.

Narrative Theory

Narrative theory has developed from several disciplines. It is still evolving, and those that analyze narratives are pushing the proverbial "envelope" of what it means to do "narratology" and how it can be applied for research purposes. Theories, models, and frameworks are being developed to meet the needs of those researching in the conflict field. It is recognized that the telling of and listening to stories are influenced by gender, race, ethnicity, age, sexual orientation, and class. These ways of telling and hearing stories are still being explored and documented. It is a given that they are not ideologically neutral.

Theoretically, narratives can tell us many things about conflicts and the people involved in them. What they can tell us is still being explored and documented. In addition to the considerations mentioned above, some of the research shows that narratives can help understand (a) the connections between the storyteller's truth and fiction, (b) differences in what the various types of narratives tell us, and (c) what narratives can tell us about the mind. These theoretical underpinnings are discussed in this section.

Narratives contain elements of both truth and fiction, but they are the story that people tell about themselves and the world around them. One important piece of this research as it applies to the study of conflicts is the fact that people, when they tell stories of any length, put *prolepses* (flashbacks) and *analepses* (flash-forwards anticipating a future situation) into their stories. These prolepses and analepses are told by choice according to Richter (1996); that is, they are specifically selected by the teller of the story in order to emphasize certain parts and perhaps convince the listener of the value of that particular part of the story. He suggests that the tellers of stories like "clean beginnings and tidy endings" (p. 98).

The individual telling the story wants it to make sense, be convincing, and wants the listener to believe that it is true. We, the listeners, tend to distrust any sign of artifice in a story. A story told out of order is likely to be a sign of the manipulation of that story. In conflict resolution, the stories that the parties tell us about conflicts are their versions of the events. If we disbelieve one portion of the story, we are likely to disregard the entire story. The researcher needs to examine the presumed factual accounts in a particular narrative and how they are used to persuade the reader of their validity. The power, position, and range of influence of the person asserting the idea have to do with how well it is accepted and transferred into everyday conversation. Also, in order to maintain the appearance of truth, the narrative must seem consistent to the teller and the hearer. The text must be plausible as it relates to everyday life. These presumed factual accounts are key features by which the researcher can construct various versions of a conflict.

There are differences in what various types of narratives can tell us about a person or the conflict. This can be observed in terms of natural versus contrived speech and natural versus artificial narratives. According to Grimshaw (1974), there are four types of narrative data: speech observed in natural settings, speech observed in contrived settings, elicited speech in response to direct inquiry, and historical and/or literary materials. One of the points of analyzing narratives would be to uncover as much "natural" speech as possible from the participants in the study, that is, to uncover the aspects of the conflict from an emic perspective (see Chapters 1 and 8). Interviewing in the field, meeting the interviewees in their natural surroundings, and letting them determine the course of the conversation would be as close as a researcher could get to speech observed in natural settings. In contrast, most research interviewing is speech elicited in response to direct inquiry, as is often done in laboratory settings.

Another distinction can be made between interviewing that produces real-time speech and written text, which is secondhand and has been pre-prepared or polished before being given to the interviewer. It can be suggested that standard questions or prepared text in an etic research tradition (see Chapter 1) may eliminate the role of certain non-verbal behaviors, emotions, and contextualized speech. If the questioning in a conflict situation is kept as spontaneous as possible, then it is more likely that the researcher would be getting the narrative truth from the interviewee, that is, how the world is seen through his or her eyes.

With regard to the distinction between artificial and natural narratives, van Dijk (1975) concludes that the former is an art form such as myth, folktale, drama, and novels, that is, they have a constructed nature and occur within a storytelling context; and the latter is everyday conversation, that is, they are stories that we tell each other about our personal experiences. It would seem logical that natural narratives would tend to be more factual than stories that were told for the purpose of entertainment. According to van Dijk (1975), actions occur in two different ways within narratives: The doing is real and factual, and the interpretation of the doing is subjective. In the case of conflict narratives, the doing is in the actions of the person in the conflict, and the interpretation of the doing can be done by both the person in the conflict and the researcher as they co-create the meaning in the interview or story. Methodologically, this can be reinforced by rechecking with the interviewee after the transcription and coding processes are complete in order to triangulate his or her findings. This process provides the interviewee with the opportunity to authenticate or repudiate the subjective interpretations of the researcher. This deep discussion of the interpretation of the narrative is where the co-creation of the narrative becomes complete.

The third theoretical underpinning addresses what narratives can tell us about the mind and its products. Chafe (1990) sees narratives as sources of insight into the mental processes and as "overt manifestations of the mind in action: as windows to both the content of the mind and its ongoing operations" (p. 79). This is also another way of looking at bias and its creation. He says that narratives give us evidence of "the fact that the mind does not record the world, but rather creates it according to its own mix of cultural and individual expectations" (p. 81). The schemas are the structures of expectations, and that another function of the mind is to process events that are contrary to those expectations. The mind also requires certain types of information in order to operate, such as space, time, social context, and ongoing events. Chafe makes an observation that is very central to the field of conflict resolution: "that different people may supply very different narratives of a physically identical input" (p. 96). This observation is certainly true of parties in a conflict. The mind does not record events factually but rather creates its own ideas of how the world works based on the schema already in place. Parties to a conflict play out these schemas through the narratives they tell about their conflicts.

There is also a connection between what is said and what is meant by what is said. Draper (1988) states, "It is widely recognized that the meaning of sentences can depend in part on the 'context' and that things may be left unsaid if the hearer can fill them in" (p. 17). If the speaker or writer thinks that the reader or listener can fill in the empty spaces, those details will be left out of the conversation. Individual narratives give us ideas about the world and the mental processes by which the storyteller came to those ideas, representing both his or her sources of information and how that information is processed.

Analysis of Narratives

Narrative researchers are faced with having to make a number of decisions about how to proceed with data collection. Five kinds of decisions can be articulated.

1. Because stories are temporally situated, a decision must be made as to whether to conduct multiple interviews with the same person over time or rather to conduct one interview with each person and ask him or her to reflect forward and backward in time.

2. Should the interviewer ask the interviewee to address specific points and questions where the researcher leads the conversation or rather let the interviewee determine the course of the discussion and simply ask appropriate follow-up questions?

3. The researcher should examine the advantages of studying the narratives in a contrived setting versus letting the interviewee determine what to him or her would be a natural setting.

4. Should the researcher study what someone involved in the conflict states publicly or rather what he or she says privately in everyday, demotic conversation? (*Demotic conversation* refers to non-specialized, non-formal, everyday language. For more on this distinction, see Johnston, 2000.)

5. Last, should the researcher question the interviewee when he or she notices inconsistencies in the stories or wait until those inconsistencies are mentioned, as an indicator of their importance?

Several researchers have offered methods for analyzing narratives and discourse. The method chosen for a particular research project depends on the type of information needed and the level of accuracy the research requires. Most models recommend that the research be conducted in the most natural situation possible and allow the interviewee to use his or her own language. Most also suggest that some attempt be made to render contextual judgments between the narrative and the situation in which it is grounded. Many suggest that some attempt be made to understand the mental processing or worldview of the interviewee. And many suggest the emphasis should be not on the exact recall of data, but rather on the interviewee's interpretation of that data.

It is also often recommended that: (1) the narratives be audiotaped to allow for more in-depth analysis, (2) they be transcribed as accurately as possible because the transcription allows for a deeper understanding of them, and (3) only the researcher decides when he or she has enough information in order to conclude the research project. Several levels of understanding are obtained from listening in several ways: conducting the interview, listening to the audiotape after the interview, transcribing the interview, and studying the interview after the transcription. If many interviews are being conducted, then a yet deeper level of understanding can be attained from comparing these interviews or by comparing different interviews with the same person over time.

The degree of accuracy to which the transcriptions are done is up to the researcher and the needs of the project. The language of the narratives can be examined down to the minutest detail, including every utterance and false start, or done more thematically, capturing more of the essence of what someone deems important. The starting point for the researcher should be the points of interest or the focus of the project itself and the issues raised by the interviewees during the process. In this sense, the themes that emerge from the research process can be both inductive and deductive.

Determining the unit of analysis, either individual words or more general themes, is a decision that needs to be made by the researcher prior to the beginning of the coding process. If words are the unit of analysis, then the researcher runs the risk of losing more general thoughts or patterns of thoughts provided by the interviewee, but gains a determination of which words are common to the language of the interviewee, which words the interviewee uses to describe things, and how often these words are used in everyday conversation. On the other hand, if thematic coding is utilized, the researcher may lose some of the intricacies of the language, but gains a broader understanding of the kinds of issues that are important to the interviewee. These issues are similar to those discussed in Chapter 9 on content analysis.

In terms of analyzing conflict narratives, other questions arise that are specific to CA&R. In the analysis of conflict narratives, the researcher can study the stories for the interviewee's perception of the following questions.

1. Who are the primary and secondary parties to the conflict, and how does the interviewee situate him- or herself in the conflict?

2. What are the parties' issues and needs?

3. How do the parties seek to resolve their conflict?

4. How do the parties link the causal and resultant factors of the conflict?

5. How do the parties explain their motivations for action?

6. What values do the parties discuss and which values are implied by what they say?

7. How does the interviewee see the conflict situated in time and place?

8. What resources are committed toward the conflict?

9. Are there any evident turning points or critical junctures in the conflict?

10. Are there inconsistencies in the narrative and does the interviewee discuss the inconsistencies?

11. Does the narrative match behaviors observed by the researcher?

12. How does the interviewee see the conflict being resolved or what does he or she view as the best-case scenario?

13. Are there latent aspects to the conflict that have yet to erupt?

14. Are there cycles apparent in the conflict and, if so, at what stage is the conflict in now?

15. Will the interviewee's goals be met by the resolution of the conflict?

The coding process can be taken one step further in order to increase reliability. Codes can be developed by a team of researchers and carried out independently by several coders. In this manner, the various coders can then compare their findings with each other. This also allows for a deeper understanding of the narratives being studied because each coder will bring to the research project his or her own biases conditioned by culture and context. Themes can then be developed from the understanding of the conflict narratives, and a deeper understanding of the conflict emerges.

A CODING EXAMPLE

The coding process described above is demonstrated with the following except from a narrative text related to the conflict over tobacco (Johnston, 2000).[1]

I: The future don't look bright.

R: Uh-huh. Would you recommend to someone that they, that they start in the business now?

I: No.

R: Like if, if your sons for instance, if one of your sons wanted to start, would you recommend that he do that?

I: In tobacco?

R: Yes.

I: No. I couldn't honestly recommend that. Ah, like I said, with my son, we were in the dairy business also. Two dairy farms. One at each, each place. And of course, we raised tobacco too, but not as much tobacco as we do now. And, ah, it, it was, even, even in the dairy business, it was, was tough to make a living. A living, [pause], living that ah, that ah, he wanted. And ah, he had this girl and he says 'this girl don't want to marry a farmer.' [laughter]. I think that that was one, one of the reasons, reasons that he, he had a different girlfriend and he was getting of the age that he wanted to settle down, get married, and raise a family. This girl just don't want to marry a damn farmer. [laughter]. And so, I, I can sort of understand why. And I think that he did too and I think that that's one of the reasons, reasons that he went back to school and went into accounting. He stayed at home and still lived on the farm. And ah, transferred what credits he could from [name of university] and took it and got a degree in accounting. And was done. He's done real well. Worked for [name of company] for several years. And then he went to work for this private concern. Helped him out. But I couldn't, I couldn't do it. You, you've got to be pretty shifty, and ah, some of them will make it, but they will have to do other things on top of it. To help get 'em along.

R: Uh-huh. You mean, grow other things or do other work?

I: Oh, yeah. Grow other things. You can't keep, there's very few people today in this area that grow tobacco, and don't do other. . . . [pause]. We, I have, we have cattle on my farm. Beef cattle. A cow calf operation. But ah, tobacco [sigh] [long pause], in the last two or three years for me has not been a sound thing. Because I bought it, I bought poundage and now there's people that are in it, and it's been, but ah, up until this time, it's been okay and I didn't raise it, that many acres.

R: Uh-huh. And you had the dairy farms and everything too.

I: Yeah. We had other but ah, we got out of the dairy business. Because it was these people would leave and that would, yes, for myself, yes, I would raise it. But physically, I couldn't. I might do a small patch, but physically I just couldn't. I couldn't do the work that's necessary to raise fifty acres. It's not as much in the flue-cured, flue-cured area, you have more of that.

Source: Johnston (2000) excerpt from Interview #3, May 13, 1999.

Using the 15 coding questions above, the researcher can discern the following information from this excerpt.

1. The interviewee sees himself as a primary party in the center of the conflict but is easing himself out of it by getting out of the dairy business and farming in general, and by encouraging his son to go to college instead of work on the farm. He is still a primary party in the sense that he continues to raise tobacco.

2. This farmer sees his issues as the need to make a living, physically not being able to do the work, and wanting something different for his son.

3. This party seeks resolution of the conflict by removing himself from tobacco growing.

4. The interviewee spoke earlier in the interview very passionately about not being able to make a living at growing tobacco any longer and the acknowledgement of tobacco as a health risk. (He had quit smoking for health reasons.) In this segment, he talks about not being able to make a living but does not expound on the reasons why.

5. He explains his motivations for action by saying that he was not getting a "sound thing." He also explains his son's motivation for going to college because his girlfriend did not want to marry a farmer.

6. The farmer refers to some people being "pretty shifty." The tone of his voice is condescending as he says this. It doesn't seem to be worth it to him to do what he sees he would have to do to "make it." He also puts a strong value on his son having done real well. He implies a value on his own health by not doing the difficult physical labor any longer.

7. The interviewee refers to the conflict over tobacco mostly in the past tense. This is probably due to the fact that he is, for the most part, retired and no longer growing as much tobacco.

8. He is no longer committing resources toward the conflict, but speaks in the past tense about buying poundage (of tobacco) and adding to his farm by also raising beef and dairy farming.

9. In this segment of the narrative, there are no evident turning points or critical junctures. However, he does speak in the past tense about several key decisions: getting out of the dairy business, no longer buying poundage, of tobacco no longer being a "sound thing," and wanting his son to have a different profession.

10. There are no apparent inconsistencies in this segment of the narrative. The interviewee did talk prior to the interview about growing tobacco and then not smoking cigarettes any longer.

11. There was no opportunity to observe the interviewee in action during this interview.

12. The interviewee does not see the conflict being resolved. He is avoiding the conflict by easing out of farming and retiring. He talks later in the interview about people still wanting to smoke and assuming, therefore, that there will probably always be a need for tobacco.

13. There are latent aspects to this conflict, such as when people lose their farms and when they are forced to take other jobs, but those aspects are not discussed in this segment.

14. The only cycle apparent in this segment of the narrative is the de-escalation of the impact of tobacco in this man's life. By retiring, he is removing himself from the dispute.

15. The goals of this interviewee are being met by retiring and having his son enter into another business. This does not represent a resolution to the conflict over tobacco but rather a resolution of the problem it poses in this interviewee's life and the life of his son.

Clearly, this interviewee is in the middle of the conflict over tobacco. He sees himself involved in a process of change, particularly related to the changes going on around him in the tobacco industry and farming in general. For his son and himself, certain choices have been made that will eventually take him out of farming altogether and discourage his son from farming at all. For this man, the conflict over tobacco is not resolved; he is, rather, choosing to distance himself from it. This man still sees himself as a farmer in terms of identity but is farming less and less. He explains this primarily in three ways: (a) the conflict over tobacco is forcing him out of farming, (b) his age is keeping him from doing the necessary labor associated with farming, and (c) he is discouraging his son from following in his footsteps and encouraging him to make other career choices.

This interview represents just one coding example of conducting narrative analysis that is useful for analyzing conflicts. Conflict themes can be developed by studying multiple interviews with many different individuals or by conducting several interviews with the same person over time. In this research project, several conflict themes developed, which the author divided into four main categories of foundational narratives (those narratives that existed prior to the beginning of the current conflict), contextual narratives (those narratives that arose out of the current conflict), tangential narratives (those narratives that are related to the contextual narratives), and resultant narratives (those narratives that result from the current conflict). In this study about the conflict over tobacco, it is claimed that the discourses and narratives people use in a conflict situation are necessary for the understanding of protracted, complex conflicts. In the case of tobacco, the narratives drive the current conflict and may in fact also augment the next phase of the conflict.

Discussion Questions

Narrative analysis is connected more explicitly to a philosophical worldview than many of the other methods discussed in this book. Within the context of this philosophical orientation, the analysis of narratives produced through interviews can provide insightful interpretations of conflicts. Despite impressions that some people have about "unsystematic" qualitative approaches (see Chapter 1, footnote 1), narrative analysis is guided by a rule structure and can be facilitated by qualitative computer programs, as noted in this chapter. We believe that you will find this approach to be useful either in combination with or instead of other forms of content analysis. To help with your learning, we have prepared eight review questions.

1. What are some of the problems that are likely to be encountered when several individuals code the same narrative material?

2. What are some of the advantages of studying transcribed interview narratives compared to narratives taken from prepared written texts?

3. Describe some of the advantages and disadvantages of using narrative analysis versus content analysis in non-laboratory settings?

4. Give some examples of how narrative analysis might aid in the analysis of conflicts related to race, gender, or ethnicity.

5. When deciding on a process for analyzing a narrative, what factors might influence how exact the transcription needs to be? When would it be appropriate to include emotions, utterances, gestures, and other sights and sounds?

6. What are some aspects of the interview process that could influence the content of the narrative produced by that interaction?

7. How might action research lead to a preference for doing a narrative analysis?

8. How might a narrative analysis be useful for distinguishing between constructive and destructive elements in a particular conflict?

Note

1. "I" indicates the interviewee and "R" indicates the researcher. Person-identifiable information has been removed.

Part VII

*Evaluating Interventions
and Applying Research*

This part of the book consists of two chapters, one on evaluation research
and another on action research and consulting. These are important topics for the CA&R researcher eager to contribute both to scholarship and practice. Thus, "A" is for analysis and "R" is for resolution. For many professionals,
this is considered to be an applied field: They seek a research paradigm that
translates easily into practice. Some examples come from evaluation research.
Others come from doing action research. The discussion in Chapter 12 also provides a glimpse into the world of the consultant, including the variety of roles,
functions, and activities performed on projects and some tips that may be useful. This topic is rarely treated in social science research methods textbooks.

In Chapter 11, I discuss evaluation research. The discussion includes both
conceptual issues and the practical ones of how to do it. The challenges and
issues of evaluation are presented with special attention to conflict interventions such as the problem-solving workshop. Some of the issues raised are
whether evaluation is to be considered research, the need to define the entity to
be evaluated, and the challenge of deciding on criteria for judging effectiveness.
These issues are confronted by the evaluator during the design of a project. The
reader also gets guidance on how to perform an evaluation in two ways. He or
she is taken through the tasks of what might be regarded a typical project. In
addition, the way a particular investigator developed a framework for evaluating workshops is presented. The guidance and the examples should help
the would-be evaluator think about the challenge. Like all the other methods
discussed, however, learning is accomplished as much or more by experience.

In Chapter 12, I discuss the role of research in practice. This is an important interface for CA&R scholars. As discussed in earlier chapters, a key motivation for these scholars is to contribute to social change or to the reduction of conflicts. Of course, there are many ways to make these contributions, and research is only one avenue. Although research is often contrasted to activism, it can be thought about as a form of active involvement in the real world. Field and evaluation research are examples of involvement, and these were discussed in Chapters 6, 7, and 8, as well as in Chapter 11 of this part. Other examples are presented in this chapter along with issues that arise in implementing the approaches. Special attention is given to the increasingly popular applied approaches of action research and policy consulting. Issues discussed are the respective roles of researchers and practitioners in implementing projects, the role of research populations in the design and information collection phases of projects, the political aspects of doing research in applied settings, and barriers to dissemination and implementation. Examples of applied projects are presented along with advice for the would-be applied researcher or consultant. Each chapter concludes with a set of discussion questions.

11

Evaluation Research

This chapter focuses on the topic of evaluating CA&R programs, projects, or interventions. Evaluation research has grown rapidly since the 1960s, spurred by investments made by agencies of the U.S. government. The importance of evaluation is reflected in the increase in societies, handbooks, annual reviews, and journals. Among the more popular sources are Patton (1981, 1982); Pawson and Tilly (1997); Weiss (1997); Rossi, Freeman, and Lipsey (2003); and the many other books that appear regularly in the Sage listings on research methodology. It is also becoming increasingly popular in the field of conflict resolution. The challenges and the methods of evaluation are discussed in this chapter. It includes sections on challenges of evaluation, tasks in an evaluation project, and issues of evaluation, concluding with an example of an intervention project. The discussion applies both to relatively long-term educational, training, or research programs on a variety of basic and applied topics and to shorter-term interventions designed to deal with specific ongoing conflicts.

Challenges of Evaluation

Like many areas of social science, CA&R has been under pressure from funding agencies, clients, consumers, and policymakers to assess the value of its services. These services include a considerable variety of interventions spanning the distinction among peacekeeping, peacemaking, and peace building. Practitioners and applied researchers are being encouraged to incorporate evaluation protocols in their designs. This satisfies the desire of clients for accountability on the part of the CA&R service providers. It generates information that can be used by the providers to improve their practices. These two purposes overlap the well-known distinction between summative and formative evaluation.

Summative evaluations are intended to assess the effects or effectiveness of an intervention. A comprehensive evaluation examines as many types of outcomes and consequences as is possible. For example, summative criteria that may be used in evaluating a CA&R research program include grants, publications, and evidence for uses of the research such as citations. *Formative evaluations* are designed to foster the development of the intervention or program. They focus on process rather than outcomes. As process is often thought to be at the heart of the field, formative evaluations would seem to be particularly useful. These might focus on the experiences of and interactions among the participants in the program. Information about these processes can come from interviews or participant observation of day-by-day activities. Relevant activities for a research program might include its thematic organization, the way that researchers work in teams, and a process for reviewing proposals and projects. These data can be regarded as intervening variables that explain the connection between a program or intervention (input) and outcomes (output). When thought about in this way, program evaluation takes the form of evaluation research. The design supplements an analysis of impacts (summative) with an inquiry into the reasons why those impacts occurred (formative).

In many ways, evaluation research is similar to other types of research with regard to design, data collection, and analysis approaches. It makes use of almost all the methods discussed in this book, especially field experiments, ethnographies and related case study methods, and surveys. It differs from other types of research, however, in its goal of being used by decision makers responsible for the implementation of programs. Utility is the first of four criteria that Robson (2002) claims needs to be satisfied before embarking on an evaluation. The others are feasibility, propriety, and technical adequacy. Utility refers to the contribution made by the evaluation to the client's problem. Feasibility refers to resources, time, and cooperation in carrying out the study. Propriety refers to protecting the participants and avoiding biases that can bring about pre-judging of the findings or recommendations. Technical adequacy refers to skills in designing and implementing the study. What remains is the important consideration of political sensitivity.

Evaluations are done usually in political contexts. Results often have implications for the way resources are distributed within organizations and the influence of various stakeholder groups. Inevitably, some members or groups gain while others lose as a result of the findings. A good deal has been written about the importance of preparing clients for the findings with sensitivity to existing cleavages or the possibility of engendering new conflicts in organizations (e.g., Robson, 2000). Many of these precautions apply also to evaluations of conflict interventions. But CA&R evaluators confront other kinds of challenges. These include protecting the anonymity of participants in the workshops or programs, being careful not to oversell the approach used, and recognizing possible attempts to sabotage the effort by those who stand to gain little from resolved conflicts. Each of these challenges is discussed briefly in turn.

Those who take part in workshops or interventions are usually recruited on a voluntary basis. Their participation depends on guarantees of anonymity. This is especially important in areas of the world considered to be war zones. Intense conflicts between groups engender extreme sensitivity to deviation from a party line that supports each group's claims. A willingness to talk to members of the "enemy" group could be very risky. Key among the risks is being labeled by one's own group a traitor. These dynamics have been shown to occur in the field of interactive conflict resolution (Fisher, 1997). Three challenges for the CA&R evaluator are (1) seeking permission to perform the needed data collection, (2) disseminating the results, and (3) influencing the course of the larger conflict taking place outside of the workshop intervention. The need to protect anonymity of participants has hindered both formative and summative evaluations and slowed progress in the development of the approach (see Rouhana, 2000). The challenge for the evaluator is to collect and analyze relevant data from the participants while protecting them from possible harm.

Many individuals in CA&R are motivated to contribute to making the world, or at least a particular area or domain within it, more peaceful. They are eager to apply their skills as conflict resolvers to a wide variety of difficult situations. At times, however, their enthusiasm for the goal transfers to enthusiasm for the approaches used to achieve that goal. Similar to entrepreneurs whose livelihoods depend on selling their goods or services, conflict resolvers' commitment to the cause may lead them to oversell their approaches. This can result in disappointed expectations for both the practitioner and his or her clients. To avoid this outcome, evaluation data on impacts would be beneficial. An evaluation approach to practice would legitimize the field without dampening the well-intentioned enthusiasm of its practitioners. Rather than overstating or making unwarranted claims for their intervention techniques, these CA&R practitioners can productively channel their excitement toward the larger enterprise and its values.

A CA&R intervention is considered effective if it is shown to reduce the intensity of a conflict, bring an end to violence, or improve relationships among combatants or clients. These goals may not be shared by all interested parties. Some of them actually stand to gain from the continuation of conflict. They believe that progress toward peace threatens their power and interests; they may use violence to undermine attempts to achieve it. These parties include disgruntled group members or extremists who see peace as a betrayal of their values, parties excluded from the agreement, and conflict entrepreneurs who profit from arms sales. Clients, including those who participate in problem-solving workshops, and peacemakers, including those who perform the evaluations, are vulnerable to attacks from these parties. In civil wars, these parties are referred to as *spoilers* (Stedman, 2000). They are an important part of the larger context of many conflicts and, thus, have implications for the evaluation process. One implication is that an intervention regarded as being successful may be jeopardized by the activities of spoiler groups. Another is that these groups must be taken into account in the presentation and dissemination of the evaluation findings. Evaluations that pay little attention to the broader context of conflicts can be misleading.

These challenges highlight the political dimensions of CA&R evaluations. But performing evaluation studies involves technical skills as well. As noted above, many of the skills are the same as those needed for conducting any kind of research. These include proposal writing, knowing a variety of design and data collection techniques, methods of analysis and interpretation, and report writing. Other skills are more specific to the tasks of evaluation. The evaluation researcher must know how to perform a needs assessment in order to clarify the purposes of the evaluation, organize and participate as a member of an evaluation team, be sensitive to the interests of multiple and often conflicting stakeholders, and foster the utilization of findings. The latter skills make evident a difference between theory-relevant research and evaluations. Unlike the researcher, an evaluator works in a client-driven environment. His or her team must be responsive to their needs and produce a product that has consequences for their organization. The technical skills of the social science researcher are combined with the social and political skills of the consultant. Chapter 12 covers more about the role of consultants. In the next sections, I outline the tasks of a typical evaluation project and raise more general issues that arise in the course of implementing evaluations.

Tasks in an Evaluation Project

My own experience in performing evaluations leads me to suggest a rough sequence of tasks. The tasks apply to a variety of types of CA&R interventions or programs.

- Define the stakeholders. These are the individuals or groups who have an interest in the intervention, project, or program and its effectiveness. They include the participants in interventions, organizational members and administrators with a stake in the outcomes, and other groups with interests in the project. Examples of stakeholders for a CA&R educational program are students, faculty, administrators (if it is a university program), advisers, community organizations (if services are provided), and the larger CA&R academic community.

- Interview the stakeholders (or representatives of each stakeholder group) to learn about the way each defines the objectives of the program. This is sometimes referred to as a *needs assessment*. For example, students may regard the primary objective of the program to be career preparation, while faculty emphasize research productivity, and administrators focus attention on enrollments and fundraising.

- Devise criteria for assessing how each objective is realized through the project or program. If the project is an intervention, then define how the approach is designed to produce the intended outcome. If it is a program, specify which activities are intended to serve which particular objective, for example, proportion of enrolled students getting degrees (students' objective), publications (faculty objective), or size of student population (administrator's objective).

- Design a project to assess impacts of the intervention or program. The impacts should include both formative and summative indicators.

  1. Include the details of a sampling frame: Who is chosen to provide needed information about the program or to participate in an intervention?
  2. Decide on the data collection techniques—interviews, survey questionnaires, expert panels, role plays—and discuss the problems associated with each.
  3. Devise a plan for organizing, coding, aggregating, and analyzing the data.
  4. Construct a budget with time lines for completion of tasks.

- Assemble a team and arrange a division of labor among its members; for example, data collection, analysis, synthesis, and writing tasks.

- Prepare a first draft of the report, placing technical details in appendices.

- Circulate the draft to outside readers, preferably non-stakeholders, for feedback.

- Revise the draft and submit it to the sponsor for review in preparation for briefings of the various stakeholder groups.

- Invite participants and stakeholders to a briefing. Consider the format, including the possibility of convening separate briefings for different groups.

- Develop an implementation plan that serves formative or program development objectives.

- If feasible, suggest a role for the team in implementing the recommendations.

The ways in which these tasks are implemented are likely to vary from project to project. For example, some CA&R projects have short-term objectives, while others have medium and long-term goals. An evaluation of a one-shot mediation to produce a settlement on a single issue is quite different from an evaluation of a peace-building program intended to help a society with its transition to democratic institutions. The approach to presenting the report's findings at briefings varies with the technical backgrounds (and patience) of the stakeholder groups in the audience. It also depends on the consequences of the recommendations for these groups. For example, a recommendation that would effectively refocus the research or practice themes of a program is likely to be perceived as threatening the sustenance of work in progress by some members of the staff. Care must be taken not to turn valued members into spoilers.

Limited time and resources make it difficult to assess the many formative impacts of a program: An evaluation restricted to summative impacts has fewer implications for program development. For some stakeholders the value of an evaluation, whether formative or summative, turns on an answer to the question, ". . . compared to what?" The value of evaluation data is increased when comparisons with similar programs are provided. Normative data—averages across many similar programs—are useful. The limited number of evaluations of CA&R programs to date has largely prevented the making of such comparisons. More comparative evaluation studies are encouraged, even when only a few similar (or matched) programs are available. Let us turn now to other broad issues confronting the evaluation researcher.

Evaluation Issues

A number of issues are weaved through the evaluation literature, many of which are relevant to CA&R. In this section, several challenges to evaluation are discussed.

EVALUATION AS RESEARCH

Many evaluations are technical exercises designed to answer the question of whether an intervention or program works. A carefully planned design and analysis should shed light on this question. It may not, however, provide much information about the reasons why the intervention did or did not work. That information comes from the control group designs discussed in earlier chapters. Those designs are intended to address the issue of counterfactuals: What would have happened if the intervention had not been tried when it was? This question is easier to answer with experimental or quasi-experimental data. However, experimental settings are usually far removed from the actual conditions under which interventions are implemented. Relevance is increased to the extent that matched cases can be identified, even when hardly any opportunities to discover no-intervention control groups exsist.

The best test, but the most difficult challenge, is to compare the effects of an intervention to a similar case where the intervention had been considered but not used. The similar case could be members of the same conflicting groups who have not experienced the intervention. Comparisons will strengthen the bases for explanation even when the ideal conditions for comparison are unlikely to be found or established. At the very least, they will suggest possible mechanisms that can be explored more systematically in the context of basic experimental research.

WHAT IS BEING EVALUATED?

CA&R interventions or programs are usually families of procedures rather than a single treatment. For example, peacekeeping missions consist of many activities serving many functions in a variety of contexts (see Diehl et al., 1998, for a typology of peacekeeping functions). Similarly, the phrases *interactive conflict resolution* and *problem-solving workshops* refer to a number of interventions that have some overall similarity but also differ in their operations and objectives (Rouhana, 2000). Even the traditional approaches of negotiation and mediation take on a variety of forms. The question of interest is whether such complex activities should be lumped together for evaluation. One answer is that it depends on the purpose of the evaluation. The "lumping" is less problematic if the evaluator's objective is program or case specific. The focus is on a particular technique used in a particular setting. For example: Does a new teaching technique work in this class? Does a peer mediation resolve the issues responsible for a fight between two schoolmates? It is evaluated from a technical rather than explanatory perspective (see the previous section).

Lumping is more of a problem if the objective is to evaluate a class of techniques or type of intervention. The interventions being evaluated are regarded as test cases sampled from a larger population of similar interventions. Differences among umbrella interventions (or programs) present problems for inference that can be reduced to some extent by large-N designs in the tradition of MDSD (see Chapter 7). The inferences are also strengthened to the extent that the cases are instances of the same general conceptual model (see Stern & Druckman, 2000, for an elaboration of these issues).

The difference between specific programs and generic techniques is also an issue in the school-based conflict resolution and peer mediation literature. Programs designed for particular schools are the focus of most evaluations. These studies provide feedback on program impacts in the schools where they are implemented. The feedback is valuable for school administrators, parents, and the students. It does not, however, address the techniques per se. A step in this direction is comparative evaluation research. The review conducted by Powell, Muir-McClain, and Halasyamani (1995) covered programs implemented in four states, finding that the programs were somewhat effective in reducing violence (discipline referrals, reports of violent incidents). A similar finding was reported more recently by Smith, Daunic, Miller, and Robinson (2002). Their analysis of three middle-school programs showed reduced violence. These sorts of findings bolster the case for generality. They do not identify which aspects of the peer-mediation package or technique contribute more, and which contribute less, to the summative outcomes. Control group designs would be needed to provide clarification for these kinds of issues.

DEFINING EFFECTIVENESS

This is both a conceptual and operational challenge. Most CA&R interventions are intended to alter the course of events in a particular direction, from violent to nonviolent interactions or to change relationships from hostile and unfriendly to friendly and enduring. (Note in this regard the distinction made by Galtung, 1969, between negative and positive peace.) Conflict analysts, including evaluators, generally agree with this broad goal. There is little agreement, however, on how to evaluate whether this goal has been achieved. Consider the various issues concerning the dimensions of success: Are interventions successful if violence is reduced without improvement in the well-being (living conditions) of the people affected by the conflict? Are interventions successful if change is assessed only in the short term? Are interventions successful if viewed only from the standpoint of elites who agree to begin negotiation? Are interventions successful if intergroup conflict subsides without changes in social justice or human rights? Are interventions successful if they encourage combatants or disputants to think in more complex ways about the conflict even though the hostilities continue? Are interventions successful if judged only on the basis of quantitative criteria (number of casualties, reports of violent incidents, frequency of interaction, number of agreements)?

Another set of questions about effectiveness addresses the reasons for success or failure. For example, school peer-mediation programs may reduce violence because of the climate created by their implementation rather than the specific techniques used. The very existence of a program may change students' expectations, which can have an impact on a prevalent school culture of violence. This is similar to the well-known Hawthorne effect in experimental research, which is regarded as a threat to internal validity (see Chapter 3). However, from an evaluation-research perspective, it is a significant indirect factor that contributes to effectiveness. But it is also the case that indirect (or unexpected) factors can contribute to effective implementation of a program. One of these factors is mediator neutrality or responsiveness to the concerns of peers. Hale and Nix (1997) found that school mediators had difficulty remaining neutral in disputes involving their peers. Many of the mediators in their sample lacked patience and were unresponsive to the disputants' stories; at times they even pressed them for specific outcomes. Although these problems are relevant specifically to peer-mediation contexts and can be corrected with training, they raise a more general issue as well. Effectiveness may be masked by inadequate preparation (including training and experience) of program administrators and implementers.

Clearly, there are multiple criteria for judging the effectiveness of an intervention. One approach is to set reasonable expectations or to avoid over-selling a procedure (see the "Challenges of Evaluation" section in this chapter). For example, if an intervention is expected to contribute to a process of resolution but is not expected to resolve the conflict by itself, the evaluation should focus specifically on that contribution. Likewise, if an intervention is expected to set conditions for eventual resolution, short-term failure should not lead to a conclusion of ineffectiveness. Evaluators should define what an intervention is expected to accomplish and over what period of time these accomplishments are expected to materialize in observable behavior. Further, the extent to which various outcomes are correlated should be explored. For example, studies of school-based peer mediation range widely across many possible outcomes, including reduced violence, increased positive attitudes, enhanced conflict resolution skills, improved self-concept, increased empathy, more respect for diversity, improved school climate, and increased achievement. Of interest are questions about relationships among these indicators of effectiveness: Is reduced violence related to increased respect for diversity or empathy? (For a discussion of effectiveness in peacekeeping missions, see Druckman & Stern, 1997.)

INTERVENTIONS AS MOVING TARGETS: DYNAMICS AND CONTINGENCIES

The impacts of any intervention depend on a variety of factors. These include the intervention itself, the particular way it is implemented, and events over which intervenors or their clients have little control. The challenge of evaluation is to sort these various influences, distinguishing between those that have stronger and weaker effects on the processes and outcomes of the intervention. This task is complicated further by the realization that the intervention is not static but changes through time, often in unexpected ways. Intervenors must adjust their strategies to circumstances. This has implications for both formative and summative evaluations. Focusing on process, an evaluator asks: (a) What is happening in the group at particular points in time? and (b) What are the factors likely to influence those interactions? Concentrating on outcomes, the question is: (c) What combination of factors contributed to the impact of the intervention on conflict resolution, attitude change, or relationship changes? These questions are difficult to answer with a small number of cases, even when no-intervention controls are devised or discovered. Progress can, however, be made by either simulating intervention processes or by reducing the number of factors thought to have substantial impacts on the effectiveness of an intervention.

Simulation has the advantage of increasing the number of cases for evaluation through replication. It has the disadvantage of leaving out possibly important factors that are part of the context of real-world interventions. This disadvantage is reduced to the extent that a simulation design captures these sorts of factors. My attempt to do this in the area of multilateral negotiation is a step in this direction. The study consisted first of developing a framework that identified the variables that influenced the negotiation process during each of four stages of negotiation. These variables were then defined and embedded within lifelike depictions of the situation at each of the stages. The effects of these variables on decisions were analyzed in each stage, leading to the paths described in the Chapter 6 section "Process Tracing" (see Druckman, 1993, for details).

A similar type of framework was constructed by Rouhana (2000) to guide evaluations of interactive conflict resolution interventions. This framework identified three major components of the intervention and the hypothesized paths between them. By so doing, the framework highlights a smaller set of critical variables that may influence effectiveness. This is a useful first step for evaluators of conflict resolution interventions. The second step—doing the evaluations—has yet to be taken. In the section to follow, this framework is used as an example of how an evaluation can be organized.

Evaluating Interventions: An Example of a Framework

One of the more popular technologies used by CA&R intervenors is the problem-solving workshop. Yet despite its popularity, it has not benefited from evaluations. In this section, Rouhana's (2000) framework is used to organize the way an evaluation might be performed. The framework connects three components of the intervention: activities within the problem-solving workshop, micro-objectives of the workshop, and macro-goals of the workshop. Let us begin with a review of the parts of this framework.

The following eight activities conducted by intervenors or organizers are listed in the first box of Rouhana's framework shown in Figure 8.1 of his chapter.

- Sensitivity training
- Training in negotiating techniques
- Training in conflict resolution
- Mutual examination of political needs
- Learning about political concerns and constraints
- Brainstorming about new political ideas
- Brainstorming about new solutions
- Writing joint concept papers

Micro-objectives refer to desired changes in the workshop participants that result from the above activities. Among the nine objectives listed in the second box are the following five.

- Increasing differentiation of the other side
- Improving interpersonal relationships
- Changing the enemy image
- Arriving at deeper understanding of psychological conflict
- Reaching mutual understanding of political ideas

Macro-goals are the desired changes in the larger conflict between the parties represented by the workshop participants. Among the nine goals listed in the third box are the following five.

- Changing societal beliefs about the adversary
- Disseminating new ideas to the public
- Influencing decision makers
- Creating or increasing trust between parties
- Changing the dynamics of the conflict

These objectives and goals were not derived from interviews with stakeholders. The author used his framework to organize a review of relevant research rather than to perform an evaluation of this type of intervention. Interviews may have revealed differences among groups such as older and younger members of the conflicting parties, decision makers and members, those constituents eager to attain a peace agreement and those less eager (including spoilers), as well as sponsors of the project and the participants themselves.

Although connections were made by Rouhana (2000) among the three boxes, no attempt was made by him to link specific activities to particular objectives or goals. An example of an hypothesized connection between the components is that conflict resolution training (a workshop activity) is intended to reduce mutual stereotypes (a micro-objective), which can result in changing the climate of the conflict (a macro-goal). Another connection is that sensitivity training leads to a deeper understanding of the psychological conflict that can improve the chances for reconciliation between the parties (a macro-goal). A third example is the connection between brainstorming about political ideas, involving potential future leaders in the workshop, and influencing decision makers. The evaluation project would assess these kinds of hypothesized connections by developing measurement criteria for assessing the objectives and goals.

A next step in the evaluation is to develop criteria for the objectives. An example is a comparison of pre- and post-workshop descriptions of the other party to detect whether change has occurred in the direction of a more differentiated image. In fact, pre- to post-workshop comparisons can be made for each of the other objectives by using ratings, behavioral-observation codes, or interviews. Some measures would address the summative evaluation question of, "What happened as a result of the workshop experience?" Other assessments would provide information that answers the formative question, "How did it happen during the workshop process?" Both types of questions concern the influences of the intervention. Evidence for those influences must take into account possible alternative explanations for observed change from pre- to post-assessments. As you know from reading the earlier chapters, this problem is addressed by experimental designs. When assessments are embedded in experimental or quasi-experimental designs, evaluations become evaluation research.

A number of research methods issues and questions come into play at this stage of the evaluation. Examples are the following:

- *The replication issue:* How many comparable interventions are available for evaluation?

- *The controls issue:* Is there a sufficient number of workshops available to assess the effects of particular activities (with and without the activities), the effects of pre-test administration (with and without pre-tests), and the effects of intervenors (with different intervenors or intervenor teams)?

- *The durability of change issue:* Can assessments be made at several points following the intervention, for example, after a month, 6 months, a year?

- *The selection issue:* Are participants with different perspectives on the conflict available for participation? Can participants be assigned randomly to matched "treatment" and control groups?

These issues are particularly relevant when attempts are being made to evaluate this type of intervention. The question of interest is, "How effective are problem-solving workshops?" They are less relevant for evaluations of particular workshop applications. The former regards each workshop as a sampled case from a larger universe of workshops. The latter regards a workshop as an approach to solving a problem involving specific participants. (See the discussion on the difference between generic and case-specific evaluations in the section "What Is Being Evaluated?") In both cases, data are analyzed for change from before to after the workshop experience. A key difference is that the former, more generic, evaluations also compare data obtained across categories or types of workshops.

At this point in the project, we are ready to prepare for an evaluation of the macro-goals. First, it is necessary to develop criteria for assessing each of the goals. Panel surveys are useful for gauging societal beliefs about the adversary. Asking the same set of questions for each wave of a public opinion poll provides data that can be used to chart trends in beliefs and perceptions. Evidence relevant to the goal of disseminating new ideas can be gathered from content analyses of media reports such as editorials, talk-show debates, and televised documentaries. Keeping track of policy statements from decision makers from both (all) parties can be used to judge the extent to which they have been influenced. The goal of increasing trust between the parties is indicated by such unobtrusive measures as frequencies of joint meetings and activities, changes in the tone of the rhetoric used in speeches (e.g., from threatening to accommodating), and changes in patterns of residential and workplace segregation. A criterion for evaluating changes in the dynamics of the larger conflict is the frequency of violent acts initiated by one or the other party.

The criteria are evaluated by research designs that allow for comparison. Time-series designs are appropriate for documenting changes in rhetoric, policy, activities, and violence. The changes can then be evaluated with various statistical techniques discussed in the Chapter 6 sections "Forecasting With Regression Techniques" and "Interrupted Time-Series Analysis." However, several interpretations of the results are possible. Lack of change may indicate that the macro-goals have not been met. But it may also reflect an inadequate choice of the time period used to evaluate change. Some criteria may take longer to show change than others. Change in the short term may only be temporary, whereas change over the long term may be attributed to factors other than the influence of the interventions. These are examples of some dilemmas facing the CA&R evaluation researcher.

A question posed by the framework is whether, and in what ways, the micro-objectives influence the macro-goals of the problem-solving workshop. This is a key challenge for designers of these sorts of interventions. It is addressed by connecting the analyses performed at each level. This can be done by using several of the techniques discussed in Chapter 6: correlations, interrupted time series, and Bayesian techniques. Change scores on the micro-objective criteria or indicators can be correlated with scaled variables from surveys of societal beliefs about the adversary or media reports of decision makers' statements. Significant positive correlations indicate that the workshop-induced changes in attitudes correspond to later changes in societal beliefs; non-significant or inverse correlations indicate either no relationship or a negative effect of the workshop experience. Because there are many indicators of change at both the micro and macro levels, a matrix of correlations would reveal distinctions among the micro-level changes that may be more or less instrumental in producing changes that occurred later at the macro level. (See Table 6.4 in the "Multiple Regression and Correlation" section of Chapter 6 for an example of a matrix that includes correlations among micro- and macro-level variables.)

Another analysis could treat the workshop intervention as an interruption in an extended time series. At the micro level, this entails stretching the assessments back (pre-tests) and forward (post-tests) in time. The additional data points enhance the evaluation of the micro-objectives. This assessment does not, however, address the macro-goals of the intervention. The impacts of the intervention on macro-goals can be addressed more directly by regarding the workshop as an interruption in a time series of macro-level assessments. Thus, panel survey data on societal beliefs about the adversary would be gathered for several time periods before and after the workshop; the macro-level data would be stretched back (pre-workshop) and forward (post-workshop) in time. Changes would indicate impacts of the intervention, although significant changes may not become manifest for a long time.

The time-series analysis can be supplemented with Bayesian techniques. Focusing on the macro-goal of policy change, the pre-workshop assessments can be used to calculate prior probabilities, for example, frequency of policy shifts by one or more parties in the past. The intervention is one of several symptoms of change used to calculate conditional probabilities; examples of others are international pressure, spoilers, schisms within the parties, and official mediations. (These symptoms are similar to those discussed in the example of forecasting the longevity of peace agreements presented in the Chapter 6 section "Bayesian Inference.") Probability estimates for each of the symptoms, generated from expert panels, provide the data needed to estimate the posterior probability of policy change. Similar calculations can be performed for the other macro-goals. This analysis peers into the future by adding a "what if" dimension to the correlation and time-series analyses. Together, these analyses shed light on the connection between the micro-objectives and macro-goals of the intervention known as the problem-solving workshop.

Interpretations of the results address three connections: the connection between workshop activities and the micro-objectives, the connection between the intervention and macro-goals, and the relationship between micro-objectives and macro-goals. With regard to summative impacts, it is important to justify the time period used for evaluation, both for the micro-objectives and the macro-goals. With regard to formative recommendations, it is important to distinguish between activities during the process that led to change, including the direction of change, and those that did not. Both types of evaluations would be included in the report to the sponsoring organization.

Technical and substantive conclusions about impacts of and improvements in the approach are not, however, the only considerations that bear on implementing the report's recommendations. The intense and often protracted conflicts dealt with by the problem-solving workshop create a sensitive political atmosphere in and around the intervention. These include, but are not limited to, the relationships between the workshop participants and their parties, various stakeholders with interests in the success or failure of the workshop, various decision makers on all sides, and the sponsoring organization. In drafting the report, the evaluation team must be sensitive to these influences. Sensitivity does not mean presenting different results or interpretations in briefings to different stakeholder groups; there should be one report. It does mean developing recommendations for implementation of the findings that acknowledge the roles played by each of the various stakeholder groups. It also means developing a strategy for implementing the recommendations that may include roles for members of the evaluation team, especially with regard to the formative suggestions.

The example of the problem-solving workshop used in this section provides an approach to evaluation largely missing from the literature. Perhaps it will stimulate practitioners in this field to devote some portion of their efforts to building evaluations into their intervention designs. The evaluations can provide useful insights into improving the technology. On this optimistic note, our treatment of issues in evaluation research is concluded, and we turn to the discussion questions for the chapter.

Discussion Questions

In this chapter, we discussed the challenges, tasks, and issues of doing evaluations of interventions or programs in conflict resolution. Evaluation shares many of the technical features of research in general. It differs from many CA&R research studies, however, with regard to the way findings are utilized. Problems arise concerning the different political sensitivities of stakeholder groups, the definition of what is being evaluated, the criteria for effectiveness, and the distinction among the factors that influence outcomes and those that do not. It is important to be aware of these issues when designing an evaluation of such activities as the problem-solving workshop. The following questions allow you to review what you have learned in this chapter.

1. Define what is meant by a summative evaluation and discuss the functions served by it.

2. Define what is meant by a formative evaluation and discuss the functions served by it.

3. In what ways is evaluation research similar to other types of research in CA&R? In what ways is it different?

4. What are some of the factors that may impede the implementation of evaluations on conflict interventions? How might you address these possible impediments in the course of designing an evaluation?

5. Who are the stakeholders in an evaluation project? How would you take their interests into account in performing the evaluation?

6. How might the politics of evaluation influence decisions about the composition of the evaluation team and the way the evaluation is performed?

7. Some evaluations are done for one-shot interventions conducted in particular settings. Other evaluations focus on a type or class of intervention. What are some differences in the way these two evaluations would be designed and performed?

8. What are some alternative ways for evaluating the success of an intervention? How can an evaluator avoid reaching conclusions such as, "It all depends on which definition of effectiveness you use."

9. What are some design and analysis strategies that can be used to deal with the problem of the multiple and changing variables that may have an impact on judgments of effectiveness?

10. The objectives of an evaluation are important to define precisely. What kinds of information would be helpful for defining objectives? How might they be evaluated?

11. Many conflict resolution interventions are intended to have impacts at both a micro and macro level of analysis. What kinds of analyses can be used to connect micro-level impacts (on participants) with macro-level changes (in society)?

12. What are some ways in which the evaluation itself can have unintended effects on the program or intervention that is being evaluated?

13. What are some examples of possible resistances that can surface when the report is released? How might these resistances be anticipated and taken into account in the report and in briefings?

14. Finally, what are some topics from your own work that could benefit from evaluation research? How might you go about designing an evaluation on one of these topics?

12

Research for Action and Consulting

The chapter begins with a discussion of basic and applied research, including the trend toward a merging of these traditions. It then divides into sections on action research and research consulting. Discussions about how to produce social change (through action research) and tips for the would-be research consultant add some practical wisdom to a book that has emphasized the more technical matters of doing basic and applied research. The chapter concludes with a final set of discussion questions.

Basic and Applied Research

At one time, it was fashionable to describe one's profession in terms of either basic or applied research. Social scientists were divided on their views regarding the uses of research. Some researchers wanted to understand the world. They were the basic researchers who measured their accomplishments in terms of contributions to the science or discipline. Other researchers were more interested in solving practical problems. These applied researchers measured their accomplishments in terms of problems solved or practices improved. In the past, it was not difficult to distinguish between these researchers: Basic research was done primarily at universities; applied research in public or private "think tanks" or consulting firms. Today, the distinction is blurred. Most social scientists construe their work in both basic and applied terms. A discernable trend toward a merging of theory, research, and practice is evident, particularly in the field of CA&R.

Yet, differences in emphasis exist among researchers. Those closer to the basic research "wing" prefer the slower pace of design, data collection, analysis, and clear writing for peer-review publication. Those closer to the applied research "wing" prefer the faster-paced enterprise of solving problems for clients or their agencies. They, too, derive rewards from publications—usually in more popular outlets—but also strive to maintain relationships with clients and are more focused on the applications of their research. The methods discussed in this book can be used profitably in both types of projects: Systematic inquiry is valued by basic and applied researchers. The differences are the goals of the research, the kinds of data collected and analyzed, and, therefore, the type of contribution made—primarily to theory or to problem solving/policy.

The question being asked can direct a project toward an application or a theoretical contribution. Many applied projects ask the evaluative question, "Does it work?" Theoretical projects are more interested in answering the question, "Why (or how) does it work?" Three examples from projects I have worked on illustrate the difference.

- **Applied question:** What are the nonverbal indicators of deception?
- **Theoretical question:** What are the mechanisms that connect nonverbal expressions to intentions?

- **Applied question:** What is the likelihood that the incumbent political regime in Country X will collapse?
- **Theoretical question:** What are the conditions under which regimes are likely to be more or less vulnerable to challenges from opposition groups?

- **Applied question:** What kinds of training are likely to be effective in changing the disparaging images (stereotypes) held by members of an ingroup toward members of other (out)groups?
- **Theoretical question:** What is the best explanation for the observed rigidity of outgroup images—cognitive (categorization), emotional (self-esteem), or social (intergroup competition)?

The applied questions ask about indicators, forecasts, and impacts of events or programs. These are technical questions that can be addressed with many of the analytical techniques discussed in this book. The tools are helpful in addressing what is likely to happen or what works. However, without the additional probes suggested by the theoretical questions, the contribution of the research to explanation or understanding is limited. Many projects can address both types of questions and, by doing so, contribute to practice and theory.

A merging of practice and theory is demonstrated by a number of projects. Our efforts to respond to clients' requests to forecast moves made by negotiating opponents and to identify areas of compromise led also to the discovery of a relationship between negotiating crises and turning points. This discovery was the basis for theoretical research on turning points (Druckman, 1986, 2001). The project also produced theoretical insights about the dynamics of alliance bargaining. Our work on political mobility in Brazil led to a more general understanding of the way regime ideologies influence appointments and promotions. These understandings contributed to the literature on political and military mobility and, more practically, insights into the way that military and civil services can be politicized (see Druckman & Vaurio, 1983). Questions asked about the chances of regime collapse in the Philippines motivated the construction of a framework for analyzing political stability. The framework was a theory of factors that influence the stability of political regimes; it also guided analyses of vulnerability to collapse and coalition formation (Druckman & Green, 1986) as well as decisions about negotiating an end to internal conflict (Druckman & Green, 1995). In addition to providing information about the practical utility of nonverbal indicators of deception and heuristics for detection, our project team performed analyses that revealed emotional states associated with various kinds of intentions. The emotional states were conceived of as the variables that intervened between the situation and the observed behaviors; this was a theoretical contribution to the literature (Druckman, Rozelle, & Baxter, 1982). Each of these projects benefited from the use of many of the techniques discussed in Chapters 4 and 6 (for example, analysis of variance, time series, regression, partial and lagged correlation, and Bayesian analyses). The techniques contributed valuable information to both the applied and basic research communities.

These examples illustrate how a study performed to address practical issues can also contribute to theoretical knowledge. Each of these studies was guided by a conceptual framework, rooted in a research literature, well designed, and carefully implemented. The practical questions pertained mostly to issues in foreign policy; the framework-driven research was relevant to issues in international relations, including negotiation, elite mobility, political stability, and peacekeeping. Because the issues were relevant to both practice and theory, it was possible to conduct research of value to both communities. For some projects, however, two versions of the report were prepared, one written for busy practitioners who prefer answers, another written for academic colleagues who prefer sound inferences derived from proper application of methods. The former satisfies the consulting assignment; the latter satisfies scientific criteria for contributions to knowledge.

The experiences gained from these projects suggest a few guidelines for the applied researcher. One is to embrace the academic work that has been done on the applied topic. Knowledge of both theoretical issues and research findings helps to ensure that a project will have broad relevance. Another is to develop expertise about the applied setting in which the research is to be performed. Knowledge of the organizational culture helps to ensure that a project will serve the client's or sponsor's needs and be implemented. A third guideline is to know what can and cannot be accomplished in the setting: know what is needed, what can be done with available resources, and how to communicate with the practitioners who request the research. Research in real-world settings depends for their success as much on the relationships developed and sustained with members of the organizations or communities as on the research skills brought to the project and refined during its execution.

Applied research can be performed by a person who has a job in the organization where the research will be done (practitioner-researcher). It can be conducted also by a researcher from outside the research setting, who is either a consultant or an independent investigator working on a dissertation or grant, or one who is not sponsored (outside researcher). This is an interesting distinction discussed by Robson (2002, Appendix B). In his treatment of these roles, Robson lists advantages and disadvantages. Essentially, these can be summarized as a tension between insider opportunities and insider biases or preconceptions and time. The existing knowledge about the setting and the opportunities for implementation are offset by worldviews shaped, at least in part, by the organization and other jobrelated commitments that take time away from the research project. Likewise, the "uncontaminated" stance of the outside researcher and the relatively uninterrupted schedule are offset by limited knowledge of the setting and opportunities for implementing research. A solution to this problem is to develop a collaborative relationship between the insider and the outsider. This relationship, if it goes smoothly, would take advantage of the complementary strengths of the roles.

A suitable division of labor can go a long way toward satisfying the dual objectives of an applied research project, namely, solving problems and contributing to theory. Whether it would contribute to the goal of social change, shared by many in the CA&R community, is less evident.

Action Research

The idea that research can be used as a vehicle for social change is not new. Lewin (1946), writing just after World War II, viewed research as an approach for bringing about democracy. Kelman (1968), writing during the turbulent period of the 1960s, emphasized the importance of human values in the process of doing research. It was not just that the values of the researcher be taken into account in the interpretation of findings, but that values regarding social change are an intrinsic part of a research process that should address and even promote them. Writing more recently, Rothman (1997a, 1997b) proposed a research paradigm that emphasizes the role of reflexivity or learning how to resolve deeply rooted conflicts from participation in research projects. Each of these writers was promoting the value of a participatory approach to research and practice known as *action research.*

There are many different approaches that fall under this umbrella term. It can be understood best perhaps in relation to other approaches discussed in this book and in terms of some commonalities that run through its various forms. Unlike experimental research conducted in a deductive tradition (see

Chapter 3), action research is flexible, relatively unstructured, and driven largely by the consumers of (or participants in) the research project. Like qualitative research in an ethnographic or grounded theory tradition, action research is inductive in the sense of acquiring insights from the ongoing participation in the process of doing the research. (See Chapter 8 for ethnographic methods; see Strauss & Corbin, 1990, for grounded theory research techniques.) Like the evaluation researchers discussed in the previous chapter, action researchers collect and analyze data about changes that occur during the period of the research. It differs, however, from these approaches in two ways: The researcher's role and perceptions are not central, and the stance taken is collaborative and democratic. The participants in the research do not simply feed information to the researchers or planners; they participate in the decisions that influence its direction in a cycle involving planning a change, acting and observing what happens following a change, reflecting on these processes and consequences, planning further action, and repeating the cycle (Kemmis & Wilkinson, 1998).

With regard to the tasks engaged in by action researchers, Bassey (1998), modified by Robson (2002) and me, specifies eight stages involved in most of these projects.

1. Define the inquiry: What are the issues? Who are the participants? When and where will it happen?

2. Describe the situation: What are we trying to do? Why are we doing this?

3. Collect evaluative data and analyze them: What do the participants understand about what is happening in this situation? Which methods are appropriate for gathering this information?

4. Review the data and look for contradictions: What are some divergences between what is happening and what we would like to see happen?

5. Tackle a contradiction by introducing change: By reflecting on the divergences, what changes can we introduce that might be beneficial?

6. Monitor the change: What happens through time after the change is introduced?

7. Analyze evaluative data about the change: How are the monitored changes through time, similar in some ways to a time series, to be interpreted? Which research methods are most useful for detecting and interpreting the changes?

8. Review the change and decide what to do next: What do we think about the change? Is it sufficient in terms of accomplishing our goals set at the beginning of the project? Have our goals changed? Will the change be sustained over time? What should we do next, if anything?

It should be evident that an action researcher is keen on bringing about change, evaluating it, and interpreting its meaning for future directions. This agenda is similar in many ways to the goals set forth by CA&R practitioners who implement problem-solving workshops. A key difference, however, is the connection made by CA&R researcher-practitioners (but not by action researchers) between micro- and macro-level processes. The changes that are encouraged, monitored, and analyzed in the workshops are regarded only as a step toward larger changes in the societies from which the participants come (Rouhana, 2000). Action research has typically been geared toward change at the level of the research participants. Of course, the approach does not proscribe thinking about larger changes. It only prescribes a process that encourages the participant-practitioners to develop ideas for change and, then, to act on those ideas if they are considered to be feasible. A strategy for bringing about macro-level changes can be developed during either the initial defining stages of the inquiry or during a later stage when next steps are being discussed.

Concerns about the contributions made by action research have been expressed by many social scientists. One concern often heard is about its status as a research paradigm: How does action research differ from other forms of practice that do not claim to be research? Another is about the model of social change advanced by these investigators: Can lasting social change result from attention paid to process rather than structures? With regard to the first concern, a number of aspects of more traditional research paradigms are missing. This includes replication (or reproducibility), cumulation of findings, comparison of matched or unmatched groups, a confusion between investigator and participant perspectives, and, more generally, a lack of a guiding paradigm or systematic implementation of a research design. Some of these limitations—from the standpoint of the critics—can be overcome by incorporating conventional data collection and analysis techniques. But for many action researchers, these considerations miss the point, which is to perform research that produces meaningful social change. The discovery and implementation functions of research are more important than the qualities of design and analysis. The method for engendering change is the primary task of the researcher. Thus, we remain in a quandary about whether this approach is practice or research.

Many action research projects have been criticized for adopting a naive conception of social change that does not consider bureaucratic processes, anti-democratic values, and inertia or a lack of desire for institutional (macro-level) change. However, there is probably nothing inherent in the approach that would preclude these considerations. In their quest for encouraging participation in research, action researchers may have overlooked how they might deal with some barriers to change. Thinking systematically about change entails having researchers and participants address the following questions.

- What specifically is to be changed? The distinction between micro-level (the group participating in the research) and macro-level (the larger society or culture) changes is useful.
- To what extent do participants agree on those particular changes? Participant agreement is essential in action research designs.
- What are some ways to bring about the changes? This discussion occurs during the second stage of the action research cycle, referred to above in Step 2 as "Describe the situation."
- What are the roles of research and fact finding in the change design? This should neither be taken for granted nor imposed by the investigator. Ideas should emerge from the discussion during the second stage.
- What are the respective roles of participants and researchers in the change research design? The idea of collaboration in action research is often vague. It would be helpful to clarify roles even in a collaborative process.
- What are some institutional and logistical barriers to implementation? This discussion should also alert participants to the difficulties of changing institutions, leading perhaps to a change strategy at the macro level.
- What are some possible ethical barriers to change? The implications of change for people not involved in the project, and therefore not part of the decision making, need to be discussed. Consent of unwitting members of the community is an issue in change designs.
- How much time and resources are available to implement the change plan? The temptation to implement ambitious plans should be tempered by the reality of available resources to pull it off.
- What criteria should be developed for evaluating whether or not change has occurred? Different criteria may be needed for evaluating short- and long-term change as well as changes that occur in the participants versus those that occur outside the research group. These criteria are discussed in Stage 3 of the action research cycle and revisited at a later stage.
- What follow-up activities are needed to sustain the changes? What can the research group do to ensure that the changes last? This entails a discussion of how to create a normative climate (or culture) that will reinforce the changes after the group has concluded its work.
- How should the research be reviewed and reported for dissemination? These are important questions for several reasons. One is the importance of public scrutiny of the project. A second is the importance of making a contribution to the research literature and influencing the way others develop action research designs. And a third is the importance of encouraging change in other communities by demonstrating the value of this project.

Another idea for connecting action research to social change is through the use of what Senehi (2002) refers to as *constructive storytelling*. She argues that storytelling can contribute to conflict resolution by the way it influences shared knowledge and identity, socialization, emotions, morality, time and memory, and geographic space. Stories are accessible, fluid, vivid, and powerful forms of expression that can bring disputants together; they can, however, also be divisive by emphasizing invidious distinctions between "us" and "them." By incorporating storytelling activities into action research projects, participants may acquire new insights that impel them to action. Whether stories actually have these effects awaits the accumulation of evidence from cases in which they have been used. Next steps include developing a typology of stories, techniques for coding them, procedures for incorporating them in an action research design, and methods for analysis (see Chapter 10 for a start along these lines).

These considerations about social change conclude our discussion of action research. For further reading about the variety of action research designs, the reader is encouraged to consult Selener (1997). For attempts to integrate action research with case studies and other qualitative approaches, see Schratz and Walker (1995). For applications to CA&R, see the work being done by Rothman's Action Evaluation Research Institute (www.aepro.org) and the articles by Rothman (1997a) and Ross (2001). The book edited by Ross and Rothman (1999) also provides perspectives on action and evaluation research related to problems of conflict and conflict resolution. I turn now to another approach that merges research and practice, research consulting.

Research Consulting

Methodology plays an important role in research consulting. It consists of the tools that social science consultants bring to assignments done for clients, including action research and related applied approaches to problem solving. By *research consulting*, I refer primarily to the broader interface between researchers or analysts and clients who are willing to pay for their services. The researchers are usually, but not always, professionals who have received advanced training in one or more social science disciplines, including CA&R. The clients include international and domestic government agencies—the largest supporter of social science research—as well as a variety of private-sector companies and public-sector nonprofit institutions. A consulting project occurs when there is a match between the needs of clients (or sponsors) and the knowledge or skills that a consultant or consulting team brings to the project. The match may happen with regard to any of several types of consulting roles and functions. These roles are discussed briefly followed by examples of methods used in various types of consulting projects on topics related to CA&R.

In a recent article, I suggested that social science consultants perform seven roles (Druckman, 2000). Some of these roles depend more on method-ological skills than others. These include the roles of technician, applied theoretician, and study director. The *technician* performs statistical analyses, designs and implements program evaluations, designs and conducts field experiments, and devises frameworks to guide research and development programs for agencies and organizations. Examples from my own experience include the use of forecasting techniques, content analysis, discriminant analysis, and mathematical models. In fact, most of the techniques discussed in Chapters 4, 6, 7, 9, and 11 have been used in consulting assignments. These consultant skills are often sought to augment the less technical backgrounds and training of agency staffs.

The role of *applied theoretician* consists of interpreting or translating research literatures for use in addressing applied problems. Focusing more on substance and theory than on tools, this role brings expertise about regional knowledge on topics such as the politics of the Middle East, the economics of South Asia, or practices in China that influence global environmental change. As an applied theoretician, the consultant would develop a framework to place the regional problem in a broader conceptual context. Many of the approaches discussed in Chapters 1 and 2, as well as the qualitative techniques described in Chapters 6, 7, and 8, are relevant to this role.

The role of *study director* is more integrative than specialized. In a consulting firm, the director may guide teams of technical specialists with both methodological and substantive expertise. This is a multifaceted role. Although directors rarely participate in projects as technicians, they must acquire an understanding of research design and analysis. Many are former technicians who progress through "the ranks" to become directors of applied research studies. They are often responsible for attracting clients, briefing them, and writing or disseminating final reports. At the U.S. National Research Council, study directors assemble committees that conduct studies that bring technical knowledge to bear on national policy (see Druckman, 2004).

Consulting roles that make fewer demands on technical skills include advisers, bridge builders, facilitators, and trainers. The *adviser* is sought to contribute to a client's strategic concerns. Advisers may, for example, be invited to be part of a panel that evaluates a federal department's intramural research program or to develop guidelines that help an agency evaluate the progress made by its programs. The *bridge builder's* function is to bring different communities together to expand networks, broaden perspectives, collaborate on projects, or even resolve ongoing disputes that arise from different professional cultural viewpoints. The *facilitator's* task is to improve communication processes in groups. This is a central role played by many conflict resolvers (e.g., Fisher, 1997; Mitchell & Banks, 1996). It includes defining problems, identifying possible solutions, helping the group to choose among the proposed solutions, and working with members to implement their decisions. It depends more on process than on technical research skills. The *trainer's* task is to help clients acquire or refine professional or other job-related skills. This often includes performing evaluations that benefit from research skills, as illustrated in an upcoming example. None of these consulting roles should be regarded as a pure type. Although each has a distinct function, there is considerable overlap in practice:

for example, the trainer who performs evaluation research or the facilitator who uses theory and frameworks in group tasks. Thus, methodological training is likely to enhance the performance of a wide variety of consulting roles and functions.

A number of consulting projects illustrate how some of these roles are played in actual practice. One project combines the roles of trainer with applied theoretician and bridge builder. Its purpose was to develop negotiating skills primarily in the context of international diplomacy. A variety of professional diplomats and advanced graduate students from a number of countries participated in the exercises. These participants evaluated their experiences in terms of the training goals: What was learned? How would the new insights be used in actual negotiations? Thus, the consultants' primary role was that of trainer. The role of applied theoretician was enacted during the period of the design phase of the project. An attempt was made to utilize research findings in the training exercises. This was done by composing research summaries, in the form of narratives, for each of 16 themes: for example, achieving integrative agreements, third-party effects, positive and negative affect, culture, and so on. Unusual or counter-intuitive research findings were highlighted in the narratives. Features of the applied theoretician role represented in this project included knowledge of a body of research literature, synthesizer of findings, and communicator for practical use of the material.

The consulting function of bridge builder is reflected in the way the exercises were developed. A sequence of role enactments provided an opportunity for trainees to apply the research knowledge in the narratives to actual cases. The applications were done in the form of three roles: analyst, strategist, and designer. Cases chosen for use in the analyst and strategist roles were those that illuminated themes from several narratives. Study guides provided direction for performing, first, the analyses and, then, the strategic role. The third role, designer, consisted of developing training exercises that would convey selected concepts and findings from the narratives. Thus, participants in the workshops had three opportunities to apply the research knowledge to real-world processes and designs (see Druckman & Robinson, 1998, for details). In this project, the consultant is building bridges between scholarship and practice. It was a rare opportunity for demonstrating the value of using basic research in practice. (See also Druckman & Ormachea [2003] for a Spanish version of the set of materials, including the complete set of narratives and case exercises.)

Other consulting projects highlight the role of technician. Projects on nonverbal communication (NVC), political elite mobility, and political stability are more in the academic research tradition. A difference, however, is that, unlike many academic projects, these are framed by clients in terms of applied goals. Each of these projects was motivated by national security concerns: The NVC project's focus on deception clues was intended to improve detection of possible security concerns in relation to employment in government agencies; the elite mobility project was a response to the practical question, "Who is likely to be in positions of leadership in country X a few years from now?" The political stability project addressed the policy issue of regime failure and, specifically, how analysts can diagnose instability. These applied frames add dimensions and activities that would not be entertained if the projects were construed only as theoretical research investigations.

The initial stage of the NVC project consisted of a state-of-the-art review of the literature on nonverbal communication. The role of the applied theoretician is illuminated in the first stage of the project, which was an attempt to cover what was known in each of five channels of communication: paralanguage, facial expressions, kinesics (body language), visual behavior, and proxemics (use of space). The role of technician is evident in the second stage, which consisted of multi-faceted research on the diagnostic value of nonverbal cues. Results of a series of experiments showed that: (a) certain nonverbal behaviors may have diagnostic value in assessing deception; (b) the diagnostic value is increased when several behaviors are considered together in combination; (c) the window into intentions (to be honest, evasive, or deceptive) operates through the arousal of emotions; (d) actors can use nonverbal behaviors to influence the impressions or attributions made by observers; (e) information-processing stages may be indicated (or diagnosed) by nonverbal behavior; and (f) observers can be trained to infer intentions from nonverbal clues with a high degree of accuracy. The role of bridge builder describes activities in the third stage of the project, which consisted of communicating the findings to the client and relevant stakeholders. To do this effectively entailed writing a report that would be widely read and conducting seminars and briefings that addressed the client's framing of the project, focusing more on implications than methods.

The political analyses were high-profile projects motivated by the events following the fall of the Shah's Iranian regime in 1979 (see Sick, 1985). One of these projects asked about the future leadership of foreign countries. Although phrased by the client as a problem of prediction (a focus on the individuals), our analyses treated the problem in terms of explanation (a focus on mobility processes). The role of applied theoretician was emphasized during the initial phase of framework design and literature review. The framework connected variables at the individual, institutional, and systems levels of analysis. It guided the empirical work to follow. The role of technician was evidenced in the analyses of data on promotions and appointments in the Brazilian military and cabinets. Results showed that different types of regimes (civilian, internationalist-military, nationalist-military) had different preferences for credentials and experiences of aspirants for top-level appointments. The bridge-builder role consisted of explaining the results to the client's applied community. This community was provided with a complex treatment of the problem that emphasized the importance of explanation rather than prediction. On the one hand, clients learned about how mobility emerges from changing aspects of politics at each of the three levels of analysis. On the other hand, they were given methods for analysis that could be used in many other country contexts.

The regime stability project also illuminates different consulting roles. The role of applied theoretician was in play during the framework-development phase of the project. The elaborate framework included a wide variety of factors thought to impinge on the vulnerability of regimes in power. It served to organize the analyses to follow. In the role of technicians, we developed analytical procedures for estimating the extent to which various political groups or coalitions of groups posed a threat to the incumbent leadership. These tools were then used to organize a data collection and make assessments of stability of the Marcos regime in the Philippines for the period 1982–1984. The results of this project answered the question posed by the client. The bridge-building role consisted of communicating these findings and the models that were developed for analysis of the problem. But, like the other projects just described, this work also made a theoretical contribution. It extended and elaborated on our conception of group politics and ways to measure concepts such as legitimacy and rectitude. Further, it contributed to conceptions of political actors as well as to the state of the art in scenario ("what if . . .") design and analysis.

A recent consulting project illustrates how the role of applied theoretician can be augmented by that of technician. The project is described in Chapter 6 on enhanced case studies. It consisted of helping the staff of a consulting firm develop an elaborate framework for analyzing international negotiation. As noted in the Chapter 6 section "Theory and Case Study," the framework captured the key conditions and processes of negotiation. These features were culled from a large research literature developed over several decades. The skills of the applied theoretician were needed, first, to identify the features—in the form of 10 sections—and, second, to elaborate the variables or questions within each of the sections. As noted earlier, a considerable effort went into reliability testing and refinement of the framework's parts. Upon completion of this phase of the project, the issue of weighting was posed by the client: Which features were more or less important influences on negotiation outcomes? Enter the technician. The challenge now was to devise a procedure for generating weights. Although regression may be the best technique for doing this (see the Chapter 6 section "Forecasting With Regression Techniques" on calculating beta weights), it was precluded by a lack of sufficient time-series or cross-sectional case data. Thus, we searched for alternatives and decided on convening an expert panel (see the Chapter 6 section "Systematic Expert Judgment").

The task consisted of, first, identifying the experts and, second, asking them to read the same negotiation case (the Panama Canal negotiations leading to an agreement in 1977). Then they were instructed to perform four exercises of making paired comparisons: first, among the five conditions; second, among the four processes; third, among all nine features, including both conditions and processes; and fourth, among six variables within the section of the framework referred to as "topics and issues." The paired-comparison data were then scaled according to the procedures described by Guilford (1954, chap. 7). In the role of technician, I developed the format for the task, prepared a set of instructions for performing the calculations, checked the calculations for accuracy, and interpreted the resulting weights. For each of the four tasks, the features being compared were arranged on a ratio scale (with a zero point as its origin) of relative importance in influencing the substantive outcome of the talks. The results indicated that what the negotiators did at the table along with the larger domestic and international environments were judged to have more impact on the treaty outcome than who they were (delegations, negotiators, or cultures). These findings were reported to the client along with the rationale for choosing the procedure. A satisfied client went a long way toward reinforcing the value of performing several functions on an assignment. These functions are facilitated by having ready access to a varied methodological tool kit.

These four projects are examples of research consulting roles that contribute both to theory and practice. Although other projects could be described, the key point is made with these examples. Research methods address the gap between theory and practice by providing results that contribute to both communities. Many of the methods discussed in this book can be used in both basic and applied projects. A difference between these projects is more in the way the question is framed than in the way the analysis is implemented. The national security frame used by the clients who commissioned these projects was not incompatible with the theoretical re-framing invented by the researchers. Thus, although the feasibility of discovering nonverbal clues to deception was demonstrated, we also learned about how various emotional states mediate the relationship between intentions and behavior (Druckman et al., 1982). Similarly, although providing tools for analyzing patterns germane to answering the succession question, the political mobility project contributed to the academic literature on recruitment and mobility processes (Druckman & Vaurio, 1983). In the course of providing country estimates of regime vulnerability, the political stability project contributed a new way of thinking about the ebb and flow of group politics (Druckman & Green, 1986). And the technician role contributed valuable analytical results in the framework project on negotiation. These and other consulting projects challenge a conventional wisdom about the separation of or, indeed, the cultural divide between, practice and theory. The nexus between them can be provided by research methods (see also Cheldelin et al., 2003).

TIPS FOR THE WOULD-BE RESEARCH CONSULTANT

Most of the consulting roles discussed in this section benefit from methodological skills. These skills are important even when performing non-technical tasks. The applied theoretician, study director, and bridge builder must understand relevant research literatures and often convey the applied implications of research. For this reason, a book of this sort should be useful as well to the communicator of research. There are, however, other skills that a consultant needs to develop as part of the craft. Many of these are discussed in books about social science consulting (e.g., Lippitt & Lippitt, 1986). A baker's dozen tips is provided here that may help you secure lucrative consulting projects and that help me bring this chapter to a close.

1. Try to avoid being one of many bidders for publicly announced contracts (e.g., those advertised as Requests for Proposals in the Commerce Business Daily). The effort put into proposals, even when highly competitive, is not justified by the probability of winning the job.

2. Be proactive. Do not wait for a request to come from a client. Often, the demand for your services must be created through active participation in stakeholder networks.

3. Cultivate a patient attitude. It often takes a while for good projects to develop and sponsors to commit resources. Thus, hedge against disappointment by developing alternatives.

4. Do not relinquish contacts with the academic community by performing projects that are unlikely to make contributions to the knowledge paradigms of larger research communities. Remember that you will need the skills developed in that community for accomplishing many types of projects. Academic reputation does count with many sponsors.

5. Do not confuse an encouraging conversation with a potential sponsor with its support for your project. Many sponsors, especially government agencies, seek many proposals as "evidence" that serves to justify their programs.

6. It is important that the proposal clearly addresses the client's needs. By including a needs assessment in the proposal, you are communicating that the client's needs will strongly influence the research.

7. Be sure the research team is shown to have task-relevant competence and experience. This often includes past projects that required technical skills.

8. Remember that most clients are interested in purchasing projects that do not duplicate what is being done in their own agency or company.

9. Be realistic about budget estimates. Gather information that will make your estimate competitive and consider taking on a project for fewer resources than desired if the promise of future work is evident.

10. Get the senior members of the client's organization or agency to buy into the project. This should be done before, during, and after the technical work is completed. But do not get involved in the internal politics of the client's organization.

11. Keep the sponsor informed of progress frequently, even if no formal request is made. Occasional briefings, milestone reports, and involving the client's staff in the project can lead to adjustments that will improve the final report and its reception.

12. Plan ahead. Do not wait until the final quarter of a project to prepare proposals for the next phase of the research.

The baker's advice: Strive to turn sponsoring clients of short-term projects into "benefactors" who are willing to sustain the program over the long term.

One message from these tips is that interpersonal skills are important in the profession of research consulting. Another is that becoming a consultant is a risky decision. On the one hand, it offers opportunities unlikely to be available to the academic social scientist, especially the chance to bring theory and research methods to bear on important practical problems. On the other hand, it can lead to disappointment—and job insecurity—in attempts to secure, perform, and implement client-sponsored projects. It is hoped that these tips ease the transition from a graduate student learning how to do research to a consultant trying to apply what has been learned in the classroom.

Discussion Questions

Research and practice are no longer considered alternative career choices for social scientists. During the past decade or so, there has been a noticeable trend toward a merging of basic and applied research. Only a few social scientists, and probably fewer CA&R researchers, think about their work in terms of this dichotomy. Many projects can be framed in both theoretical and applied terms, and a number of them have addressed both types of questions in their implementation. Some of these projects have the dual aim of learning about conflict dynamics and contributing to its resolution. Others use research to promote a more ambitious agenda of social change. These aims are served by an approach known as action research, which breaks down the distinction between the researchers and those being researched by encouraging equal participation of both in all phases of the project. They are also served in the practice of research consulting, which highlights responsiveness to client-driven questions and agendas. In this chapter, both approaches are discussed as popular examples of how CA&R research and practice are merged. The following questions provide you with an opportunity to review what you have learned.

1. Discuss some differences and similarities between research that is motivated by theoretical questions and research that addresses applied issues.

2. Choose a topic that interests you and, first, frame the research question in theoretical terms, then reframe it in applied terms.

3. What are some advantages and disadvantages of conducting research on the organizations in which you work? What are the advantages and disadvantages of the outside-researcher role?

4. What is action research? Describe the common features of the various approaches that fall under this rubric.

5. What are some possibilities and limitations of bringing about social change through action research?

6. What are some differences between doing action research and conducting third-party interventions such as the problem-solving workshop?

7. What distinguishes research consulting from other types of research projects?

8. Discuss the various functions often performed by social scientists in consulting roles. Which functions involve more and which involve fewer research skills?

9. Show how some of these functions are performed in the context of a project. For example, describe the parts of a project that emphasize technician, applied-theoretician, and bridge-builder skills.

10. How might research methods serve to reduce the gaps between applied and theory-driven research projects?

11. What are some lessons from theory that might be useful in a CA&R practice? What are some lessons from applied work that may contribute to CA&R theory?

Part VIII

Concluding

This final part of the book consists of a concluding section that does several things. It begins by highlighting the main thrust of the book, which is a philosophy that provides a foundation for the way methodologies can be used for doing social science research. This approach—like all approaches to research—raises some issues that need to be addressed, and these are discussed in the next section. I then summarize the key aspects of each of the research methods discussed in the earlier chapters, 11 in all. These summaries illuminate complementarities among the methods. This should be useful for the researcher who contemplates doing a multi-method project. The key issues discussed in each chapter are also summarized.

The three pillar methodologies—experiments, case studies, and surveys—are emphasized in comparisons made on eight criteria in the next section. This discussion is intended to give the reader some guidance in making what is for many researchers a first-level decision: Which general approach best addresses my problem? Among the decisions made at the next level are data collection strategies. To help with these decisions, I provide an overview of the strengths and weaknesses for each of 12 sources of information collected in conjunction with experiments, case studies, or surveys. The section wraps up with some problems that have surfaced in student research proposals written for methods courses. Advice on how these problems may be avoided is provided with the intention of improving the quality of social science research.

From Philosophies to Research Methods: The Value of Doing Research in Conflict Analysis and Resolution

DOING RESEARCH: PHILOSOPHIES AND METHODOLOGIES

This book opened with a discussion of philosophical issues that influence the way research is conducted in the social sciences. The issues were presented as tensions between opposing approaches. The approaches are manifest in varying degrees in the methodologies treated in the following chapters. Some of the methods are more etic or comparative than others. Some are more emic or case specific. Abstract skills are needed more for certain methods, such as modeling, whereas more experiential skills are emphasized by other methods, such as action research and ethnographies. Quantification is a hallmark of experimentation and large-N surveys or comparative studies, whereas qualitative understanding is highlighted in many case studies, some forms of content analysis, and in discourse analysis. The tension that exists between competing approaches is a source of creative energy and vision. Each provides a window through which to view the etiology and course of conflict processes. It is when several of these approaches are used together that a larger picture—seen from windows in different corners of the scholar's edifice—emerges. This is the kind of synthesis that could not be obtained from the standpoint of one perspective or application of one methodology. It is derived from a multi-method approach to research advanced by a post-positivist generation of scholarship and integrates the different contributions made by the methodologies.

The approach that I am describing can be illustrated with three recent projects in CA&R. Each of these projects is an attempt to forge a connection between micro-level processes and macro-level contexts. The project described by Rouhana (2000), and discussed in detail in Chapter 11, consisted of developing a framework for linking the activities, micro-objectives, and macro-goals of the problem-solving workshop. The primary contribution made by this project was to articulate the linkages. He does this by conceptualizing theoretical paths, first from the intervention to the micro-objectives and then from the micro-objectives to the macro-goals. This is a taxonomic effort that moves us closer to answering the questions about which intervention procedures work, in what types of conflict, at what stage in the conflict, and under what societal or international conditions. Providing the basis for empirical research, these questions are not answered by Rouhana's taxonomy.

Progress toward addressing the questions would be made by a multi-method research program done in three phases. As noted in Chapter 11, the first phase consists of a quasi-experimental evaluation of the micro-objectives: What are the impacts of the workshop procedures (e.g., sensitivity training, writing joint papers) on the objectives (e.g., changing the enemy image, improving relationships)? Of course, stronger inferences about impacts would result from a larger number of workshops, distinguished perhaps in terms of the approach to intervention. A second phase consists of conducting surveys and/or interviews to assess the macro-goals (e.g., changing societal beliefs, influencing decision makers). Sensitivity to time lags is needed to bolster confidence in the relationship between what happened at the micro (workshop) and macro (societal) levels.

A third phase applies process-tracing methods to the data collected in the earlier phases. A key connection made by the paths is between attitude changes that occur in workshop participants and changes in public opinion and behaviors. The path could be traced in a chronological time line similar to the several examples shown in Chapter 6. A more ambitious study would add the feature of most similar and most different systems design comparisons. Paths could be compared for workshops conducted in both similar and different conflict regions during roughly the same time period. Other indicators of macro-level effects are the more general climate of the conflict, increased evidence of official and nonofficial cooperative activities, reduced expenditures on defense and mobilization in both (all) the societies, and the emergence of new regimes signaling a transition from war to peace zones.

Fast's (2002) study of NGO security in three countries illustrates another attempt to connect micro- and macro-level factors. She was interested in learning about why some NGOs are more insecure than others. Using reported incidents of violence as a dependent variable, she coded a variety of organizational attributes in a sample of NGOs from three countries: for example, impartiality, engagement, types of activities, provision of material aid, and organizational mission. The correlational and discriminant-function analyses uncovered relationships among impartiality, engagement, and security. More impartial and more engaged NGOs were more insecure. These were regarded as micro-level findings.

The next question asked was whether context mattered: Do the micro-level relationships between organizational attributes and insecurity transcend country setting? This question was answered with a focused-comparison methodology. The most-similar comparison between Angola and Sierra Leone was complemented by a most-different comparison between these countries and Ecuador during roughly the same period of time. She discovered differences due to context: Insecurity levels—referred to by Fast (2002) as *ambient insecurity*— were higher in the countries experiencing ongoing war (Angola, Sierra Leone). Further, the profiles of more and less insecure NGOs differed for these countries, referred to by Fast as *situational insecurity*. The relationships found between organizational attributes and insecurity across the countries were shown to be moderated by the type of country. This multi-level, multi-method study underscores the importance of context in CA&R.

Irmer's (2003) study is another example of an attempt to connect levels with multiple methods. She was interested in the relationship between negotiation processes and outcomes. This relationship was explored by performing a large-N comparative case analysis (26 cases) and a small-n focused comparison. The large-N correlational analysis examined relationships among both process and contextual variables with negotiation outcomes. Process and outcome variables were aggregated indices of scaled codes that reflected the distinction between distributive or competitive and integrative or cooperative bargaining. Four contextual variables were codes for regime type, geographic proximity, alliances among the parties, and regional stability. Process correlated strongly with outcome ($r = .79$); only geographical proximity correlated significantly with process ($r = .45$) and outcome ($r = .51$). More interesting, however, were the results of a partial correlation analysis. The process-outcome relationship was not diminished when each—or a combination—of these contextual variables was controlled. (For example, controlling for geographical proximity, the process-outcome correlation was .75.) Thus, context in this study was less important. This then led to further probes of the process-outcome relationship.

The probes were designed to detect causality. By juxtaposing most-similar and most-different systems logic on a small set of cases, she demonstrated that the process indicators (distributive bargaining) lagged behind the outcomes (less comprehensive agreement): This was shown to occur in both types of comparisons. Going a step further, she conducted a plausibility probe—a type of process tracing—on these cases. The probe identified a mechanism that tied the process indicators to the outcomes. It was the development of trust through the course of the talks. This project is a good example of a step-by-step logical progression aided by both quantitative and qualitative methods. It demonstrated the prevalence, across contexts, of a causal link between negotiation process and outcomes.

The three studies just discussed may be considered part of a trend in social science, and in CA&R, toward complex multi-level, multi-method analysis. The hallmarks of this trend are recognizing the importance of context, sensitivity to achieving a balance between the concerns of internal and external validity or relevance, and a merging of theoretical and applied priorities. The importance of these features was recognized early, in the 1960s, when laboratory research incorporated context through the design of experimental simulations. Realizing that simulations could reproduce only some aspects of non-laboratory settings, researchers became increasingly interested in doing case studies that, for a number of us, were conducted primarily to validate the simulations. These were efforts to check and then improve the external validity of the research. This was, however, a limited contribution. External validity would be improved only by expanding the case database. This realization led many researchers to develop and refine comparative approaches, in both the qualitative and quantitative traditions.

Nonetheless, the applied value of this research was still a nagging concern. It encouraged investigators to adapt various methods to address problems of evaluation and social change. Evaluation and action research approaches have been very popular additions to the tool kit for CA&R consultants. Moving around in this landscape of approaches and methods may well become the modus operandi for CA&R scholar-practitioners. It is the defining feature of a post-positivist era in social science.

RESEARCH ISSUES

We have learned that research is conducted primarily within particular methodological traditions. Each of these traditions has strengths and weaknesses. A preference for multi-methods (as well as perspectives) stems from a recognition that no single approach can provide knowledge that transcends the limitations of time and place. These limitations are reduced to some extent when complementary approaches are used in a study or in a research program. For example, when a randomized control group experiment is conducted within the context of a sample survey, both internal and external validity are strengthened. (See Wall & Druckman, 2003, for an example of an experiment embedded in interviews of a purposive sample of peacekeepers.) Similarly, when small-*n*–focused case comparisons are augmented by large-*N* case comparative analyses, internal and external validity are strengthened along with providing relatively deep and broad insights (see Irmer, 2003, for an example). Further, the external validity of laboratory experiments is strengthened when the experiment is carried out in the context of a simulated social process.

Validity is one of the issues highlighted in this book. When we addressed it, we have referred to various concerns. In the arena of experimentation, the primary concern is whether alternative explanations for findings are plausible. Some refer to this as *analytical specificity.* In the arena of simulation, the concern is whether the situation captured in the laboratory (or in a model) represents the context or domain being simulated. With regard to survey research and content analysis, the questions asked have to do with whether a sample represents a larger population or universe of people or material. And, with regard to ethnographic research and discourse analysis, the question often asked is whether the descriptions are authentic. Issues of internal and external validity framed in a positivist tradition are supplemented by the concerns of authenticity raised in the constructivist tradition.

Other issues concern matters of confidence and type of contribution made by the research. Confidence is, of course, related to validity but also brings into play other considerations. One is whether the research issue being addressed is important in the sense of its contribution to the field. A valid but trivial experiment is unlikely to get published: Some journals refer to this as the substantive or theoretical importance of the study. Another concern is the heuristic value of the study. This refers to whether it is likely to generate further research as evidenced by frequency of citations. A third is the way the study is written and, then, revised in response to a journal peer review. An acceptance is more likely if the author "leaves no stone unturned" in preparing the revised manuscript. Nothing bolsters confidence more than an acceptance in a peer-reviewed publication.

CA&R researchers contribute both to theory and practice. Theoretical contributions are sensitive to validity issues as discussed in the chapters on experiments, case studies, and surveys. Applied contributions are sensitive to consumers of the research as discussed in the chapters on evaluation and action research, including research consulting. These different goals are joined when applied researchers or consultants use their theoretical knowledge to address the problems posed by practitioners and clients. A number of examples of such bridge building were given in the previous chapter. More recently, a government client requested tools that could assist professional diplomats negotiate more effectively. This problem was tackled by developing a framework, based on the academic research literature, that would guide decisions and diagnose the possible impacts of strategies contemplated by the professionals in the context of particular cases. The bridges built between these communities are not very different from those imagined by action researchers eager to bring about social change. They also value the contributions that social science theory and basic research can make to the practical challenges of solving problems that involve conflict.

SUMMARY OF METHODS COVERED

Many other issues about methodology have been raised in this book. They are addressed largely in the context of particular approaches. Here is a summary of the methods in terms of their primary purpose and the key issues addressed by them. This list may have value as a quick reference for the researcher who is contemplating the implementation of a multi-method project. Let us start with experimentation.

Experimental Design

The primary purpose of laboratory experiments is to strengthen the internal validity of the evidence produced by the design. This is done by creating control groups that address the various threats to validity. Experimentalists have shown considerable ingenuity in creating controls for many of these threats. They have also been sensitive to cumulation issues, particularly with the advent of meta-analytic techniques. The foundation for these innovations has been provided by advances in statistical analysis: Recall the discussion of the measurement-power trade-offs in Chapter 4. Many of these advances have also been useful for strengthening the inferences made from results obtained in quasi and field experiments.

Simulation

In this book, we focused primarily on the use of simulation for experimentation. The discussion in Chapter 3 emphasized the way that experimental designs can be embedded in scenarios of social processes. A goal of these designs is to enhance external validity without forfeiting internal validity: To the extent that the scenario reproduces a particular non-laboratory context, it contributes to the external validity of situations rather than populations as in survey research. To the extent that a randomized control group design is used, the study contributes to internal validity. These advantages are, however, purchased at the possible cost of highlighting role players' sensitivity to the hypotheses of the study. Role playing may make the study's purpose or hypotheses easier to detect, leading participants to behave in terms of their suspicions or expectations. This has been referred to as *demand characteristics.*

Modeling

Like simulation, modeling is an attempt to capture key features of a social process. Unlike simulation, models depict these processes in a mathematical (rather than operational) form. Many of the models that are relevant to CA&R consist of preference functions that maximize desired outcomes such as minimal winning coalitions or a balance of constituents' or stakeholders' interests. Some models attempt to capture conflict dynamics in the form of rates of transition to new states. Empirical data are often used to evaluate them by performing sensitivity analyses (assessing the relative impacts of the model's components) or by conducting gaming experiments. However, many formal models are restricted to situations that satisfy the assumptions and measurement requirements of the model and, thus, may not apply to a wide variety of cases.

Survey Research

The most sophisticated treatment of sampling is found in books about survey research. Developed in conjunction with probability theory and statistical inference, techniques for drawing random samples from defined populations have been devised by survey researchers: The key idea of random sampling is that each member of a population has a known calculable (not necessarily equal) chance of being selected for inclusion in the sample. This idea is also the basis for the more complex forms of random sampling such as stratified (strata created by demographic variables) and cluster (captive populations for convenience) sampling. It is often the case, however, that circumstances pose obstacles to random sampling, leading researchers to seek purposive samples. Although these samples can be representative of a larger population, they preclude calculating reliable estimates of sampling error through statistical analysis and, thus, pose threats to external validity. This is one of the reasons why surveys have been under-utilized in CA&R research. The discussion in Chapter 5 about relationships between sample size, response variability, and sampling error provides useful tips for making decisions about a survey design.

Response rates to survey questions differ depending on the way a survey is conducted. Higher rates are obtained from face-to-face interviews than from mail or telephone surveys. A problem is that the resulting sample differs from the planned sample and may not be representative of a larger population. Response biases are also sensitive to the way a survey is administered as well as to question wording. Face-to-face interviews may accentuate interviewer influence on the way questions are answered and social-desirable responding. Further, questions worded in the same direction—all low scores are scaled as positive, high scores are negative—encourage acquiescent responding. Long surveys with precisely gradated questions (7- or 10-step scales, for example) risk fatigue, leading to less thoughtful answers from the sampled respondents.

Single Case Studies

Two types of case studies are the enhanced case study (Chapter 6) and ethnographies (Chapter 8). The former consists of superimposing theoretical frameworks on documented (secondary data) cases: The case is interpreted through the lens of one or more theories. This deductive approach enhances the theoretical relevance of cases. The advantage of the approach is, however, "purchased" at the cost of precluding other possible interpretations not covered by the chosen theories. Ethnographies are deeper probes into a culture through various participant-observer (primary data) techniques. The many advantages of sharing experiences with local citizens may be offset by sampling problems. The fieldworker is limited by his or her own exposure to events and activities, including the particular informants interviewed. Time and resources are needed to acquire the deeper insights that can be induced from immersion in the daily lives of members of particular cultures. A broad sampling of events and informants is needed to acquire the representative insights that can also come from immersion.

Comparative Case Studies, Small-n

Two types of small-n comparative approaches, discussed in Chapter 7, are the most-similar (focused comparison) and most-different systems designs (MDSD). The former is an attempt to apply the logic of experimentation to case studies. This logic is based on the idea of reducing threats to internal validity through the use of control groups. The case study counterpart to controls is matching on independent variables. This is accomplished by selecting two or more cases on dimensions of similarity: The cases are similar on all independent variables except those (usually one or two) hypothesized to influence the dependent variables of interest. (Note the use of experimental terminology for this methodology.) The difficulty of attaining this objective has not prevented some investigators from "pulling it off." However, even those excellent studies are vulnerable to threats to external validity.

The MDSD approach is based on the opposite logic. An attempt is made to select cases that differ on many independent variables. The reason for this is to discover contrasting profiles or to distinguish between "extremes" in a typology of conflict processes or structures. The examples of Nagorno Karabakh and Mozambique illustrate a comparison between negative and positive peace processes. Of course, the very small number of cases and lack of a control group strategy render this approach vulnerable to both external and internal validity threats.

Comparative Case Studies, Large-N

Two large-N comparative research strategies discussed in Chapters 6 and 7 are time-series and multiple-case cross-sectional designs. Both of these strategies provide sufficient data points for statistical analysis. Time-series designs capture the dynamics of conflict processes, which is also known as *diachronic variation*. Comparisons between two or more time series can be done in a number of ways: regression for scaled data points, Bayesian analysis for probabilities, or qualitative process tracing for categorical data. One problem that arises with these analyses is correlated (or non-independent) data points, referred to as *autocorrelation*. Other problems are the comprehensiveness and precision of the chronologies used for scaling or categorizing events. These matters do not intrude on cross-sectional analyses of many cases.

This approach is in the MDSD (concomitant variation) tradition but, unlike the small-n version, captures variability across a sampled series of case observations. These comparative studies are less vulnerable to external validity threats. They are, however, more problematic with regard to causal inference, especially when most of the measured variables are correlated with each other—referred to as *multicollinearity*. This problem was addressed in the Chapter 6 discussion of partial, lagged correlational analyses.

Content Analysis

The systematic analysis of textual material is becoming increasingly popular in CA&R research. It is often easier, and less expensive, to acquire documented accounts of cases than to conduct interviews on site. Both types of data collections benefit from a sampling design: Informants or respondents and text are sampled data from a larger universe. With regard to text, the sampling unit varies from the word or sentence to larger thematic units. The size of the unit has implications for reliability and validity. Typically, the smaller the unit, the more agreement between coders in assigning a category to the statement. Small units are, however, often taken out of context, which poses a threat to validity. The trade-off for the content analyst is to balance ease of coding with meaning that derives from understanding the larger themes in a text.

Texts are not, however, the only source of material for content analysis. Interaction processes are also valuable data for conflict analysts. This is primary data that can be transcribed or videotaped for more deliberate coding (as compared to making on-the-spot decisions). A good deal of our knowledge of negotiations and related interactions comes from process analysis, notably from the category system referred to as *bargaining process analysis*. More complex forms of content analysis include attempts to capture the ebb and flow of ongoing conversations with the help of coding-category distinctions made in the research tradition of narrative or discourse analysis. This approach to analysis is also becoming increasingly popular in CA&R research. It is rooted in a constructivist philosophical tradition that emphasizes the importance of subjective experience (see the "Epistemological Foundations" section in Chapter 1). A key criterion for validity is the authenticity of a subject's narrative, which is usually constructed from interviews. Although limited in terms of generality, narrative analysis has the advantage of probing more deeply into a subject's interpretation of conflict than most content-analysis systems. Progress is being made in developing a rule-based structure for analyzing the transcribed stories about conflicts as told by the persons being interviewed.

Evaluation Research

Evaluations are done primarily to ascertain the effectiveness of interventions. Effectiveness has been defined in terms of both outcomes (summative evaluation) and processes (formative evaluation). A focus on processes for CA&R researchers and practitioners makes formative evaluations particularly valuable. Evaluations can contribute to the improvement of problem-solving workshops. They inform design choices and the extent to which impacts are sustained. Although most of the research techniques discussed in this book are relevant to the conduct of evaluations, other considerations may be more important.

Evaluations are performed for clients, as distinct from sponsors of research, who often use the results to improve or change the organizations they direct. For this reason, evaluations are politically sensitive. They have implications for a variety of stakeholder groups. This means that the evaluation researcher must perform a needs assessment to ascertain their interests and make an effort to address their sometimes conflicting concerns when making recommendations. This challenge is met when the evaluator realizes that he or she functions in dual roles, as researcher who collects and evaluates data and as consultant who is sensitive to the practical implications of the findings. The value of the evaluation turns on the way these roles are performed.

Action Research

This is another approach to doing research that is receiving attention from the CA&R community. It is an example of applied research that addresses the nexus between research and application. Action researchers emphasize the discovery and implementation aspects of research more than design and analysis. The early work in this tradition (going back to the years following World War II) was actually more concerned with social change than with new knowledge. In recent years, efforts have been made to make the investigations more systematic while maintaining the key element of collaboration between the investigator and the participants (research subjects). Unlike other approaches to doing research, participants take part in the decisions that influence its direction, including planning a change, observing what happens after the change occurs, reflecting on these consequences, and planning further action. Three issues raised about this approach are its status as a research paradigm (the action component may trump the research contribution), its focus on processes rather than structures, and the lack of a connection between the micro-processes analyzed in a project and macro-level changes that would be expected to occur. These are some of the issues currently being debated in discussions about the approach. CA&R researchers are making important contributions to these discussions.

Research and Policy Consulting

This may be one of the few research methods texts, if not the only one, that includes the topic of research and policy consulting. An increasing demand for advice from social scientists and from conflict analysts makes this a relevant topic. Consulting has become a viable alternative to an academic career for many graduate students. The challenges posed by consulting assignments often require technical skills, particularly a knowledge of modeling social processes, survey design, and evaluation techniques. These skills are used to solve practical problems rather than to contribute to theory. However, the same data can often be analyzed to provide answers to more general (less applied) questions. For example, in the course of providing clients with estimates of a political regime's vulnerability to being overthrown or with projections of a country's future leadership, a consulting analyst can also shed light (using the same techniques) on group politics or mobility processes. As in evaluation research, being responsive to a client's interests is paramount—and this is stressed in the

Chapter 12 section "Tips for the Would-Be Research Consultant"—but this sensitivity does not prevent making contributions to more general theoretical issues as well. With this thought, the summary review of methods covered in the earlier chapters concludes.

The accompanying box lists the set of issues identified in the overviews of each of the methodologies covered in this book. This is a handy list of 31 issues that directs the reader to the chapter where each is discussed in some detail.

Issues Addressed by Chapter

Chapter 1: Emic and etic approaches to doing research

Chapter 1: Abstract and concrete perspectives and related philosophical issues

Chapter 2: Research literature coverage as a basis for new studies

Chapter 2: Finding a match between questions asked and research method chosen

Chapter 3: Threats to internal validity and the use of control groups (discussed also in Chapter 4)

Chapter 3: Threats to external validity and representative designs

Chapter 3: Cumulation of research findings for meta-analysis

Chapter 4: Measurement/power trade-offs for statistical analysis

Chapter 4: Within- and between-group variation in experimental designs

Chapter 5: Sample size, response variability, and sampling error

Chapter 5: Response rates for survey returns

Chapter 5: Response biases for survey questions and administration

Chapter 6: Framework standardization and coding consistency for time series (also for aggregate analyses in Chapter 7)

Chapter 6: Autocorrelation for time-series designs

Chapter 6: Multicollinearity in correlation and regression

Chapter 7: Case matching and mismatching for most-similar and most-different systems designs

Chapter 7: Accurate chronologies of events for process tracing (and for time series)

Chapter 7: Sufficient number of cases or events for aggregate statistical analyses

Chapter 7: Sampling from a universe of cases for aggregate statistical analyses

Chapter 8: Informant sampling and authentic accounts for ethnographies

---

COMPARING THE METHODOLOGIES: EXPERIMENTS, SURVEYS, AND CASE STUDIES

The various methodologies discussed in this book can be compared in terms of a number of criteria. Running through the criteria is the distinction made by Robson (2002) between fixed and flexible designs. As discussed in Chapters 3 and 4, laboratory experiments represent the most fixed or structured approach to doing research. Each of the other methodologies is more flexible but in varying degrees, ranging from the relatively fixed simulation experiment or random sample survey to the flexible ethnography or single case study. In this section, the methodologies are compared on each of several criteria. The comparison is made in terms of the extent to which an approach deviates from the fixed-design experiment. Let us start with the form of the approach.

Form

Four aspects of form are structure, stability of design through research stages, control over independent variables, and deductive in the sense of being theory based. A successful laboratory experiment is one that is highly structured, maintains its pre-planned structure throughout the phases, has tight control over the independent variables, and is designed to evaluate hypotheses derived a priori from a theory. It is the prototype for the fixed design. Some of these aspects are compromised for quasi or field experiments and for simulations: In the former, random assignment and control are compromised;

in the latter, some structure is forfeit for providing role players with a realistic scenario. Like the laboratory experiment, the focused-comparison case study is highly structured in order to evaluate theory-derived hypotheses. At the other extreme is the relatively unstructured ethnography intended primarily for discovery rather than theory testing. Large-N comparative case studies fall in between these approaches: Coding standardization (fixed design) is balanced by the many differences between the sampled cases (flexible design). The mechanical form of random-sample surveys, with regard to both respondent selection and administration of questions, renders this method highly structured in all ways except control over independent variables. Deviations from the structured format of these surveys are found in low response-rate mail and telephone surveys as well as in non-probability, purposive samples.

Role of Researcher

Experiments and action research present contrasting roles for the researcher. The experimenter plays a passive role in data collection. The action researcher, as the name suggests, is active. Other approaches vary between these extremes. Generally, the more mechanical the procedures, the less that the researcher intrudes on the process of doing the research. Experiments, mail surveys, precoded (non-interpretive) category systems used to code texts or cases, game models, and forced-choice responses to interview questions are examples of very limited researcher involvement. Ethnographies, discourse analysis, open-ended interviews used in evaluation research or surveys, and action research are examples of researcher involvement in the process. The former approaches, in the etic tradition, emphasize the role of researcher as technician who is keen on ensuring that different cases can be compared. The latter, mostly in an emic or constructivist tradition, emphasize the role of researcher as interpreter who seeks understanding of conflict processes within their larger social context.

Logistics

Good research is done with considerable care. Logistics are important for any of the approaches discussed in this book, but they are not the same for different approaches. About half of them require very careful preparation up front, before the data collection begins. These are the more deductive theory-testing methods of experimentation, focused-case comparisons, random-sample surveys, and some forms of content analysis. Much of the "production" (data collection, analysis) is orchestrated: Data are collected according to a script prepared for the experimenter or the survey interviewer; analysis is closely coordinated to the design. The other half involves at least some degree of invention during data collection. These are the more inductive discovery methods of ethnography, action research, correlational analyses of multiple cases, discourse analysis, and other interpretive approaches in the tradition of grounded theory (e.g., Strauss & Corbin, 1990). Less is done up front as orchestration gives way to learning or improvisation during the research process. Of course, this does not mean that these are more casual approaches to doing research. Careful note taking, keeping track of progress, technical skills, and the preparation of reports that survive peer-review processes are essential aspects of doing these kinds of projects.

Sampling

Many kinds of sampling issues and designs were covered in this book. Issues of comparison are paramount in experimental approaches. It is addressed through random assignment of subjects to different treatments and control groups or through selecting matched cases. Issues of generality are central in surveys and simulations. Survey researchers sample from a defined population of respondents. Simulation researchers design scenarios that represent types of situations. Similarly, time periods, events, and texts are sampled to increase confidence that apply to more general populations of these units. But we also learned about sampling informants for representative perspectives on cultural history, sampling stories produced by narrative methods for capturing larger meanings produced in interviews, and sampling concepts or variables for valid models. In all of these ways, samples provide opportunities for collecting and analyzing data that strengthen the argument that results have relevance also to non-sampled groups or situations. The case for relevance (or generality) is strengthened further if the sampling is random. Better yet, it would be advantageous to use several types of sampling frames in a project—sampling from populations, situations, and time periods, for example. This sort of triangulation of sampling frames is similar to triangulation of methods. Together, these are complementary ways to bolster validity.

Validity

Validity has been discussed in a number of different ways. The traditional distinction between internal and external validity was highlighted: Threats to internal validity are best addressed by randomized control group experiments or simulations; threats to external validity are best addressed by random sample surveys. The variations on random designs, such as quasi-experiments or purposive sampling frames, leave open the possibility of alternative explanations and limited generality for findings. These are not, however, the only ways in which the term has been used. Research approaches developed in a constructivist tradition, like narrative analysis, emphasize the importance of authenticity. Validity is evaluated from the standpoint of the participants in the research process or in terms of the joint vantage points of researcher and participants. This kind of subjective validity reflects an attempt to capture the meaning of experiences or interactions. Another kind of validity has been defined in the context of applied research or consulting. Validity refers to policy relevance, usefulness, or even client satisfaction. It is evaluated by feedback from those being served by the research projects and, thus, is also a form of subjective validity. As with sampling, a research project would benefit from incorporating multiple kinds of validity perspectives and criteria.

Analysis

The approaches differ also on the way each conceives of data analysis. These differences can be regarded as deviations from the classical analysis paradigm that has been tied to the experimental method: analytic (vs. holistic), quantitative (vs. qualitative), deductive (vs. inductive), causal (vs. correlational), replicable (vs. unique), and cumulative (vs. case specific). Many of the research approaches discussed are attempts by the researchers to unbridle themselves from the strictures of the fixed, pre-planned design. Ethnography may be the best example of deviation from the classic paradigm. It features more of a holistic approach and is qualitative, inductive, and primarily emic in the sense of emphasizing uniqueness rather than comparability. (Note, however, the argument for comparability made in Chapter 8.) Small-n case studies, discourse analysis, and action research are also deviations in varying degrees. But some of the more quantitative approaches are deviations as well. The inductive "fishing expeditions" illustrated by many correlation analyses of cases are attempts to discover patterns or dimensions from the matrices. Exploratory surveys are carried out to generate hypotheses that can be evaluated with more confirmatory approaches. These kinds of projects are quite popular in fields such as CA&R, where theories are less well developed. A large number of term papers submitted in my methods classes are subtitled (correctly) "An Exploratory Study."

Research and Practice

A key difference among the methods is the extent to which practical considerations are incorporated in the research paradigm. These considerations are addressed directly by evaluation and action research. In fact, these approaches were designed to bridge research and practice. A question asked about both these approaches is whether the concern for practical contributions has led to a compromise of standards for doing research: Although this may be the case for particular projects, the approaches do not prevent contributions to both research and practice. A distinction, however, between evaluation and action research concerns the respective roles of researcher and participant in the study. These roles are separated in evaluation research (as well as in research consulting). They are joined through collaborative models in action research.

The other approaches discussed—experimentation and modeling, case studies, surveys, content analysis—do not incorporate practical considerations into the design. Research questions are posed by the researcher (based often on theory) rather than by a consumer or participant in the research process. Contributions to practice are indirect. Examples include utilizing experimental research findings in training programs, addressing policy issues with results from relevant case studies, and using surveys that reveal values or preferences of groups represented in a multilateral negotiation. The methodologies were used for basic research; the findings were used by policy and training practitioners.

Foundations and Disciplines

The approaches do not divide in clear ways by philosophical foundation or by social science discipline. Although experimentation is primarily associated with positivism and has a very long history in psychology, it has been used also to gain insights into subjective processes and is gaining popularly in all of the other social sciences except anthropology. Similarly, survey methodologies were developed and refined by sociologists (and statisticians) but are used by many political scientists and economists as well. Case studies were developed initially in qualitative and applied social science (including clinical) traditions. They have a long history in anthropology. More recently, however, cases have been considered as units of analysis in the comparative statistical studies performed by many international relations investigators. Notable exceptions to this diversity—or plasticity—are discourse or narrative analysis and action research. These approaches are tied more closely to particular philosophical and analytical traditions: constructivism for discourse analysis and democratic orientations for action research; both approaches have a strong preference for qualitative analysis. For CA&R, I suggest an approach referred to as *disciplined eclecticism*. It is disciplined because an investigator has a plan for combining the methodologies in research projects. It is eclectic because it is not confined to any one approach, philosophy, or discipline. This is indeed the richness of multi-method research.

The discussion of similarities and differences among the approaches now concludes. Many kinds of data are collected within and across these approaches. It would seem useful to provide guidance about the relative strengths and weaknesses of the various sources of data used in CA&R studies. These are summarized in the next section.

TYPES OF DATA

Data take many forms in CA&R research and, more generally, in social science. Many types of data have been discussed in this book in conjunction with the different design and analysis approaches. Twelve popular sources of information are covered in the following box.

• Information Source	Strengths	Weaknesses
• Behavioral observations	Easy to observe. Relatively reliable coding for analysis.	Does not reveal motives or explanations for the behavior. More difficult to record in studies of groups or other large units of analysis.
• Self-reported perceptions, opinions, or attitudes	An important source for subjective data that can be assessed on scales for quantitative analyses. Primary data from survey questionnaires.	Relatively weak correlations with behavioral observations. Difficult to control for various response biases.
• Expert judgments	Informed judgments based on experience with a topic or area.	Can be inaccurate despite expressed confidence by the experts (sometimes over-confidence). Subject to response biases.
• Informant observations	As with experts, informants are often skilled and experienced observers. If sampled, accounts can be representative of a larger population.	Inaccurate memory for events that occurred in the distant past. If not sampled, observations are limited to particular vantage points. Comparability across informants can be problematic.
• Events	A source for historical, time-series analyses. Relatively easy to code reliably. Though not always apparent, the meaning of events can be inferred from interviews with actors.	Subject to observer biases. Intentions of actors are rarely revealed. Comparability across events can be problematic.
• Verbal statements from documents	Often the only record of past activities or events. Suitable for content analysis.	Lack of control over the production of the material. Often incomplete coverage on variables of interest. Difficult to evaluate importance of missing information.
• Narrative accounts	Information about perceptions and subjective meaning of experiences and events.	Subject to interviewer influence. Lack of comparability.

	Elaborations may provide more complex interpretations than other verbal accounts.	Non-representative accounts of events.
• Oral histories and other introspective reporting	Valuable for documenting an actor's role in a process, institution, or career. Can provide an elaborate account of historical events.	Inaccurate—and sometimes self-serving— recall of distant events. Subject to attribution biases and limitations of vantage point. Difficult to compare different reports of similar activities, especially if the interviews are open ended.
• Unobtrusive data	Avoids subject reactivity. Can capture trails (or traces) not recoverable by asking questions. Indicators of activities not known by other methods, as in archaeology.	A lack of control over the data production. Interpretations may be ambiguous, especially when other data are not available. Subject to observer biases.
• Aggregate data	Indicators of societal or systems-level variables. Major source for demographic or population data. Useful for capturing cyclical political or economic processes.	May mask small group or individual variables. Controversial rules for aggregating data obtained from smaller units (groups, organizations, cities, or regions).
• Computer simulation data	Direct and controlled evaluation of competing theoretical interpretations or assumptions. Useful for evaluating alternative policy scenarios. Can be compared to empirical cases.	Eliminates human or cultural factors. Analyses can be based on fairly simple assumptions about human behavior, such as consistent utility-maximizing actors.
• Secondary data	Often the only source of available data. The basis for research syntheses, including meta-analyses. Useful as baseline data for comparison with new (primary) data collections.	Lack of control over the conditions of collection. Often collected for other purposes. Lack of coverage of variables, which may be of interest to analysts.

WRAPPING UP

In this chapter, I have summarized the book's coverage. This has included an overall philosophical theme emphasizing the use of multiple methods in investigations and recognizing multiple levels of analysis. The theme is compatible with Cook's (1985) idea of a post-positivist approach in social science and Boudreau's (2003) multiplex methodology for conflict analysis, as well as with the argument that the various methods are complementary rather than competing (e.g., George & Bennett, 2004). The flexibility needed to move among the approaches should not be purchased at the expense of validity. In designing their studies, CA&R researchers must be cognizant of threats to internal and external validity. Indeed, the use of multiple complementary methods may strengthen validity claims by offsetting the weaknesses of one approach with the strengths of another. To help the researcher navigate through the various approaches, I have provided a summary of each approach and offered comparisons of advantages and disadvantages of the various methodologies, emphasizing the broad umbrella approaches of experiments, surveys, and case studies. Focusing on data collections, I have also offered an appraisal of their strengths and weaknesses. Although none of this is intended to be a rule of thumb for the researcher, all of it is intended to raise the consciousness of both new and experienced investigators. By doing so, the challenge of doing research ought to be less daunting and even less burdensome.

Some of the challenges are evident in the term papers that I have read through my years as a teacher of research methods. I regard many of these as confusions that can remedied by careful attention to the discussion questions following each chapter. Here are 10 examples.

1. Students often propose experimental designs with small numbers of subjects (dyads, groups) in each cell. The small ns make it difficult to attain statistical significance. Smaller statistical ratios are needed for larger numbers of subjects. My advice is as follows: When it is feasible, strive for large Ns.

2. Often, students do not appreciate the value of randomization. They are tempted to substitute convenience samples for those drawn randomly from populations or assigned randomly to experimental groups. Statistical inference depends on the random-sampling or assignment assumption. Convenience in the short run may be inconvenience over the course of a project.

3. The measurement-power trade-off may not be intuitive. Many proposals treat scaled data as ordinal or ranked data as interval. When it is feasible, measure variables in gradations; when it is not, rely on appropriate nonparametric tests.

4. Simple random sampling is often confused with representative sampling. Randomization does not ensure that key subgroups will be adequately or proportionately represented in the research sample. Stratified random sampling addresses this problem. Purposive, nonrandom sampling is a poor substitute.

5. Causal reasoning differs from correlational hypotheses. The independent-dependent variable terminology should be reserved for designs that lag one variable behind the other in time. Although statistical methods have been developed for inferring cause from correlational data, they do not substitute for well-designed time-lagged experiments. The idea of building experiments into surveys facilitates causal analysis of large-N sample surveys. However, the experimental design should not be confused with the survey design.

6. Identifying threats to validity in a study is important. However, defining these threats is not the same as developing a design or analysis strategy to reduce them. Many proposals go no further than the identification.

7. Similarly, gauging the response rate to a mail survey alerts the investigator to a problem of inference. It does not solve the problem. The researcher must ask two questions: How does a small response rate change the representativeness of the sample? What can be done to improve the response?

8. Surveys are sometimes confused with case studies. There appears to be a preference among CA&R researchers for conducting questionnaire or interview surveys with selected groups even when broader sampling is possible. The broader sampling, as in sample surveys or comparative case studies, can make a larger contribution to knowledge, especially when the questions being asked are inspired by theory.

9. Many students limit their definition of qualitative research to interpretive or thematic analysis. This should be recognized as being only one of many qualitative approaches. Qualitative research ranges widely along a spectrum of framework or rule-drive procedures. Contrasting examples in this tradition are process tracing and some forms of action research. Both are covered in this book.

10. It is a mistake to assume that the more systematic approaches to research are also more demanding on the researcher. Flexible designs may indeed be more demanding than fixed designs. Of all the approaches discussed in this book, the most demanding may be the least systematic, action research and ethnographic methods. This is because the researcher is at the center of knowledge creation and change. His or her judgments, often made on the

spot, are critical to the next phase of data collection and interpretation. A distinction between approaches that are demanding in the conduct of the study and those that are demanding in learning complex, and often abstract, skills may be useful.

I now give you the wrap-up but not the final word, which I reserve for the epilogue to follow. Doing research on problems of conflict or related social science topics entails developing a variety of skills. If we think about these skills in broad categories, they include an understanding of the philosophical foundations for various methodological approaches, appreciating the lessons of previous research, crafting research questions, constructing research designs, producing or discovering appropriate data, knowing how to perform analyses, and writing for peer-review publications. If we break down the categories into sets of skills, they would include, for example, library search methods (for reviews and research questions); sampling strategies (for data collection); listening, language, and interviewing skills (for many forms of qualitative research); mathematical and statistical knowledge for modeling and simulation; learning about political cultures for evaluation research; and designing coding systems for content analysis. Textbooks can provide guidance for each of these types of skills. I have tried to do this with examples of projects from the field of conflict analysis. The skills are further developed and refined with experience, including graduate-student apprenticeships. This part of the learning process I leave to my colleagues and hope that they provide many learning opportunities on projects that encourage you to develop rewarding careers as social scientists.

Epilogue

O ne impression conveyed by this book is that conflict analysis is a field searching for an identity. Like many other interdisciplinary fields, CA&R has been shopping for theories and methods that can be adapted to its problems. Some projects can be housed comfortably in departments of psychology, sociology, or political science. Others seem to transcend the boundaries between traditional disciplines, and several of these projects—particularly dissertations—were used as examples in this book. Thus, the first textbook on methods is presented as a multiplex, where several "messages" (approaches, techniques, levels of analysis) are transmitted over the same "circuit" (CA&R). My choice to present the field in this way was based on my long teaching and research experiences as well as on the conjecture that creative work is fostered by the tensions that arise from the intellectual diversity of the topic and the professional and social diversity of the community.

In searching for an identity, CA&R professionals struggle with the idea of paradigmatic coherence. As discussed in "Features, Norms, and Assumptions" in Chapter 1, coherence has several advantages. These include ease of communication among researchers, accepted standards for evaluating contributions to knowledge or practice as well as for charting the growth of a field, and legitimacy in the academic community. But coherence also has some limitations. One is that it may discourage lines of investigation that do not fit into the paradigm. Another limitation is that research projects may be more derivative than original as a next step in a preprogrammed sequence. A third limitation is that coherence encourages risk aversion by investigators. And a fourth is that it could lead to attrition due to the uncertainties of both funding and tenure decisions. For these reasons, I suggest that we rejoice rather than bemoan our plight of the elusive paradigm. Our challenge is to sustain the momentum generated from fledgling status, realizing that the best work may be done during the earliest stages of a field. (In this regard, note the set of articles published in the first issue of the *Journal of Conflict Resolution,* appearing in 1957.) This book's emphasis on using established methodologies in new ways or inventing new methods of investigation addresses this challenge. It is an emphasis that should also help other social scientists expand their portfolio of skills and contributions.

The state of the field has implications as well for graduate training. The elusive paradigm encourages a more eclectic and diversified program than is likely to be found in most of the other social sciences. This kind of program provides opportunities for a less specialized education, at least to the point where students begin work on their dissertations: At George Mason's ICAR, students take required courses in micro- and macro-level theories, qualitative and quantitative research approaches, and reflective practice and choose courses within streams of electives on culture, structure, and process. Although this type of training places them at a competitive disadvantage in a market-place that values competent specialists, they have the competitive advantage of flexibility in offering a variety of courses and conducting research on a broad array of problems: They may have trouble securing academic offers but, after securing an appointment, may become highly valued members of the department or research unit that hires them. It should not be surprising that this book has been written with this type of student-researcher in mind.

The *flexibility* that emanates from participation in the CA&R "enterprise" is augmented by the *discipline* that is instilled from absorbing the lessons of this book. Together, these features may well contribute to a full social science career. Despite the impression that there are few employment opportunities compared to other fields, the CA&R professional is prepared to take advantage of many more opportunities. Consider that he or she is trained to perform basic and applied research, do modeling and framework development, synthe-size a wide array of research findings, lead study teams, perform evaluations of interventions and other practices, consult, and teach. Moreover, the graduate has been encouraged to be innovative with both qualitative and quantitative techniques, connect micro-level processes to macro-level structures or institu-tions in contributing to knowledge, and move comfortably between academic and practitioner roles. These skills should also enable him or her to survive, if not transcend, the bureaucratic structures of the academy as well as the peer-review process. Indeed, this is the profile of the complete scholar-practitioner. It is my hope that this book contributes to fulfilling that aspiration for CA&R scholars as well as for professionals in other social science disciplines. I believe that enough has been said to promote the endeavor. Now, let us move forward with the tasks of *doing research.*

References

Achen, C. H. (1982). *Interpreting and using regression* (Sage University Paper series on Quantitative Applications in the Social Sciences, series no. 07–029). Beverly Hills, CA: Sage.

Agar, M. H. (1996). *The professional stranger: An informal introduction to ethnography* (2nd ed.). San Diego, CA: Academic Press.

Agresti, A., & Finlay, B. (1997). *Statistical methods for the social sciences* (3rd ed.). Upper Saddle River, NJ: Prentice Hall.

Allen Nan, S. (1999). *Complementarity and coordination of conflict resolution efforts in the conflicts over Abkhazia, South Osetia, and Transdniestria.* Unpublished doctoral dissertation, George Mason University, Fairfax, VA.

Anderson, J. R., Reder, L. M., & Simon, H. A. (1998). Radical constructivism and cognitive psychology. In D. Ravitch (Ed.), *Brookings papers on educational policy.* Washington, DC: Brookings.

Antaki, C. (Ed.). (1988). *Analyzing everyday explanation: A casebook of methods.* Newbury Park, CA: Sage.

Appadurai, A. (1996). *Modernity at large: Cultural dimensions of globalization.* Minneapolis: University of Minnesota Press.

Armstrong, R. R. (1995). Gaming-simulation in perspective. In D. Crookall & K. Arai (Eds.), *Simulation and gaming across disciplines and cultures: ISAGA at a watershed.* Thousand Oaks, CA: Sage.

Atran, S., Medin, D., Ross, N., Lynch, E., Coley, J., Edilberto, U. E., & Vapnarsky, V. (1999). Folkecology and commons management in the Maya Lowlands. *Proceedings of the National Academy of Sciences, 96,* 7598–7603.

Aubert, V. (1963). Competition and dissensus: Two types of conflict and of conflict resolution. *Journal of Conflict Resolution, 7,* 26–42.

Avruch, K. (2003). Type I and Type II errors in culturally sensitive conflict resolution practice. *Conflict Resolution Quarterly, 20,* 351–371.

Ayres, W. R. (1997). Modeling international conflict: Is image change necessary? *Journal of Peace Research, 34,* 431–447.

Bales, R. F. (1950). *Interaction process analysis.* Reading, MA: Addison-Wesley.

Bales, R. F., & Strodtbeck, F. L. (1951). Phases in group problem solving. *Journal of Abnormal and Social Psychology, 46,* 485–495.

Bartos, O. J. (1995). Modeling distributive and integrative negotiations. *Annals of the American Academy of Political and Social Science, 542,* 48–60.

Baruch, R., May, H., Turner, H., Lavenberg, J., Petrosino, A., DeMoya, D., Grimshaw, J., & Foley, E. (2004). Estimating the effects of interventions that are deployed in many places: Place-randomized trials. *American Behavioral Scientist, 47,* 608–633.

Bassey, M. (1998). Action research for improving educational practice. In R. Halsall (Ed.), *Teacher research and school improvement: Opening doors from the inside.* Buckingham, England: Open University Press.

Bayes, T. (1764). An essay towards solving a problem in the doctrine of chances. *Philosophical Transactions of the Royal Society of London, 53.*

Becker, H. S., & Geer, B. (1960). Latent culture: A note on the theory of latent social roles. *Administrative Science Quarterly, 5,* 304–313.

Bell, S. E. (1988). Becoming a political woman: The reconstruction and interpretation of experience through stories. In A. D. Todd & S. Fisher (Eds.), *Gender and discourse: The power of talk.* Norwood, NJ: Ablex Press.

Bendahmane, D., & McDonald, J. W., Jr. (Eds.). (1986). *Perspectives on negotiation: Four case studies and interpretations.* Washington, DC: Foreign Service Institute.

Bercovitch, J., & Houston, A. (1996). The study of international mediation: Theoretical issues and empirical evidence. In J. Bercovitch (Ed.), *Resolving international conflicts: The theory and practice of mediation.* Boulder, CO: Lynne Reinner.

Bercovitch, J., & Langley, J. (1993). The nature of the dispute and the effectiveness of international mediation. *Journal of Conflict Resolution, 37,* 670–691.

Beriker, N., & Druckman, D. (1991). Models of responsiveness: Lausanne peace negotiations (1922–23). *Journal of Social Psychology, 131,* 297–300.

Beriker, N., & Druckman, D. (1996). Simulating the Lausanne peace negotiations, 1922–23: Power asymmetries in bargaining. *Simulation & Gaming, 27,* 162–183.

Birkhoff, J. E. (2001). *Mediators' perspectives on power: A window into a profession?* Unpublished doctoral dissertation, George Mason University, Fairfax, VA.

Blalock, H. M. (1960). *Social statistics.* New York: McGraw-Hill.

Blalock, H. M. (1979). *Social statistics* (2nd ed.). New York: McGraw-Hill.

Bloomfield, L. P., & Beattie, R. (1971). Computers and policy making: The CASCON experiment. *Journal of Conflict Resolution, 15,* 33–46.

Bonham, G. M. (1971). Simulating international disarmament negotiations. *Journal of Conflict Resolution, 15,* 299–318.

Bottom, W. P. (2003). *Smoke and mirrors: Cognitive illusions and the origins of appeasement at the Paris Peace Conference 1919.* Paper presented at the First Biennial International Conference on Negotiation, Paris.

Boudreau, T. (2003). Intergroup conflict reduction through identity affirmation: Overcoming the image of the ethnic or enemy other. *Peace and Conflict Studies, 10,* 87–107.

Brewer, M. B., & Kramer, R. M. (1985). The psychology of intergroup attitudes and behavior. *Annual Review of Psychology, 36,* 219–243.

Briley, D. A., Morris, M., & Simonson, I. (2000). Reasons as carriers of culture: Dynamic vs. dispositional models of cultural influence on decision making. *Journal of Consumer Research, 27,* 157–178.

Brown, G., & Yule, G. (1983). *Discourse analysis.* Cambridge: Cambridge University Press.

Buller, P. F., & Bell, C. H., Jr. (1986). Effects of teambuilding and goal setting on productivity: A field experiment. *Academy of Management Journal, 29,* 305–328.

Burton, J. W. (1986). The history of international conflict resolution. In E. E. Azar & J. W. Burton (Ed.), *International conflict resolution: Theory and practice.* Boulder, CO: Lynne Rienner.

Cameron, M., & Tomlin, B. (2000). *The making of NAFTA: How the deal was done.* Ithaca, NY: Cornell University Press.

Campbell, D. T., & Stanley, J. C. (1963). *Experimental and quasi-experimental designs for research.* Boston: Houghton-Mifflin.

Campbell, J. C. (1976). *Successful negotiation: Trieste, 1954.* Princeton, NJ: Princeton University Press.

Carment, D., & Rowlands, D. (1998). Evaluating third-party intervention in interstate conflict. *Journal of Conflict Resolution, 42,* 572–599.

Carstarphen, N. (2003). *Shift happens: Transformations during small group interventions in protracted social conflicts.* Unpublished doctoral dissertation, George Mason University, Fairfax, VA.

Chafe, W. (1990). Some things that narratives tell us about the mind. In B. K. Britton & A. D. Pellegrini (Eds.), *Narrative thought and narrative language.* Hillsdale, NJ: Lawrence Erlbaum.

Chagnon, N. (1968). *Yanomamo: The fierce people.* New York: Holt, Rinehart and Winston.

Cheldelin, S., Druckman, D., & Fast, L. (Eds.). (2003). *Conflict: From analysis to intervention.* London: Continuum.

Clarke, K. (2003). Nonparametric model discrimination in international relations. *Journal of Conflict Resolution, 47,* 72–93.

Clifford, J., & Marcus, G. E. (Eds.). (1986). *Writing culture: The poetics and politics of ethnography.* Berkeley: University of California Press.

Cohen, J. (1968). Multiple regression as a general data-analytic system. *Psychological Bulletin, 70,* 426–443.

Cohen, R., & Westbrook, R. (Eds.). (2000). *Amarna diplomacy: The beginnings of international relations.* Baltimore: Johns Hopkins University Press.

Coleman, J. S. (1973). *The mathematics of collective action.* Chicago: Aldine.

Conlon, D. E., Carnevale, P., & Ross, W. H. (1994). The influence of third-party power and suggestions on negotiation: The surface value of a compromise. *Journal of Applied Social Psychology, 24,* 1084–1113.

Converse, J., & Presser, S. (1986). *Survey questions: Handcrafting the standardized questionnaire.* Beverly Hills, CA: Sage.

Cook, T. D. & Campbell, D. T. (1979). *Quasi-experimentation.* Boston: Houghton- Mifflin.

Cook, T. D. (1985). Post-positivist critical multiplism. In R. L. Shotland & M. M. Marks (Eds.), *Social science and social policy.* Beverly Hills, CA: Sage.

Cooper, H. M. (1998). *Synthesizing research: A guide for literature reviews.* Thousand Oaks, CA: Sage.

Cortazzi, M. (1993). *Narrative analysis.* Washington, DC: Falmer Press.

Coser, L. (1956). *The functions of social conflict.* Glencoe, IL: The Free Press.

Cushman, D. P. (1977). The rules perspective as a theoretical basis for the study of human communication. *Communication Quarterly, 23,* 30–45.

Creswell, J. W. (1994). *Research design: Qualitative and quantitative approaches.* Thousand Oaks, CA: Sage.

Crookall, D., & Arai, K. (Eds.). (1995). *Simulation/gaming across disciplines and cultures: ISAGA at a watershed.* Thousand Oaks, CA: Sage.

Crump, L. (2003). *Inter-organizational negotiation: Team dynamics and goal attainment.* Paper presented at the First Biennial International Conference on Negotiation, Paris.

Czaja, R., & Blair, J. (1995). *Designing surveys: A guide to decisions and procedures.* Thousand Oaks, CA: Pine Forge Press.

Dasgupta, S. (Ed.). (2003a). Symposium: Internet-mediated simulation and gaming. *Simulation & Gaming, 34*(1).

De Callieres, F. (2000). *On the manner of negotiating with princes* (A. F. Whyte, Trans.). Boston: Houghton Mifflin.

De Dreu, C. K. W., Weingart, L. R., & Kwon, S. (2000). Influence of social motives on integrative negotiation: A meta-analytic review and test of two theories. *Journal of Personality and Social Psychology, 78*, 889–905.

Diehl, P. F., Druckman, D., & Wall, J. (1998). International peacekeeping and conflict resolution: A taxonomic analysis with implications. *Journal of Conflict Resolution, 42*, 33–55.

Dillman, D. A. (2000). *Mail and internet surveys: The tailored design method* (2nd ed.). New York: John Wiley.

Dixon, W. J., & Massey, F. J. (1957). *Introduction to statistical analysis.* New York: McGraw-Hill.

Donohue, W. A. (1981). Development of a model of rule use in negotiation interaction. *Communication Monographs, 48*, 106–120.

Donohue, W. A. (1991). *Communication, marital dispute and divorce mediation.* Hillsdale, NJ: Lawrence Erlbaum.

Donohue, W. A., & Roberto, A. J. (1993). Relational development as negotiated order in hostage negotiations. *Human Communication Research, 20*, 175–198.

Drabek, T. E., & Haas, J. E. (1967). Realism in laboratory simulation: Myth or method? *Social Forces, 45*, 337–346.

Drakos, K., & Kutan, A. M. (2003). Regional effects of terrorism on tourism. *Journal of Conflict Resolution, 47*, 621–641.

Draper, S. W. (1988). What's going on in everyday explanation? In C. Antaki (Ed.), *Analyzing everyday explanation: A casebook of methods.* Newbury Park, CA: Sage.

Druckman, D. (1967). Dogmatism, prenegotiation experience, and simulated group representation as determinants of dyadic behavior in a bargaining situation. *Journal of Personality and Social Psychology, 6*, 279–290.

Druckman, D. (1970). Double agreement with reversed items: The plausibility of an alternative explanation to response bias. *Journal of General Psychology, 82*, 63–75.

Druckman, D. (1971). The influence of the situation in inter-party conflict. *Journal of Conflict Resolution, 15*, 523–554.

Druckman, D. (1973). *Human factors in international negotiations: Social-psychological aspects of international conflict* (Sage Professional Papers in International Studies Number 02–020). Beverly Hills, CA: Sage.

Druckman, D. (1977a). The person, role, and situation in international negotiation. In M. G. Hermann with T. W. Milburn (Eds.), *A psychological examination of political leaders.* New York: The Free Press.

Druckman, D. (1977b). Social-psychological approaches to the study of negotiation. In D. Druckman (Ed.), *Negotiations: Social-psychological perspectives.* Beverly Hills, CA: Sage.

Druckman, D. (1986). Stages, turning points and crises: Negotiating military base rights, Spain and the United States. *Journal of Conflict Resolution, 30*, 327–360.

Druckman, D. (1990). Three cases of base-rights negotiations: Lessons learned. In J. W. McDonald & D. B. Bendahmane (Eds.), *U.S. bases overseas: Negotiations with Spain, Greece, and the Philippines.* Boulder, CO: Westview.

Druckman, D. (1993). The situational levers of negotiating flexibility. *Journal of Conflict Resolution, 37,* 236–276.

Druckman, D. (1994a). Determinants of compromising behavior in negotiation: A meta-analysis. *Journal of Conflict Resolution, 38,* 507–556.

Druckman, D. (1994b). Tools for discovery: Experimenting with simulations. *Simulation & Gaming, 25,* 446–455.

Druckman, D. (1995). Situational levers of position change: Further explorations. *Annals of the American Academy of Political and Social Science, 542,* 61–80.

Druckman, D. (1997a). Dimensions of international negotiation: Structures, processes, and outcomes. *Group Decision and Negotiation, 6,* 395–420.

Druckman, D. (1997b). Negotiating in the international context. In I. W. Zartman & J. L. Rasmussen (Eds.), *Peacemaking in international conflict: Methods and techniques.* Washington, DC: United States Institute of Peace Press.

Druckman, D. (2000). Frameworks, techniques, and theory: Contributions of research consulting in social science. *American Behavioral Scientist, 43,* 1635–1666.

Druckman, D. (2001). Turning points in international negotiation: A comparative analysis. *Journal of Conflict Resolution, 45,* 519–544.

Druckman, D. (with Hopmann, P. T.). (2002a). Content analysis. In V. A. Kremenyuk (Ed.), *International negotiation: Analysis, approaches, issues.* San Francisco: Jossey-Bass.

Druckman, D. (2002b). Case-based research on international negotiation: Approaches and data sets. *International Negotiation, 7,* 17–37.

Druckman, D. (2002c). Settlements and resolutions: Consequences of negotiation processes in the laboratory and in the field. *International Negotiation, 7,* 313–338.

Druckman, D. (2003). Puzzles in search of researchers: Processes, identities, and situations. *International Journal of Conflict Management, 14,* 3–22.

Druckman, D. (2004). Be all that you can be: Enhancing human performance. *Journal of Applied Social Psychology, 34,* 2234–2260.

Druckman, D., & Bonoma, T. V. (1976). Determinants of bargaining behavior in a bilateral monopoly situation II: Opponent's concession rate and attraction. *Behavioral Science, 21,* 252–262.

Druckman, D., & Broome, B. (1991). Value differences and conflict resolution: Familiarity or liking? *Journal of Conflict Resolution, 35,* 571–593.

Druckman, D., Broome, B., & Korper, S. (1988).Value differences and conflict resolution: Facilitation or delinking? *Journal of Conflict Resolution, 32,* 489–510.

Druckman, D., & Druckman, J. (1996). Visibility and negotiating flexibility. *Journal of Social Psychology, 136,* 117–120.

Druckman, D., & Green, J. (1986). *Political stability in the Philippines: Framework and analysis* (Denver Monograph Series in World Affairs No. 22, Book 3). Denver, CO: University of Denver.

Druckman, D., & Green, J. (1995). Playing two games: Internal negotiations in the Philippines. In I. W. Zartman (Ed.), *Elusive peace: Negotiating an end to civil wars.* Washington, DC: Brookings.

Druckman, D., & Guner, S. (2000). A social-psychological analysis of Amarna diplomacy. In R. Cohen & R. Westbrook (Eds.), *Amarna diplomacy: The beginnings of international relations.* Baltimore: Johns Hopkins University Press.

Druckman, D., & Harris, R. (1990). Alternative models of responsiveness in international negotiation. *Journal of Conflict Resolution, 34,* 234–251.

Druckman, D., & Hopmann, P. T. (1989). Behavioral aspects of negotiations on mutual security. In P. Tetlock, J. Husbands, R. Jervis, P. Stern, & C. Tilly (Eds.), *Behavior, society, and nuclear war*. New York: Oxford University Press.

Druckman, D., Husbands, J., & Johnston, K. (1991). Turning points in the INF negotiations. *Negotiation Journal, 6,* 55–67.

Druckman, D., & Iaquinta, L. (1974). Toward bridging the international negotiation/ mediation information gap. *International Studies Notes, 1,* 6–14.

Druckman, D., & Lyons, T. (2004). Negotiation processes and post-settlement relations: Comparing Nagorno-Karabakh with Mozambique. In I. W. Zartman (Ed.), *Forward-looking outcomes in negotiation*. Boulder, CO: Rowman & Littlefield.

Druckman, D., Martin, J., Allen Nan, S., & Yagcioglu, D. (1999). Dimensions of international negotiation: A test of Iklé's typology. *Group Decision and Negotiation, 8,* 89–108.

Druckman, D., & Ormachea, I. (2003). *Negociacion: de la teoria a la practica*. Lima, Peru: Instituto de Estudos Internacionales de la Pontificia Universidad Catolica del Peru.

Druckman, D., Ramberg, B., & Harris, R. (2002). Computer-assisted international negotiation: A tool for research and practice. *Group Decision and Negotiation, 11,* 231–256.

Druckman, D., & Robinson, V. (1998). From research to application: Utilizing research findings in training programs. *International Negotiation, 3,* 7–38.

Druckman, D., Rozelle, R., & Baxter, J. (1982). *Nonverbal communication: Survey, theory, and research*. Beverly Hills, CA: Sage.

Druckman, D., Rozelle, R., & Zechmeister, K. (1977). Conflict of interest and value dissensus: Two perspectives. In D. Druckman (Ed.), *Negotiations: Social-psychological perspectives*. Beverly Hills, CA: Sage.

Druckman, D., Solomon, D., & Zechmeister, K. (1972). Effects of representational role obligations on the process of children's distribution of resources. *Sociometry, 35,* 387–410.

Druckman, D., & Stern, P. (1997). Evaluating peacekeeping missions. *Mershon International Studies Review, 41,* 151–165.

Druckman, D., & Vaurio, E. (1983). Regimes and selection of political and military leaders: Brazilian cabinet ministers and generals. *Journal of Political and Military Sociology, 11,* 301–324.

Druckman, D., & Zechmeister, K. (1973). Conflict of interest and value dissensus: Propositions in the sociology of conflict. *Human Relations, 26,* 449–466.

Druckman, D., Zechmeister, K., & Solomon, D. (1972). Determinants of bargaining behavior in a bilateral monopoly situation: Opponent's concession rate and relative defensibility. *Behavioral Science, 17,* 514–531.

Dumont, J. P. (1992). Ideas on Philippine violence: Assertions, negations, and narrations. In C. Nordstrom & J. Martin (Eds.), *The paths to domination, resistance and terror*. Berkeley: University of California Press.

Duncan, G. T., & Job, B. L. (1980). *Probability forecasting in international affairs*. Final report to the Defense Advanced Research Projects Agency, Washington, DC.

Duranti, A. (1988). Ethnography of speaking: Toward a linguistics of the praxis. In F. J. Newmeyer (Ed.), *Linguistics: The Cambridge survey: Vol. 4. Language: The socio-cultural context*. Cambridge, UK: Cambridge University Press.

Edmonds, D., & Eidinow, J. (2001). *Wittgenstein's poker: The story of a ten-minute argument between two great philosophers*. New York: Ecco.

Edwards, A. (1960). *Experimental design in psychological research*. New York: Holt, Rinehart, and Winston.

Ember, C. R., & Ember, M. (1992). Resource unpredictability, mistrust, and war: A cross-cultural study. *Journal of Conflict Resolution, 36*, 242–262.

Evans-Pritchard, E. E. (1976). *Witchcraft, oracles, and magic among the Azande*. Oxford, UK: Clarendon Press.

Fast, L. (2002). *Context matters: Identifying micro- and macro-level factors contributing to NGO insecurity*. Unpublished doctoral dissertation. George Mason University, Fairfax,VA.

Faure, A. M. (1994). Some methodological problems in comparative politics. *Journal of Comparative Politics, 6*, 307–322.

Feinstein, A. H., & Cannon, H. M. (2002). Constructs of simulation evaluation. *Simulation & Gaming, 33*, 425–440.

Ferguson, R. B. (1995). *Yanomami warfare: A political history*. Santa Fe, NM: School of American Research.

Fern, E. F. (2001). *Advanced focus group research*. Thousand Oaks, CA: Sage.

Fink, A. (2004). *Conducting research literature reviews: From the internet to paper* (2nd ed.). Thousand Oaks, CA: Sage.

Firth, A. (Ed.). (1994). *The discourse of negotiation: Studies of language in the workplace*. Tarrytown, NY: Elsevier Science.

Fisher, R. (1964). Fractionating conflict. In R. Fisher (Ed.), *International conflict and behavioral science: The Craigville papers*. New York: Basic Books.

Fisher, R. A. (1934). Discussion on Dr. Wishart's paper. *Journal of the Royal Statistical Society Supplement, 1*, 51–53.

Fisher, R. J. (1997). *Interactive conflict resolution*. Syracuse, NY: Syracuse University Press.

Fowler, F. J., Jr. (1995). *Improving survey questions: Design and evaluation*. Thousand Oaks, CA: Sage.

Fox, R. J., Crask, M. R., & Kim, J. (1988). Mail survey response rate: A meta-analysis of selected techniques for inducing response. *Public Opinion Quarterly, 52*, 467–491.

Frederiksen, N. (1971). *Toward a taxonomy of situations*. Paper presented at the annual meeting of American Psychological Association, Washington, DC.

Frei, D., & Ruloff, D. (1989). *Handbook of foreign policy analysis*. Dordrecht, the Netherlands: Martin Nijhoff.

Galtung, J. (1969). Violence, peace and peace research. *Journal of Peace Research, 6*, 167–191.

Garris, R., Ahlers, R., & Driskell, J. E. (2002). Games, motivation, and learning: A research and practice model. *Simulation & Gaming, 33*, 441–467.

Genette, G. (1980). *Narrative discourse: An essay on method*. Ithaca, NY: Cornell University Press.

George, A. L. (1979). Case studies and theory development: The method of structured, focused comparison. In P. G. Lauren (Ed.), *Diplomacy: New approaches in history, theory, and policy*. New York: The Free Press.

George, A. L., & Bennett, A. (2004). *Case studies and theory development in the social sciences*. Cambridge: MIT Press.

Gergen, K. J. (1982). The healthy, happy human being wears many masks. In D. Krebs (Ed.), *Readings in social psychology: Contemporary perspectives* (2nd ed.). New York: Harper & Row.

Gergen, K. J. (1984). Experimentation and the myth of the incorrigible. In V. Sarris & A. Parducci (Eds.), *Perspectives in psychological experimentation: Toward the year 2000.* Hillsdale, NJ: Lawrence Erlbaum Associates.

Girden, E. (2001). *Evaluating research articles from start to finish* (2nd ed.). Thousand Oaks, CA: Sage.

Goldstein, J. S., & Pevehouse, J. C. (1997). Reciprocity, bullying, and international cooperation: A time-series analysis of the Bosnia conflict. *American Political Science Review, 91,* 515–530.

Graham, J. L., Mintu, A. T., & Rodgers, W. (1994). Explorations of negotiations in ten foreign cultures using a model developed in the United States. *Management Science, 40,* 72–95.

Green, D. P., & Gerber, A. S. (Eds.). (2004). Experimental methods in the political sciences. *American Behavioral Scientist, 47.*

Green, J. J., & Druckman, D. (1986). Experts in political risk analysis: A risky basis for estimates. In J. Rogers (Ed.), *Global risk assessments: Issues, concepts, and applications.* Riverside, CA: Global Risk Assessments, Inc.

Greenbaum, T. L. (1997). *The handbook for focus group research* (2nd ed.). Thousand Oaks, CA: Sage.

Greene, J. (1986). *Language understanding: A cognitive approach.* Philadelphia: Open University Press.

Greeno, J. G., Smith, D. R., & Moore, J. R. (1993). Transfer of situated learning. In D. K. Detterman & R. J. Sternberg (Eds.), *Transfer on trial: Intelligence, cognition, and instruction.* Norwood, NJ: Ablex.

Grimshaw, A. D. (1974). Data and data use in an analysis of communicative events. In R. Bauman & J. Sherzer (Eds.), *Explorations in the ethnography of speaking.* Cambridge, UK: Cambridge University Press.

Groves, R. M. (1989). *Survey errors and survey costs.* New York: John Wiley.

Guetzkow, H. (1957). Isolation and collaboration: A partial theory of inter-nation relations. *Journal of Conflict Resolution, 1,* 48–68.

Guetzkow, H., & Valadez, J. J. (Eds.). (1981). *Simulated international processes: Theories and research in global modeling.* Beverly Hills, CA: Sage.

Guilford, J. P. (1954). *Psychometric methods* (2nd ed.). New York: McGraw-Hill.

Guner, S., & Druckman, D. (2000). Identification of a princess under incomplete information: An Amarna story. *Theory and Decision, 48,* 383–410.

Gupta, A., & Ferguson, J. (Eds.). (1997). *Culture, power, place: Explorations in critical anthropology.* Durham, NC: Duke University Press.

Hale, C. L., & Nix, C. (1997). Achieving neutrality and impartiality: The ultimate communication challenge for peer mediators. *Mediation Quarterly, 14,* 337–352.

Hancock, L. E. (2003). *Peace from the people: Identity salience and the Northern Irish peace process.* Unpublished doctoral dissertation, George Mason University, Fairfax, VA.

Harris, K. L. (1996). Content analysis in negotiation research: A review and guide. *Behavior Research Methods, Instruments, and Computers, 28,* 458–467.

Harris, M. (1990). Emics and etics revisited. In T. N. Headland, K. L. Pike, & M. Harris (Eds.), *Emics and etics: The insider/outsider debate.* Newbury Park, CA: Sage.

Harris, M. (1994). Cultural materialism is alive and well and won't go away until something better comes along. In R. Borofsky (Ed.), *Assessing cultural anthropology.* New York: McGraw-Hill.

Harris, M. J., & Rosenthal, R. (1985). Mediation of interpersonal expectancy effects: 31 meta-analyses. *Psychological Bulletin, 97,* 363–386.

Hart, C. (2001). *Doing a literature search: A comprehensive guide for the social sciences.* Thousand Oaks, CA: Sage.

Haskel, B. (1974). Disparities, strategies, and opportunity costs. *International Studies Quarterly, 18,* 3–30.

Henkel, R. E. (1976). *Tests of significance* (Sage University Paper on Quantitative Applications in the Social Sciences, series no. 07–004). Beverly Hills, CA: Sage.

Henry, G. T. (1990). *Practical sampling.* Newbury Park, CA: Sage.

Hodson, R., Welsh, S., Rieble, S., Jamison, C. S., & Creighton, S. (1993). Is worker solidarity undermined by autonomy and participation? Patterns from the ethnographic literature. *American Sociological Review, 58,* 398–416.

Holsti, O. R. (1969). *Content analysis for the social sciences and humanities.* Reading, MA: Addison-Wesley.

Hopmann, P. T. (1995). Two paradigms of negotiation: Bargaining and problem solving. *The Annals of the American Academy of Political and Social Science, 542,* 24–47.

Hopmann, P. T., & Walcott, C. (1977). The impact of external stresses and tensions on negotiations. In D. Druckman (Ed.), *Negotiations: Social-psychological perspectives.* Beverly Hills, CA: Sage.

Iklé, F. C. (1964). *How nations negotiate.* New York: Harper & Row.

Insko, C. A., Hoyle, R. H., Pinkley, R. L., Hong, G.-Y., & Slim, R. M. (1988). Individual-group discontinuity: The role of a consensus rule. *Journal of Experimental Social Psychology, 24,* 505–519.

Irmer, C. G. (2003). *The promise of process: Evidence on ending violent international conflict.* Unpublished doctoral dissertation, George Mason University, Fairfax, VA.

Jackson, S. H. (2001). *Children's conflict management: Preferences and perceived control beliefs.* Unpublished doctoral dissertation, George Mason University, Fairfax, VA.

Johnston, L. M. (2000). *The tobacco dispute: A study in the use of discourse and narrative theory in the understanding of health-related conflicts.* Unpublished doctoral dissertation, George Mason University, Fairfax, VA.

Jones, S. E. (1979). Integrating etic and emic approaches in the study of intercultural communication. In M. K. Asante, E. Newmark, & C. A. Blake (Eds.), *Handbook of intercultural communication.* Beverly Hills, CA: Sage.

Jost, J. T., & Kruglanski, A. W. (2002). The estrangement of social constructionism and experimental social psychology: History of the rift and prospects for reconciliation. *Personality and Social Psychology Review, 6,* 168–187.

Keashly, L., & Fisher, R. J. (1996). A contingency perspective on conflict intervention: Theoretical and practical considerations. In J. Bercovitch (Ed.), *Resolving international conflicts: The theory and practice of mediation.* Boulder, CO: Lynne Rienner.

Keeter, S., Miller, C., Kohut, A., Groves, R. M., & Presser, S. (2000). Consequences of reducing nonresponse in a national telephone survey. *Public Opinion Quarterly, 64,* 125–148.

Kelman, H. C. (1967). Human use of human subjects: The problem of deception in social psychological experiments. *Psychological Bulletin, 67,* 1–11.

Kelman, H. C. (1968). *A time to speak: On human values and social research.* San Francisco: Jossey-Bass.

Kemmis, S., & Wilkinson, M. (1998). Participatory action research and the study of practice. In B. Atweh, S. Kemmis, & P. Weeks (Eds.), *Action research in practice: Partnerships for social justice in education*. London: Routledge.

King, G., Keohane, R. O., & Verba, S. (1994). *Designing social inquiry: Scientific inference in qualitative research*. Princeton, NJ: Princeton University Press.

King, G., Keohane, R. O., & Verba, S. (1995). The importance of research design in political science. *American Political Science Review, 89*, 475–481.

Klabbers, J. H. D., Swart, R. J., Van Ulden, A. P., & Vellinga, P. (1995). Climate policy: Management of organized complexity through gaming. In D. Crookall & K. Arai (Eds.), *Simulation and gaming across disciplines and cultures: ISAGA at a watershed*. Thousand Oaks, CA: Sage.

Klecka, W. R. (1980). *Discriminant analysis* (Sage University Paper Series in Quantitative Applications in the Social Sciences, series no. 07–019). Beverly Hills, CA: Sage.

Kolb, D. M. (1984). *Experiential learning: Experience as the source of learning and development*. Englewood Cliffs, NJ: Prentice Hall.

Krause, R. M., Druckman, D., Rozelle, R., & Mahoney, R. (1975). Components of value and representation in coalition formation. *Journal of Peace Science, 1*, 141–158.

Kressel, K., Frontera, E., Forlenza, S., Butler, F., & Fish, L. (1994). The settlement orientation vs. the problem-solving style in custody mediation. *Journal of Social Issues, 50*, 67–84.

Kruskal, J. B., & Wish, M. (1990). *Multidimensional scaling* (Sage University Paper series on Quantitative Applications in the Social Sciences, series no. 07–011). Beverly Hills, CA: Sage.

Kydd, A. (2003). Which side are you on?: Bias, credibility and mediation. *American Journal of Political Science, 47*, 597–611.

Landsberger, H. A. (1955). Interaction process analysis of the mediation of labor-management disputes. *Journal of Abnormal and Social Psychology, 51*, 552–558.

Larson, M. (2003). Low-power contributions in multilateral negotiations: A framework analysis. *Negotiation Journal, 19*, 133–149.

Lebedeva, M. (1991). *The analysis of negotiating behavior in simulations*. Paper presented at the annual meeting of the International Studies Association, Vancouver, Canada.

LeCompte, M., & Goetz, J. (1982). Problems of reliability and validity in ethnographic research. *Review of Educational Research, 52*, 31–60.

Leizerov, S. (2001). *The institutionalization of conflicts in cyberspace: A study of conflict over online privacy*. Unpublished doctoral dissertation, George Mason University, Fairfax, VA.

Leng, R. J. (1993). *Interstate crisis behavior, 1816–1980: Realism versus reciprocity*. Cambridge, UK: Cambridge University Press.

Leng, R. J. (1998). Reciprocity in recurring crises. *International Negotiation, 3*, 197–226.

Lepgold, J., & Shambaugh, G. (1998). Rethinking the notion of reciprocal exchange in international negotiation: Sino-American relations, 1969–1997. *International Negotiation, 3*, 227–252.

LeVine, R. A., & Campbell, D. T. (1972). *Ethnocentrism. Theories of conflict, ethnic attitudes, and group behavior*. New York: John Wiley.

Lewin, K. (1946). Action research and minority problems. *Journal of Social Issues, 10*, 34–46.

Lewis-Beck, M. S. (1980). *Applied regression: An introduction* (Sage University Paper series on Quantitative Applications in the Social Sciences, series no. 07–022). Beverly Hills, CA: Sage.

Lewontin, R. C. (1995, April 20). Sex, lies, and social science. *New York Review of Books.*

Lijphart, A. (1975). The comparable-cases strategy in comparative research. *Comparative Political Studies, 8,* 158–177.

Likert, R. (1932). A technique for measurement of attitudes. *Archives of Psychology, 140.*

Lippitt, G., & Lippitt, R. (1986). *The consulting process in action.* Amsterdam: Pfeiffer.

Locke, L., Silverman, S., & Spirduso, W. (2004). *Reading and understanding research.* Thousand Oaks, CA: Sage.

MacLeod, R. B. (1964). Phenomenology: A challenge to experimental psychology. In T. W. Wann (Ed.), *Behaviorism and phenomenology: Contrasting bases for modern psychology.* Chicago: University of Chicago Press.

Mahoney, R., & Druckman, D. (1975). Simulation, experimentation and context: dimensions of design and inference. *Simulation and Games, 6,* 235–270.

Marcus, G. (1998). *Ethnography through thick and thin.* Princeton, NJ: Princeton University Press.

Martin, W. (1986). *Recent theories of narrative.* Ithaca, NY: Cornell University Press.

McClelland, C. A. (1976). *World event interaction survey code book* (ICPSR 5211). Ann Arbor, MI: Inter-University Consortium for Political and Social Research.

McClendon, M. (1991). Acquiescence and recency-order effects in interview surveys. *Sociological Methods & Research, 20,* 60–101.

McClintock, C. G., & Nuttin, J. (1969). Development of competitive behavior in children across two cultures. *Journal of Experimental Social Psychology, 5,* 282–294.

McDonald, J. W., Jr., & Bendahmane, D. (Eds.). (1990). *U.S. base rights overseas: Negotiations with Spain, Greece, and the Philippines.* Boulder, CO: Westview.

McGillicuddy, N. B., Welton, G. L., & Pruitt, D. G. (1987). Third-party intervention: A field experiment comparing three different models. *Journal of Personality and Social Psychology, 53,* 104–112.

Midgaard, K. (1974). *Some topics in the theory of negotiation on whaling regulation.* Paper presented at the European Consortium for Political Research Workshop on Political Theory, Strasbourg, France.

Mill, J. S. (1843). *A system of logic.* London: Parker.

Mish, F. C., et al. (Eds.). (2001). *Merriam-Webster's collegiate dictionary* (10th ed.). Springfield, MA: Merriam-Webster.

Mishler, E. G. (1986). *Research interviewing: Context and narrative.* Cambridge, MA: Harvard University Press.

Mitchell, C., & Banks, M. (1996). *Handbook of conflict resolution: The analytical problem solving approach.* London: Pinter/Cassel.

Mooradian, M., & Druckman, D. (1999). Hurting stalemate or mediation? The conflict over Nagorno-Karabakh, 1990–95. *Journal of Peace Research, 36,* 709–727.

Mosher, J. S. (2003). Relative gains concerns when the number of states in the international system increases. *Journal of Conflict Resolution, 47,* 642–668.

Nash, J. F., Jr. (1950). The bargaining problem. *Econometrica, 18,* 155–162.

Neu, J., & Graham, J. L. (1994). A new methodological approach to the study of interpersonal influence tactics: A "test drive" of a behavioral scheme. *Journal of Business Research, 29,* 131–144.

Newhouse, J. (1973). *Cold dawn: The story of SALT.* New York: Holt.

Nisbett, R. E., Peng, K., Choi, I., & Norenzayan, A. (2001). Culture and systems of thought: Holistic vs. analytical cognition. *Psychological Review, 108,* 291–310.

Nordstrom, C. (1992). The backyard front. In C. Nordstrom & J. Martin (Eds.), *The paths to domination, resistance and terror.* Berkeley: University of California Press.

Nordstrom, C. (1997). *A different kind of war story.* Philadelphia: University of Pennsylvania Press.

Nordstrom, C., & Martin, J. (Eds.). (1992). *The paths to domination, resistance and terror.* Berkeley: University of California Press.

Olekalns, M., & Smith, P. (2003). *Moments in time: Turning points, trust, and outcomes in dyadic negotiation.* Unpublished paper, Melbourne Business School, University of Melbourne, Melbourne, Australia.

Orne, M. T. (1962). On the social psychology of the psychology experiment. *American Psychologist, 17,* 776–783.

Osborne, M. J. (2004). *An introduction to game theory.* New York: Oxford University Press.

Osgood, C. E., Suci, C. J., & Tannenbaum, P. H. (1957). *The measurement of meaning.* Urbana: University of Illinois Press.

Ozcelik, S. (2004). *Influence of power and knowledge on negotiation processes, perceptions, and outcomes: Environmental regime negotiations.* Unpublished doctoral dissertation, George Mason University, Fairfax, VA.

Patchen, M., & Bogumil, D. D. (1995). Testing alternative models of reciprocity against interaction during the cold war. *Conflict Management and Peace Science, 14,* 163–195.

Patton, M. Q. (1981). *Creative evaluation.* Beverly Hills, CA: Sage.

Patton, M. Q. (1982). *Practical evaluation.* Beverly Hills, CA: Sage.

Pawson, R., & Tilly, N. (1997). *Realistic evaluation.* London: Sage.

Pearson, E. S., & Kendall, M. G. (1970). *Studies in the history of statistics and probability.* London: Griffin.

Peng, K., & Nisbett, R. E. (1999). Culture, dialectics, and reasoning about contradiction. *American Psychologist, 54,* 741–754.

Pennings, P., Keman, H., & Kleinnijenhuis, J. (1999). *Doing research in political science: An introduction to comparative methods and statistics.* London: Sage.

Petit, M. (2003). Les enjeux des négociations agricoles internationales et les fondements du libre-échange. *Options Méditerranéenes, Serie A, 52,* 41–50.

Pew Case Studies in International Affairs. (1999). *The ISD compendium of case study abstracts and indexes.* Washington, DC: Institute for the Study of Diplomacy, Edmund A. Walsh School of Foreign Service, Georgetown University.

Powell, K. E., Muir-McClain, L., & Halasyamani, L. (1995). A review of selected school-based conflict resolution and peer mediation projects. *Journal of School Health, 65,* 426–441.

Pruitt, D. G. (1981). *Negotiation behavior.* New York: Academic Press.

Pruitt, D. G. (in press). Escalation, readiness for negotiation, and third party functions. In I. W. Zartman & G. O. Faure (Eds.), *Escalation and negotiation.* Cambridge, England: Cambridge University Press.

Pruitt, D. G., McGillicuddy, N. B., Welton, G. L., & Fry, W. R. (1989). Process of mediation in dispute settlement centers. In K. Kressel & D. G. Pruitt (Eds.), *Mediation research.* San Francisco: Jossey-Bass.

Putnam, R. (1993). *Making democracy work: Civic traditions in modern Italy.* Princeton, NJ: Princeton University Press.

Ramberg, B. (1978). Tactical advantages of opening positioning strategies: Lessons from the Seabeds Arms Control Talks 1967–1970. In I. W. Zartman (Ed.), *The negotiation process: Theories and applications.* Beverly Hills, CA: Sage.

Reder, L. M., & Klatsky, R. (1994). Transfer: Training for performance. In D. Druckman & R. A. Bjork (Eds.), *Learning, remembering, believing: Enhancing human performance.* Washington, DC: National Academy Press.

Richter, D. H. (1996). *Narrative theory.* White Plains, NY: Longman Press.

Riessman, C. K. (1993). *Narrative analysis.* Newbury Park, CA: Sage.

Robson, C. (1993). *Real world research: A resource for social scientists and practitioner-researchers.* Oxford, UK: Blackwell.

Robson, C. (2000). *Small-scale evaluation: Principles and practice.* London: Sage.

Robson, C. (2002). *Real world research: A resource for social scientists and practitioner-researchers* (2nd ed.). Oxford, UK: Blackwell.

Roemer, C., Garb, P., Neu, J., & Graham, J. L. (1999). A comparison of American and Russian patterns of behavior in buyer-seller negotiations using observational methods. *International Negotiation, 4,* 37–61.

Rokeach, M. (1963). The double agreement phenomenon: Three hypotheses. *Psychological Review, 70,* 304–309.

Rosenthal, R. (1964). The effects of experimenter on the results of psychological research. In B. A. Maher (Ed.), *Progress in experimental personality research* (Vol. 1). New York: Academic Press.

Rosenthal, R. (1984). *Meta-analytic procedures for social research.* London: Sage.

Ross, M. H. (2001). Action evaluation in the theory and practice of conflict resolution. *Peace and Conflict Studies, 8,* 1–15.

Ross, M. H., & Rothman, J. (Eds.). (1999). *Theory and practice in ethnic conflict management: Conceptualizing success and failure.* London: Macmillan.

Rossi, P. H., Freeman, H. E., & Lipsey, M. W. (2003). *Evaluation: A systematic approach* (7th ed.). Thousand Oaks, CA: Sage.

Rothman, J. (1997a). Action evaluation and conflict resolution training. *International Negotiation, 2,* 451–470.

Rothman, J. (1997b). *Resolving identity-based conflicts in nations, organizations, and communities.* San Francisco: Jossey-Bass.

Rouhana, N. N. (2000). Interactive conflict resolution: Theoretical and methodological issues. In P. Stern & D. Druckman (Eds.), *International conflict resolution after the Cold War.* Washington, DC: National Academy Press.

Rubin, J. Z. (Ed.). (1981). *Dynamics of third party intervention: Kissinger in the Middle East.* New York: Praeger.

Salant, P., & Dillman, D. A. (1994). *How to conduct your own survey.* New York: John Wiley.

Sandler, T., & Arce M., D. G. (2003). Terrorism and game theory. *Simulation & Gaming, 34,* 319–337.

Sandole, D. J. D. (1998). *Toward a common and comprehensive security model for Europe in the 21st century: The views of CSCE/OSCE negotiators, 1993–1997.* Paper presented at the joint meeting of the Third Pan-European International Relations Conference and the International Studies Association, Vienna, Austria.

Sandole, D. J. D. (2003). Typology. In S. Cheldelin, D. Druckman, & L. Fast (Eds.), *Conflict: From analysis to intervention.* London: Continuum.

Sanjek, R. (Ed.). (1990). *Fieldnotes: The makings of anthropology.* Ithaca, NY: Cornell University Press.

Sawyer, J., & Guetzkow, H. (1965). Bargaining and negotiations in international relations. In H. C. Kelman (Ed.), *International behavior: A social-psychological analysis.* New York: Holt, Rinehart, & Winston.

Schellenberg, J. A., & Druckman, D. (1986). Bargaining and gaming. *Society, 23,* 65–71.

Schelling, T. C. (1960). *The strategy of conflict.* Cambridge, MA: Harvard University Press.

Scheub, H. (1975). Oral narrative process and the use of models. *New Literary History, 6,* 353–377.

Schotz, R. W., & Tietje, O. (2002). *Embedded case study methods: Integrating quantitative and qualitative knowledge.* Thousand Oaks, CA: Sage.

Schratz, M., & Walker, R. (1995). *Research as social change: New opportunities for qualitative research.* London: Routledge.

Schrodt, P. A., & Gerner, D. J. (2004). An event data analysis of third-party mediation in the Middle East and Balkins. *Journal of Conflict Resolution, 48,* 310–330.

Schuman, H., & Presser, S. (1996). *Questions and answers in attitude surveys: Experiments in question form, wording and context.* Thousand Oaks, CA: Sage.

Scott, J. C. (1985). *Weapons of the weak: Everyday forms of peasant resistance.* New Haven, CT: Yale University Press.

Scott, J. C. (1992). Domination, acting, and fantasy. In C. Nordstrom & J. Martin (Eds.), *The paths to domination, resistance and terror.* Berkeley: University of California Press.

Secord, P. F., & Backman, C. W. (1964). *Social psychology.* New York: McGraw-Hill.

Selener, D. (1997). *Participatory action research and social change* (2nd ed.). Ithaca, NY: Cornell University Press.

Seligmann, L. J. (1995). *Between reform and revolution, political struggles in the Peruvian Andes, 1969–1991.* Stanford, CA: Stanford University Press.

Seligmann, L. J., & Bunker, S. G. (1994). An Andean irrigation system: Ecological visions and social organization. In D. Guillet & W. Mitchell (Eds.), *Irrigation at high altitudes: The social organization of water control systems in the Andes.* Washington, DC: American Anthropological Association.

Sells, S. B. (1966). A model for the social system for the multi-man extended duration space ship. *Aerospace Medicine, 37,* 1130–1135.

Senehi, J. (2002). Constructive storytelling: A peace process. *Peace and Conflict Studies, 9,* 41–63.

Sick, G. (1985). *All fall down: America's tragic encounter with Iran.* New York: Random House.

Siegel, S., & Castellan, N. J. (1988). *Nonparametric statistics for the behavioral sciences* (2nd ed.). New York: McGraw-Hill.

Simon, H. A. (1954). Spurious correlation: A causal interpretation. *Journal of the American Statistical Association, 49,* 467–479.

Skinner, B. F. (1964). Behaviorism at fifty. In T. W. Wann (Ed.), *Behaviorism and phenomenology: Contrasting bases for modern psychology.* Chicago: University of Chicago Press.

Sluka, J. (1992). The politics of painting: Political murals in Northern Ireland. In C. Nordstrom & J. Martin (Eds.), *The paths to domination, resistance and terror.* Berkeley: University of California Press.

Smith, S. W., Daunic, A. P., Miller, M. D., & Robinson, T. R. (2002). Conflict resolution and peer mediation in middle schools: Extending the process and outcome knowledge base. *Journal of Social Psychology, 142,* 567–586.

Smith, T. (1984). Nonattitudes: A review and evaluation. In C. Turner & E. Martin (Eds.), *Surveying subjective phenomena.* New York: Russell Sage.

Sniderman, P. M., & Grob, D. (1996). Innovations in experimental design in general population attitude surveys. *Annual Review of Sociology, 22,* 377–399.

Snyder, G. H., & Diesing, P. (1977). *Conflict among nations: Bargaining, decision making and system structure in international crises.* Princeton, NJ: Princeton University Press.

Solomon, D., & Druckman, D. (1972). Age, representatives' prior performance and the distribution of winnings with teammates. *Human Development, 15,* 244–252.

Stedman, S. J. (2000). Spoiler problems in peace processes. In P. Stern & D. Druckman (Eds.), *International conflict resolution after the cold war.* Washington, DC: National Academy Press.

Stern, P., & Druckman, D. (2000). Evaluating interventions in history: The case of international conflict resolution. *International Studies Review, 2,* 33–63.

Stevahn, L., Johnson, D., Johnson, R., & Schultz, R. (2002). Effects of conflict resolution training integrated into a high school social studies curriculum. *Journal of Social Psychology, 142,* 305–331.

Stoll, R. J., & McAndrew, W. (1986). Negotiating strategic arms control, 1969–79: Modeling the bargaining process. *Journal of Conflict Resolution, 30,* 315–326.

Strauss, A. (1978). *Negotiations: Varieties, contexts, processes, and social order.* San Francisco: Jossey-Bass.

Strauss, A., & Corbin, J. (1990). *Basics of qualitative research: Grounded theory procedures and techniques.* Newbury Park, CA: Sage.

Stringer, E. (1999). *Action research.* Thousand Oaks: Sage.

Suárez-Orozco, M. (1992). A grammar of terror: Psychocultural responses to state terrorism in dirty war and post-dirty war Argentina. In C. Nordstrom & J. Martin (Eds.), *The paths to domination, resistance and terror.* Berkeley: University of California Press.

Swearingen, C. J. (1990). The narration of dialogue and narration within dialogue: The transition from story to logic. In B. K Britton & A.D Pellegrini (Eds.), *Narrative thought and narrative language.* Hillsdale, NJ: Lawrence Erlbaum.

Tarrow, S. (1996). Making social science work across space and time: A critical reflection on Robert Putnam's *Making democracy work. American Political Science Review, 90,* 389–397.

Thurstone, L. L., & Chave, E. J. (1929). *The measurement of attitude.* Chicago: University of Chicago Press.

Tomlin, B. W. (1989). The stages of prenegotiation: The decision to negotiate North American free trade. In J. G. Stein (Ed.), *Getting to the table: The processes of international prenegotiation.* Baltimore: Johns Hopkins University Press.

Toolan, M. J. (1988). *Narrative: A critical linguistic introduction.* New York: Routledge.

Tourangeau, R., Rips, L. J., & Rasinski, K. (2000). *The psychology of survey response.* Cambridge, UK: Cambridge University Press.

Tufte, E. R. (1990). *Envisioning information.* Cheshire, CT: Graphics Press.

Underdal, A. (1973). Multilateral negotiation parties: The case of the European community. *Cooperation and Conflict, 8,* 173–182.

van Dijk, T. A. (1975). Action, action description, and narrative. *New Literary History,* 6, 274–294.

Wagner, L. M. (1998). *Problem solving and convergent bargaining: An analysis of negotiation processes and their outcomes.* Unpublished doctoral dissertation, Paul H. Nitze School for Advanced International Studies, Baltimore Johns Hopkins University, Baltimore.

Walcott, C., & Hopmann, P. T. (1978). Interaction analysis and bargaining behavior. In R. T. Golembiewski (Ed.), *The small group in political science: The last two decades of development.* Athens: University of Georgia Press.

Wall, J., & Druckman, D. (2003). Mediation in peacekeeping missions. *Journal of Conflict Resolution, 47,* 693–705.

Walton, R. E., & McKersie, R. B. (1965). *A behavioral theory of labor negotiations: An analysis of a social interaction system.* New York: McGraw-Hill.

Webb, E. J., Campbell, D. T., Schwartz, R. D., & Sechrest, L. (1966). *Unobtrusive measures: Nonreactive research in the social sciences.* Chicago: Rand McNally.

Weiss, C. H. (1997). *Evaluation: Methods for studying programs and policies* (2nd ed.). Upper Saddle River, NJ: Prentice Hall.

Weiss, J. N. (2002). *Which way forward: Mediator sequencing strategies in intractable communal conflicts.* Unpublished doctoral dissertation, George Mason University, Fairfax, VA.

Weitzman, E., & Miles, M. (1995). *Computer programs for qualitative data analysis: A software sourcebook.* Thousand Oaks, CA: Sage.

White, H. (1980). The value of narrativity in the representation of reality. In W. J. T. Mitchell (Ed.), *On narrative.* Chicago: University of Chicago Press.

Winham, G. (1977). Complexity in international negotiation. In D. Druckman (Ed.), *Negotiations: Social-psychological perspectives.* Beverly Hills, CA: Sage.

Winslade, J., & Monk, G. (2000). *Narrative mediation: A new approach to conflict resolution.* San Francisco: Jossey-Bass.

Wolf, F. M. (1986). *Meta-analysis: Quantitative methods for research synthesis* (Sage University Paper series on Quantitative applications in the social sciences, 07–059). Newbury Park, CA: Sage.

Wolfe, J. (1995). The use of simulations/games to fill Russia's managerial needs. In D. Crookall & K. Arai (Eds.), *Simulation and gaming across disciplines and cultures: ISAGA at a watershed.* Thousand Oaks, CA: Sage.

Young, K. T. (1968). *Negotiating with the Chinese Communists: The United States experience.* New York: McGraw-Hill.

Zartman, I. W. (1994). *International multilateral negotiation.* San Francisco: Jossey-Bass.

Zartman, I. W. (2000). Ripeness: The hurting stalemate and beyond. In P. C. Stern & D. Druckman (Eds.), *International conflict resolution after the Cold War.* Washington DC: National Academy Press.

Zartman, I. W., & Rasmussen, J. L. (Eds.). (1997). *Peacemaking in international conflict: Methods and techniques.* Washington, DC: U.S. Institute of Peace Press.

Index

About the Author

Daniel Druckman is a 2004–2005 visiting Professor at the University of Queensland's Australian Centre for Peace and Conflict Studies in Brisbane, Australia. He is the Vernon M. and Minnie I. Lynch Professor of Conflict Resolution at George Mason University, where he has coordinated the doctoral program at the Institute for Conflict Analysis and Resolution (ICAR). He is also a member of the faculty at Sabanci University in Istanbul and has held senior positions at several consulting firms as well as at the U.S. National Academy of Sciences. He received a Ph.D. from Northwestern University and was awarded a best-in-field prize from the American Institutes for Research for his doctoral dissertation. He has published widely (approximately 150 publications, including 12 authored or edited books) on such topics as negotiating behavior, nationalism and group identity, human performance, peacekeeping, political stability, nonverbal communication, and methodology, including simulation. He is a board member or associate editor of eight journals. He received the 1995 Otto Klineberg Award for Intercultural and International Relations from the Society for the Psychological Analysis of Social Issues for his work on nationalism, a Teaching Excellence award in 1998 from George Mason University, and an award for outstanding article published in 2001 from the International Association for Conflict Management. He is the recipient of the 2003 Lifetime Achievement Award from the International Association for Conflict Management.